Course   Taking Sides: Clashing Views
           in Management, 4/e
           by Barnes/Smith

http://create.mcgraw-hill.com

ISBN-10: 1121844839   ISBN-13: 9781121844834

Contents

Credits

Preface

He who knows only his side of the case knows little of that. His reasons may have been good, and no one may have been able to refute them. But if he is equally unable to refute the reasons on the opposite side he has no ground for preferring either opinion.

John Stuart Mill

The United States criminal system is adversarial in nature; two sides with incompatible goals meet in front of a judge and/or jury to determine the fate of an individual charged with a crime. Underlying this process is the presupposition that truth can be reached through the presentation of conflicting viewpoints. This book, the 4th edition of *Taking Sides: Clashing Views in Management*, is predicated on this presupposition. Each of the debates presented here mimics the courtroom: There are two opposing sides, each vigorously presenting its evidence and questioning its opponent's case; there is a judge—the reader—who considers the relative merits of each side, hopefully maintaining objectivity while searching for truth; and there is a time for rendering an opinion which may signal vindication for one side or perhaps leave the decision open for debate and consideration on another day and time.

This text consists of debates on controversial issues in the field of business management. Each issue consists of opposing viewpoints presented in a pro and con format. It is your role as judge to give each side a fair and unbiased hearing. This will be a difficult task, for the authors of each of the articles is an expert and defends his or her position with great vigor.

To help in this task, we suggest that you ask difficult questions, make notes on troubling points, and interact with the material. If you have a preconceived opinion about an issue, force yourself to look critically at the side you support. This, too, is difficult to do as it's much easier to find the weaknesses in the opposing point of view than in your own. None the less, doing so helps protect against self-deception and, frequently, strengthens your original belief. Perhaps most importantly, it makes you think!

Book Organization

The text is divided into five units, each addressing a different aspect of management. At the beginning of each unit is a unit opener that briefly identifies the specific issues in the section. Next are the issues themselves, each of which starts with an introduction that sets the stage for the debate as it is argued in the YES and NO selections. An exploring the issue section follows the selections and provides some final observations and comments about the topic. The exploring the issue section contains critical thinking and reflection questions, the common ground between the two viewpoints, and print and Internet suggestions for further reading.

We'd like to make a few observations regarding this new edition. Those familiar with the 3rd edition will notice that we have made several significant changes in this 4th edition. First, we dropped six issues from the 3rd edition that proved too inaccessible, not particularly controversial, somewhat outdated, or too similar to another topic. Second, of the 12 topics carried over from the third edition, 3 have been updated with newer articles by different authors. Finally, and perhaps most significantly, we have added 6 new, topical issues that address some of the many contemporary controversies and discussions existing in management today.

Overall, 15 articles are new to this edition, making this 4th edition a significant revision. Our overarching goal with this work has been to contribute to the development of critical thinkers who are willing to question their own values and beliefs to get to the "truth" of difficult questions and matters. We hope that this work contributes to that goal and that you find the topics to be not only controversial, but interesting and educational as well. Thank you for your interest in and support of our work!

Editors of This Volume

KATHLEEN J. BARNES is an associate professor of business management at East Stroudsburg University. She teaches principles of management, human resource management, organizational behavior, organizational leadership, and organizational strategy. Barnes received her PhD from the University at Albany, SUNY. Her current research interests include experiential learning and education, organizational culture, and individual and team empowerment.

GEORGE E. SMITH is an associate professor of business at Albright College. He regularly teaches principles of management, business, government, and society, and the capstone course in management. Smith received his PhD from The Rockefeller College of Public Affairs & Policy at the University at Albany, SUNY. His current areas of research interest include experiential learning and education, ethics education, and exploring management history's place in the management/business education curriculum.

Acknowledgments

We extend our heartfelt thanks to our McGraw-Hill editor, Debra Henricks for her professionalism and flexibility in making the completion of this work possible. We'd also like to thank our family and friends for their continued support and encouragement. Thank you!

We dedicate this text to our Mothers—Joyce Barnes and Lana Smith. Joyce and Lana actively promoted, modeled, and rewarded the intellectual curiosity and critical thinking skills required to make this work possible. Their support and love helped us become the successful people that we are today.

Editors/Academic Advisory Board

Members of the Academic Advisory Board are instrumental in the final selection of articles for each edition of TAKING SIDES. Their review of articles for content, level, and appropriateness provides critical direction to the editors and staff. We think that you will find their careful consideration well reflected in this volume.

Academic Advisory Board Members

Yoa A. Amewokunu
Virginia State University

Sally Andrews
Linn-Benton Community College

Robert Atkin
University of Pittsburgh

Derek D. Bardell
Delgado Community College

Kathleen J. Barnes
East Stroudsburg University

David Binder
Brenau University

Barbara Boerner
Brevard College

John Boulmetis
University of Rhode Island

Glenn W. Briggs
Webster University

Barry Brock
Barry University

Dennis Brode
Sinclair Community College

Marilyn Brooks-Lewis
Warren County Community

Dean Bruce
Northwest College

Buck Buchanan
Defiance College

Mark C. Butler
University of Dubuque

Kalyan S. Chakravarty
California State University

Bonnie Chavez
Santa Barbara City College

Rachna Condos
American River College

Gary Corona
Florida Community College

William L. Corsover
Barry University

Dale Cox
Gadsden State Community College

Kevin W. Cruthirds
The University of Texas–Brownsville

Kevin Cruz
University of Texas–El Paso

Anthony D'Ascoli
Miami Dade College

Elizabeth Danon-Leva
University of Texas at Austion

Charles E. Davies, Jr.
Hillsdale College

Miles K. Davis
Shenandoah University

Gary M. Donnelly
Casper College

Donald Doty
Northwest University

Arthur Duhaime
Nichols College

Mary Dunn
University of Texas at Austin

Karen Eboch
Bowling Green State University

Thomas Eveland
DeVry University

Diane Fagan
Webster University

Jeffrey Fahrenwald
Rockford College

Janice Feldbauer
Schoolcraft College

Charles Feldhaus
Indiana University-Purdue University

Martin Felix
Johnson & Wales University

Anthony Fruzzetti
Johnson & Wales University

James Glasgow
Villanova University

Joel Goldhar
Illinois Institute of Technology

David S. Greisler
York College of Pennsylvania

M. Ray Grubbs
Millsaps College

Semere Haile
Grambling State University

Bruce L. Haller
Dowling College

Jon Harbaugh
Southern Oregon University

Michael A. Heel
SUNY–Brockport

John Heller
Laramie County Community College

Jim Henderson
Alverno College

P. L. "Rick" Hogan
Pierce College

Betty Hoge
Bridgewater College

Phillip A. Jeck
University of Central Oklahoma

Masud Kadri
University of Phoenix

James Katzenstein
California State University, Dominguez Hills

F. Jeffrey Keil
Mary Baldwin College

Gary F. Kelly
Clarkson University

Carolyn Kelly Ottman
Milwaukee School of Engineering

Charles Kitzmiller
Indian River Community College

Clark Lambert
Adelphi University

Jane LeMaster
University of Texas–Pan American

Ken Levitt
East Stroudsburg University

Victor Lipe
Trident Technical College

David Little
High Point University

Nick Lockard
Texas Lutheran University

Jayme Long
Delta State University

Susan Losapio
Southern New Hampshire University

Ed Maglisceau
Santa Fe University of Art and Design

Kenyetta McCurty
Amridge University

Ellen McMahon
National Louis University

Jeanne McNett
Assumption College

Joseph B. Mosca
Monmouth University

Tim Muth
Florida Institute of Technology

Tina Nabatchi
Syracuse University

J.R. Ogden
Kutztown University of Pennsylvania

Don A. Okhomina
Fayetteville State University

David Olson
California State University

Floyd Ormsbee
Clarkson University

Mary Jo Payne
University of Phoenix

Pedro David Perez
Cornell University–Ithaca

Richard J. Pilarski
Empire State College

Renee Porter
Lindenwood University

Lynn Powell
James Madison University

Michael J. Provitera
Barry University

Eivis Qenani-Petrela
Cal Poly–San Luis Obispo

Kathryn Ready
Winona State University

Al C. Restivo
California State University, Los Angeles

Juan E. Riojas
Laredo Community College

Ray Rodgers
Harcum College

Robert K. Rowe
Park University

Raymond Ruetsch
Columbia College

Mark J. Safferstone
Mary Washington College

Janet Salmons
Capella University

Jean Sampson
McKendree University

Jan Napoleon Saykiewicz
Duquesne University

Catharine Schauer
Embry-Riddle Aeronautical University

Calvin Scheidt
Tidewater Community College

Michael Scheuermann
Drexel University

Peter Schneider
College of St. Elizabeth

Bruce Schultz
Brooklyn College

Greg Schultz
Carroll College

Lakshmy Sivaratnam
Kansas City Community College

Anthony W. Slone
Elizabethtown Community and Technical College

Gerald Smith
University of Northern Iowa

Katrina Stark
University of Great Falls

Ira Teich
Lander College for Men

Eric Teoro
Lincoln Christian College

Wanda Tillman
North Greenville University

John Turpen
Fairmont State University

Elionne Walker
University of Saint Thomas

Ruth M. Weatherly
Simpson College

Timothy L. Weaver
Moorpark College

Caroline Shaffer Westerhof
California National University, Kaplan University

Dennis R. Williams
Pennsylvania College of Technology

Mary I. Williams
College of Southern Nevada–North Las Vegas

Otis G. Wilson
Northwood University

Debra D. Woods
Westmoreland County Community College

Mary Wright
Hope International University

Correlation Guide

The Taking Sides series presents current issues in a debate-style format designed to stimulate student interest and develop critical thinking skills. Each issue is thoughtfully framed with an issue summary, an issue introduction, and an exploring the issue section. The pro and con essays—selected for their liveliness and substance—represent the arguments of leading scholars and commentators in their fields.

Taking Sides: Clashing Views in Management, 4/e, is an easy-to-use reader that presents issues on important topics such as *anti-fraternization, social media monitoring, CEO compensation,* and *creating sustainable businesses.*

Organizational Behavior

This convenient guide matches the issues in **Taking Sides: Management, 4/e,** with the corresponding chapters in three of our best-selling McGraw-Hill Organizational Behavior textbooks by Colquitt, Lepine, and Wesson; Kreitner & Kinicki; and McShane & Von Glinow.

TAKING SIDES: Management, 4/e	Organizational Behavior: Improving Performance and Commitment in the Workplace, 3/e by Colquitt, Lepine, and Wesson	Organizational Behavior, 10/e by Kreitner and Kinicki	Organizational Behavior: Emerging Knowledge. Global Reality, 16/e by McShane and Von Glinow
Issue: Can Managerial Behavior Be Controlled in the Same Manner as Other "Professions"?	**Chapter 16:** Organizational Culture	**Chapter 3:** Organizational Culture, Socialization, and Mentoring	**Chapter 2:** Individual Behavior, Personality, and Values
Issue: Do Corporations Have a Responsibility to Society Beyond Maximizing Profit?	**Chapter 16:** Organizational Culture	**Chapter 9:** Improving Job Performance with Goals, Feedback, Rewards, and Positive Reinforcement	**Chapter 14:** Organizational Culture
Issue: Are U.S. CEOs Paid More Than They Deserve?	**Chapter 6:** Motivation	**Chapter 8:** Motivation	**Chapter 5:** Foundations of Employee Motivation
Issue: Can Ethical Malaise Be Remedied Through Ethics Education?	**Chapter 7:** Trust, Justice, and Ethics	**Chapter 11:** Developing and Leading Effective Teams	**Chapter 12:** Leadership in Organizational Settings
Issue: Does an Employer's Need to Monitor Workers Trump Employee Privacy Concerns?	**Chapter 7:** Trust, Justice, and Ethics	**Chapter 6:** Values, Attitudes, Job Satisfaction, and Counterproductive Work	**Chapter 11:** Conflict and Negotiation in the Workplace
Issue: Is Workplace Drug Testing a Wise Corporate Policy?	**Chapter 7:** Trust, Justice, and Ethics	**Chapter 6:** Values, Attitudes, Job Satisfaction, and Counterproductive Work	**Chapter 11:** Conflict and Negotiation in the Workplace
Issue: Is Social Media a Tool of Expression or Trouble for Businesses?	**Chapter 16:** Organizational Culture	**Chapter 3:** Organizational Culture, Socialization, and Mentoring	**Chapter 14:** Organizational Culture
Issue: Is Growth Always an Inherent Corporate Value?	**Chapter 15:** Organizational Structure	**Chapter 17:** Organizational Design, Effectiveness, and Innovation	**Chapter 15:** Designing Organizational Structures
Issue: Is Outsourcing a Wise Corporate Strategy?	**Chapter 15:** Organizational Structure	**Chapter 17:** Organizational Design, Effectiveness, and Innovation	**Chapter 15:** Designing Organizational Structures
Issue: Will the Use of Reshoring/ Insourcing by Corporations Increase?	**Chapter 15:** Organizational Structure	**Chapter 17:** Organizational Design, Effectiveness, and Innovation	**Chapter 15:** Designing Organizational Structures
Issue: Does Expanding via Mergers and Acquisitions Make for Sound Corporate Strategy?	**Chapter 15:** Organizational Structure	**Chapter 17:** Organizational Design, Effectiveness, and Innovation	**Chapter 15:** Designing Organizational Structures
Issue: Should Corporations Adopt Environmentally Friendly Policies of Corporate Social Responsibility (CSR) and Sustainable Development?	**Chapter 15:** Organizational Structure	**Chapter 17:** Organizational Design, Effectiveness, and Innovation	**Chapter 15:** Designing Organizational Structures

(Continued)

TAKING SIDES: Management, 4/e	Organizational Behavior: Improving Performance and Commitment in the Workplace, 3/e by Colquitt, Lepine, and Wesson	Organizational Behavior, 10/e by Kreitner and Kinicki	Organizational Behavior: Emerging Knowledge. Global Reality, 16/e by McShane and Von Glinow
Issue: Is Corporate Sustainability Reporting a Valuable Corporate Reporting Tool?	**Chapter 15:** Organizational Structure	**Chapter 17:** Organizational Design, Effectiveness, and Innovation	**Chapter 15:** Designing Organizational Structures
Issue: Is It Really Possible to Create Sustainable Businesses?	**Chapter 15:** Organizational Structure	**Chapter 17:** Organizational Design, Effectiveness, and Innovation	**Chapter 15:** Designing Organizational Structures
Issue: Are Cap-and-Trade Policies Effective?	**Chapter 15:** Organizational Structure	**Chapter 4:** International OB: Managing Across Cultures	**Chapter 15:** Designing Organizational Structures
Issue: Do Unskilled Immigrants Hurt the American Economy?	**Chapter 10:** Ability	**Chapter 4:** International OB: Managing Across Cultures	**Chapter 6:** Applied Performance Practices
Issue: Is Economic Globalization Good for Humankind?	**Chapter 15:** Organizational Structure	**Chapter 4:** International OB: Managing Across Cultures	**Chapter 15:** Designing Organizational Structures
Issue: Are Protectionist Policies Beneficial to Business?	**Chapter 15:** Organizational Structure	**Chapter 4:** International OB: Managing Across Cultures	**Chapter 15:** Designing Organizational Structures

Human Resource Management

This convenient guide matches the issues in **Taking Sides: Management, 4/e**, with the corresponding chapters in three of our best-selling McGraw-Hill Human Resource Management textbooks by Cascio; Ivancevich and Konopaske; and Noe, Hollenbeck, Gerhart, and Wright.

TAKING SIDES: Management, 4/e	Managing Human Resources: Productivity, Quality of Life, Profits, 9/e by Cascio	Human Resource Management, 12/e by Ivancevich and Konopaske	Human Resource Management: Gaining A Competitive Advantage, 8/e by Noe, Hollenbeck, Gerhart, and Wright
Issue: Can Managerial Behavior Be Controlled in the Same Manner as Other "Professions"?	**Chapter 10:** Managing Careers	**Chapter 13:** Training and Development	**Chapter 9:** Employee Development
Issue: Do Corporations Have a Responsibility to Society Beyond Maximizing Profit?	**Chapter 3:** The Legal Context of Employment Decisions	**Chapter 3:** Legal Environment of Human Resource Management: Equal Employment Opportunity	**Chapter 3:** The Legal Environment: Equal Employment Opportunity and Safety
Issue: Are U.S. CEOs Paid More Than They Deserve?	**Chapter 9:** Performance Management; **Chapter 11:** Pay and Incentive Systems	**Chapter 10:** Compensation: An Overview **Chapter 11:** Compensation: Methods and Policies	**Chapter 11:** Pay Structure Decisions **Chapter 12:** Recognizing Employee Contributions with Pay
Issue: Can Ethical Malaise Be Remedied Through Ethics Education?	**Chapter 8:** Workplace Training	**Chapter 13:** Training and Development	**Chapter 7:** Training
Issue: Does an Employer's Need to Monitor Workers Trump Employee Privacy Concerns?	**Chapter 3:** The Legal Context of Employment Decisions	**Chapter 3:** Legal Environment of Human Resource Management: Equal Employment Opportunity	**Chapter 3:** The Legal Environment: Equal Employment Opportunity and Safety
Issue: Is Workplace Drug Testing a Wise Corporate Policy?	**Chapter 7:** Staffing	**Chapter 8:** Selecting Effective Employees	**Chapter 6:** Selection and Placement
Issue: Is Social Media a Tool of Expression or Trouble for Businesses?	**Chapter 3:** The Legal Context of Employment Decisions	**Chapter 3:** Legal Environment of Human Resource Management: Equal Employment Opportunity	**Chapter 3:** The Legal Environment: Equal Employment Opportunity and Safety
Issue: Is Growth Always an Inherent Corporate Value?	**Chapter 15:** International Dimensions of Human Resource Management	**Chapter 4:** Global Human Resource Management	**Chapter 15:** Managing Human Resources Globally
Issue: Is Outsourcing a Wise Corporate Strategy?	**Chapter 1:** Human Resources in a Globally Competitive Business	**Chapter 2:** A Strategic Approach to Human Resource Management	**Chapter 2:** Strategic Human Resource Management
Issue: Will the Use of Reshoring/ Insourcing by Corporations Increase?	**Chapter 1:** Human Resources in a Globally Competitive Business	**Chapter 2:** A Strategic Approach to Human Resource Management	**Chapter 2:** Strategic Human Resource Management
Issue: Does Expanding via Mergers and Acquisitions Make for Sound Corporate Strategy?	**Chapter 1:** Human Resources in a Globally Competitive Business	**Chapter 2:** A Strategic Approach to Human Resource Management	**Chapter 2:** Strategic Human Resource Management

TAKING SIDES: Management, 4/e	*Managing Human Resources: Productivity, Quality of Life, Profits, 9/e by Cascio*	*Human Resource Management, 12/e by Ivancevich and Konopaske*	*Human Resource Management: Gaining A Competitive Advantage, 8/e by Noe, Hollenbeck, Gerhart, and Wright*
Issue: Should Corporations Adopt Environmentally Friendly Policies of Corporate Social Responsibility (CSR) and Sustainable Development?	**Chapter 1:** Human Resources in a Globally Competitive Business	**Chapter 2:** A Strategic Approach to Human Resource Management	**Chapter 2:** Strategic Human Resource Management
Issue: Is Corporate Sustainability Reporting a Valuable Corporate Reporting Tool?	**Chapter 1:** Human Resources in a Globally Competitive Business	**Chapter 2:** A Strategic Approach to Human Resource Management	**Chapter 2:** Strategic Human Resource Management
Issue: Is It Really Possible to Create Sustainable Businesses?	**Chapter 1:** Human Resources in a Globally Competitive Business	**Chapter 2:** A Strategic Approach to Human Resource Management	**Chapter 2:** Strategic Human Resource Management
Issue: Are Cap-and-Trade Policies Effective?	**Chapter 1:** Human Resources in a Globally Competitive Business	**Chapter 2:** A Strategic Approach to Human Resource Management	**Chapter 2:** Strategic Human Resource Management
Issue: Do Unskilled Immigrants Hurt the American Economy?	**Chapter 1:** Human Resources in a Globally Competitive Business	**Chapter 2:** A Strategic Approach to Human Resource Management	**Chapter 2:** Strategic Human Resource Management
Issue: Is Economic Globalization Good for Humankind?	**Chapter 1:** Human Resources in a Globally Competitive Business	**Chapter 2:** A Strategic Approach to Human Resource Management	**Chapter 2:** Strategic Human Resource Management
Issue: Are Protectionist Policies Beneficial to Business?	**Chapter 1:** Human Resources in a Globally Competitive Business	**Chapter 2:** A Strategic Approach to Human Resource Management	**Chapter 2:** Strategic Human Resource Management

Strategic Management

This convenient guide matches the issues in **Taking Sides: Management, 4/e,** with the corresponding chapters in five of our best-selling McGraw-Hill Strategic Management textbooks by Dess, Lumpkin, Eisner, and McNamara; Gamble, Thompson, and Peteraf; Pearce and Robinson; Rothaermel; and Thompson, Peteraf, Gamble, and Strickland.

TAKING SIDES: Management, 4/e	*Strategic Management: Creating Competitive Advantage, 4/e by Dess, Lumpkin, Eisner, and McNamara*	*Essentials of Strategic Management: The Quest for Competitive Advantage, 3/e by Gamble, Thompson, and Peteraf*	*Strategic Management: Planning for Domestic and Global Competition, 13/e by Pearce and Robinson*	*Strategic Management: Cases and Concepts, 3/e by Rothaermel*	*Crafting & Executing Strategy: The Quest for Competitive Advantage Concepts and Cases, 18/e by Thompson, Peteraf, Gamble, and Strickland*
Issue: Can Managerial Behavior Be Controlled in the Same Manner as Other "Professions"?	**Chapter 11:** Strategic Leadership: Creating a Learning Organization and an Ethical Organization	**Chapter 9:** Strategy, Ethics, and Corporate Social Responsibility	**Chapter 3:** Corporate Social Responsibility and Business Ethics	**Chapter 12:** Corporate Governance, Business Ethics, and Strategic Leadership	**Chapter 9:** Ethics, Corporate Social Responsibility, Environmental Sustainability, and Strategy
Issue: Do Corporations Have a Responsibility to Society Beyond Maximizing Profit?	**Chapter 11:** Strategic Leadership: Creating a Learning Organization and an Ethical Organization	**Chapter 9:** Strategy, Ethics, and Corporate Social Responsibility	**Chapter 3:** Corporate Social Responsibility and Business Ethics	**Chapter 12:** Corporate Governance, Business Ethics, and Strategic Leadership	**Chapter 9:** Ethics, Corporate Social Responsibility, Environmental Sustainability, and Strategy
Issue: Are U.S. CEOs Paid More Than They Deserve?	**Chapter 11:** Strategic Leadership: Creating a Learning Organization and an Ethical Organization	**Chapter 10:** Superior Strategy Execution—Another Path to Competitive Advantage	**Chapter 12:** Leadership and Culture	**Chapter 11:** Organizational Design: Structure, Culture, and Control	**Chapter 10:** Building an Organization Capable of Good Strategy Execution: People, Capabilities, and Structure
Issue: Can Ethical Malaise Be Remedied Through Ethics Education?	**Chapter 11:** Strategic Leadership: Creating a Learning Organization and an Ethical Organization	**Chapter 9:** Strategy, Ethics, and Corporate Social Responsibility	**Chapter 3:** Corporate Social Responsibility and Business Ethics	**Chapter 12:** Corporate Governance, Business Ethics, and Strategic Leadership	**Chapter 9:** Ethics, Corporate Social Responsibility, Environmental Sustainability, and Strategy
Issue: Does an Employer's Need to Monitor Workers Trump Employee Privacy Concerns?	**Chapter 11:** Strategic Leadership: Creating a Learning Organization and an Ethical Organization	**Chapter 10:** Superior Strategy Execution—Another Path to Competitive Advantage	**Chapter 12:** Leadership and Culture	**Chapter 11:** Organizational Design: Structure, Culture, and Control	**Chapter 11:** Managing Internal Operations: Actions That Promote Good Strategy Execution

(Continued)

TAKING SIDES: Management, 4/e	Strategic Management: Creating Competitive Advantage, 4/e by Dess, Lumpkin, Eisner, and McNamara	Essentials of Strategic Management: The Quest for Competitive Advantage, 3/e by Gamble, Thompson, and Peteraf	Strategic Management: Planning for Domestic and Global Competition, 13/e by Pearce and Robinson	Strategic Management: Cases and Concepts, 3/e by Rothaermel	Crafting & Executing Strategy: The Quest for Competitive Advantage Concepts and Cases, 18/e by Thompson, Peteraf, Gamble, and Strickland
Issue: Is Workplace Drug Testing a Wise Corporate Policy?	**Chapter 11:** Strategic Leadership: Creating a Learning Organization and an Ethical Organization	**Chapter 10:** Superior Strategy Execution—Another Path to Competitive Advantage	**Chapter 12:** Leadership and Culture	**Chapter 11:** Organizational Design: Structure, Culture, and Control	**Chapter 11:** Managing Internal Operations: Actions That Promote Good Strategy Execution
Issue: Is Social Media a Tool of Expression or Trouble for Businesses?	**Chapter 11:** Strategic Leadership: Creating a Learning Organization and an Ethical Organization	**Chapter 10:** Superior Strategy Execution—Another Path to Competitive Advantage	**Chapter 12:** Leadership and Culture	**Chapter 11:** Organizational Design: Structure, Culture, and Control	**Chapter 11:** Managing Internal Operations: Actions That Promote Good Strategy Execution
Issue: Is Growth Always an Inherent Corporate Value?	**Chapter 6:** Corporate-Level Strategy: Creating Value Through Diversification	**Chapter 6:** Supplementing the Chosen Competitive Strategy—Other Important Strategy Choices	**Chapter 7:** Long-Term Objectives and Strategies	**Chapter 9:** Corporate Strategy: Acquisitions, Alliances, and Networks	**Chapter 6:** Strengthening a Company's Competitive Position: Strategic Moves, and Scope of Operations
Issue: Is Outsourcing a Wise Corporate Strategy?	**Chapter 6:** Corporate-Level Strategy: Creating Value Through Diversification	**Chapter 6:** Supplementing the Chosen Competitive Strategy—Other Important Strategy Choices	**Chapter 7:** Long-Term Objectives and Strategies	**Chapter 6:** Business Strategy: Differentiation, Cost Leadership, and Integration	**Chapter 6:** Strengthening a Company's Competitive Position: Strategic Moves, and Scope of Operations
Issue: Will the Use of Reshoring/Insourcing by Corporations Increase?	**Chapter 6:** Corporate-Level Strategy: Creating Value Through Diversification	**Chapter 6:** Supplementing the Chosen Competitive Strategy—Other Important Strategy Choices	**Chapter 7:** Long-Term Objectives and Strategies	**Chapter 8:** Corporate Strategy: Vertical Integration and Diversification	**Chapter 6:** Strengthening a Company's Competitive Position: Strategic Moves, and Scope of Operations
Issue: Does Expanding via Mergers and Acquisitions Make for Sound Corporate Strategy?	**Chapter 6:** Corporate-Level Strategy: Creating Value Through Diversification	**Chapter 6:** Supplementing the Chosen Competitive Strategy—Other Important Strategy Choices	**Chapter 7:** Long-Term Objectives and Strategies	**Chapter 9:** Corporate Strategy: Acquisitions, Alliances, and Networks	**Chapter 6:** Strengthening a Company's Competitive Position: Strategic Moves, and Scope of Operations
Issue: Should Corporations Adopt Environmentally Friendly Policies of Corporate Social Responsibility (CSR) and Sustainable Development?	**Chapter 11:** Strategic Leadership: Creating a Learning Organization and an Ethical Organization	**Chapter 9:** Strategy, Ethics, and Corporate Social Responsibility	**Chapter 3:** Corporate Social Responsibility and Business Ethics	**Chapter 12:** Corporate Governance, Business Ethics, and Strategic Leadership	**Chapter 9:** Ethics, Corporate Social Responsibility, Environmental Sustainability, and Strategy
Issue: Is Corporate Sustainability Reporting a Valuable Corporate Reporting Tool?	**Chapter 11:** Strategic Leadership: Creating a Learning Organization and an Ethical Organization	**Chapter 9:** Strategy, Ethics, and Corporate Social Responsibility	**Chapter 3:** Corporate Social Responsibility and Business Ethics	**Chapter 12:** Corporate Governance, Business Ethics, and Strategic Leadership	**Chapter 9:** Ethics, Corporate Social Responsibility, Environmental Sustainability, and Strategy
Issue: Is It Really Possible to Create Sustainable Businesses?	**Chapter 11:** Strategic Leadership: Creating a Learning Organization and an Ethical Organization	**Chapter 9:** Strategy, Ethics, and Corporate Social Responsibility	**Chapter 3:** Corporate Social Responsibility and Business Ethics	**Chapter 12:** Corporate Governance, Business Ethics, and Strategic Leadership	**Chapter 9:** Ethics, Corporate Social Responsibility, Environmental Sustainability, and Strategy
Issue: Are Cap-and-Trade Policies Effective?	**Chapter 7:** International Strategy: Creating Value in Global Markets	**Chapter 7:** Strategies for Competing in International Markets	**Chapter 5:** The Global Environment	**Chapter 10:** Global Strategy: Competing Around the World	**Chapter 7:** Strategies for Competing in International Markets
Issue: Do Unskilled Immigrants Hurt the American Economy?	**Chapter 7:** International Strategy: Creating Value in Global Markets	**Chapter 7:** Strategies for Competing in International Markets	**Chapter 5:** The Global Environment	**Chapter 10:** Global Strategy: Competing Around the World	**Chapter 7:** Strategies for Competing in International Markets

TAKING SIDES: Management, 4/e	Strategic Management: Creating Competitive Advantage, 4/e by Dess, Lumpkin, Eisner, and McNamara	Essentials of Strategic Management: The Quest for Competitive Advantage, 3/e by Gamble, Thompson, and Peteraf	Strategic Management: Planning for Domestic and Global Competition, 13/e by Pearce and Robinson	Strategic Management: Cases and Concepts, 3/e by Rothaermel	Crafting & Executing Strategy: The Quest for Competitive Advantage Concepts and Cases, 18/e by Thompson, Peteraf, Gamble, and Strickland
Issue: Is Economic Globalization Good for Humankind?	**Chapter 7:** International Strategy: Creating Value in Global Markets	**Chapter 7:** Strategies for Competing in International Markets	**Chapter 5:** The Global Environment	**Chapter 10:** Global Strategy: Competing Around the World	**Chapter 7:** Strategies for Competing in International Markets
Issue: Are Protectionist Policies Beneficial to Business?	**Chapter 7:** International Strategy: Creating Value in Global Markets	**Chapter 7:** Strategies for Competing in International Markets	**Chapter 5:** The Global Environment	**Chapter 10:** Global Strategy: Competing Around the World	**Chapter 7:** Strategies for Competing in International Markets

Management

This convenient guide matches the issues in **Taking Sides: Management, 4/e**, with the corresponding chapters in five of our best-selling McGraw-Hill Management textbooks by Bateman and Snell; Ghillyer; Jones and George; Kinicki and Williams.

TAKING SIDES: Management, 4/e	M: Management, 3/e by Bateman and Snell	Management: Leading & Collaborating in a Competitive World, 10/e by Bateman and Snell	Management Now: Skills for 21st Century Management, 1/e by Ghillyer	Contemporary Management, 7/e by Jones and George	Management: A Practical Introduction, 6/e by Kinicki and Williams
Issue: Can Managerial Behavior Be Controlled in the Same Manner as Other "Professions"?	**Chapter 14:** Managerial Control	**Chapter 16:** Managerial Control	**Chapter 11:** Management Control	**Chapter 11:** Organizational Control and Change **Chapter 13:** Motivation and Performance	**Chapter 14:** Power, Influence, & Leadership: From Becoming a Manager to Becoming a Leader
Issue: Do Corporations Have a Responsibility to Society Beyond Maximizing Profit?	**Chapter 4:** Ethics and Corporate Responsibility	**Chapter 5:** Ethics and Corporate Responsibility	**Chapter 13:** Staying Legal and Ethical: Ethical and Social Responsibilities	**Chapter 4:** Ethics and Social Responsibility	**Chapter 3:** The Manager's Changing Work Environment & Ethical Responsibilities: Doing the Right Thing
Issue: Are U.S. CEOs Paid More Than They Deserve?	**Chapter 11:** Motivating People	**Chapter 13:** Motivating for Performance	**Chapter 10:** Motivating People	**Chapter 13:** Motivation and Performance **Chapter 10:** Managing Organizational Structure and Culture	**Chapter 12:** Motivating Employees: Achieving Superior Performance in the Workplace
Issue: Can Ethical Malaise Be Remedied Through Ethics Education?	**Chapter 4:** Ethics and Corporate Responsibility	**Chapter 5:** Ethics and Corporate Responsibility	**Chapter 13:** Staying Legal and Ethical: Ethical and Social Responsibilities	**Chapter 4:** Ethics and Social Responsibility **Chapter 10:** Managing Organizational Structure and Culture	**Chapter 3:** The Manager's Changing Work Environment & Ethical Responsibilities: Doing the Right Thing
Issue: Does an Employer's Need to Monitor Workers Trump Employee Privacy Concerns?	**Chapter 14:** Managerial Control	**Chapter 16:** Managerial Control	**Chapter 11:** Management Control	**Chapter 11:** Organizational Control and Change **Chapter 10:** Managing Organizational Structure and Culture	**Chapter 3:** The Manager's Changing Work Environment & Ethical Responsibilities: Doing the Right Thing
Issue: Is Workplace Drug Testing a Wise Corporate Policy?	**Chapter 14:** Managerial Control	**Chapter 16:** Managerial Control	**Chapter 11:** Management Control	**Chapter 11:** Organizational Control and Change **Chapter 10:** Managing Organizational Structure and Culture	**Chapter 3:** The Manager's Changing Work Environment & Ethical Responsibilities: Doing the Right Thing
Issue: Is Social Media a Tool of Expression or Trouble for Businesses?	**Chapter 14:** Managerial Control	**Chapter 16:** Managerial Control	**Chapter 11:** Management Control	**Chapter 11:** Organizational Control and Change **Chapter 10:** Managing Organizational Structure and Culture	**Chapter 3:** The Manager's Changing Work Environment & Ethical Responsibilities: Doing the Right Thing

(Continued)

TAKING SIDES: Management, 4/e	M: Management, 3/e by Bateman and Snell	Management: Leading & Collaborating in a Competitive World, 10/e by Bateman and Snell	Management Now: Skills for 21st Century Management, 1/e by Ghillyer	Contemporary Management, 7/e by Jones and George	Management: A Practical Introduction, 6/e by Kinicki and Williams
Issue: Is Growth Always an Inherent Corporate Value?	**Chapter 5:** Strategic Planning and Decision Making	**Chapter 4:** Planning and Strategic Management	**Chapter 4:** Strategic Management	**Chapter 6:** Managing in the Global Environment	**Chapter 4:** Strategic Management: How Exceptional Managers Realize a Grand Design
Issue: Is Outsourcing a Wise Corporate Strategy?	**Chapter 5:** Strategic Planning and Decision Making	**Chapter 4:** Planning and Strategic Management	**Chapter 4:** Strategic Management	**Chapter 6:** Managing in the Global Environment	**Chapter 4:** Strategic Management: How Exceptional Managers Realize a Grand Design
Issue: Will the Use of Reshoring/Insourcing by Corporations Increase?	**Chapter 5:** Strategic Planning and Decision Making	**Chapter 4:** Planning and Strategic Management	**Chapter 4:** Strategic Management	**Chapter 6:** Managing in the Global Environment	**Chapter 4:** Strategic Management: How Exceptional Managers Realize a Grand Design
Issue: Does Expanding via Mergers and Acquisitions Make for Sound Corporate Strategy?	**Chapter 5:** Strategic Planning and Decision Making	**Chapter 4:** Planning and Strategic Management	**Chapter 4:** Strategic Management	**Chapter 6:** Managing in the Global Environment	**Chapter 4:** Strategic Management: How Exceptional Managers Realize a Grand Design
Issue: Should Corporations Adopt Environmentally Friendly Policies of Corporate Social Responsibility (CSR) and Sustainable Development?	**Chapter 4:** Ethics and Corporate Responsibility	**Chapter 5:** Ethics and Corporate Responsibility	**Chapter 13:** Staying Legal and Ethical: Ethical and Social Responsibilities	**Chapter 4:** Ethics and Social Responsibility	**Chapter 3:** The Manager's Changing Work Environment & Ethical Responsibilities: Doing the Right Thing
Issue: Is Corporate Sustainability Reporting a Valuable Corporate Reporting Tool?	**Chapter 4:** Ethics and Corporate Responsibility	**Chapter 5:** Ethics and Corporate Responsibility	**Chapter 13:** Staying Legal and Ethical: Ethical and Social Responsibilities	**Chapter 4:** Ethics and Social Responsibility	**Chapter 3:** The Manager's Changing Work Environment & Ethical Responsibilities: Doing the Right Thing
Issue: Is It Really Possible to Create Sustainable Businesses?	**Chapter 5:** Strategic Planning and Decision Making	**Chapter 4:** Planning and Strategic Management	**Chapter 4:** Strategic Management	**Chapter 6:** Managing in the Global Environment	**Chapter 4:** Strategic Management: How Exceptional Managers Realize a Grand Design
Issue: Are Cap-and-Trade Policies Effective?	**Chapter 5:** Strategic Planning and Decision Making	**Chapter 4:** Planning and Strategic Management	**Chapter 4:** Strategic Management	**Chapter 6:** Managing in the Global Environment	**Chapter 4:** Strategic Management: How Exceptional Managers Realize a Grand Design
Issue: Do Unskilled Immigrants Hurt the American Economy?	**Chapter 9:** Managing Diversity and Inclusion	**Chapter 11:** Managing the Diverse Workforce	**Chapter 13:** Staying Legal and Ethical: Ethical and Social Responsibilities	**Chapter 5:** Managing Diverse Employees in a Multicultural Environment	**Chapter 9:** Human Resource Management: Getting the Right People for Managerial Success
Issue: Is Economic Globalization Good for Humankind?	**Chapter 1:** Managing Effectively in a Changing World	**Chapter 6:** International Management	**Chapter 5:** Global Management	**Chapter 6:** Managing in the Global Environment	**Chapter 4:** Global Management: Managing Across Borders
Issue: Are Protectionist Policies Beneficial to Business?	**Chapter 1:** Managing Effectively in a Changing World	**Chapter 6:** International Management	**Chapter 5:** Global Management	**Chapter 6:** Managing in the Global Environment	**Chapter 4:** Global Management: Managing Across Borders

International Business

This convenient guide matches the issues in **Taking Sides: Management, 4/e,** with the corresponding chapters in two of our best-selling McGraw-Hill International Business textbooks by Ball, Geringer, McNett, and Minor; and Hill.

TAKING SIDES: Management, 4/e	International Business: The Challenge of Global Competition, 13/e by Ball, Geringer, McNett, and Minor	International Business: Competing in the Global Marketplace, 9/e by Hill
Issue: Can Managerial Behavior Be Controlled in the Same Manner as Other "Professions"?	**Chapter 17:** Managing Human Resources in an International Context	**Chapter 19:** Global Human Resource Management

TAKING SIDES: Management, 4/e	International Business: The Challenge of Global Competition, 13/e by Ball, Geringer, McNett, and Minor	International Business: Competing in the Global Marketplace, 9/e by Hill
Issue: Do Corporations Have a Responsibility to Society Beyond Maximizing Profit?	**Chapter 11:** Strategic Leadership: Creating a Learning Organization and an Ethical Organization	**Chapter 5:** Ethics in International Business
Issue: Are U.S. CEOs Paid More Than They Deserve?	**Chapter 17:** Managing Human Resources in an International Context	**Chapter 19:** Global Human Resource Management
Issue: Can Ethical Malaise Be Remedied Through Ethics Education?	**Chapter 11:** Strategic Leadership: Creating a Learning Organization and an Ethical Organization	**Chapter 5:** Ethics in International Business
Issue: Does an Employer's Need to Monitor Workers Trump Employee Privacy Concerns?	**Chapter 17:** Managing Human Resources in an International Context	**Chapter 19:** Global Human Resource Management
Issue: Is Workplace Drug Testing a Wise Corporate Policy?	**Chapter 17:** Managing Human Resources in an International Context	**Chapter 19:** Global Human Resource Management
Issue: Is Social Media a Tool of Expression or Trouble for Businesses?	**Chapter 17:** Managing Human Resources in an International Context	**Chapter 19:** Global Human Resource Management
Issue: Is Growth Always an Inherent Corporate Value?	**Chapter 9:** International Competitive Strategy	**Chapter 13:** The Strategy of International Business
Issue: Is Outsourcing a Wise Corporate Strategy?	**Chapter 9:** International Competitive Strategy	**Chapter 13:** The Strategy of International Business
Issue: Will the Use of Reshoring/Insourcing by Corporations Increase?	**Chapter 9:** International Competitive Strategy	**Chapter 13:** The Strategy of International Business
Issue: Does Expanding via Mergers and Acquisitions Make for Sound Corporate Strategy?	**Chapter 9:** International Competitive Strategy	**Chapter 13:** The Strategy of International Business
Issue: Should Corporations Adopt Environmentally Friendly Policies of Corporate Social Responsibility (CSR) and Sustainable Development?	**Chapter 9:** International Competitive Strategy	**Chapter 13:** The Strategy of International Business
Issue: Is Corporate Sustainability Reporting a Valuable Corporate Reporting Tool?	**Chapter 5:** Natural Resources and Environmental Sustainability	**Chapter 5:** Ethics in International Business
Issue: Is It Really Possible to Create Sustainable Businesses?	**Chapter 5:** Natural Resources and Environmental Sustainability	**Chapter 5:** Ethics in International Business
Issue: Are Cap-and-Trade Policies Effective?	**Chapter 6:** Political and Trade Forces	**Chapter 2:** National Differences in Political Economy
Issue: Do Unskilled Immigrants Hurt the American Economy?	**Chapter 17:** Managing Human Resources in an International Context	**Chapter 19:** Global Human Resource Management
Issue: Is Economic Globalization Good for Humankind?	**Chapter 6:** Political and Trade Forces	**Chapter 2:** National Differences in Political Economy
Issue: Are Protectionist Policies Beneficial to Business?	**Chapter 6:** Political and Trade Forces	**Chapter 2:** National Differences in Political Economy

Topic Guide

Selected, Edited, and with Issue Framing Material by:
Kathleen J. Barnes, *East Stroudsburg University*
and
George E. Smith, *Albright College*

This topic guide suggests how the selections in this ExpressBook relate to the subjects covered in your course. You may want to use the topics listed on these pages to search the web more easily.

All the issues that relate to each topic are listed below the bold-faced term.

Cap-and-Trade Policy

Are Cap-and-Trade Policies Effective?

CEO Compensation

Are U.S. CEOs Paid More Than They Deserve?

Corporate Social Responsibility

Do Corporations Have a Responsibility to Society Beyond Maximizing Profit?
Is Corporate Sustainability Reporting a Valuable Corporate Reporting Tool?
Should Corporations Adopt Environmentally Friendly Policies of Corporate Social Responsibility (CSR) and Sustainable Development?

Corporate Strategy

Do Corporations Have a Responsibility to Society Beyond Maximizing Profit?
Does Expanding via Mergers and Acquisitions Make for Sound Corporate Strategy?
Is Growth Always an Inherent Corporate Value?
Is it Really Possible to Create Sustainable Businesses?
Is Outsourcing a Wise Corporate Strategy?
Should Corporations Adopt Environmentally Friendly Policies of Corporate Society Responsibility (CSR) and Sustainable Development?
Will the Use of Reshoring/Insourcing by Corporations Increase?

Drug Testing

Is Workplace Drug Testing a Wise Corporate Policy?

Education

Can Ethical Malaise Be Remedied Through Ethics Education?

Employee Monitoring

Does an Employer's Need to Monitor Workers Trump Employee Privacy Concerns?
Is Workplace Drug Testing a Wise Corporate Policy?

Employee Privacy

Does an Employer's Need to Monitor Workers Trump Employee Privacy Concerns?
Is Workplace Drug Testing a Wise Corporate Policy?

Employment

Do Unskilled Immigrants Hurt the American Economy?

Does an Employer's Need to Monitor Workers Trump Employee Privacy Concerns?

Environment

Is Corporate Sustainability Reporting a Valuable Corporate Reporting Tool?
Are Cap-and-Trade Policies Effective?
Is it Really Possible to Create Sustainable Businesses?
Should Corporations Adopt Environmentally Friendly Policies of Corporate Social Responsibility (CSR) and Sustainable Development?

Ethics

Are U.S. CEOs Paid More Than They Deserve?
Can Ethical Malaise Be Remedied Through Ethics Education?
Do Corporations Have a Responsibility to Society Beyond Maximizing Profit?
Does an Employer's Need to Monitor Workers Trump Employee Privacy Concerns?
Can Managerial Behavior Be Controlled in the Same Manner as Other "Professions"?

Global Issues

Are Cap-and-Trade Policies Effective?
Is Economic Globalization Good for Humankind?

Globalization

Are Protectionist Policies Beneficial to Business?
Is Economic Globalization Good for Humankind?

Government

Are Protectionist Policies Beneficial to Business?
Are Cap-and-Trade Policies Effective?

Human Resource Management

Can Ethical Malaise Be Remedied Through Ethics Education?
Does an Employer's Need to Monitor Workers Trump Employee Privacy Concerns?
Is Workplace Drug Testing a Wise Corporate Policy?
Is Social Media a Tool of Expression or Trouble for Businesses?

Human Rights

Do Unskilled Immigrants Hurt the American Economy?
Does an Employer's Need to Monitor Workers Trump Employee Privacy Concerns?
Is Workplace Drug Testing a Wise Corporate Policy?

(Continued)

Immigration

Do Unskilled Immigrants Hurt the American Economy?

Insourcing

Is Outsourcing a Wise Corporate Strategy?
Will the Use of Reshoring/Insourcing by Corporations Increase?

International Management

Are Protectionist Policies Beneficial to Business?
Do Unskilled Immigrants Hurt the American Economy?
Is Economic Globalization Good for Humankind?

Mergers and Acquisitions

Does Expanding via Mergers and Acquisitions Make for Sound
    Corporate Strategy?
Is Social Media a Tool of Expression or Trouble for Businesses?

Outsourcing

Is Outsourcing a Wise Corporate Strategy?
Will the Use of Reshoring/Insourcing by Corporations Increase?

Policy

Does an Employer's Need to Monitor Workers Trump Employee Privacy
    Concerns?
Is Workplace Drug Testing a Wise Corporate Policy?
Is Social Media a Tool of Expression or Trouble for Businesses?

Pollution

Are Cap-and-Trade Policies Effective?
Should Corporations Adopt Environmentally Friendly Policies of
    Corporate Social Responsibility (CSR) and Sustainable Development?

Professionalization

Can Managerial Behavior Be Controlled in the Same Manner as Other
    "Professions"?

Protectionism

Are Protectionist Policies Beneficial to Business?

Reshoring

Is Outsourcing a Wise Corporate Strategy?
Will the Use of Reshoring/Insourcing by Corporations Increase?

Social Media

Is Social Media a Tool of Expression or Trouble for Businesses?

Strategic Management

Does Expanding via Mergers and Acquisitions Make for Sound
    Corporate Strategy?
Is Growth Always an Inherent Corporate Value?
Is Outsourcing a Wise Corporate Strategy?
Will the Use of Reshoring/Insourcing by Corporations Increase?

Sustainability

Is Corporate Sustainability Reporting a Valuable Corporate Reporting
    Tool?
Is It Really Possible to Create Sustainable Businesses?
Should Corporations Adopt Environmentally Friendly Policies of
    Corporate Social Responsibility (CSR) and Sustainable Development?

Technology

Does an Employer's Need to Monitor Workers Trump Employee Privacy
    Concerns?
Is Social Media a Tool of Expression or Trouble for Businesses?

Training

Can Ethical Malaise Be Remedied Through Ethics Education?

Unskilled Immigrants

Do Unskilled Immigrants Hurt the American Economy?

Workplace Monitoring

Does an Employer's Need to Monitor Workers Trump Employee Privacy
    Concerns?

Introduction

Controversial Issues in Management

This introduction consists of five units, each of which briefly discusses a different area of business management. Each unit provides important information about a specific management area and sets the stage for the debate topics that comprise the five parts of this book. This introduction is organized paralleling the debate topics presentation in the text: the first unit discusses business ethics–related issues; the second unit covers human resource management–related issues; strategic management–related issues are discussed in the third unit; environment-related issues are covered in the fourth unit; and international management–related issues are discussed in the fifth unit.

Business Ethics and Management

Many business ethics scholars analyze this complex management topic at two levels. The macro-level involves issues broad in nature and relevant for analysis at the organizational level. At the micro-level of analysis, business ethics is concerned primarily with the ethical decision-making process of individuals in the workplace.

Business Ethics and Taking Sides

The first unit of this book consists of four debates—two at the macro and two at the micro-levels of analyses. Each topic is in a debate format and presents articles supportive of each side.

The first micro-level issue involves the question of why managerial behavior can't be controlled in the same manner as other "professions." Changes have occurred over the past 150 years in the fields of medicine, law, and accounting that specifically address these issues and this behavior. While one author indicates that it is his belief that the discipline of management is a profession, the opposing author in this section makes the observation that management is not a profession based on the fact that various facets of recognized and accepted "professions" are absent. At the heart of this issue is the ongoing debate of how to best control managerial behavior.

The second issue presents the macro-level corporate social responsibility (CSR) versus profit maximization controversy. Advocates of free-market capitalism believe that the only responsibility an organization has is to maximize profits for its shareholders, whereas stakeholder theory states that managers have obligations that go beyond profit maximization since they are concerned with satisfying the needs of all of stakeholders. Thus, those firms that do not place the interests of one set of stakeholders above the rest are acting in a *socially responsible* manner, whereas firms that stick to the traditional emphasis of maximizing profit with disregard of other stakeholder interests are frequently viewed as irresponsible and immoral.

The next issue examines another highly controversial micro-level topic, the issue of executive pay. In recent years, the business and news media have portrayed numerous examples of U.S. CEOs receiving millions of dollars in salary and benefits while their organizations were posting losses, laying off workers, and, in some instances, even declaring bankruptcy. As a result of the public outrage generated by these stories, the question of top-level management compensation has taken on greater significance in the field of management. The specific question addressed in this issue is whether or not CEO pay is just.

The final topic in this section is the macro-level issue of whether ethical malaise can be remedied through ethics education. While there are different approaches for potentially improving ethical decision making and behavior in our corporations, many of these corporations have elected to pursue improvement via formal ethics education and training. This trend has been instituted by the business schools that supply much of the labor pool to these corporations as well. The two articles comprising this debate examine whether ethical education can remedy ethical malaise. As is the case with other issues in this text, it seems that the more learns about this topic the more difficult it becomes to draw a conclusion!

Human Resource Management

Human resource management (HRM) is the design and implementation of formal systems that utilize human resources to accomplish organizational goals (Mathis and Jackson, *Human Resource Management*, 12th ed., South-Western Thompson, 2008). Although the fields of organizational behavior and human resource management are both conducted primarily at the individual level of analysis, HRM is a much more practical area of management characterized by laws, regulations, and formal systems.

Human Resource Management and Taking Sides

The second unit of this book consists of three debates. Each topic is in a debate format and presents articles supportive of each side.

The first issue addresses whether an employer's need to monitor workers trumps employee privacy concerns. The authors in this issue present arguments defending an employer's need to monitor employee behavior and criticizing the practice. One particularly challenging question in this issue is that of the rights of employers and employees when using electronic media such as email and social media tools.

The second topic in this unit asks if workplace drug testing is a wise corporate strategy, particularly in light of the seemingly obvious concerns about privacy rights. This issue examines the benefits and costs of drug testing as well as the rationale for conducting these tests.

A discussion regarding a company's right to monitor its employees is presented in the final issue of this section. A later issue furthers this discussion by specifically questioning whether or not social media are tools of expression for employees or potential trouble for businesses. Social media have become a marketing tool used by many organizations. It seems like every company has a Facebook page and wants to be "liked." The issue here is what are the concerns that social media presents for corporations and how do corporations attempt to negotiate those concerns.

Strategic Management

While HRM is primarily concerned with understanding, motivating, and managing individual employees in the workplace, the focus of strategic management is on the organization as a whole. The basic unit of strategic management is a *strategy*. A strategy is a plan designed to achieve a specific goal or organizational target. In the business world, strategic management refers to the process of effectively developing and executing the collection of plans designed to achieve the organization's goals. Typically, the goals of the organization reflect the overall purpose of the company as spelled out in the firm's mission statement. In most large companies, top-level executives and managers are responsible for the development of the organization's strategies, while mid-level managers and supervisors are typically in charge of making sure the strategies are implemented successfully. Thus, the executives are involved in *strategy formulation*, while the managers and supervisors are concerned with *strategy implementation*.

Strategic Management and Taking Sides

The third unit of this text contains four issues particularly relevant to the topic of strategic management. U.S. firms have been adopting the view that reducing costs through labor force reductions—downsizing—should not be reserved only for desperate firms on the edge of bankruptcy. Indeed, many organizations now routinely reduce their workforce even when the firm is profitable and its future prospects appear positive. Closely related to downsizing is the corporate strategy of outsourcing. While moving domestically expensive operational functions to a country with lower wage rates may reduce costs, many have argued that it is an unpatriotic strategy and should not be condoned, particularly when the economy is in bad shape. Interestingly, one of the issues in this section explores corporations' increased use of reshoring (sometimes called "backshoring," which is when jobs that were offshored are brought back onshore) and insourcing (a management decision made to maintain control of critical production processes or competencies).

Important topics in section three are growth and mergers and acquisitions (M&As) as corporate initiatives and whether growth is always an inherent corporate value. Additionally, although M&A as a mode of corporate expansion has been around since at least the Industrial Revolution, it exploded in the early 1980s. Presently, merger activity seems to be continuing unabated as firms seek strength and security in size. Here, inquiry as to whether or not expanding via mergers and/or acquisitions really is wise strategy is explored.

Environmental Management

Over the last quarter century, environmental managerial challenges have grown in importance so dramatically that executives in corporate America have no alternative but to take them into account when formulating organizational strategy. Specifically, U.S. organizations now face the difficult challenge of maintaining financial success while recognizing obligations to protect and maintain the world's physical environment.

Environmental Management and Taking Sides

An underlying assumption of the environmental movement in the United States and abroad is that the health of the planet is deteriorating and that business activity is primarily responsible. An important idea that emerged in the 1980s in response to this assumption is the concept of sustainable development. This idea, a conceptual child of corporate social responsibility, holds that corporations should conduct their business activities and develop their plans and goals within a framework that recognizes that the earth's resources are limited and must be preserved. Consequently, corporations should take into account the needs of future generations when mapping out future growth strategies. Not surprisingly, however, this concept is controversial to many. Sustainability-related topics and corporate sustainability reporting's practice and value are some of the topics explored. One issue questions the goal of sustainability for business and the potential for creating sustainable businesses. Finally, the last issue in this section addresses cap-and-trade policies. This issue examines the history and mechanics of cap-and-trade policies as well as the potential barriers and challenges to expanding the use of these policies.

International Management

In response to the tremendous growth of competition from international firms, corporations all over the world have embraced the idea of globalization by extending sales and/or production operations to markets abroad. Globalization offers firms many advantages: access to new sources of cheap labor; access to new sources of highly skilled labor; access to established markets; and access to emerging markets (e.g., China, Russia, and

India). These advantages come at a cost, as globalization, by its very definition, means greater competition. Thus, a second critical challenge facing U.S. managers is responding successfully to the tremendous growth of competition from international firms, both here and abroad.

International Management and Taking Sides

One of the most important and controversial social issues of our time is the growing number of illegal aliens in the United States. This issue poses a serious problem to the nation and is likely to be an important political, social, and economic issue for the foreseeable future. In the next we ask whether U.S. firms should be allowed to tap into this reservoir of labor legally or whether doing so hurts the American economy. Passions run high when this topic is raised, so it's no surprise that the two articles presented come to completely different conclusions.

A growing number of countries around the world have embraced the idea of globalization as a means of raising the standard of living for their citizens. Despite the fact that much evidence attests to the economic benefits that accrue as a result of globalization, there are those who question whether globalization on the whole is a positive occurrence. The question, "Is Economic Globalization Good for Humankind?" provides two competing answers. There are a growing number of politicians, media pundits, and business experts who are calling for the U.S. president to help the U.S. economy by enacting a wide range of protectionist economic policies. On the other hand, the vast majority of economists is skeptical of protectionism and seemingly appears to have much empirical and historical evidence on hand to support their view. This leads to the text's final topic, "Are Protectionist Policies Beneficial to Business?"

UNIT 1

UNIT

Ethical Issues for Managers

*A*n old saying holds that business ethics is an oxymoron. For years, the generally accepted view on morality and business was that they don't mix, that business is a game played by a different set of rules. To act morally was to act weakly. And in the business arena, weak firms were dead firms.

    Things certainly change. In today's business arena, firms are finding that immoral behavior can prove fatal. The financial industry's recent experiences amid the financial meltdown that began Fall 2008 appear to lend credence to those who believe that ethical behavior is an afterthought in corporate boardrooms. Ethical behavior is certainly not an afterthought in this unit, which examines several ethically laden issues of importance to many managers in corporate America.

Selected, Edited, and with Issue Framing Material by:
Kathleen J. Barnes, *East Stroudsburg University*
and
George E. Smith, *Albright College*

ISSUE

Can Managerial Behavior Be Controlled in the Same Manner as Other "Professions"?

YES: **Charles D. Ellis**, from "Is Management Becoming a Profession?" *Qn* (Spring 2007, pp. 51–56)

NO: **Richard Barker**, from "No, Management Is *Not* a Profession," *Harvard Business Review* (July/August 2010, pp. 52–60)

Learning Outcomes

After reading this issue you should be able to:

- Provide a definition of what a profession is.
- Discuss whether or not management is a profession.
- Explain the problem(s) and limitations of controlling management in the same manner as other professions.
- Understand the challenge of controlling and insuring ethical and moral behavior in the field and practice of management.

ISSUE SUMMARY

YES: Charles D. Ellis opens this selection by acknowledging changes that have occurred over the past 150 years in the fields of medicine, law, and accounting. Ellis indicates in this selection that it is his belief that the discipline of management is a profession.

NO: Professor Barker of Cambridge University makes the observation that management is not a profession based on the fact that various facets of recognized and accepted "professions" are absent.

The challenge of maintaining morally sound and correct ethical principles of business conduct has been an ongoing one. For example, Ronald W. Clement notes that "In recent years, the business news in the United States has been rife with reports of misconduct by American corporations" (Clement, 2006, p. 313). To this Al Gini pessimistically notes that "Conventional wisdom paradoxically tells us that even though change is constant, certain things never really change. Or even when things appear to change, they wind up coming back again" (Gini, 2004, p. 9). Both of these scholars proceed to outline contemporary and historical ethical lapses to illustrate their theses and in the case of Gini's article he notes the historical presence of Ponzi-like schemes in the 1920s, 1970s, and 1980s as he illustrates how society and business repeat behavior—good and bad—throughout time.

The first issue in this text *Taking Sides: Clashing Views in Management* explores the challenge of regulating managerial behavior and promoting and maintaining ethical standards. As management students and practitioners we may have wondered why it is that some "professions" experience many challenges and calls for reform while others quietly go about their business avoiding public scrutiny. The approach taken in this first issue is to question whether managers and those practicing management should be formally considered "professionals." Put simply, the question is, Is management a profession similar in nature to other professions such as law and medicine? The answer to this question may have implications for how to control and monitor those pursuing managerial activities.

While some may argue that this is a purely academic debate, the underlying theme of this discussion is the question of how best to manage and control the behavior of managers. The fundamental argument being made here is, if managers are formally trained and often pursue and receive graduate degrees such as the Master of

Business Administration (MBA), why then can't managers be controlled in the same fashion that doctors, lawyers, and architects are? After all, individuals practicing their craft in all of these fields are thought of or referred to as professionals by the public.

In exploring this issue, the two authors address the similarities and differences of the field of management and its study and practice to other accepted professional fields. One of the foundational points of discussion is what is meant by the word "profession." This discussion is shaped by defining what a profession is or should include.

In discussing this issue, Ellis notes that professions possess four levels or components. In his estimation professions must consist of or include:

- Mastery of specific skills.
- Knowledge and understanding of numerous concepts and analytical models.
- Understanding of core and enduring principles of good practice.
- Establishment of core values or ethics that guide behavior when facing the new and unfamiliar.

Based on these elements, Ellis makes his argument that management currently is or is becoming a formal profession. To support this position Ellis provides some evidence that other fields currently recognized as professions have had to pass through a transitory period of time in similar fashion to what management is experiencing.

In contrast, Professor Barker is not sympathetic to Mr. Ellis's claim that management is a profession. In his estimation, management as a field of study and practice is lacking many facets associated with recognized and accepted "professions." An argument that Professor Barker makes is that there are ideas and practices that cannot be effectively taught in a classroom setting and this distances management—as practiced—from attaining the formal status of "profession."

While the academic and theoretical discussion of whether or not management is a profession is intriguing in and of itself, one of the anticipated outcomes of an examination of these selections and this topic is that the reader begins to understand the difficulties of defining professions and more importantly defining management, its educational and certification process, and the controlling and monitoring of the field. Ultimately, it is hoped that you will begin to understand the difficulty of controlling entrance into the field and defining and enforcing of professional standards for not just management, but all "professional" fields.

YES ↵   **Charles D. Ellis**

Is Management Becoming a Profession?

Times change: 150 years ago, most doctors did not go to medical school; 100 years ago, few lawyers thought law school necessary; 75 years ago, most accountants were not CPAs; and 50 years ago, most business leaders had no MBA. Today, most corporate leaders would advise the best and brightest intent on careers in management to study in business school, future doctors to go to medical school, and lawyers to law school. In management, as in other professions, the accumulated knowledge and understanding requisite to great career success have become so extensive and complex—and so very worth understanding—that it is wise to carve out several years for serious study before practicing. While inexperienced people don't recognize that reality, experienced people understand and know it to be true.

Is there enough evidence to say that management is becoming a profession? At least four levels of a profession can be considered: mastery of specific skills; knowledge and understanding of numerous concepts and analytical models; understanding of core and enduring principles of good practice; and establishment of core values or ethics that guide behavior when facing the new and unfamiliar. Skills can be taught and learned—and so can most forms of knowledge. But an understanding of core principles and of the overriding importance of ethics must be internalized by each individual, because ethics and values matter most when dealing with the new and unfamiliar—and when nobody's looking.

Whether business management has become a profession depends, to put it candidly, on the individual professional, and the key factor is a commitment to serve others and to serve one's organization. Not all skillful and hardworking business managers are noble; some are despicable. But the very best—Alfred Sloan, Tom Watson, Herman Abs, Joe Wilson, Marvin Bower, Lou Gerstner, John Brown, Warren Buffett, Indra Nooyi, Jeff Immelt, Fred Smith, etc.—clearly serve others inside their organizations and in their communities and nations. (I've written a biography of Joe Wilson, because I think he's such an exemplary role model.)

Buffett, America's favorite business professional, has combined his knowledge and understanding as an investor to increase his effectiveness as a businessman and his knowledge and understanding as a businessman to increase his effectiveness as an investor. The third side of his professional triangle is a rigorous commitment to assertive business ethics because he sees principled behavior as a requirement for superb results. People want to do business—as employees, customers, and suppliers—with ethically strong business organizations. And the people who care the most are the employees, because we all want to be proud of our work organizations and we know ourselves by the companies we keep.

Here at Yale, the obvious illustration of professionalism in business is chief investment officer David Swensen, who has foregone spectacular personal financial compensation to produce the world's best record of investment management with all the consequential benefits to the strength of a great university. He is of course rivaled by his president, Richard C. Levin.

The profession of management is threatened by an absurd oversimplification: money. Sure, we all want to earn enough to provide well for our families, but equally surely, for the very talented in our society, that's not really a problem. Realistically, the "problem of money" is more accurately and usefully framed in two parts: (1) How will I protect my family from the harms of surplus income which may tempt us away from our real values? (2) If I achieve more than my family really wants to spend, how will I invest it in the best philanthropic purposes to advance scientific discovery, healthcare, education, and the arts, or to serve others who are less fortunate?

All of us with careers in business management would do well to consider that some of our society's greatest managers are in fields without prospects of high pay or wealth accumulation—the military, the judiciary, civil service, education—including the leaders of complex, multibillion-dollar universities and other institutions we treasure because they enrich our lives.

Management in business is and will be recognized as a profession to the extent that those engaged see it as a service—and a calling. For those who are so fortunate to see their work in leadership and management as a service, the familiar guideline applies: "You get out of it at least what you put into it—and often much more."

It is ironic that as management—usually thought of as business management—is shifting toward being a profession, some of the traditional learned professions are shifting toward "business" disciplines. As their organizations get larger and more concerned with economics and billable hours, lawyers express concerns about losing the treasured traditions of the legal profession, and medical doctors complain about insurance costs, fixed overheads, and pressures for "productivity." While most professions are only now learning how to work effectively in large groups, business management has long worked with large groups and is now learning how to develop greater depth and expertise in achieving intended results reliably and predictably.

Words migrate disruptively in meaning, so we must not be distracted by phrases like "she's a real pro" meaning self-disciplined, or "he acted very professionally," meaning calmly and unemotionally despite severe pressures, or "professional" as opposed to "amateur" in athletics.

> "People want to do business—as employees, customers, and suppliers—with ethically strong business organizations. And the people who care the most are the employees, because we all want to be proud of our work organizations and we know ourselves by the companies we keep."

Ethics of leadership, like pornography, is easier to recognize than to define, but it's fair to say that in business you are doing ethical things when you do them because they're right—even though it's costing you money. In *Profiles in Courage*, JFK focused on describing politicians who took actions because they believed those actions were right even though they lost votes or advancement. Two dimensions of ethics are important to management professionals: the hygienic or nonnegative ethics of not doing wrong and the affirmative ethics of deliberately doing what's really right and reaching to a higher standard. Rising to a higher standard of true professionalism is what George Marshall did when he was privately keen to lead the invasion of Europe—and everyone knew he was best qualified—but he insisted on giving FDR the choice, knowing he would be kept in Washington because his president and his nation needed him. Holding to a higher professional standard is what American Funds did when they decided not to offer a money-market fund or, later on, an emerging-market fund when each "product" was in hot demand but investors would, over the long term, have made unwise decisions.

Other aspects of a maturing profession include self-regulatory powers to certify the competence of practitioners and disciplinary powers to punish those who don't get it. As much as I believe management as a discipline is indeed a profession, I do not believe that SRO status will ever come to the management profession. As a part of holding managers accountable to and responsible for the real interests of laymen, I do hope to see individual and institutional commitments to continuous study and learning (as the military professionals so splendidly exemplify with their commitments to war colleges and civilian PhD programs) to keep up with the burgeoning knowledge and to develop cumulative mastery, with rigorous examinations to demonstrate requisite mastery.

Michael Bloomberg is a professional's professional in leadership and management. As block trading and capital markets were developing in the 1970s, he led Salomon Brothers to the top of a very competitive league. Then, having had some experience with computers, he conceptualized and created a global high-tech information business of such dynamism that it outperformed all competitors. More recently, as mayor of New York City, he has been one of America's most successful political leaders. Among the panoply of challenges facing the mayor of our largest city, one of the easiest to ignore must be the appointment of judges for the city's Family Courts—traditionally a dumping ground for political hangers-on—but Mayor Bloomberg has insisted on selecting those judges with care because those courts impact kids' lives. As a very busy man, he spends two full days each year with a group of experienced lawyers and child psychologists interviewing candidates. He said, "We couldn't care less about their political parties. We just want to know how much they know and understand about kids. If they're really good on understanding kids in peril, they get appointed."

Professions are simultaneously a cluster of intellectual disciplines, a community of shared ethical values, and a commitment to serve. In business, the appropriate term for the superior professional at work is "servant-leader"—a leader who is in service to the organization and its achievement of the highest satisfactions for customers, workers, and the community. If we are not achieving substantial results on all three dimensions, we should ask the obvious question: Why not?

CHARLES D. ELLIS is a consultant in investing; director; and former managing partner of Greenwich Associates.

PLEASE NOTE: To access the "NO" selection, please refer to "No, Management Is Not a Profession," by Richard Barker immediately following this issue.

EXPLORING THE ISSUE

Can Managerial Behavior Be Controlled in the Same Manner as Other "Professions"?

Critical Thinking and Reflection

1. What should a manager's formal academic curriculum look like or consist of?
2. Should management be recognized as a "profession"? Why or why not?
3. How should management be formally controlled if it were to be recognized as a profession?
4. Should the "professional" status of management really change managers' behavior?
5. Is formal education a requirement of management practice? Should it be?
6. Are there other solutions that could be used to attempt to ensure ethical and moral managerial behavior and practice?

Is There Common Ground?

Both selections of this debate make strong cases for their positions. The crux of this debate hinges on the issues of access to the field of management and the formal educational requirements of a practicing manager (if any). The common ground that exists with this issue is answering the question of how to effectively monitor and control individual/managerial behavior. A formal profession like law or medicine has known, formalized mechanisms in place that guarantee a level of competency; maintain some level of control; and if necessary provide for censure and exclusion from practicing within the field. At present, no such mechanism exists in the field of management. Thus, while the profession debate may not continue to resonate loudly going forward, the debate of how to control managerial behavior will continue to be ever present.

Additional Resources

Barker, R. (2010). "Management Is Not and Can Never Be a Profession," *Financial Times*, September 5.

Bowen, H.R. (1955). "Business Management: A Profession?" *Annals of the American Academy of Political and Social Science*, January, pp. 112–117.

Clement, R.W. (2006). "Just How Unethical Is American Business?" *Business Horizons*, p. 313.

Cogan, M.L. (1955). "The Problems of Defining a Profession," *Annals of the American Academy of Political and Social Science*, January, pp. 105–111.

Donaldson, T. (2000). "Are Business Managers 'Professionals'"? *Business Ethics Quarterly*, January, pp. 83–94.

Gini, A. (2004). "Business, Ethics, and Leadership in a Post Enron Era," *Journal of Leadership & Organizational Studies*, p. 9.

Khurana, R. and Nohria, N. (2008). "Time to Make Management a Profession," *Harvard Business Review*, October, pp. 70–77.

Pfeffer, J. (2011). "Management a Profession? Where's the Proof?" *Harvard Business Review*, September, p. 38.

Podolny, J.M. (2009). "Buck Stops (and Starts) at Business School," *Harvard Business Review*, June, pp. 62–67.

Internet References . . .

Should Management Be a Profession?

Iniguez, S. (2010). "Should Management Be a Profession?"

www.deanstalk.net/files/santiago-iniguez-global-focus-of-efmd.pdf

Management as a Profession

Stern, S. (2009). "Management as a Profession," September 23.

www.managers.org.uk/practical-support/management-community/blogs/management-profession

Why Management Is Not a Profession

Sutton, B. (2007). "Why Management Is Not a Profession."

http://bobsutton.typepad.com/my_weblog/2007/09/more-evidence-t.html

www.hbr.org

THE BIG IDEA

Some business skills can't be taught in a classroom. They have to be learned through experience.

No, Management Is *Not* a Profession

by Richard Barker

Included with this full-text *Harvard Business Review* article:

Reprint R1007C

THE BIG IDEA

No, Management Is *Not* a Profession

Idea in Brief

The big idea: Although managers can be formally trained and qualified, and their social status is similar to that of doctors and lawyers, management is not a profession.

The argument: We rely on professional bodies to define what their members should know and to certify them as fit for practice. But the abilities and learning required to be a good manager don't lend themselves to such oversight—and business education is more about acquiring the skill of integration than about mastering a set body of knowledge.

A better approach: The key is to recognize that integration is learned rather than taught: It takes place in the minds of MBA students, who link the various elements of the program. Business education is not one-size-fits-all, and, most important, it should be collaborative rather than competitive.

Some business skills can't be taught in a classroom. They have to be learned through experience.

THE BIG IDEA

No, Management Is *Not* a Profession

by Richard Barker

It is natural to view management as a profession. Managers' status is similar to that of doctors or lawyers, as is their obligation to contribute to the well-being of society. Managers can also be formally trained and qualified, notably by earning an MBA. If management is a profession, the business school is a professional school.

That perception has fueled criticism of business schools during the recent economic crisis. They have come under fire for allegedly failing in their obligation to educate socially responsible business leaders. The same perception has informed the schools' response, which has been to work toward greater professionalism. Writing in the June 2009 issue of *Harvard Business Review*, Joel Podolny, a former dean of the Yale School of Management, argued, "An occupation earns the right to be a profession only when some ideals, such as being an impartial counsel, doing no harm, or serving the greater good, are infused into the conduct of people in that occupation. In like vein, a school becomes a professional school only when it infuses those ideals into its graduates."

Podolny is in sympathy with Harvard Business School professors Rakesh Khurana and Nitin Nohria, who argued in the October 2008 issue of HBR that it was time to make management a true profession. In their view, "True professions have codes of conduct, and the meaning and consequences of those codes are taught as part of the formal education of their members." Yet, they wrote, "unlike doctors and lawyers," managers don't "adhere to a universal and enforceable code of conduct."

These calls to professionalism are hardly new. Writing in the very first issue of HBR, in 1922, HBS professor John Gurney Callan claimed, "Business...may be thought of as a profession [and] we may profitably spend a good deal of time in considering what is the best professional training for [those] who are to take important executive positions in the coming generation."

A. Lawrence Lowell, the president of Harvard University, was even more assertive in his 1923 HBR essay "The Profession of Business" (adapted from his address to the incoming class at HBS the previous September). He attributed the very creation of HBS to the emergence of business management as a distinct profession.

In contrast with these views, I will argue that management is not a profession at all and can never be one. Therefore, business schools are not professional schools. Moreover, laudable and beguiling though professional standards and ethics may be, and however appealing professional status is, hanging the mantle "professional" on business education fosters inappropriate analysis and misguided prescriptions.

Let's begin by examining what actually constitutes a profession.

What Is a Profession?

Professions are made up of particular categories of people from whom we seek advice and services because they have knowledge and skills that we do not. A doctor, for example, can recommend a course of treatment for an illness; a lawyer can advise us on a course of legal action. We cannot make these judgments ourselves—and often we cannot judge the quality of the advice we receive. The Nobel laureate Kenneth Arrow wrote about the medical profession, "The value of information is frequently not known in any meaningful sense to the buyer; if, indeed, he knew enough to measure the value of information, he would know the information itself. But information, in the form of skilled care, is precisely what is being bought from most physicians, and, indeed, from most professionals."

It is true, of course, that most nonprofessional providers of goods and services also have knowledge that we don't. We cannot, for instance, manufacture a computer or operate a train service. Nevertheless, we can judge whether or not our demand has been met: We know what to expect from our computer, and we know if our train is delayed. The difference is that we might act on a lawyer's advice and not know its quality, even after the case has been completed. Perhaps she gave us good advice but the case was lost, or vice versa. The outcome might have been more or less favorable had her advice been different. We are in no position to know, because the professional is the expert and we are not. There is an asymmetry of knowledge.

In some cases the knowledge asymmetry is relatively transient. A taxi driver in a foreign town provides us with a service, using his knowledge of the local geography. Once we arrive at our destination, however, we can ask a local whether the driver's route was the most direct, and thus reduce the asymmetry. But who evaluates legal advice for us? Although we could ask another lawyer, he couldn't offer a second opinion without being informed of the details of our case—which would amount to hiring two lawyers to do the work of one. Furthermore, the two lawyers might advise us differently, and we'd be unable to distinguish the better advice.

In practice, our lawyer herself implicitly assures us that we can rely on the legal advice she is giving. This relatively permanent knowledge asymmetry is the mark of the true profession; as consumers, we have no option but to trust the professionals with whom we transact. Nevertheless, we might be unwilling to transact at all without some guarantee that the services we receive meet a minimum quality threshold. That requires the existence of professional bodies, whose regulatory role enables consumers to trust their advisers, thereby making a market for professional services feasible.

For a professional body in any given field to function, a discrete body of knowledge for that field must be defined, and the field's boundaries must be established: When, for example, is something a medical or legal issue, and when is it not? There must also be a reasonable consensus within the field as to what the knowledge should consist of: If physicians cannot agree on how the human body functions, or lawyers on the nature of a contract, no discrete body of knowledge can be said to exist. The boundaries and consensus for any profession will evolve over time, but at any given moment they can be defined—which is what enables formal training and certification. Certification signals competence to consumers who would benefit from it.

Professional bodies hold a trusted position. They have, in effect, a contract with society at large: They control membership in the professions through examination and certification, maintain the quality of certified members through ongoing training and the enforcement of ethical standards, and may exclude anyone who fails to meet those standards. Society is rewarded for its trust with a professional quality that it would otherwise be unable to ensure. This is the model for the legal and medical pro-

Richard Barker (r.barker@jbs.cam.ac.uk) is a professor at Cambridge University's Judge Business School in England, where he served as director of the MBA program from 2003 to 2008.

fessions and others, including accounting, architecture, and engineering.

As I will argue, neither the boundaries of the discipline of management nor a consensus on the requisite body of knowledge exists. No professional body is granted control, no formal entry or certification is required, no ethical standards are enforced, and no mechanism can exclude someone from practice. In short, management is not a profession. Moreover, management can never be a profession, and policies predicated on the assumption that it can are inherently flawed.

Why Not Management?

One might ask, If medicine can reach agreement on the requisite body of knowledge for becoming a physician, why can't business do the same for management? After all, isn't the MBA a general-management qualification, and isn't there a reasonable consensus on MBA curriculum content? It is generally agreed that nobody should be allowed to practice medicine without schooling and certification; is society not also at risk from a business leader with no license to operate? Moreover, don't several organizations, including the Graduate Management Admission Council and the Association to Advance Collegiate Schools of Business, play roles similar to those of established professional bodies? And why shouldn't we introduce and enforce ethical standards?

Asking whether a consensus can be reached on the body of knowledge that qualifies someone to be a manager—on the basis of which society would delegate control of the training for, certification in, and practice of management to a professional body—is not the same as asking whether consensus is possible on the MBA curriculum. That is a narrower question of whether business schools can agree on what they should teach. The real issue is whether what the schools do teach qualifies students to manage, in the way that an MD qualifies someone to practice medicine. I will argue that the answer is no, and that therefore management cannot become a profession.

Consider the nature of a business contract, which in its narrowest form is a detailed, precisely worded document, drafted by a professional lawyer and specifying the terms of an agreement, including prescribed remedies in the event of certain outcomes. The contract is the re-

sult of a professional service delivered to managers. Managers also seek the services of accounting firms for internal audits, of engineering consultancies for capital expenditure projects, and so on. Each transaction requires the specialized skills of a professional. Each is also an output from the professional's perspective and an input from the manager's perspective.

The manager, however, is responsible for bringing together many inputs. The lawyer is always concerned with matters of law, whereas

---

The MBA Debate: It's Not Over Yet

Business schools are under attack as a result of the economic crisis. MBAs, perhaps especially those from our parent, Harvard Business School, have come under fire for supposedly putting their own interests ahead of those of employees, customers, and even shareholders. Management education is broken, the indictment reads, and we need to make fundamental changes to it.

Many people believe there's some truth to these charges. The debate, therefore, is really about how business schools should respond. A number of experts, including Nitin Nohria, the new dean of HBS, argue that management should have a rigorous professional code. In a landmark HBR article, Nohria and HBS professor Rakesh Khurana eloquently called for a return to the intent of HBS's founders, which was to create a cadre of managers as skilled and disciplined in their field as Harvard-trained lawyers and doctors were in theirs.

Some experts view the issue differently. McGill University's Henry Mintzberg, for example, believes that MBA programs already straitjacket managers—by encouraging the development of narrow functional expertise rather than the integrative skills that define effective management. (See his HBR article "The Five Minds of a Manager," written with Jonathan Gosling.) This month's Big Idea feature is very much in this vein. Richard Barker, a former director of the MBA program at Cambridge University's Judge Business School, argues that manage-

ment by its very nature cannot be defined as narrowly and precisely as a profession, and that the essence of an MBA resides not in professional training but in the broader experience of the business school as a learning environment.

Other commentators weigh in somewhere in the middle. A former dean of the Yale School of Management, Joel Podolny, asserted in his HBR article "The Buck Stops (and Starts) at Business School" that although MBA programs need to inculcate professional standards akin to those for lawyers and doctors, the curriculum should be designed along lines that Barker and Mintzberg would probably agree with.

Harvard Business Review has been a leading forum for discussion of the MBA's future. In addition to publishing the articles mentioned here, the magazine has hosted a fascinating online debate (see http://blogs.hbr.org/how-to-fix-business-schools/) joined by B-school deans and educators from around the world. The exchanges have been spirited and sometimes even testy. We urge readers to engage with them. Management education will never become more responsive to the needs of business in particular and society in general without the involvement of the practitioners who graduate and recruit from business schools.

We have invited Nohria and Khurana to comment on Barker's article at hbr.org. Please join the debate.

—The Editors

the manager's focus may change significantly and unpredictably from one day to the next. In general, the professional is an expert, whereas the manager is a jack-of-all-trades and master of none—the antithesis of the professional.

The argument can be taken further. The lawyer writes a contract and charges for her time; her work is finite. Even when she has an ongoing relationship with a corporate client, her contribution is always a specialized input, measurable in terms of the amount billed. But the manager is responsible for the combined value generated by all inputs to the firm. Inputs are managed at varying stages in a product's life cycle, and at any given time products are at different stages in that life cycle—meaning the manager's job is never done. The manager's contribution is inherently difficult to measure and has an indeterminable impact on a variety of outcomes. The difference between the lawyer's world and the manager's is rather like that between the value of a single revenue transaction and the value of a company as a whole. As a completed output with a monetary value, the revenue transaction is relatively objective. A company's share price is subjective—dependent on imprecise assumptions concerning a range of inputs, and ultimately a best guess about the future.

All this accords, of course, with the reality that no true professional bodies have emerged in the field of management. Consider again an analogy with medicine: Although we cannot expect an unqualified person to successfully conduct brain surgery, successful businesses are frequently run by people without MBAs. It is unthinkable that society would allow an unqualified person to even attempt brain surgery, but nobody would seriously suggest that an MBA be required for entry to management. We can, of course, offer business education, including certification in the form of MBAs and other degrees, and such education can reasonably be assumed to generate better managers. Yet the difference between a business education and a professional education is stark and fundamental: The former may help individuals improve their performance, but it cannot certify their expertise. The role of the manager is inherently general, variable, and indefinable.

Business Education

The inherent differences between the professions and management have direct implications for the design of education in each. Professional education enables an individual to master the body of knowledge deemed requisite for practice. It comprises three stages: admission, during which potential entrants are screened for intellectual ability and aptitude; a taught program, during which educators impart knowledge of the subject; and formal assessment, which leads to certification. Business education also involves admission, a taught program, and assessment, but the similarity is superficial only. If business educators, imbued with notions of professionalism, fail to recognize the fundamental differences in the business education model will inevitably result.

Admission. Professional education is about taking a given individual on the journey from having little or no knowledge or experience to becoming qualified. But business education is

A Code of Business Ethics?

A professional body determines and enforces a code of ethics. This process is fundamental to the very existence of any profession, because it enables society to trust that members of the body are serving the public interest.

Management is not a profession. It has no code of ethics, much less a mechanism to enforce one. Does that make business ethics a lost cause?

A code of business ethics is in principle achievable, albeit challenging because of management's broad and undefined scope. HBS professors Rakesh Khurana and Nitin Nohria offer a prototype in their 2008 HBR article "It's Time to Make Management a True Profession," which could no doubt provide the basis for a generally accepted code. The greater problem is enforcement. The professions have monopoly control over membership; they can restrict entry and force exit. No such model is available in management, which doesn't require a license.

Business schools can make a difference by building on core strengths rather than emulating the professions. The subject of ethics provides excellent raw material in an environment where students are learning as much about themselves as about technical or functional subjects, and where the learning comes as much from interaction with their peers, inside and outside class, as from classroom interaction with the professor. In that environment, discussion of an ethical issue such as conflict of interest has great value: Students must consider what they would do if faced with the issue and think through the consequences. Equally important, they experience firsthand how their peers would react to their choosing one road rather than another. If a certain behavior is unacceptable to your peers, and if they are important to you personally and to your career, unethical business practice becomes less likely.

Business ethics belongs in the curriculum but can be learned effectively only in the right environment. Business schools should ensure that students understand the situations in which ethical decisions are made, and in particular that they grasp the personal implications of such decisions. The focus, in short, should be on the core strength of the business school as a learning environment.

—R.B.

typically post-experience, meaning that participants are not novices. An MBA program offers them an opportunity to share, conceptualize, and better understand workplace experiences; to build on the skill of working with others; and to open up new career opportunities. To admit only students with little or no work experience, as the professions normally do, would be to misunderstand the nature and purpose of the learning experience.

A second difference is that although professional education is concerned exclusively with the individual, a quality business education depends in a distinctive way on the peer group. Thus no given candidate can be effectively evaluated independent of all the other candidates.

Suppose you wanted to provide a course in international business. Most people would probably agree that learning international business is not about the textbook acquisition of technical knowledge but, rather, about a concentrated exposure to the breadth of experience and understanding that helps make someone a better global manager. A prerequisite for learning is therefore diversity in the classroom—which requires that the nature of admissions be rethought.

This is particularly a problem for management education in the United States. A typical class in a top-tier U.S. school might be made up of 70% American students, 20% international students with close ties to the U.S., and 10% genuine "outsiders." International business is taught by means of case studies, which allow students to discuss subjects ranging from trade relationships with China to cross-cultural management in Eastern Europe to outsourcing in India. This process, unfortunately but inevitably, is superficial. It is unrealistic to think that American students who have had American experiences—even when they have the benefits of a good textbook and a great professor—can conjure up a meaningful understanding of international business through class discussion, however academically gifted they may be.

Because a student at business school has a direct impact on the learning of others, the strongest class is likely to be the strongest combination of individuals. Many graduates recognize the truth of this. Jacklyn Sing, an alumna of the MIT Sloan School of Management, describes a view among alumni: "Some of the classes proved useful to their current work [but] the specifics fade in the memory. It is the people in the program that shape the experience and make all the difference."

This view will be familiar to anyone who has studied or worked at a business school. For technical training to fade in the memory would be alarming in a medical doctor, but it is understandable in business school alumni. Again, that is because business education is not about mastering a body of knowledge.

The program. Consider the following finding from a formal review of the MBA program at London Business School: "The corporate leaders we interviewed indeed produced an extensive list of qualities they desired in future recruits, but almost none involved functional or technical knowledge. Rather, virtually all their requirements could be summed up as fol-

The Value of the MBA Program

In a survey about their experience in Cambridge University's MBA program, alumni were asked to rate the usefulness in their current careers of the aspects below, on a scale of 1 to 5. They valued most highly what they had learned outside the classroom. As for classroom subjects, they valued the general skills of strategy and leadership above more-focused disciplines such as marketing, operations, and finance.

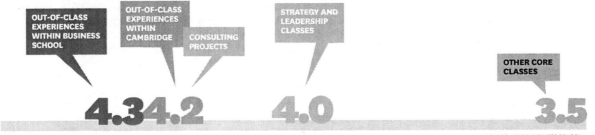

OUT-OF-CLASS EXPERIENCES WITHIN BUSINESS SCHOOL — OUT-OF-CLASS EXPERIENCES WITHIN CAMBRIDGE — CONSULTING PROJECTS — STRATEGY AND LEADERSHIP CLASSES — OTHER CORE CLASSES

4.3 4.2 4.0 3.5

SOURCE JUDGE BUSINESS SCHOOL

lows: the need for more thoughtful, more aware, more sensitive, more flexible, more adaptive managers, capable of being moulded and developed into global executives." LBS summarizes these requirements as attributes rather than skills. They are intrinsically soft and indefinable. They can probably be learned, especially in a business school environment, but it is not obvious that they can be taught, which is what would be expected from a professional school.

The exhibit "The Value of the MBA Program" shows some findings from a survey of approximately 600 MBA alumni of Cambridge University. In terms of its usefulness in their careers, the alumni valued the learning environment above the curriculum itself. They ranked learning that took place outside the business school classroom, and more broadly in the university, as the most useful. Next came company-based consulting projects, which are not part of the taught curriculum but are a component of small-group learning. Within the curriculum itself the softer skills of strategy and leadership were most prized. Clearly, the environment within which people learn can be more powerful than the specific material taught.

None of this is to say that functional areas are unimportant. Rather, we need to broaden our perspective on business education. Any business needs effective execution in functional areas, but that is not the role of the general manager, of the business leader. The general manager should have an understanding of these areas, and the combination of textbook learning and classroom discussion is an effective way to achieve it. But it would be a mistake to think that business education stops there. The manager must also acquire the core skill of integration and decision making across various functional areas, groups of people, and circumstances.

The skill of integration distinguishes managers and is at the heart of why business education should differ from professional education. Yet business schools have always wrestled with how best to help students acquire this skill. The difficulty is partly structural. Faculty members almost universally specialize in one functional area and typically lack the expertise to teach (or sometimes even to cross-reference) material from others. Case studies, which are typically written from a functional perspective,

The typical U.S. MBA class is made up of 70% Americans, 20% internationals with close ties to the U.S., and 10% "outsiders."

reinforce this limitation. The Yale School of Management has pioneered a curriculum based on the co-teaching of integrated classes, but this is a challenging model that others are unlikely to follow.

The key here is to recognize that integration is not taught but learned. It takes place in the minds of the students rather than in the content of program modules. The students themselves link the various elements of the program. Thus it is vital that business schools understand themselves primarily as learning environments, where individuals develop attributes, rather than as teaching environments, where students are presented with a body of functional and technical content.

First and foremost, business education should be collaborative. Consider Oxford University's MBA program, in which a class has about 240 students, each with about six years of work experience, who represent nearly 50 countries and almost all sectors of the economy. That amounts to some 1,500 years of experience. The pedagogical opportunities in sharing it are obvious—and they require an environment in which students actively work together and learn from one another. This goes much deeper than networking, the much-cited benefit of business schools. Networking is important in the professions, too, and doctors and lawyers are equally likely to look back on school relationships with a warm glow. But in a collaborative learning environment the people around you are more than just colleagues and friends; they are an explicit and valuable part of your educational experience. It follows from this that effective business education cannot be delivered exclusively online, because online delivery is a teaching mechanism, not a learning environment. Dick Schmalensee, a former dean of MIT Sloan, has acknowledged, "We're trying to maximize the quality of what we deliver and don't feel going online will help us achieve that." Implicit is the recognition that business education is about more than the acquisition of textbook knowledge.

Moreover, business education is explicitly not one-size-fits-all. Most MBA students have prior work experience; each of them is building in a unique way on a unique foundation and will experience the program differently, learn different things, and emerge to pursue a different career. An important implication is that learning needs differ according to the stage of a student's career. For example, a younger student might gain little from studying the responsibilities and functions of boards of directors but might need precisely that knowledge 15 or 20 years later. In other words, business education is best delivered in doses throughout a career, rather than in a single shot at the beginning.

In this regard, the Insead model is exemplary. The one-year MBA program, which was pioneered by Insead, is successful in part because some of the fundamental benefits of immersion in a business school environment can be captured within one year; the second year conveys primarily technical or functional knowledge. Exposure to the learning environment over time, however, continues to bring benefits, so Insead also runs one of the largest executive education programs in the world. It is a lifelong learning partner, not a one-stop certification shop. That is precisely what business education should be.

Assessment. Evaluation is actually neither problematic nor contentious in technical and functional areas. It is perfectly possible—and appropriate—for ability to be measured in finance or accounting, and for students to compete for the highest grades. But we have seen that business education is about more than clearly defined subsets of knowledge like these; its essence is in softer, indefinable attributes and experiences that have relevance in interpersonal contexts. Thus we should not be surprised that an academic grading system cannot reliably predict managerial ability.

Assessment in these softer areas is problematic in two respects: It is difficult and thus perhaps arbitrary, and it risks being counterproductive because it can damage a learning environment. If a business school is a competitive environment, in which the myth is maintained that the best future business leaders will score the highest grades, dysfunctional behav-

ior inevitably results. Why learn collaboratively if doing so helps your competitors score higher grades? Why develop attributes of leadership, of interpersonal impact, if you are graded on individual performance in functional subjects? Why immerse yourself in the learning environment if you can get better grades by immersing yourself in a textbook? How can business schools embrace the diversity of candidates' prior experiences and learning opportunities if everything comes down to performance under a homogenized grading system?

Grading is important in technical and functional areas, but the distinctiveness and vitality of business education require that a grading culture be downplayed. Students are there to contribute to and benefit from a rich learning environment; they are there to be empowered rather than ranked.

Management educators need to resist the siren song of professionalism. Functional and technical knowledge is an important component of business school curricula, but it is not the essence of management or the substance of business leadership. Nor is it what makes a business school like Harvard or Stanford great. Business schools do not uniquely certify managers, enabling them to practice. Nor do they regulate the conduct of those managers according to a professional code of practice. What they do is provide learning environments that consolidate, share, and build business experience, that accelerate personal development and growth, and that help equip managers to deal with their diverse working environments. Business schools are not professional schools. They are incubators for business leadership.

Reprint R1007C
To order, call 800-988-0886 or 617-783-7500
or go to www.hbr.org

The skill of integration is at the heart of why business education should differ from professional education.

To Order

For *Harvard Business Review* reprints and subscriptions, call 800-988-0886 or 617-783-7500. Go to www.hbr.org

For customized and quantity orders of *Harvard Business Review* article reprints, call 617-783-7626, or e-mail customizations@hbsp.harvard.edu

Harvard Business Review

www.hbr.org

U.S. and Canada
800-988-0886
617-783-7500
617-783-7555 fax

Selected, Edited, and with Issue Framing Material by:
Kathleen J. Barnes, *East Stroudsburg University*
and
George E. Smith, *Albright College*

ISSUE

Do Corporations Have a Responsibility to Society Beyond Maximizing Profit?

YES: **Peter F. Drucker,** from "Conclusion: The Responsibilities of Management," in *The Practice of Management* (Harper & Row, 1986, pp. 381–392)

NO: **Milton Friedman,** from "The Social Responsibility of Business Is to Increase Its Profits," *The New York Times Magazine,* September 13, 1970

Learning Outcomes

After reading this issue, you should be able to:

- Appreciate the conflicts businesses face as they attempt to balance the demands of various stakeholders.
- Understand why businesses are expected to do more than simply generate profit.
- Explain why businesses may have a limited response in terms of their contributions to society.
- Understand the challenge of implementing or practicing corporate responsibility beyond profit generation.

ISSUE SUMMARY

YES: Peter Drucker maintains that if corporations are to continue to enjoy success and have access to requisite resources for that success, managers must step beyond self-interested behavior and assume responsibility for the public good.

NO: In his classical defense of the profit motive, Nobel laureate Milton Friedman attacks social responsibility, arguing that spending shareholders' property against their wishes is immoral, illegal, and ultimately unproductive.

Not surprisingly, in the wake of the subprime mortgage, housing-bubble meltdown, and the associated chaos in the financial services industry, attitudes toward U.S. corporations have turned decidedly negative. A 2008 survey conducted by Gallup found that a third of those polled believe that big business represents the single largest threat to our country's future (www.gallup.com/poll/5248/Big-Business.aspx). Additionally, in a Fall 2008 Pew Research Center poll, nearly 6 in 10 respondents (59 percent) indicated that business corporations make too much profit. This survey also reported that 62 percent of those polled believe that financial executives in America are "more greedy than they were in the past" (http://people-press.org/report/7pageicM399). Indeed, at the end of 2008, social commentators and political analysts placed the blame for the debacle on the pursuit of profit.

An interesting outcome of this attention on corporate behavior has been a renewed interest in the question of what the purpose of business is in general. While this is not a new topic, it is one that generates passionate debate. As a result of the renewed interest in defining and understanding corporate responsibility, this issue focuses on examining the question, "Do corporations have a responsibility to society beyond maximizing profit?"

Those who answer in the affirmative usually provide a two-pronged response. The first response is based on stakeholder theory and the second on practical observations and assertions. Stakeholder theory argues that the manager's job is to balance interests among the various groups with a stake in the company's survival. Consequently, management's obligations have been expanded beyond focusing primarily on financial gain for shareholders to include satisfying the needs and concerns of all of its stakeholders. Organizations that recognize this expansion and act on it accordingly are said to be acting in a socially responsible manner, whereas firms that stick to the traditional emphasis of increasing share price as priority one are deemed irresponsible and immoral.

The second prong in the "yes" response consists of more practical arguments. One point often raised is that because corporations are the source of many problems in society—pollution, corruption, discrimination, and so on—they should be required to resolve those problems. After all, the community in which the corporation resides is a legitimate stakeholder of the firm. Also, business organizations are members of society and, as such, should assume the responsibilities of membership. Another argument holds that organizations frequently have a lot of financial resources and, therefore, are in a position to use the money for social good and not just for increasing the power and wealth of the firm and its shareholders.

On the other side of the debate, the strongest and most consistent defender of shareholder theory has been free-market economist and Nobel laureate Milton Friedman. In his anti-stakeholder approach, Friedman argues that shareholders—not employees, customers, or suppliers—own the companies in which they invest and, consequently, have the legal right to expect management to comply with their desires (which is usually to maximize the value of their investments). Consider the example of a corporation whose management, without shareholder consent, wants to use some of the company's profits on its local community by contributing to the creation of a park project. If management chooses to reduce profit distribution to its shareholders and spend it on the project, its members have acted both immorally and illegally because they have, in effect, stolen from the shareholders. If they choose to pay shareholders out-of-profit and instead finance the project by reducing labor costs, the employees will suffer. If they choose to avoid antagonizing shareholders and employees and contribute to the park by raising product prices, they will hurt their customers and possibly price themselves out of the market. Thus according to Friedman, doing anything other than increasing shareholder wealth is tantamount to theft, is immoral, and is ultimately self-defeating for the organization.

The following two selections address the question of whether or not corporations have responsibilities to society that extend beyond profit maximization. The "pro" selection is by Peter F. Drucker, who focuses on emphasizing to management that it wields great power in society and as a result possesses the potential to do both much good and conversely cause much harm. At the heart of Drucker's work is a reminder to management to remember the public (stakeholders) when corporate decisions—big and small—are made. While Drucker originally published this work in 1954, it is illustrative of the direction contemporary society is attempting to push business in.

For the "con" side, Milton Friedman's classic anti-stakeholder article was selected. Originally written in 1970, Friedman emphasizes that responsible management seeks to maximize profit. While Friedman doesn't deny that good can be accomplished through profitability—namely via the acts of individuals—he is concerned that any responsibility or expectation beyond the pursuit of profit detracts from the mission of business.

YES ↵

Peter F. Drucker

Conclusion: The Responsibilities of Management

Our discussion has so far treated the business enterprise as primarily existing by and for itself. True, we have stressed the relationship to the outside—to customers and market, to the labor union, to the social, economic and technological forces at work in our society. But these relations have been viewed somewhat like the relationship between a ship and the sea which engirds it and carries it, which threatens it with storm and shipwreck, which has to be crossed, but which is yet alien and distinct, the environment rather than the home of the ship.

But society is not just the environment of the enterprise. Even the most private of private enterprises is an organ of society and serves a social function.

Indeed the very nature of the modern business enterprise imposes responsibilities on the manager which are different in kind and scope from those of yesterday's businessman.

Modern industry requires an organization of basic resources which is radically different from anything we have known before. In the first place, the time span of modern production and of business decisions is so long that it goes way beyond the life span of one man as an active factor in the economic process. Secondly, the resources have to be brought together into an organization—both of material objects and of human beings—which has to have a high degree of permanence to be productive at all. Next, resources, human and material, have to be concentrated in large aggregations—though there is of course a question how large they have to be for best economic performance and how large they should be for best social performance. This in turn implies that the people who are entrusted with the direction of this permanent concentration of resources—the managers—have power over people, that their decisions have great impact upon society, and that they have to make decisions that shape the economy, the society and the lives of individuals within it for a long time to come. In other words, modern industry requires the business enterprise, which is something quite different and quite new.

Historically, society has always refused to allow such permanent concentrations of power, at least in private hands, and certainly for economic purposes. However, without this concentration of power which is the modern enterprise, an industrial society cannot possibly exist. Hence society has been forced to grant to the enterprise what it has always been most reluctant to grant, that is, first a charter of perpetuity, if not of theoretical immortality to the "legal person," and second a degree of authority to the managers which corres-ponds to the needs of the enterprise.

This, however, imposes upon the business and its managers a responsibility which not only goes far beyond any traditional responsibility of private property but is altogether different. It can no longer be based on the assumption that the self-interest of the owner of property will lead to the public good, or that self-interest and public good can be kept apart and considered to have nothing to do with each other. On the contrary, it requires of the manager that he assume responsibility for the public good, that he subordinate his actions to an ethical standard of conduct, and that he restrain his self-interest and his authority wherever their exercise would infringe upon the commonweal and upon the freedom of the individual.

And then there is the fact that the modern business enterprise for its survival needs to be able to recruit the ablest, best educated and most dedicated of young men into its service, To attract and to hold such men a promise of a career, of a living, or of economic success is not enough. The enterprise must be able to give such men a vision and a sense of mission. It must be able to satisfy their desire for a meaningful contribution to their community and society. It must in other words embrace public responsibility of a high order to live up to the demands the manager of tomorrow must make on himself.

No discussion of the practice of management could therefore leave out those functions and responsibilities of management that arise out of the social character and the public existence of even the most private of enterprises. In addition the enterprise itself must demand that management think through its public responsibilities. For public policy and public law set the range for the actions and activities of the enterprise. They decide what forms of organization are open to it. They prescribe marketing, pricing, patent and labor policies. They control the ability of the enterprise to obtain capital and its price. They decide altogether whether private enterprise is to remain private and autonomous and to be governed by managements of its own choosing.

The responsibility of management in our society is decisive not only for the enterprise itself but for management's public standing, its success and status, for the very future of our economic and social system and the survival of the enterprise as an autonomous institution. The public responsibility of management must therefore underlie all its behavior. Basically it furnishes the ethics of management.

The discussion of management's public responsibility tends today, at least in this country, to begin with the consideration of management as a leading group in society. But properly it should begin with management's responsibility to the enterprise of which it is an organ. This responsibility cannot be compromised or side-stepped. For the enterprise is management's specific trust; everything else arises out of this trust.

The first responsibility which management owes to the enterprise in respect to public opinion, policy and law is to consider such demands made by society on the enterprise (or likely to be made within the near future) as may affect attainment of its business objectives. It is management's job to find a way to convert these demands from threats to, or restrictions on, the enterprise's freedom of action into opportunities for sound growth, or at least to satisfy them with the least damage to the enterprise.

Even the staunchest friend of management would not claim that the job done so far could not be improved upon.

One illustration should suffice. It should have been clear ten years ago that the changing age structure of the American population, coupled with the steady drop in the purchasing power of the dollar, would produce an irresistible demand on business to do something for old employees. Some managements faced the problem years ago; we have good pension plans going back to 1900. But many more refused to see the inevitable. As a result they were forced to accept demands for employee pensions which tend to impose the greatest rather than the least burden on the enterprise though they do not actually meet the issue. For it is becoming increasingly obvious that pensions will not solve the problem of the old employee. If one fifth of the work force is of pensionable age, as it soon will be in our society, compulsory pensioning of the older people puts an all but unbearable burden on the production of the younger men. At the same time the great bulk of the people who reach what used to be considered old age are both able physically to continue work and eager to do so. What management should have done was to work out plans for keeping employed those older people who want to work and are able to do so. with pensions as something to fall back on for those who are unable or unwilling to keep on working. At the same time these plans would have to make sure that the older employees who are retained do not bottle up the promotional opportunities for younger men or endanger their employment security. Having failed to think through the problem, managements will almost certainly find themselves faced with compulsory employment programs for older people—imposed by unions or by government—which will mean additional cost and new restrictions.

American managements are on the verge of making the same mistake in respect to the stability of income and employment. That this demand will have to be met can hardly be disputed any more. It expresses not only the need of the worker for income security, but the need of our society to symbolize the worker's middle-class status. Also the demand has behind it the force of the deep "depression psychosis" that we inherited from the thirties.

I have tried to show earlier that this demand could be satisfied in such a way as to improve and strengthen the enterprise, increase its productivity and raises its overall profits. If managements, however, refuse to face the responsibility to make the inevitable productive for the enterprise, they will only saddle their businesses with the guaranteed annual wage—both the most expensive and the least effective way to take care of a real social need.

Management is also responsible for making sure that the present actions and decisions of the business enterprise will not create future public opinion, demands and policies that threaten the enterprise, its freedom and its economic success.

During the last years many companies have dispersed their plants geographically. In doing so many of them have simply built, in a new location, a replica of the original plant, turning out the same product for the same market. In many cases both the old and the duplicate plants are the main source of employment in their respective communities. Examples are a rubber company with old plants in Akron and a new plant in a small southern town; a ball-bearing company with an old plant in a small New England town and a new plant in a small town in Ohio; a shirt maker with old plants in upstate New York and a new plant in rural Tennessee.

In a depression this can only lead to serious public reaction. For management will then be forced to decide which of these plants to close down and which to keep open—the new plants which represent a high capital investment, have by and large a high break-even point and thus require capacity operations to be profitable, or the old plants around which a whole community may have grown up. But will any community, no matter how eager it was to obtain the new industry, take quietly a decision to deprive it of its main source of income so as to keep up employment in some other place? If the market and the forces of the business cycle bring about unemployment, that is one thing. But if management, by unilateral action, does so, it is quite another. It may therefore be a vital management responsibility to organize new plants so that they have their own market and their own product rather than only be separated geographically. Otherwise expansion will lead to a clash between management and the community, between the requirements of the business and of public policy.

Other practices which may tend to breed public opinion and policies hostile to the enterprise, are the exclusive hiring of college graduates for management positions, thus cutting off chances for men inside the company; the narrowing of promotional opportunities for foremen, thus cutting off the most important rungs on the traditional American ladder of success; or the policy of not hiring older workers or disabled people. To discharge its responsibility to the enterprise management must carefully think through these practices and their impact upon the public welfare.

In brief, management, in every one of its policies and decisions, should ask: What would be the public reaction if everyone in industry did the same? What would be the public impact if this behavior were general business behavior? And this is not just a question for the large corporations. In their totality, small businesses and their managements have fully as much of an impact on public opinion and policy. And all, large and small, should remember that if they take the easy way out and leave these problems to "the other fellow," they only assure that their solution will eventually be imposed by government.

The Social Impact of Business Decisions

This discussion should have made it clear that the impact of management's decisions on society is not just "public" responsibility but is inextricably interwoven with management's responsibility to the enterprise. Still, there is a responsibility of management to the public interest as such. This is based on the fact that the enterprise is an organ of society, and that its actions have a decisive impact on the social scene.

The first responsibility to society is to operate at a profit, and only slightly less important is the necessity for growth. The business is the wealth-creating and wealth-producing organ of our society. Management must maintain its wealth-producing resources intact by making adequate profits to offset the risk of economic activity. And it must besides increase the wealth-creating and wealth-producing capacity of these resources and with them the wealth of society.

> It may seem paradoxical that this responsibility of management is most clearly recognized in the Soviet Union. Profitability is the first and absolute law for Soviet management and the essence of what the Russians proudly proclaim to be their great economic discovery; "management by the ruble." But a source which the Kremlin would hardly admit as authority has said as much; I refer, of course, to Our Lord's Parable of the Talents.

This responsibility is absolute and cannot be abdicated. No management can be relieved of it. Managements are in the habit of saying that they have a responsibility to the shareholder for profits. But the shareholder, at least in a publicly owned company, can always sell his stock. Society, however, is stuck with the enterprise. It has to take the loss if the enterprise does not produce adequate profits, has to take the impoverishment if the enterprise does not succeed in innovation and growth.

For the same reason management has a public responsibility to make sure of tomorrow's management

without which the resources would be mismanaged, would lose their wealth-producing capacity and would finally be destroyed.

Management is responsible for conducting the enterprise so as not to undermine our social beliefs and cohesion. This implies a negative responsibility: not to usurp illegitimate authority over citizens by demanding their absolute and total allegiance.

In a free society the citizen is a loyal member of many institutions; and none can claim him entirely or alone. In this pluralism lies its strength and freedom. If the enterprise ever forgets this, society will retaliate by making its own supreme institution, the state, omnipotent.

The tendency today of so many, especially of our larger, enterprises to assume paternal authority over their management people and to demand of them a special allegiance, is socially irresponsible usurpation, indefensible on the grounds alike of public policy and the enterprise's self-interest. The company is not and must never claim to be home, family, religion, life or fate for the individual. It must never interfere in his private life or his citizenship. He is tied to the company through a voluntary and cancellable employment contract, not through some mystical and indissoluble bond.

But responsibility for our social beliefs and cohesion also has a positive component. At least in this country it imposes on management the duty to keep open the opportunity to rise from the bottom according to ability and performance. If this responsibility is not discharged, the production of wealth will, in the long run, weaken rather than strengthen our society by creating social classes, class hatred and class warfare.

There are other areas in which responsibilities can be asserted, I would, for instance, consider it a responsibility of the management of the large company to develop a capital-expenditure policy which tends to counteract the extremes of the business cycle (with Automation such a policy becomes a business necessity). I believe that management has a responsibility to develop policies that will overcome the deep-seated hostility to profits, for the simple reason that this is a threat to our economic and social system. I finally believe that any business, in the present world situation, has the responsibility to make its best contribution to the defensive strength of its country.

But what is most important is that management realize that it must consider the impact of every business policy and business action upon society. It has to consider whether the action is likely to promote the public good, to advance the basic beliefs of our society, to contribute to its stability, strength and harmony.

Management as a Leading Group

Only now can we raise the question of the responsibility that management should assume by virtue of being one of the leading groups in society—responsibilities over and above those grounded in the business itself.

Hardly a day goes by when a spokesman of management does not assert a new public responsibility of this kind. We have been told that management should hold itself responsible for the survival of the liberal arts colleges, for the economic education of workers, for religious tolerance or for a free press, for strengthening the United Nations or for abolishing it, for "culture" in its broadest form and for every one of the arts in particular.

There is no doubt that being a leading group entails heavy responsibility; and there is nothing more destructive than to shirk these responsibilities. There is also, however, nothing more destructive than to assert responsibilities for a group which it does not have, nothing more dangerous than to usurp responsibilities. The present management approach tends to do both: it shirks responsibilities that exist and usurps others that do not and must not exist.

For whoever says "responsibility" also implies "authority." One does not exist without the other. To assert management's responsibility in any area is therefore to assign it authority in the area in question. Is there any reason to believe that management in a free society should have any authority over the colleges, over culture and the arts, over the freedom of the press or over our foreign policy? To raise the question is to answer it: such authority would be intolerable. Even the impassioned twaddle permitted, by hoary custom, to the commencement speaker or the boss at the annual employees' picnic should avoid such a claim.

Managament's public responsibility as one of the leading groups should therefore be restricted to areas in which management can legitimately claim authority.

As a "rule of thumb" I recommend that management religiously avoid asserting or assuming responsibility for any activities it does not want to see controlled either by the union leader or by government. These are the activities which should be free, that is, organized by spontaneous, local, pluralist action of the citizens, not by any one group or any governing organ. If management does not want the union leader to control an activity, it is a fair assumption that the union leader (and his sizable following) would not want management to control the activity either. And it would be reasonable to assume that society would find sole control of such an activity by either management or union leader intolerable. It would demand the obvious and easy substitute for non-control of these areas: control by the organized government as the representative of the entire people.

And if the business enterprise becomes a source of financial support for important causes and institutions—as our tax laws force it increasingly to be—management must take scrupulous care not to let financial support become "responsibility," not to let itself be misled into usurping authority where it has and should have none.

But from the fact that responsibility and authority go together, it follows also that management owes to society responsibility wherever its special competence gives it authority.

One major area here is that of fiscal policy. Because we have not modernized our tax structure even though it was built when the maximum income tax was 4 per cent (and that rate applied to millionaires only), we have today an illogical, unmanageable, indeed an immoral system of taxation that encourages and rewards irresponsible actions and decisions of businesses and private individuals alike. Here management can make a major contribution—and it has therefore a major responsibility. But it has responsibility for positive action.

It is not enough to scream that taxes are too high as some people in management have been doing. What we need is a policy that reconciles the necessity of continuing high government expenditures, in the world we live in, with the requirements of society and economy. As long as management confines itself to shouting "down with taxes" it will not have discharged its responsibility for fiscal policy. In fact, it will have been totally ineffectual and will only have made itself look irresponsible.

Wherever management's competence gives it authority, wherever therefore management has a responsibility, this responsibility must be discharged on the basis of the public interest. It is not good enough to start out with the premise that "what is good for the business is good for the country," even though the assertion may be substantially correct for the very large company which is in effect a cross section of the American economy. For while its competence is the basis for management's authority, the only basis on which this authority can be used is the public interest. What is good for the business—or even for all businesses—is irrelevant.

But the final conclusion from the consideration of management's public responsibility as one of the leading groups is the most important one: It is management's public responsibility to *make* whatever is genuinely in the public good *become* the enterprise's own self-interest.

To be disinterested is not enough for a leading group in society. It is not even enough that the group subordinate its own interests to the common good. It must succeed in harmonizing public and private interest by making what is the common good coincide with its own self-interest. "This company must be so managed as to make everything likely to strengthen our country, or to advance its prosperity, add strength to the company and advance its prosperity"; thus the management of one of our most successful companies. Sears, Roebuck. In economic fact, "what is good for the country must be made to be good for Sears" may not be so different from "what is good for the business is good for the country." In spirit, in essence, in assertion of responsibility, however, it is completely different.

The Sears statement does not imply pre-established harmony between the private self-interests of a group and the commonweal. On the contrary; to make what is good for the country good for the enterprise requires hard work, great management skill, high standards of responsibility and broad vision. It is a counsel of perfection. To carry it out completely would require the philosopher's stone that can transmute the basest element into pure gold. But if management is to remain a leading group—indeed, if it is to remain autonomous management running free enterprises—it must make this rule the lodestar of its conduct, must consciously strive to live up to it, and must actually do so with a fair degree of success.

Two hundred and fifty years ago an English pamphleteer, de Mandeville, summed up the spirit of the new commercial age in the famous epigram: "private vices become public benefits"—selfishness unwittingly and automatically turns into the common good. He may have been right; economists since Adam Smith have been arguing the point without reaching agreement.

But whether he was right or wrong is irrelevant; no society can lastingly be built on such belief. For in a good, a moral, a lasting society the public good must always rest on private virtue. No leading group can be accepted on de Mandeville's foundation. Every leading group must, on the contrary, be able to claim that the public good determines its own interest. This assertion is the only legitimate basis for leadership; to make it reality is the first duty of the leaders.

That "capitalism," as the nineteenth century understood the term (and as Europe still too prevalently understands it), was based on de Mandeville's principle may explain its material success. It certainly explains the revulsion against capitalism and capitalists that has swept the Western world during the last hundred years. The economic doctrines of the enemies of capitalism have been untenable and often childish. Their political doctrines have carried the threat of tyranny. But these answers have not been sufficient to quiet the critics of capitalism. Indeed they have usually appeared quite irrelevant to the

critics, as well as to the people at large. For the hostility to capitalism and capitalists is moral and ethical. Capitalism is being attacked not because it is inefficient or misgoverned but because it is cynical. And indeed a society based on the assertion that private vices become public benefits cannot endure, no matter how impeccable its logic, no matter how great its benefits.

Fifty years ago de Mandeville's principle was as fully accepted here as it still is in Europe. But today it has become possible if not commonplace in this country to assert the opposite principle that the business enterprise must be so managed as to make the public good become the private good of the enterprise. In this lies the real meaning of the "American Revolution" of the twentieth century. That more and more of our managements claim it to be their responsibility to realize this new principle in their daily actions is our best hope for the future of our country and society, and perhaps for the future of Western society altogether.

To make certain that this assertion does not remain lip service but becomes hard fact it the most important, the ultimate responsibility of management: to itself, to the enterprise, to our heritage, to our society and to our way of life.

PETER F. DRUCKER has published articles in professional journals and publications including *The Economist, Harvard Business Review, The Atlantic Monthly, Financial Times, Foreign Affairs, Fortune, Inc.,* and *Harpers.* As a consultant, Dr. Drucker specialized in strategy and policy for governments, businesses, and nonprofit organizations. Finally, Drucker's special focus was on the organization and work of top management.

Milton Friedman

 **NO**

The Social Responsibility of Business Is to Increase Its Profits

When I hear businessmen speak eloquently about the "social responsibilities of business in a free-enterprise system," I am reminded of the wonderful line about the Frenchman who discovered at the age of 70 that he had been speaking prose all his life. The businessmen believe that they are defending free enterprise when they declaim that business is not concerned "merely" with profit but also with promoting desirable "social ends; that business has a social conscience" and takes seriously its responsibilities for providing employment, eliminating discrimination, avoiding pollution and whatever else may be the catchwords of the contemporary crop of reformers. In fact they are—or would be if they or anyone else took them seriously—preaching pure and unadulterated socialism. Businessmen who talk this way are unwitting puppets of the intellectual forces that have been undermining the basis of a free society these past decades.

The discussions of the "social responsibilities of business" are notable for their analytical looseness and lack of rigor. What does it mean to say that "business" has responsibilities? Only people can have responsibilities. A corporation is an artificial person and in this sense may have artificial responsibilities, but "business" as a whole cannot be said to have responsibilities, even in this vague sense. The first step toward clarity in examining the doctrine of the social responsibility of business is to ask precisely what it implies for whom.

Presumably, the individuals who are to be responsible are businessmen, which means individual proprietors or corporate executives. Most of the discussion of social responsibility is directed at corporations, so in what follows I shall mostly neglect the individual proprietor and speak of corporate executives.

In a free-enterprise, private-property system, a corporate executive is an employee of the owners of the business. He has direct responsibility to his employers. That responsibility is to conduct the business in accordance with their desires, which generally will be to make as much money as possible while conforming to the basic rules of the society, both those embodied in law and those embodied in ethical custom. Of course, in some cases his employers may have a different objective. A group of persons might establish a corporation for an eleemosynary purpose—for example, a hospital or a school. The manager of such a corporation will not have money profit as his objective but the rendering of certain services.

In either case, the key point is that, in his capacity as a corporate executive, the manager is the agent of the individuals who own the corporation or establish the eleemosynary institution, and his primary responsibility is to them.

Needless to say, this does not mean that it is easy to judge how well he is performing his task. But at least the criterion of performance is straightforward, and the persons among whom a voluntary contractual arrangement exists are clearly defined.

Of course, the corporate executive is also a person in his own right. As a person, he may have many other responsibilities that he recognizes or assumes voluntarily—to his family, his conscience, his feelings of charity, his church, his clubs, his city, his country. He may feel impelled by these responsibilities to devote part of his income to causes he regards as worthy, to refuse to work for particular corporations, even to leave his job, for example, to join his country's armed forces. If we wish, we may refer to some of these responsibilities as "social responsibilities." But in these respects he is acting as a principal, not an agent; he is spending his own money or time or energy, not the money of his employers or the time or energy he has contracted to devote to their purposes. If these are "social responsibilities," they are the social responsibilities of individuals, not of business.

What does it mean to say that the corporate executive has a "social responsibility" in his capacity as businessman? If this statement is not pure rhetoric, it must mean that he is to act in some way that is not in the interest of his employers. For example, that he is to refrain from increasing the price of the product in order to contribute to the social objective of preventing inflation, even though a price increase would be in the best interests of the corporation. Or that he is to make expenditures on reducing pollution beyond the amount that is in the best interests of the corporation or that is required by law in order to contribute to the social objective of improving the environment. Or that, at the expense of corporate profits, he is to hire "hard-core" unemployed instead of better-qualified available workmen to contribute to the social objective of reducing poverty.

In each of these cases, the corporate executive would be spending someone else's money for a general social interest. Insofar as his actions in accord with his "social responsibility" reduce returns to stockholders, he is spending their money. Insofar as his actions raise the price to customers, he is spending the customers' money. Insofar as his actions lower the wages of some employees, he is spending their money.

The stockholders or the customers or the employees could separately spend their own money on the particular action if they wished to do so. The executive is exercising a distinct "social responsibility," rather than serving as an agent of the stockholders or the customers or the employees, only if he spends the money in a different way than they would have spent it.

But if he does this, he is in effect imposing taxes, on the one hand, and deciding how the tax proceeds shall be spent, on the other.

This process raises political questions on two levels: principle and consequences. On the level of political principle, the imposition of taxes and the expenditure of tax proceeds are governmental functions. We have established elaborate constitutional, parliamentary and judicial provisions to control these functions, to assure that taxes are imposed so far as possible in accordance with the preferences and desires of the public—after all, "taxation without representation" was one of the battle cries of the American Revolution. We have a system of checks and balances to separate the legislative function of imposing taxes and enacting expenditures from the executive function of collecting taxes and administering expenditure programs and from the judicial function of mediating disputes and interpreting the law.

Here the businessman—self-selected or appointed directly or indirectly by stockholders—is to be simultaneously legislator, executive and jurist. He is to decide whom to tax by how much and for what purpose, and he is to spend the proceeds—all this guided only by general exhortations from on high to restrain inflation, improve the environment, fight poverty and so on and on.

The whole justification for permitting the corporate executive to be selected by the stockholders is that the executive is an agent serving the interests of his principal. This justification disappears when the corporate executive imposes taxes and spends the proceeds for "social" purposes. He becomes in effect a public employee, a civil servant, even though he remains in name an employee of a private enterprise. On grounds of political principle, it is intolerable that such civil servants—insofar as their actions in the name of social responsibility are real and not just window-dressing—should be selected as they are now. If they are to be civil servants, then they must be selected through a political process. If they are to impose taxes and make expenditures to foster "social" objectives, then political machinery must be set up to guide the

assessment of taxes and to determine through a political process the objectives to be served.

This is the basic reason why the doctrine of "social responsibility" involves the acceptance of the socialist view that political mechanisms, not market mechanisms, are the appropriate way to determine the allocation of scarce resources to alternative uses.

On the grounds of consequences, can the corporate executive in fact discharge his alleged "social responsibilities"? On the one hand, suppose he could get away with spending the stockholders' or customers' or employees' money. How is he to know how to spend it? He is told that he must contribute to fighting inflation. How is he to know what action of his will contribute to that end? He is presumably an expert in running his company—in producing a product or selling it or financing it. But nothing about his selection makes him an expert on inflation. Will his holding down the price of his product reduce inflationary pressure? Or, by leaving more spending power in the hands of his customers, simply divert it elsewhere? Or, by forcing him to produce less because of the lower price, will it simply contribute to shortages? Even if he could answer these questions, how much cost is he justified in imposing on his stockholders, customers and employees for this social purpose? What is the appropriate share and what is the appropriate share of others?

And, whether he wants to or not, can he get away with spending his stockholders', customers' or employees' money? Will not the stockholders fire him? (Either the present ones or those who take over when his actions in the name of social responsibility have reduced the corporation's profits and the price of its stock.) His customers and his employees can desert him for other producers and employers less scrupulous in exercising their social responsibilities.

This facet of "social responsibility" doctrine is brought into sharp relief when the doctrine is used to justify wage restraint by trade unions. The conflict of interest is naked and clear when union officials are asked to subordinate the interest of their members to some more general social purpose. If the union officials try to enforce wage restraint, the consequence is likely to be wildcat strikes, rank-and-file revolts and the emergence of strong competitors for their jobs. We thus have the ironic phenomenon that union leaders—at least in the U.S.—have objected to Government interference with the market far more consistently and courageously than have business leaders.

The difficulty of exercising "social responsibility" illustrates, of course, the great virtue of private competitive enterprise—it forces people to be responsible for their own actions and makes it difficult for them to "exploit" other people for either selfish or unselfish purposes. They can do good—but only at their own expense.

Many a reader who has followed the argument this far may be tempted to remonstrate that it is all well and good to speak of government's having the responsibility to impose taxes and determine expenditures for such "social" purposes as controlling pollution or training the hard-core unemployed, but that the problems are too urgent to wait on the slow course of political processes, that the exercise of social responsibility by businessmen is a quicker and surer way to solve pressing current problems.

Aside from the question of fact—I share Adam Smith's skepticism about the benefits that can be expected from "those who affected to trade for the public good"—this argument must be rejected on grounds of principle. What it amounts to is an assertion that those who favor the taxes and expenditures in question have failed to persuade a majority of their fellow citizens to be of like mind and that they are seeking to attain by undemocratic procedures what they cannot attain by democratic procedures. In a free society, it is hard for "good" people to do "good," but that is a small price to pay for making it hard for "evil" people to do "evil," especially since one man's good is another's evil.

I have, for simplicity, concentrated on the special case of the corporate executive, except only for the brief digression on trade unions. But precisely the same argument applies to the newer phenomenon of calling upon stockholders to require corporations to exercise social responsibility (the recent G.M. crusade, for example). In most of these cases, what is in effect involved is some stockholders trying to get other stockholders (or customers or employees) to contribute against their will to "social" causes favored by the activists. Insofar as they succeed, they are again imposing taxes and spending the proceeds.

The situation of the individual proprietor is somewhat different. If he acts to reduce the returns of his enterprise in order to exercise his "social responsibility," he is spending his own money, not someone else's. If he wishes to spend his money on such purposes, that is his right, and I cannot see that there is any objection to his doing so. In the process, he, too, may impose costs on employees and customers. However, because he is far less likely than a large corporation or union to have monopolistic power, any such side effects will tend to be minor.

Of course, in practice the doctrine of social responsibility is frequently a cloak for actions that are justified on other grounds rather than a reason for those actions.

To illustrate, it may well be in the long-run interest of a corporation that is a major employer in a small community to devote resources to providing amenities to that community or to improving its government. That may make it easier to attract desirable employees, it may reduce the wage bill or lessen losses from pilferage and sabotage or have other worthwhile effects. Or it may be that, given the laws about the deductibility of corporate charitable contributions, the stockholders can contribute more to charities they favor by having the corporation make the gift than by doing it themselves, since they can in that way contribute an amount that would otherwise have been paid as corporate taxes.

In each of these—and many similar—cases, there is a strong temptation to rationalize these actions as an exercise of "social responsibility." In the present climate of opinion, with its widespread aversion to "capitalism," "profits," the "soulless corporation" and so on, this is one way for a corporation to generate goodwill as a by-product of expenditures that are entirely justified in its own self-interest.

It would be inconsistent of me to call on corporate executives to refrain from this hypocritical window-dressing because it harms the foundations of a free society. That would be to call on them to exercise a "social responsibility"! If our institutions, and the attitudes of the public, make it in their self-interest to cloak their actions in this way, I cannot summon much indignation to denounce them. At the same time, I can express admiration for those individual proprietors or owners of closely held corporations or stockholders of more broadly held corporations who disdain such tactics as approaching fraud.

Whether blameworthy or not, the use of the cloak of social responsibility, and the nonsense spoken in its name by influential and prestigious businessmen, does clearly harm the foundations of a free society. I have been impressed time and again by the schizophrenic character of many businessmen. They are capable of being extremely far-sighted and clear-headed in matters that are internal to their businesses. They are incredibly short-sighted and muddleheaded in matters that are outside their businesses but affect the possible survival of business in general. This short-sightedness is strikingly exemplified in the calls from many businessmen for wage and price guidelines or controls or income policies. There is nothing that could do more in a brief period to destroy a market system and replace it by a centrally controlled system than effective governmental control of prices and wages.

The short-sightedness is also exemplified in speeches by businessmen on social responsibility. This may gain them kudos in the short run. But it helps to strengthen the already too prevalent view that the pursuit of profits is wicked and immoral and must be curbed and controlled by external forces. Once this view is adopted, the external forces that curb the market will not be the social consciences, however highly developed, of the pontificating executives; it will be the iron fist of Government bureaucrats. Here, as with price and wage controls, businessmen seem to me to reveal a suicidal impulse.

The political principle that underlies the market mechanism is unanimity. In an ideal free market resting on private property, no individual can coerce any other, all cooperation is voluntary, all parties to such cooperation benefit or they need not participate. There are no "social" values, no "social" responsibilities in any sense other than the shared values and responsibilities of individuals. Society is a collection of individuals and of the various groups they voluntarily form.

The political principle that underlies the political mechanism is conformity. The individual must serve a more general social interest—whether that be determined by a church or a dictator or a majority. The individual may have a vote and a say in what is to be done, but if he is overruled, he must conform. It is appropriate for some to require others to contribute to a general social purpose whether they wish to or not.

Unfortunately, unanimity is not always feasible. There are some respects in which conformity appears unavoidable, so I do not see how one can avoid the use of the political mechanism altogether.

But the doctrine of "social responsibility" taken seriously would extend the scope of the political mechanism to every human activity. It does not differ in philosophy from the most explicitly collectivist doctrine. It differs only by professing to believe that collectivist ends can be attained without collectivist means. That is why, in my book "Capitalism and Freedom," I have called it a "fundamentally subversive doctrine" in a free society, and have said that in such a society, "there is one and only one social responsibility of business—to use its resources and engage in activities designed to increase its profits so long as it stays within the rules of the game, which is to say, engages in open and free competition without deception or fraud."

MILTON FRIEDMAN was the winner of the 1974 Nobel Prize in Economics and is recognized as one of the most important economists of the twentieth century. Friedman was the author of numerous academic publications as well as several highly influential books written primarily from a free-market, pro-capitalism perspective.

EXPLORING THE ISSUE

Do Corporations Have a Responsibility to Society Beyond Maximizing Profit?

Critical Thinking and Reflection

1. What do corporations "owe" society?
2. Does my stake in an organization change my view or outlook on what corporations should do for society?
3. In what types of activities should corporations become more involved? Do corporations possess knowledge, skills, and abilities that could prove beneficial to society?
4. Are there limits that should be placed on corporate involvement in society?
5. Given the power corporations already possess, should they be granted additional power via the corporate responsibility issues discussed in these articles?

Is There Common Ground?

The common ground that exists with this issue is the recognition of business as a powerful societal actor. Both sides of this debate recognize and acknowledge the existence of business or corporate power, but vary in their views of what this power or influence means in terms of corporate responsibility or responsiveness to broader society and societal issues. As evidenced by the original dates of publication of these contrasting works, this is a discussion that has already spanned several decades. In light of contemporary challenges and public sentiment, it is anticipated that this topic will be the subject of continued discussion and debate for decades to come.

Additional Resources

Barro, R.J. (1998). "Milton Friedman: Being Right Is the Best Revenge," *Business Week*, July 13, p. 11.

Freeman, R.E. (2002). "Fixing the Ethics Crisis in Corporate America," *Miller Center Report*, Fall, pp. 13–17.

Hartman, L.P. (2004). *Perspectives in Business Ethics*, 3rd ed., New York: McGraw-Hill.

Internet References . . .

Making the Case for Social Responsibility

Cavett-Goodwin, D. (2007). "Making the Case for Social Responsibility." *Cultural Shifts*, December.

http://culturalshifts.com/archives/181

The Social Responsibility of Profit

Driessen, P. (2007). "The Social Responsibility of Profit."

www.eco-imperialism.com/content/article. php3?id=242

Big Business

Gallup Poll (2008). "Big Business."

www.gallup.com/poll/5248/Big-Business.aspx

What Is a Business for?

Handy, C. "What Is a Business for?"

http://ssrn.com/abstract=932676

The Case Against Corporate Social Responsibility

Henderson, D. (2001). "The Case Against Corporate Social Responsibility." *Policy*, Winter, 17(2). The Center for Independent Studies.

http://www.cis.org.au/images/stories/policy-magazine/2001-winter/2001-17-2-david-henderson.pdf

Milton Friedman Was Right

Mann, H.G. (2006). "Milton Friedman Was Right," *The Wall Street Journal*, November 24.

http://online.wsj.com/article/SB116432800408631539 .html

Pew Research Center

Pew Research Center (2008).

http://www.pewresearch.org/

Selected, Edited, and with Issue Framing Material by:
Kathleen J. Barnes, *East Stroudsburg University*
and
George E. Smith, *Albright College*

ISSUE

Are U.S. CEOs Paid More Than They Deserve?

YES: Sarah Anderson et al., from "Executive Excess 2008: How Average Taxpayers Subsidize Runaway Pay" (Institute for Policy Studies, 2008), www.ips-dc.org/reports/#84

NO: Ira T. Kay, from "Don't Mess with CEO Pay," *Across the Board* (January/February 2006)

Learning Outcomes

After reading this issue, you should be able to:

- Understand the positive and negative consequences of executive pay in the workplace.
- Understand how executive pay can be used as a workplace tool.
- Understand policies that might be implemented concerning executive pay.
- Appreciate the legal implications of executive pay's use in the workplace.

ISSUE SUMMARY

YES: Arguing that U.S. CEOs are substantially overpaid in a 2008 study conducted for the Institute for Policy Studies (IPS) are compensation expert and IPS Fellow Sarah Anderson and her colleagues.

NO: Ira T. Kay is an expert in executive compensation and a consultant at Watson Wyatt Worldwide. He argues persuasively that market forces play an important role in determining executive compensation, which is, on the whole, fair and equitable.

On February 4, 2009, in what must have been a tremendously rewarding moment for those who believe that American CEO pay is out of control, President Obama placed a ceiling on the amount of pay top executives at financial institutions receiving federal bailout funds can receive. Imposing a cap of $500,000 on top executive pay, President Obama stated that Americans are angry "at executives being rewarded for failure." He also pointed out that "For top executives to award themselves these kinds of compensation packages in the midst of this economic crisis is not only in bad taste, it's a bad strategy—and I will not tolerate it as president" (*The Seattle Times*, 2009).

Less than six weeks later, the issue of excessive CEO pay achieved even greater attention when it was reported that senior level executives at AIG, a huge U.S. insurance company based in New York City, doled out more than $160 million in bonuses using funds they received as part of the federal government's massive bailout of the financial industry. Again, Obama expressed outrage, declaring that his administration would "pursue every single legal avenue to block those bonuses and make the American taxpayers whole" (Sweet, 2009).

Clearly, the topic of U.S. CEO compensation is one that invokes much emotion and, if President Obama's behavior is any indication, significant political attention as well. And who doubts that the average American citizen believes that American CEOs are paid more than they deserve? Nevertheless, as is so often the case, closer scrutiny of this topic suggests that things are not so simple. In fact, even in the aftermath of the financial debacle of 2008, many academicians, public intellectuals, and business observers strongly believe that U.S. CEO pay is not excessive. Furthermore, and as you shall soon learn, they have very compelling reasons for advocating this view. As the purpose of this text is to have you decide where you stand on controversial issues in management, let's consider Are U.S. CEOs paid more than they deserve?

Those who argue that U.S. CEOs are overpaid raise several interesting points in support of their position. One emotionally powerful point involves the apparent irrational act of paying a CEO millions of dollars while her or his firm is simultaneously reducing its workforce via layoffs and downsizing. Why should a CEO be rewarded for cutting the workforce? Additionally, some boards of directors have shown a willingness to award large bonuses not only to high-performing CEOs but also to CEOs whose organizations were clear under-performers the previous year. Such actions suggest that an individual CEO's pay may not be tied to how well he or she performs, a situation that most would agree is not fair. Perhaps the strongest argument put forth by those who think U.S. CEOs are overpaid is based on a comparison of the CEO pay-to-worker pay ratio in America to that of other industrialized countries. Critics frequently point out that U.S. executives typically make several hundred times more in annual income than the lowest paid employees in their firms. In other countries, however, the ratio is considerably smaller. For example, in Japan the typical CEO makes only about 15 times the lowest worker, and many member countries of the European Union restrict top executive pay to around 20 times the lowest worker's pay.

On the other side of the debate, supporters of current U.S. CEO pay levels argue that CEO pay is, like most jobs in America, subject to labor market influences. Currently, the market for quality CEOs is very tight, and wage-increasing bidding wars are the norm. Thus, CEO pay is clearly subject to labor market conditions. In response to the layoff issue, proponents of existing CEO pay levels argue that CEOs are paid to make and execute difficult decisions. They point out that often the alternative to downsizing and staying in business is not downsizing and going out of business entirely. Proponents also point out that U.S. CEOs, in many instances, are actually *underpaid* because U.S. CEOs and their organizations have created an incredible amount of wealth over the past two decades. In other words, when compared to the wealth U.S. CEOs have made for shareholders, their compensation packages typically look very reasonable.

The following selections represent opposite sides of our CEO pay debate. The affirmative position in this debate is provided by a 2008 study conducted for the Institute for Policy Studies by Sarah Anderson and her colleagues. The negative position put forward by Ira T. Kay, an expert in executive compensation and a consultant at Watson Wyatt Worldwide, argues that CEOs are not paid more than they deserve.

YES ↵

Sarah Anderson et al.

Executive Excess 2008: How Average Taxpayers Subsidize Runaway Pay

Tax Subsidies for Executive Excess

The U.S. tax code currently is riddled with loopholes that allow top corporate and financial leaders to avoid paying their fair share of taxes. Still other loopholes allow corporations to claim unwarranted deductions for exorbitant executive pay. Ordinary taxpayers wind up picking up the bill. That's why this report defines such loopholes as "subsidies for executive excess."

This section focuses on five such subsidies. For each one, analysts have been able to calculate an estimated annual cost to taxpayers. The first three of these subsidies put money directly into executive pockets. The final two give employers an incentive for doling out excessive executive rewards. All five have become targets for legislative reform action.

Estimated Annual Cost to Taxpayers of the Five Most Direct Tax Subsidies for Excessive Executive Pay	
1. Preferential capital gains treatment of carried interest	$2,661,000,000
2. Unlimited deferred compensation	$80,600,000
3. Offshore deferred compensation	$2,086,000,000
4. Unlimited tax deductibility of executive pay	$5,249,475,000
5. Stock option accounting double standard	$10,000,000,000
Total	$20,077,075,000

Subsidy #1

Preferential capital-gains treatment of carried interest
Annual cost: $2,661,000,000

The top 50 highest-paid private equity and hedge fund managers last year made $558 million on average, according to the business trade journal *Alpha*.[1] The top five each collected over $1 billion. These private investment fund magnates hardly seem to need taxpayer assistance. Yet they get it—in massive amounts. Our current tax code allows top private investment fund managers to pay taxes, as investor Warren Buffett has repeatedly noted, at lower rates than their office receptionists.[2]

This tax loophole plays off the peculiarities of pay practices in the investment fund industry. In a publicly traded corporation, a CEO pay package typically includes salary, bonus, perks, and stock awards of various sorts. Private investment fund managers take their rewards through two distinctly different revenue streams. They first collect annual management fees, usually set at 2 percent of the capital they oversee. But these managers also collect a share of the profits realized when they sell fund assets. Within the financial industry, this share goes by the label of "carried interest." Private investment fund managers usually claim, for themselves, a 20 percent "carried interest" share.

Fund managers report this carried interest as a capital gain, not ordinary income. This categorization, critics note, distorts marketplace reality. Carried interest, they point out, clearly represents payment for the delivery of a professional service, the managing of other people's money. Such professional fees, everywhere else in the economy, face the same tax rate as ordinary wage and salary income, up to 35 percent for income in the highest tax bracket.

The capital gains tax rate, by contrast, now sits at only 15 percent. On every $1 million pocketed in "carried interest," in other words, an investment fund manager saves about $200,000 in taxes.

KKR: TAX BREAK BONANZA

Corporate buyout king Henry Kravis earned $450 million as the head of the KKR private equity fund in 2006, *Forbes* reports.[3] A labor group, using public documents, has estimated that Kravis saved somewhere between $58.6 million and $96 million in taxes on that income, thanks to the carried interest loophole.[4] *Forbes* currently ranks Kravis as the 178th wealthiest individual in the world, with a net worth of $5.5 billion.[5]

KKR has launched a vigorous lobbying campaign to "defend" the carried interest loophole — and preferential tax treatment for Henry Kravis. In 2007, the fund paid more than $2 million to advance its interests in Congress. Kravis himself went to Capitol Hill to lobby Senators in July 2007, a job he has traditionally left to those further down the totem pole.[6]

KKR is also a key player in an industry lobby group formed principally to protect tax preferences for investment fund managers. The Private Equity Council opened up shop in early 2007 and spent over $2 million on lobbying before the year ended. The Council's member firms, including the high-profile Blackstone and Carlyle investment funds, spent an additional $7.9 million.[7] In the year's first six months alone, Blackstone shelled out what *The Washington Post* subsequently called the "heftiest six-month payment to any lobbyist ever reported."[8]

Pending reform: Subject carried interest to the same tax rate as ordinary income.

Last November, the U.S. House of Representatives passed a tax reform bill that would have closed the carried interest loophole.[9] But an aggressive lobbying campaign by deep-pocketed investment fund industry movers and shakers — current and potential major campaign donors all — halted the initiative in the Senate.[10]

If the reform had been adopted, the Joint Committee on Taxation estimates, the federal government would have garnered an additional $2,661,000,000 in 2008.[11]

Subsidy #2

Unlimited deferred compensation
Annual cost: $80,600,000

The vast majority of CEOs at large companies now legally shield unlimited amounts of compensation from taxes through special deferred accounts set up by their employers.

According to researchers at Equilar, a compensation analytics firm, 83.4 percent of S&P 500 companies offered such accounts for their top brass in 2007.[12] Equilar found that deferred compensation plan balances increased by 54.3 percent last year, to a median value of $4,517,488.

By contrast, ordinary taxpayers face strict limits on how much income they can defer from taxes via 401(k) plans — $15,500 max per year for most workers.

What makes special deferred pay accounts such a desirable perk for top executives? These accounts offer, of course, the standard economic advantage of pretax compounding. Dollars stashed in deferred-pay pots grow and grow, untaxed, until executives start withdrawing from them. Down the road, at that withdrawal time, the executives might just face a lower tax rate than they do now. Today's top executives, after all, have watched top federal marginal tax rates fall sharply since their careers began. These rates, they have reason to hope, could sink even lower.

Executive deferred pay accounts boast another appealing feature. Many corporations guarantee executives an above-market rate of return on the dollars in their deferred pay accounts. American Express CEO Kenneth I. Chenault, the Associated Press notes, collected $1.55 million in above-market returns on his deferred compensation in 2007.[13] Average corporate employees, by contrast, enjoy no guarantees on the dollars in their deferred-pay 401(k)s. The funds in 401(k)s grow and compound tax-free. But if an employee's investment choices go sour, the funds may not grow at all.

Over recent decades, by forcing workers out of traditional "defined-benefit" pension plans into "defined-contribution" plans like 401(k)s, corporations in the United States have shifted the risk of retirement funding onto workers. Increasingly, in our new American economy, only executives rate retirement security.

Tax Benefits of Deferring Compensation

A hypothetical based on two taxpayers in the top income tax bracket:

Taxpayer who *can* defer compensation

1. Receives compensation in the amount of $100
2. Defers compensation for 5 years, earning 10% return on investment each year, for a total of $161.05
3. Amount the taxpayer can pocket after paying a one-time tax of 35%: **$104.68**

Taxpayer who *cannot* defer compensation

1. Receives compensation in the amount of $100
2. Pays a tax of $35, leaving only $65 to invest
3. Amount available to the taxpayer after earning an after-tax return of 6.5% per year (10% return—35% tax on earnings per year) for five years: **$89.06**

Source: Based on analysis by the Joint Committee on Taxation.[14]

TARGET'S TREASURE CHEST

Before retiring in January 2008, Target CEO Robert Ulrich amassed a treasure chest of $140,791,549 in deferred compensation — all of this over and beyond the dollars in his regular pension and 401(k). Last year alone Ulrich contributed $9,511,070 to his pay-deferral pot.

Ulrich can clearly afford to set aside millions in his deferred-pay stash and still easily maintain the style of life to which he has become accustomed. Last year he cashed in $93,497,000 in stock options.[15]

Pending reform: Cap the amount of pay executives can have deferred.

In 2007, Senate Finance Committee chairman Max Baucus (D-Montana) and the panel's ranking minority member, Senator Charles Grassley (R-Iowa), pushed all the way to a House-Senate conference committee legislation that would have limited annual executive pay deferrals to $1 million.[16] This extremely modest cap, if enacted, would have generated an estimated $806 million over 10 years.[17] Attacked fiercely by corporate interests, this proposal did not survive the conference committee deliberations, but Senator Baucus has pledged to revisit it.

Subsidy #3

Offshore deferred compensation
Annual cost: $2,086,000,000

U.S.-based corporations do incur a tax cost when they allow their executives to stash massive sums in deferred accounts. Until executives begin to withdraw from the accounts, the company cannot claim a tax deduction for the executive compensation deferred.

Businesses registered in offshore tax havens, on the other hand, have little or nothing to lose by allowing their employees to accumulate boatloads of compensation in deferred accounts, since registering in such havens allows them to sidestep the U.S. tax liabilities they would otherwise face.

Offshore maneuvering creates particularly lucrative tax-avoidance opportunities for hedge funds, since most of them have already created offshore subsidiaries. Hedge Fund Research, a Chicago-based analyst firm, estimates that of the total $1.86 trillion invested in hedge funds, $1.25 trillion is kept in funds registered offshore.[18] According to the Joint Committee on Taxation on Capitol Hill, 92 percent of offshore hedge funds have situated themselves in the notorious tax havens of the Cayman Islands, the British Virgin Islands, Bermuda, and the Bahamas.[19]

Deferring pay in offshore accounts represents only one way that the wealthy use tax havens to avoid paying their fair share of taxes. The practice of stashing funds in offshore banks, one Senate investigation has found, costs U.S. taxpayers an estimated $100 billion dollars each year.[20] The data so far available do not reveal how many of these billions benefit business executives, the focus of this report, as opposed to other rich tax-dodgers.

CITADEL: PROTECTING PAY FROM TAXES

Kenneth Griffin, the head of Citadel Investment Group, made $1.5 billion in 2007, up from $1.2 billion in 2006.[21] Citadel's largest fund, the Bermuda-registered Citadel Kensington Ltd.,[22] manages about $10 billion in assets and has reported over 20 percent annual gains for the past nine years.[23] Information on Griffin's tax-deferred offshore accounts is not publicly available, and the investment kingpin lustily defends the tax breaks he enjoys.

"I am proud to be an American," he told the *New York Times* last year. "But if the tax became too high, as a matter of principle, I would not be working this hard."[24]

To help maintain Griffin's work ethic, Citadel has spent more than $1.1 million since the beginning of 2007 lobbying to preserve tax loopholes for private investment managers. Griffin is also hedging his political bets. He has hosted fund-raisers for both Senators Obama and McCain and acted as a "bundler" to collect more than $50,000 for each candidate.[25]

Pending reform: Prevent executives from using offshore tax-deferred compensation accounts.

The Joint Committee on Taxation estimates that American hedge fund managers have amassed so much wealth in offshore deferred accounts that if this tax-dodging scheme had been eliminated this year, the federal government would have received an additional $2,086,000,000 in revenue.[26] A bill that would have closed this loophole passed this year in the House, but stalled in the Senate.[27]

Subsidy #4

Unlimited tax deductibility of executive pay
Annual cost: $5,249,475,000

Tax law allows corporations to deduct the cost of executive compensation from their income taxes, as a business expense, so long as this compensation remains "reasonable." But what's reasonable? The IRS has no clear definition.

In 1993, the Clinton Administration sought to provide some guidance here by promoting legislation designed to cap executive pay deductions at $1 million.

But this attempt to define executive pay reasonableness has proved wholly ineffective because the legislation, as enacted, allows an exception for "performance-based" pay. Most companies simply limit top executive salaries to $1 million or so and then add on to that total various assortments of "performance-based" bonuses, stock awards, and other long-term compensation that increases overall executive pay about an average ten times over.

This tax loophole operates as a powerful subsidy for excessive compensation. The more corporations pay out in executive compensation, the less they owe in taxes. And average taxpayers wind up paying the bill.

WAL-MART: "WE DEDUCT FOR MORE"

In 2007, Wal-Mart CEO H. Lee Scott, Jr. made $29,682,000 — 1,314 times as much as the company's average full-time workers. The discount giant refuses to disclose pay levels for its thousands of part-time workers, but reports that full-time workers make an average of $10.86 per hour.

If Wal-Mart had been required to pay corporate income taxes on the portion of Scott's compensation that exceeded 25 times the value of the firm's average full-time compensation, the company's tax bill would have increased by $10,191,069 in 2007.[28]

This seems a small price to pay, given that taxpayers have provided billions of dollars in subsidies to Wal-Mart over the years in the form of public assistance for the retailer's poorly compensated employees.[29]

Pending reform: Deny corporations deductions on any executive pay that runs over 25 times the pay of a company's lowest-paid worker.

This legislation, the Income Equity Act, has been pending before Congress since the early 1990s, introduced first by the now retired Martin Sabo (D-Minn.) and currently by Barbara Lee (D-Calif.).[30]

The Income Equity Act would not set a ceiling on, or dictate in any way, how much corporations can pay their executives. The legislation would instead place a cap on the amount of pay that corporations can deduct off their taxes. Corporations could still freely pay their executives outlandishly large sums. But the federal government—and America's average taxpayers—would no longer reward them for their excessive generosity.

The bill could have an important impact on lower-level workers as well. By tying pay at the top of the corporate ladder to pay at the bottom, the Income Equity Act would encourage corporations to raise pay at the bottom, since the greater the pay for a company's lowest-paid worker, the higher the tax-deductible pay for the company's highest-paid executives.

The Income Equity Act would, if enacted, also require corporations to annually reveal the pay gap between their highest- and lowest-paid workers. American taxpayers and consumers currently have no way of knowing exactly how much companies squeeze their least powerful workers to create windfalls for executives at the top.

Government estimates of the tax revenue implications of this bill are not available. The Institute for Policy Studies has calculated a conservative estimate, based on a limited sample of the top five executives at 1,500 U.S. firms. The current subsidy, by these calculations is: $5,249,475,000.[31]

Subsidy #5

Stock option accounting double standard
Annual cost: $10,000,000,000

Stock options—the most lucrative of all executive pay categories—come with a magical accounting and tax double standard that makes them nearly irresistible to both executives and the corporations that employ them.

Current *accounting* rules value stock options on their grant date. The current *tax code* values stock options on the day that executives decide to cash them in. The two numbers rarely match, and in recent years, the actual "in-the-pocket" value has been significantly higher than the grant date estimate. As a result, companies can lower their tax bill by claiming deductions for options-related costs that are much higher than what they report in their financial statements.

At the same time, by reporting a low expense for stock options on financial statements, corporations can show higher quarterly net earnings. That keeps Wall Street investors happy, share prices high, and executive rewards flowing at ever more ample levels.

Internal Revenue Service research shows that corporations claimed 2005 stock option tax deductions that were collectively $61 billion larger than the expenses shown on company books.[32]

"By eliminating this outdated and overly generous corporate tax deduction," notes Senator Carl Levin (D-Michigan), "we would eliminate a tax incentive that encourages corporate boards to hand out huge executive stock option pay which, in turn, fuels the growing chasm between executive pay and the earnings of rank and file workers."[33]

UNITEDHEALTH'S STOCK-OPTION SLEIGHT OF HAND

Between 2002 and 2006, a Congressional inquiry has found, UnitedHealth Group, one of the nation's largest health insurance companies, claimed a tax deduction of $317.7 million on 9 million stock options exercised by CEO William McGuire.

In its financial statement, UnitedHealth recorded zero expenses related to those options.[34] The stock option accounting double standard offers all corporations, not just UnitedHealth, an incentive to dole out generous helpings of executive stock options. At UnitedHealth, corporate board members took this doling out to the extreme.

In 2006, the company became one of the top culprits in a rash of stock option backdating scandals after news reports revealed that McGuire and other high-level executives had been allowed to pick the grant dates for their options to maximize payouts.

Continued

"Backdating" itself does not break the law, but improper reporting does. Government investigators nailed UnitedHealth for improperly reporting the real cost of its executive options. As a result, McGuire had to forfeit about $618 million worth of options to help settle shareholder and federal government claims and paid a record $7 million fine to the SEC.[35]

In July 2008, the company announced it was settling one shareholder suit for $895 million and cutting costs by laying off 4,000 employees.[36] McGuire technically "lost" his job, too, but he still retired into the sunset with hundreds of millions in dubiously acquired compensation.

Pending reform: Mandate a single standard for reporting stock options.[37]

Neither the Joint Committee on Taxation nor the Congressional Budget Office has analyzed the revenue implications of this reform. In 2007, Senator Levin cited an estimate of $5 billion to $10 billion in additional revenues that could be generated by eliminating what he calls "unwarranted and excess stock option deductions."

Levin chairs the Senate's Permanent Subcommittee on Investigations, the panel that has led the examination of the stock option accounting double standard. Levin based his estimate on partial-year numbers for 2004 that were considerably lower than the IRS findings for 2005. This report uses the high-end estimate.[38]

Additional Subsidies for Executive Excess

The tax and accounting loopholes noted above actually deliver a relatively small piece of the taxpayer largesse that every year plops into corporate coffers. The federal government also encourages and supports excessive executive pay indirectly, through a variety of supports that range from procurement contracts to handouts that go by the label of "corporate welfare." A recent report revealed that two-thirds of U.S. companies paid no federal income taxes between 1998 and 2005, in part because of tax credits.[39] How much of this taxpayer money winds up in the pockets of top executives? No researchers have yet calculated a specific figure. But the sum likely dwarfs the executive pay subsidies that flow through tax loopholes.

Nearly every major corporation in the United States owes a significant chunk of its profitability to interactions with federal, state, and local governing bodies. Executives regularly claim credit — and huge rewards — for their corporate "performance." Without taxpayer dollars, executives would "perform" nowhere near as well.

That reality creates an opportunity that executive pay reformers have seldom appreciated. Government policies today encourage executive excess. But governments at all levels, if they so chose, could leverage the power of the public purse to discourage such excess and encourage instead the more equitable pay differentials that nurture effective and efficient enterprises and healthy economies.

We describe here a small sampling of today's indirect subsidies for executive excess and the opportunities that ending these subsidies would create for real executive pay reform.

I. Government Procurement and Executive Excess

By law, the U.S. government denies contracts to companies that discriminate, in their employment practices, by race or gender. Our tax dollars, Americans agree, should not subsidize racial or gender inequality. But billions of taxpayer dollars flow annually to companies that increase economic inequality — by paying CEOs hundreds of times more than their workers.

In theory, existing law prevents government contractors from pouring tax dollars, at excessive levels, into executive pockets. Every year, the Office of Management and Budget establishes a maximum benchmark for contractor compensation, $612,196 in FY 2008. But this benchmark only limits the executive pay a company can directly bill the government for reimbursement. The benchmark in no way curbs windfalls that contracts generate for companies and their top executives.

One bill before Congress, the Patriot Corporations Act, would discourage these windfalls.[40] This legislation offers a preference in the evaluation of bids or proposals for federal contracts to companies that meet a series of benchmarks for good corporate citizenship. Among the benchmarks: paying executives no more than 100 times the pay of their lowest-paid employee.

Most top contractors do not currently meet this standard.

The Institute for Policy Studies has analyzed the data available for the top 100 U.S. federal government contractors in 2006. Together, these contractors received over $226 billion in taxpayer-funded contracts.[42] Of these 100 contractors, 47 operate as publicly traded U.S.

LOCKHEED MARTIN CEO: GETTING RICH ON THE DOLE

Perennial top-ranking defense contractor Lockheed Martin took in $32.1 billion from the federal government in 2006, most of it from the Pentagon. These taxpayer dollars made up more than 80 percent of the aerospace giant's total revenues.

In 2007, Lockheed Martin CEO Robert Stevens took home more than $24 million — 787 times the annual pay of a typical U.S. worker ($30,617). That placed the company far over the 100-to-1 standard for good corporate citizenship the pending Patriot Corporations Act proposes.

To make matters worse, at the same time CEO Stevens and his fellow executives were lining his pockets with taxpayer dollars, government auditors were accusing the aerospace firm of more than $8 billion in cost overruns on weapons development projects.[41]

---

corporations, a distinction that requires these companies to report the annual earnings of their top five executives. In 2006, 40 of the 47 (85 percent) paid their CEOs more than 100 times the pay of a typical U.S. worker.[43]

The privately held U.S. companies on this list have not been required to report their executive pay to the SEC. At an October 2007 hearing, members of Congress pushed the CEO of one of these private contactors, Blackwater's Erik Prince, to disclose his personal compensation. Blackwater has received over $1 billion to provide security services in Iraq and Afghanistan, but Prince refused to give a specific figure for his own compensation, defiantly noting that he collected "more than $1 million."[44]

Congress recently passed legislation, the Government Contractor Accountability Act, which will now require executive pay disclosure of all major contractors that receive more than 80 percent of their revenues from federal contracts.[45]

2. Bailouts and Executive Excess

Shortly after the 9/11 attacks, lawmakers in Congress established an important precedent to limit windfall profit-taking in industries that receive substantial government assistance. The $15 billion airline industry bailout Congress okayed in 2001 required that airline companies accepting bailout dollars ban raises and limit severance for all executives who had taken home over $300,000 the previous year.

Unfortunately, lawmakers have not applied strict limits on executive pay in other bailout situations.

This year, the Federal Reserve Board has taken aggressive action to prop up the troubled U.S. financial sector, injecting hundreds of billions of dollars of liquidity into the system — with no restrictions whatsoever on pay for the executives who had reaped massive personal gains while engaging in behaviors that created the credit crisis. The Federal Reserve also agreed to buy up to $29 billion in shaky mortgage bonds to facilitate JPMorgan Chase's purchase of beleaguered Bear Stearns, a move that put taxpayers at risk while placing no restrictions on the benefits that executives might reap from the subsidy.[49]

In late July, Congress followed up this Federal Reserve action by passing a rescue package for Fannie Mae and Freddie Mac that contained only loose controls over the executive pay practices of these private sector "government-sponsored enterprises." The bill created a new regulator for the two mortgage firms and gives this regulator the authority to limit or withhold "golden parachutes" and to ensure that executive pay levels are "reasonable." But the legislation does not define "reasonable," a decision that allows regulators considerable latitude.[50]

FANNIE AND FREDDIE: RISKY FOR TAXPAYERS, NOT CEOS

In 2007, the heads of Freddie Mac and Fannie Mae both earned far more than the average for large company CEOs—despite their utter failure to recognize the housing bubble or avert the mortgage crisis.[46] At Freddie Mac, chief Richard Syron took in nearly $19.8 million, while presiding over a 50 percent drop in the company's stock.[47] Fannie Mae head Daniel Mudd made $13.4 million, 27 percent more than the average for S&P 500 CEOs, according to the Associated Press.[48]

During the debate over a taxpayer bailout for the firms, Senator Bob Casey (D-Pennsylvania) urged the mortgate firms' boards to sue to recover the bonuses that Syron and Mudd pocketed while failing to do their jobs.

Executive Pay Subsidies: What's At Stake?

Fiscal Trade-offs

Our ongoing — and deepening — U.S. economic downturn is forcing governments at every level to make painful choices on which problems to address and which to ignore. In this political climate, taxpayer subsidies for executive excess take on an even greater significance.

All subsidies involve trade-offs. Each time we allow executives and their employers to avoid paying taxes they would otherwise owe, we reduce government's capacity to deliver needed services that taxpayers and their families would otherwise receive.

Tax subsidies for excessive executive pay represent a particularly indefensible waste of government resources. At the moment, no serious observer of the American scene is arguing that top business executives, as a group, earn too little in compensation. So why then should government, in any manner, be encouraging corporations and investment firms to pay their executives even more?

Those tax dollars that currently go to encouraging and rewarding corporate America's most advantaged could, if redirected, go a long way toward addressing *real* problems.

Consider, for instance, one of America's weakest and most vulnerable populations: children with disabilities and other special needs. In the 2007 fiscal year, the federal government distributed not quite $10.8 billion in state aid for special education.[51] Top business executives this year will enjoy nearly twice that amount in federal subsidies for excessive executive compensation.

Or consider federal support for risk taking. Ample rewards for business executives, defenders of contemporary American executive pay often argue, serve as an important incentive for the risk taking necessary to keep an economy innovative and growing.

CEO PAY AND WORKER RIGHTS: WITHOUT LABOR LAW REFORM, CEO-WORKER PAY GAP LIKELY TO GROW

The divide between CEO and worker pay is on course to grow even wider, since industries projected to have the largest employment growth in the next decade show pay gaps that are far wider than industries that are losing the most jobs. One reason for the difference: union representation. In the expanding service sectors, only a tiny percentage of workers have the power to bargain collectively for fair compensation.

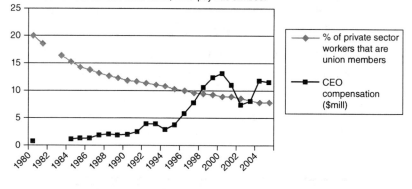

Executive Pay and Unionization, 1980–2005
As unionization rates have fallen, CEO pay has climbed.

Legend: % of private sector workers that are union members; CEO compensation ($mill)

According to the Labor Department, the top job growth industry, food services, will add over 1 million jobs by 2016. The 9.3 million non-management workers in this sector—only 1.2 percent of whom are union members—earn an average of $18,877 per year.[56] The CEOs of the top 10 firms in this industry—McDonald's, YUM Brands (owner of KFC, Taco Bell, Pizza Hut), and other major employers that set industry-wide pay standards—averaged 354 times that amount in 2007.

In retail, another fast-growing industry with low unionization, the CEO-worker pay gap runs even wider, 453-to-1.

By contrast, in industries like auto parts and pulp and paper, where unionization rates are above 20 percent, CEO-worker pay gaps stand at 173-to-1 and 219-to-1 respectively. These manufacturing workers have used union leverage over the years to bargain for decent compensation. Today, however, "free trade" agreements and other factors are slashing employment in these traditional union strongholds.

Without legislative action to allow more workers the right to organize, the divide between compensation for top executives and the rest of us will only continue to grow.

Chart sources: Unionization: Bureau of National Affairs, Union Membership And Earnings Data Book. CEO pay: *Business Week* and *Wall Street Journal* surveys.[57]

But executives hardly make up the only risk-takers on our economic scene today. Many Americans, every day they walk into work, risk their lives. In 2006, 5,320 private-sector workers died on the job. Nearly half a million more lost workdays to on-the-job falls and back injuries.[52]

What's government doing about this real problem? In 2006, the federal government spent $264 million enforcing workplace safety standards. The government is devoting 75 times more than that $264 million, every year, encouraging higher paychecks for top executives, precious few of whom will ever face real "risk" in the workplace.[53]

Additional Economic Costs of a Pay System out of Control

Subsidies for excessive executive pay don't just involve fiscal trade-offs. These subsidies have deep consequences for the economy as a whole—and the economic well-being of America's families.

Senator McCain has not yet endorsed any of the five. In 2002, he co-sponsored a bill similar to the pending proposed fix for the stock option accounting double standard. But McCain has declined, according to Senator Levin's office, to take a position on the current bill.[54]

In 2007, both candidates voted in favor of a minimum wage bill that included an amendment to cap executive deferred compensation. But neither has spoken out about this measure specifically, and the proposal is still pending, since a House-Senate Conference Committee stripped the deferred-pay limit from the minimum wage bill.[55]

None of these five reforms will, either individually or as a group, fully correct the power imbalances in the American economy that have tilted rewards so far up the corporate ladder. The first step needed to restore some modicum of balance? That would be passage of the **Employee Free Choice Act**, the legislation now pending in Congress that would expand collective bargaining throughout the American economy. Senator McCain opposes this legislation, Senator Obama supports it.

Conclusion

Journalists have been writing about rising executive pay since the early 1980s. Over the past quarter-century, poll after poll has shown widespread public opposition to our contemporary CEO pay levels. Almost every high-ranking political leader in the United States has, at one time or another, expressed dismay over pay at America's corporate summit. Surveys have found that even those individuals directly responsible for setting executive pay levels—the members of corporate boards of directors—feel we have a serious executive pay problem.

Yet, year after year, nothing changes. Executive pay continues to rise much faster than compensation elsewhere in the U.S. economy. Does all this mean that rising executive pay reflects some inexorable natural economic phenomenon? Not at all. Public policies, we have detailed in this edition of *Executive Excess*, have fueled the executive pay explosion. We can change public policies.

Historically, troubled economic times in the United States have helped generate long-overdue public policy reforms. We have now entered troubled economic times, likely our worst since executive pay started ballooning in the 1980s. Ballooning executive pay has helped create our current economic woes. Deflating that excess can help end them.

Notes

1 *Alpha* magazine, April 22, 2008.

2 Buffett disclosed to NBC's Tom Brokaw that he paid 17.7 percent of his income in federal income and payroll taxes. His office employees paid an average of 32.9 percent of their income. Buffett attributed this difference to the special treatment of capital gains income. See: www.cnbc.com/id/21543506/site/14081545/

3 Michael K. Ozanian and Peter J. Schwartz, "Top Guns," *Forbes*, May 21, 2007.

4 Services Employees International Union, "Buyout Industry Tax Loopholes That Cost Billions Should be Closed in 2009," (press release) Apr 15, 2008. See: www.reuters.com/article/pressRelease/idUS218165+15-Apr-2008+PRN20080415

5 "Billionaires 2008," *Forbes*, March 24, 2008.

6 Stephen Labaton and Jenny Anderson, "Mr. Kravis Goes to Washington (Capra Rolls Over)," *New York Times*, July 11, 2007. See: www.nytimes.com/2007/07/11/business/11tax.html?_r=1&pagewanted=print&oref=slogin

7 Richard Rubin and Emily Cadei, "Private Equity's Lobby Shop Ramping Up for Renewed Tax Battle," *Congressional Quarterly Today*, March 28, 2008. See: www.cqpolitics.com/wmspage.cfm?docID=news-000002693578

8 Jeffrey H. Birnbaum, "Wall Street Paying High Price to Keep Cash," Washington Post, August 21, 2007. See: www.washingtonpost.com/wp-dyn/content/article/2007/08/20/AR2007082001761.html

9 Temporary Tax Relief Act of 2007 (H.R.3996).

10 Charlie Cray and Christopher Hayes, "Executive Excess on Capitol Hill," *The Nation*, November 12, 2007. See: www.thenation.com/doc/20071126/cray_hayes

11 Joint Committee on Taxation, JCX-105-07, October 31, 2007. See: www.house.gov/jct/x-105-07.pdf

12 Equilar, "S&P 500 CEO Compensation Rises 1.3% to $8.8 Million," April 10, 2008. See: www.equilar.com/Executive_Compensation_Knowledge_Center.php.

13 Associated Press, "Clarification: American Express CEO pay story," May 6, 2008. See: http://news.moneycentral.msn.com/provider/providerarticle.aspx?feed=AP&date=20080506&Id=8596806

14 Joint Committee On Taxation, "Present Law and Analysis Relating to Tax Treatment of Partnership Carried Interests and Related Issues, Part II," September 4, 2007, p. 8.

15 Target proxy statement, May 22, 2008. See: www.sec .gov/Archives/edgar/data/27419/000104746908004184/ a2183269zdef14a.htm

16 The Small Business and Work Opportunity Act (S. 349).

17 Democratic Policy Committee (press release) January 23, 2007. see: dpc.senate.gov/dpc-new .cfm?doc_name=lb-110-1-11. Note: We divided the 10-year projected revenue by 10 to obtain an annual cost to taxpayers.

18 Imogen Rose-Smith, "Offshore Fantasy?" *Alpha*, April 2008.

19 Joint Committee On Taxation, "Present Law And Analysis Relating To Tax Treatment Of Partnership Carried Interests And Related Issues, Part II," (JCX-63-07) September 4, 2007.

20 Permanent Subcommittee On Investigations Issues Report On Tax Haven Banks Hiding Billions From The IRS (press release) July 17, 2008. See: http://hsgac .senate.gov/public/index.cfm?Fuseaction=PressReleases. View&PressRelease_id=c9724a6a-1135-4cb8-9584-d474499e8131&Affiliation=R

21 The 2006 figure is from *Forbes*, May 21, 2007, while the 2007 figure is from *Alpha*, April 22, 2008.

22 See: www.alacrastore.com/storecontent/spcred/ 575725

23 Marcia Vickers, "A hedge fund superstar," FORTUNE Magazine, April 3 2007. See: http://money .cnn.com/magazines/fortune/fortune_archive/2007/ 04/16/8404298/

24 Louis Uchitelle, "The Richest Of The Rich, Proud Of A New Gilded Age," *New York Times Magazine*, July 15, 2007.

25 Michael Luo and Kitty Bennett, "McCain Names More Top Fund-Raisers, Including Lobbyists," *New York Times*, July 16, 2008. See: www.nytimes .com/2008/07/16/us/politics/16donate.html

26 Joint Committee on Taxation, JCX-105-07, October 31, 2007. See: www.house.gov/jct/x-105-07.pdf

27 Temporary Tax Relief Act of 2007 (H.R.3996).

28 Formula: $22,589 (annual average pay for full-time Wal-Mart workers) × 25 = $564,725 (amount above which Wal-Mart could not claim a deduction under the proposed Income Equity Act). $29,682,064 (Wal-Mart CEO pay in 2007)— $564,275 (amount above which Wal-Mart could not claim a deduction under the proposed law) = $29,117,339 (unallowable corporate deduction) × 35 percent (maximum corporate tax rate) = $10,191,069 (taxpayer savings related to CEO's pay)

29 See, for example: Arindrajit Dube, Dave Graham-Squire, Ken Jacobs and Stephanie Luce, "Living Wage Policies and Wal-Mart: How a Higher Wage Standard Would Impact Wal-Mart Workers and Shoppers," UC Berkeley Labor Center, December 2007,

and Democratic Staff of the Committee on Education and the Workforce, U.S. House of Representatives, "Everyday Low Wages: The Hidden Price We All Pay For Wal-Mart: Wal-Mart's Labor Record," February 16, 2004.

30 Income Equity Act (H.R. 3876).

31 Methodology: $5.2 billion is the additional revenue that the federal government would have received if a deductibility cap of no more than 25 times a company's lowest-paid worker pay had been in place in 2003 for the companies that comprise the S&P 500, MidCap400, and SmallCap600. Pay figures for the top five executives in each of these groups drawn from Bebchuk and Grinstein, "The Growth of Executive Pay" (2005). Formula: $12,168 (annual pay for full-time minimum wage workers) × 25 = $304,200 (amount above which corporations could not claim a deduction under the proposed Income Equity Act). $4,280,000 (average pay for top 5 execs in S&P 500)— $304,200 (amount above which corporations could not claim a deduction under the proposed law) = $3,975,800 (unallowable corporate deduction) × 35 percent (maximum corporate tax rate) = $1,391,530 (tax payer savings per executive) × 2,500 (5 execs in 500 companies = $3,478,825,000 in total taxpayer savings. (repeated for MidCap400 and SmallCap600). Note: This calculation uses the minimum wage as the lowest-pay rate but the estimate is conservative in that it only applies to 1,500 companies of varying sizes.

32 Senate Permanent Subcommittee on Investigations (press release), April 21, 2008. See: http://levin.senate .gov/newsroom/release.cfm?id=296455

33 Senate Committee on Homeland Security and Governmental Affairs, press release, September 28, 2007. See: http://hsgac.senate.gov/public/index .cfm?Fuseaction=PressReleases.View&PressRelease_ id=661bf7cc-b067-4cf4-a02a-136ed7ed9160& Affiliation=R

34 Hearing Before the Permanent Subcommittee on Investigations of the Committee on Homeland Security and Governmental Affairs, "Executive Stock Options: Should the Internal Revenue Service and Stockholders Be Given Different Information?" June 5, 2007. See: frwebgate.access .gpo.gov/cgi-bin/getdoc.cgi?dbname=110_senate_ hearings&docid=f:36611.pdf

35 David Phelps, "McGuire pays again, ends SEC's inquiry," *Star Tribune* (Minneapolis, MN), December 7, 2007.

36 MarketWatch, July 2, 2008.

37 Ending Corporate Tax Favors For Stock Options Act (S. 2116).

38 Senate Committee on Homeland Security and Governmental Affairs (press release), September 28, 2007. See: http://hsgac.senate .gov/public/index.cfm?Fuseaction=PressReleases .View&PressRelease_id=661bf7cc-b067-4cf4-a02a-136ed7ed9160&Affiliation=R

39 Government Accountability Office, "Comparison of the Reported Tax Liabilities of Foreign- and U.S.-Controlled Corporations, 1998–2005," GAO-08-957, July 24, 2008. See: http://gao.gov/docsearch/abstract.php?rptno=GAO-08-957

40 Patriot Corporations of America Act of 2007 (H.R.3319).

41 Government Accountability Office, "Defense Acquisitions: Assessments of Selected Weapon Programs," March 2008, p. 25, Table 5. See: www.gao.gov/new.items/d08467sp.pdf

42 List compiled by OMB Watch: See: www.fedspending.org/fpds/tables.php?tabtype=t2&subtype=t&year=2006

43 CEO pay figures were calculated from information in corporate proxy statements, based on the Associated Press formula for total compensation, which includes: salary, bonuses, perks, above-market interest on deferred compensation and the value of stock and option awards. Stock and options awards were measured at their fair value on the day of the grant. Worker pay is based on U.S. Department of Labor, Bureau of Labor Statistics, Employment, Hours, and Earnings from the Current Employment Statistics Survey. Average hourly earnings of production workers ($17.42) × average weekly hours of production workers (33.8 hours) × 52 weeks = $30,617.

44 Transcript, House Oversight and Government Reform Committee hearing, October 2, 2007. See: http://oversight.house.gov/documents/20071127131151.pdf

45 OMB Watch, August 5, 2008. See: www.ombwatch.org/article/articleview/4324/

46 Dean Baker, "Paying for Fannie and Freddie's mistakes," *The Guardian*, July 21, 2008.

47 Associated Press, "Freddie Mac CEO paid almost $20M last year," July 18, 2008. See: http://money.cnn.com/2008/07/18/news/newsmakers/Freddiemac_CEO.ap/index.htm?section=money_latest

48 AP inter-active compensation survey. See: hosted.ap.org/dynamic/files/specials/interactives/_business/executive_compensation/index.html?SITE=YAHOO&SECTION=HOME

49 Bob David, Damian Paletta and Rebecca Smith, "Amid Turmoil, U.S. Turns Away From Decades of Deregulation," *Wall Street Journal*, July 25, 2008. See: http://online.wsj.com/article/SB121694460456283007.html

50 Housing and Economic Recovery Act of 2008 (H.R.3221).

51 U.S. Department of Education, Fiscal Year 2001–2009 State Tables. See: www.ed.gov/about/overview/budget/statetables/09stbyprogram.pdf

52 Bureau of Labor Statistics, "Injuries, Illnesses, and Fatalities." See: www.bls.gov/iif/home.htm

53 OMB Watch, "Workers Threatened by Decline in OSHA Budget, Enforcement Activity," Jan. 23, 2008. See: www.ombwatch.org/article/articleview/4143 - 1b

54 E-mail communication with Levin aide Elise Bean, August 5, 2008.

55 Voting record on the Fair Minimum Wage Act of 2007: http://www.senate.gov/legislative/LIS/roll_call_lists/roll_call_vote_cfm.cfm?congress=110&session=1&vote=00042

56 Wage and employment: Based on Bureau of Labor Statistics figures. See: www.bls.gov/oes/current/oessrci.htm. Unionization: Bureau of National Affairs, "Union Membership and Earnings Data Book," 2007, p. 54.

57 Sources: Unionization: Bureau of National Affairs, Union Membership And Earnings Data Book, 2007 Edition, Table 1b, p. 12. CEO pay for 1980–2004: Business Week surveys. For 2005: Wall Street Journal survey. (both surveys covered about 350 large companies). Note: The data end in 2005 because SEC reporting changes make subsequent data not directly comparable. Gaps reflect years for which data were not available.

Sarah Anderson is the director of the Global Economy Project at the Institute for Policy Studies and a coauthor of 14 previous IPS annual reports on executive compensation.

John Cavanagh is the director of the Institute for Policy Studies and coauthor of *Development Redefined: How the Market Met Its Match* (Paradigm Publishers, 2008).

Chuck Collins is a senior scholar at the Institute for Policy Studies where he directs the Program on Inequality and the Common Good. He was a cofounder of United for a Fair Economy, and his latest book, the coauthored *The Moral Measure of the Economy,* appeared earlier this year (Orbis, 2008).

Mike Lapham is the project director of the Responsible Wealth program at United for a Fair Economy. Responsible Wealth organizes business leaders and wealthy individuals to raise their voices in support of tax fairness and corporate accountability.

Sam Pizzigati is an associate fellow of the Institute for Policy Studies and the author of *Greed and Good: Understanding and Overcoming the Inequality That Limits Our Lives* (Apex Press, 2004). He edits *Too Much,* an online weekly on excess and inequality.

Ira T. Kay

NO

Don't Mess with CEO Pay

For years, headlines have seized on dramatic accounts of outrageous amounts earned by executives—often of failing companies—and the financial tragedy that can befall both shareholders and employees when CEOs line their own pockets at the organization's expense. Images of lavish executive lifestyles are now engraved in the popular consciousness. The result: public support for political responses that include new regulatory measures and a long list of demands for greater shareholder or government control over executive compensation.

These images now overshadow the reality of thousands of successful companies with appropriately paid executives and conscientious boards. Instead, fresh accusations of CEOs collecting huge amounts of undeserved pay appear daily, fueling a full-blown mythology of a corporate America ruled by executive greed, fraud, and corruption.

This mythology consists of two related components: the myth of the failed pay-for-performance model and the myth of managerial power. The first myth hinges on the idea that the link between executive pay and corporate performance—if it ever existed—is irretrievably broken. The second myth accepts the idea of a failed pay-for-performance model and puts in its service the image of unchecked CEOs dominating subservient boards as the explanation for decisions resulting in excessive executive pay. The powerful combination of these two myths has captured newspaper headlines and shareholder agendas, regulatory attention and the public imagination.

This mythology has spilled over into the pages of *Across the Board,* where the September/October cover story links high levels of CEO pay to the country's growing income inequality and wonders why U.S. workers have not taken to the streets to protest "the blatant abuse of privilege" exercised by CEOs. In "The Revolution That Never Was," James Krohe Jr. manages to reference Marie Antoinette, Robespierre, Adam Smith, Alexis de Tocqueville, Andrew Jackson, Kim Jong II, Jack Welch, guerrilla warfare, "economic apartheid," and police brutality, in Selma, Ala., in an article that feeds virtually every conceivable element of the myth of executive pay and wonders why we have not yet witnessed calls for a revolution to quash the "financial frolics of today's corporate aristocrats."

In a very different *Across the Board* feature story published a few months earlier, the myth of managerial power finds support in an interview with one of the myth's creators, Harvard professor Lucian Bebchuk, who believes that the pay-for-performance model is broken and that executive control over boards is to blame. Bebchuk is a distinguished scholar who has significant insights into the executive-pay process, but he greatly overestimates the influence of managerial power in the boardroom and ignores empirical evidence that most companies still operate under an intact and explicit pay-for-performance model. And although he acknowledges in his interview with *ATB* editor A.J. Vogl that "American companies have been successful and executives deserve a great deal of credit," his arguments about managerial power run counter to the realities of this success.

Fueling the Fiction

These two articles, in different ways, contribute to what is now a dominant image of executives collecting unearned compensation and growing rich at the expense of shareholders, employees and the broader community. In recent years, dozens of reporters from business magazines and the major newspapers have called me and specifically asked for examples of companies in which CEOs received exorbitant compensation, approved by the board, while the company performed poorly. Not once have I been asked to comment on the vast majority of companies—those in which executives are appropriately rewarded for performance or in which boards have reduced compensation or even fired the CEO for poor performance.

I have spent hundreds of hours answering reporters' questions, providing extensive data and explaining the pay-for-performance model of executive compensation, but my efforts have had little impact: The resulting stories feature the same anecdotal reporting on those corporations for which the process has gone awry. The press accounts ignore solid research that shows that annual pay for most executives moves up and down significantly with the company's performance, both financial and stock-related. Corporate wrongdoings and outlandish executive pay packages make for lively headlines, but the reliance on purely anecdotal reporting and the highly prejudicial language adopted are a huge disservice to the companies, their executives and employees, investors, and the public. The likelihood of real economic damage to the U.S. economy grows daily.

For example, the mythology drives institutional investors and trade unions with the power to exert enormous pressure on regulators and executive and board practices. The California Public Employees' Retirement System—the nation's largest public pension fund—offers a typical example in its Nov. 15, 2004, announcement of a new campaign to rein in "abusive compensation practices in corporate America and hold directors and compensation committees more accountable for their actions."

The AFL-CIO's website offers another example of the claim that managerial power has destroyed the efficacy of the pay-for-performance model: "Each year, shocking new examples of CEO pay greed are made public. Investors are concerned not just about the growing size of executive compensation packages, but the fact that CEO pay levels show little apparent relationship to corporate profits, stock prices or executive performance. How do CEOs do it? For years, executives have relied on their shareholders to be passive absentee owners. CEOs have rigged their own compensation packages by packing their boards with conflicted or negligent directors."

The ROI of the CEO

As with all modern myths, there's a grain of truth in all the assumptions and newspaper stories. The myths of managerial power and of the failed pay-for-performance model find touchstones in real examples of companies where CEOs have collected huge sums in cash compensation and stock options while shareholder returns declined. (You know the names—there's no need to mention them again here.) Cases of overstated profits or even outright fraud have fueled the idea that executives regularly manipulate the measures of performance to justify higher pay while boards default on their oversight responsibilities. The ability of executives to time the exercise of their stock options and collect additional pay through covert means has worsened perceptions of the situation both within and outside of the world of business.

These exceptions in executive pay practices, however, are now commonly mistaken for the rule. And as Krohe's article demonstrates, highly paid CEOs have become the new whipping boys for social critics concerned about the general rise in income inequality and other broad socioeconomic problems. Never mind that these same CEOs stand at the center of a corporate model that has generated millions of jobs and trillions of dollars in shareholder earnings. Worse, using CEOs as scapegoats distracts from the real causes of and possible solutions for inequality.

The primary determinant of CEO pay is the same force that sets pay for all Americans: relatively free—if somewhat imperfect—labor markets, in which companies offer the levels of compensation necessary to attract and retain the employees who generate value for shareholders. Part of that pay for most executives consists of stock-based incentives. A 2003 study by Brian J. Hall and Kevin J. Murphy shows that the ratio of total CEO compensation to production workers' average earnings closely follows the Dow Jones Industrial Average. When the Dow soars, the gap between executive and non-executive compensation widens. The problem, it seems, is not that CEOs receive too much performance-driven, stock-based compensation, but that non-executives receive too little.

The key question is not the actual dollar amount paid to a CEO in total compensation or whether that amount represents a high multiple of pay of the average worker's salary but, rather, whether that CEO creates an adequate return on the company's investment in executive compensation. In virtually every area of business, directors routinely evaluate and adjust the amounts that companies invest in all inputs, and shareholders directly or indirectly endorse or challenge those decisions. Executive pay is no different.

Hard Realities

The corporate scandals of recent years laid bare the inner workings of a handful of public companies where, inarguably, the process for setting executive pay violated not only the principle of pay-for-performance but the extensive set of laws and regulations governing executive pay practices and the role of the board. But while I condemn illegal actions and criticize boards that reward executives who fail to produce positive financial results, I know that the vast majority of U.S. corporations do much better by their shareholders and the public. I have worked directly with more than a thousand publicly traded companies in the United States and attended thousands of compensation-committee meetings, and I have *never* witnessed board members straining to find a way to pay an executive more than he is worth.

In addition, at Watson Wyatt I work with a team of experts that has conducted extensive research at fifteen hundred of America's largest corporations and tracked the relationship between these pay practices and corporate performance over almost twenty years. In evaluating thousands of companies annually, yielding nearly twenty thousand "company years" of data, and pooling cross-sectional company data over multiple years, we have discovered that for both most companies and the "typical" company, there is substantial pay-for-performance sensitivity. That is, high performance generates high pay for executives and low performance generates low pay. Numerous empirical academic studies support our conclusions.

Our empirical evidence and evidence from other studies have produced the following key findings:

1. Executive pay is unquestionably high relative to low-level corporate positions, and it has risen dramatically over the past ten to fifteen years, faster than inflation and faster than average employee pay. But executive compensation generally tracks total returns to shareholders—even including the recent rise in pay.
2. Executive stock ownership has risen dramatically over the past ten to fifteen years. High levels of CEO stock ownership are correlated with and most likely the cause of companies' high financial and stock-market performance.

3. Executives are paid commensurate with the skills and talents that they bring to the organization. Underperforming executives routinely receive pay reductions or are terminated—far more often than press accounts imply.
4. CEOs who are recruited from outside a company and have little influence over its board receive compensation that is competitive with and often higher than the pay levels of CEOs who are promoted from within the company.
5. At the vast majority of companies, even extraordinarily high levels of CEO compensation represent a tiny fraction of the total value created by the corporation under that CEO's leadership. (Watson Wyatt has found that U.S. executives receive approximately 1 percent of the net income generated by the corporations they manage.) Well-run companies, it bears pointing out, produce significant shareholder returns and job security for millions of workers.

Extensive research demonstrates a high and positive correlation between executive pay and corporate performance. For example, high levels of executive stock ownership in 2000, created primarily through stock-option awards, correlated with higher stock-market valuation and long-term earnings per share over the subsequent five-year period. In general, high-performing companies are led by highly paid executives—with pay-for-performance in full effect. Executives at low-performing companies receive lower amounts of pay. Reams of data from other studies confirm these correlations.

Why CEOs Are Worth the Money

The huge gap between the realities of executive pay and the now-dominant mythology surrounding it has become even more evident in recent years. Empirical studies show that executive compensation has closely tracked corporate performance: Pay rose during the boom years of the 1990s, when U.S. corporations generated huge returns, declined during the 2001–03 profit slowdown, and increased in 2004 as profits improved. The myth of excessive executive pay continued to gain power, however, even as concrete, well-documented financial realities defied it.

The blind outrage over executive pay climbed even during the slowdown, as compensation dropped drastically. During this same period, in the aftermath of the corporate scandals, Congress and the U.S. regulatory agencies instituted far-reaching reforms in corporate governance and board composition, and companies spent millions to improve their governance and transparency. But the critics of executive pay and managerial power were only encouraged to raise their voices.

It might surprise those critics to learn that CEOs are not interchangeable and not chosen by lot; they are an extremely important asset to their companies and generally represent an excellent investment. The relative scarcity of CEO talent is manifested in many ways, including the frenetic behavior of boards charged with filling the top position when a CEO retires or departs. CEOs have significant, legitimate, market-driven bargaining power, and in pay negotiations, they use that power to obtain pay commensurate with their skills. Boards, as they should, use their own bargaining power to retain talent and maximize returns to company shareholders.

Boards understand the imperative of finding an excellent CEO and are willing to risk millions of dollars to secure the right talent. Their behavior is not only understandable but necessary to secure the company's future success. Any influence that CEOs might have over their directors is modest in comparison to the financial risk that CEOs assume when they leave other prospects and take on the extraordinarily difficult task of managing a major corporation, with a substantial portion of their short- and long-term compensation contingent on the organization's financial success.

Lucian Bebchuk and other critics underestimate the financial risk entailed in executive positions when they cite executives' large severance packages, derided as "golden parachutes." Top executive talent expects and can command financial protections commensurate with the level of risk they assume. Like any other element of compensation, boards should and generally do evaluate severance agreements as part of the package they create to attract and retain talent. In recent years, boards have become more aware of the damage done when executive benefits and perquisites are excessive and not aligned with non-executive programs, and are now reining in these elements.

Properly designed pay opportunities drive superior corporate performance and secure it for the future. And most importantly, many economists argue, the U.S. model of executive compensation is a significant source of competitive advantage for the nation's economy, driving higher productivity, profits, and stock prices.

Resetting the Debate

Companies design executive pay programs to accomplish the classic goals of any human-capital program. First, they must attract, retain, and motivate their human capital to perform at the highest levels. The motivational factor is the most important, because it addresses the question of how a company achieves the greatest return on its human-capital investment and rewards executives for making the right decisions to drive shareholder value. Incentive-pay and pay-at-risk programs are particularly effective, especially at the top of the house, in achieving this motivation goal.

Clearly, there are exceptions to the motivational element—base salaries, pensions, and other benefits, for example—that are more closely tied to retention goals and are an essential part of creating a balanced portfolio for the employee. The portfolio as a whole must address the need for income and security and the opportunity for creating significant asset appreciation.

A long list of pressures, including institutional-investor pushback, accounting changes, SEC investigations, and scrutiny from labor unions and the media, are forcing companies to rethink their executive-compensation programs, especially their stock-based incentives. The key now is to address the real problems in executive compensation without sacrificing the performance-based model and the huge returns that it has generated. Boards are struggling to achieve greater transparency and more rigorous execution of their pay practices—a positive move for all parties involved.

The real threat to U.S. economic growth, job creation, and higher living standards now comes from regulatory overreach as proponents of the mythology reject market forces and continue to push for government and institutional control over executive pay. To the extent that the mythology now surrounding executive pay leads to a rejection of the pay-for-performance model and restrictions on the risk-and-reward structure for setting executive compensation, American corporate performance will suffer.

There will be more pressure on boards to effectively reduce executive pay. This may meet the social desires of some constituents, but it will almost surely cause economic decline, for companies and the U.S. economy. We will see higher executive turnover and less talent in the executive suite as the most qualified job candidates move into other professions, as we saw in the 1970s, when top candidates moved into investment banking, venture-capital firms, and consulting, and corporate performance suffered as a result.

Our research demonstrates that aligning pay plans, incentive opportunities, and performance measures throughout an organization is key to financial success. Alignment means that executives and non-executives alike have the opportunity to increase their pay through performance-based incentives. As new regulations make it more difficult to execute the stock-based elements of the pay-for-performance model, for example, by reducing broad-based stock options, we will see even less alignment between executives' compensation and the pay packages of the rank-and-file. We are already witnessing the unintended consequences of the new requirement for stock-option expensing as companies cut the broad-based stock-option plans that have benefited millions of workers and given them a direct stake in the financial success of the companies for which they work.

Instead of changing executive pay plans to make them more like pay plans for employees, we should be reshaping employee pay to infuse it with the same incentives that drive performance in the company's upper ranks. A top-down regulatory approach to alignment will only damage the entire market-based, performance-management process that has worked so well for most companies and the economy as a whole. Instead of placing artificial limits on executive pay, we should focus squarely on increasing performance incentives and stock ownership for both executive and non-executive employees and rewarding high performers throughout the organization, from top to bottom. Within the context of a free-market economy, equal opportunity—not income equality by fiat—is the goal.

The short answer to James Krohe's question of why high levels of executive pay have not sparked a worker revolution is that the fundamental model works too well. Workers vote to support that model every day when they show up for work, perform well, and rely on corporate leadership to pursue a viable plan for meeting payroll and funding employee benefits. Shareholders vote to support the model every time they purchase shares or defeat one of the dozens of proposals submitted in recent years to curb executive compensation. Rejecting the pay-for-performance model for executive compensation means returning to the world of the CEO as caretaker. And caretakers—as shown by both evidence and common sense—do not create high value for shareholders or jobs for employees.

In some ways, the decidedly negative attention focused on executive pay has increased the pressure that executives, board members, HR staffs, and compensation consultants all feel when they enter into discussions about the most effective methods for tying pay to performance and ensuring the company's success. The managerial-power argument has contributed to meaningful discussions about corporate governance and raised the level of dialogue in boardrooms. These are positive developments.

When the argument is blown into mythological proportions, however, it skews thinking about the realities of corporate behavior and leads to fundamental misunderstandings about executives, their pay levels, and their role in building successful companies and a flourishing economy. Consequently, the mythology now surrounding executive compensation leads many to reject a pay model that works well and is critical to ongoing growth at both the corporate and the national economic level. We need to address excesses in executive pay without abandoning the core model, and to return the debate to a rational, informed discussion. And we can safely leave Marie Antoinette out of it.

IRA T. KAY is an expert in executive compensation and a consultant at Watson Wyatt Worldwide.

EXPLORING THE ISSUE

Are U.S. CEOs Paid More Than They Deserve?

Critical Thinking and Reflection

1. Would guidelines on executive compensation mitigate potential legal challenges?
2. Would different executive compensation packages change executives' behavior?
3. Will an executive compensation control policy spur other methods to compensate executives?
4. Can executive compensation effectively be contained?
5. Should the executive compensation be changed?

Is There Common Ground?

One reason the issue of CEO pay is so contentious is that both sides can easily cite data in support of their position. Even an issue as seemingly straightforward as determining actual CEO pay levels can be difficult. While finding common ground on even basic aspects of this important management topic is difficult, there is consensus that executive compensation is a highly charged topic that will be debated for quite some time.

Additional Resources

Bebchuk, L. and Ginstein, Y. (2005). "The Growth of Executive Pay," *Oxford Review of Economic Policy*, Summer, pp. 283–303.

Hayes, R.M. and Schaefer, S. (2009). "CEO Pay and the Lake Wobegon Effect," *Journal of Financial Economics*, November, pp. 280–290.

Jensen, M.C. and Murphy, K.J. (2010). "CEO Incentives—It's Not What You Pay, but How," *Journal of Applied Corporate Finance*, Winter, pp. 64–76.

Internet References . . .

2009 Executive PayWatch

AFL-CIO. "2009 Executive PayWatch."

www.aflcio.org/corporatewatch/paywatch/

Executive Pay Isn't That Excessive and Some CEOs Really Deserve It

Angur, M. (2009). "Executive Pay Isn't That Excessive and Some CEOs Really Deserve It," IBDeditorials, March 23.

www.ibdeditorials.com/IBDArticles .aspx?id=322697364171124

Nothing Wrong with CEOs Making Top Dollar

Balaker, T. (2006). "Nothing Wrong with CEOs Making Top Dollar," *Los Angeles Business Journal*, November 6.

www.reason.org/news/show/122437.html

Don't Cap CEO Pay: End Bailouts

Brook, Y. (2008). "Don't Cap CEO Pay: End Bailouts," *Ayn Rand Center for Individual Rights*, September 23.

www.aynrand.org/site/News2?page=NewsArticle&id= 21359&news_iv_ctrl=2528

Say on Pay Rules Won't Satisfy Public's Salary Bloodlust

Jaffe, C. (2009). "Say on Pay Rules Won't Satisfy Public's Salary Bloodlust," *FoxBusiness*, April 1.

www.foxbusiness.com/story/markets/industries/ finance/say-pay-rules-wont-satisfy-publics-salary- bloodlust/

Fixing Executive Compensation Excesses

Lawler, III, E. (2009). "Fixing Executive Compensation Excesses," *BusinessWeek*, February 5.

www.businessweek.com/managing/content/feb2009/ ca2009025_072667.htm

CEO Pay Sinks Along with Profits

Lubin, J. (2009). "CEO Pay Sinks Along with Profits," *Wall Street Journal Online*, April 6.

http://online.wsj.com/article/SB123870448211783759 .html

Obama's AIG Bonus Outrage; AIG Unites Democrats, Republicans

Sweet, L. (2009). *"Obama's AIG Bonus Outrage; AIG Unites Democrats, Republicans," Chicago Sun-Times,* March 17.

http://blogs.suntimes.com/sweet/2009/03/obamas_ aig_bonus_outrage_aig_u.html

Goal of Obama's CEO Pay Cap: Make Wall St. Accountable

Associated Press and McClatchy Newspapers. (2009) *"Goal of Obama's CEO Pay Cap: Make Wall St. Accountable,"The Seattle Times* February 5.

http://seattletimes.nwsource.com/html/ politics/2008709424_pay05.html

Selected, Edited, and with Issue Framing Material by:
Kathleen J. Barnes, *East Stroudsburg University*
and
George E. Smith, *Albright College*

ISSUE

Can Ethical Malaise Be Remedied Through Ethics Education?

YES: Verne E. Henderson, from "Can Business Ethics Be Taught?" *Management Review* (August 1998, pp. 52–53)

NO: John Hooker, from "The Case Against Business Ethics Education: A Study in Bad Arguments," *Journal of Business Ethics Education* (vol. 1, no. 1, 2004, pp. 75–88)

Learning Outcomes
After reading this issue, you should be able to: • Discuss and explain the benefits and limitations of ethical instruction as a tool for addressing ethical problems.   • Explain why corporations and educational institutions have widely adopted ethics instruction as a tool for addressing real and potential ethics problems.   • Understand that ethics knowledge does not necessarily equate to ethical and moral behavior.   • Appreciate the challenge of ensuring employee adherence to ethical and moral behavior in organizations.

ISSUE SUMMARY

YES: Verne Henderson's article indicates that we don't question whether students "learn" in other areas if they pass a course. However, Henderson observes that we do question learning and what is learned in ethics education. The real question is what are our expectations for learning and its outcomes in ethics education and why is it so hard to measure these.

NO: John Hooker presents several arguments against the teaching of business ethics and discusses his approach to addressing these arguments in his own teaching.

As national and global financial markets crashed, a cry for ethical reform of the business environment emerged. The underlying claims driving this cry were the beliefs that management practices were immoral, that managerial morals and ethics were lacking, and that management education had failed its students by not inculcating in them a sense of moral responsibility and obligation. Common sentiment held that management education had done little to assuage this present state and taught and promoted little more than the pursuit of self-interested behavior and short-sighted profit maximization.

Of late, the fervor and furor surrounding business education's perceived negligence and culpability has taken center stage and it has been observed in the popular press that "Indicting business schools and management educa-

tion has become a bloodsport" (Kaplan, 2009, p. 27). This cry has even gone so far as to question the "degree of contrition" shown by business schools, executives, and companies in light of the "magnitude of the offense" that has been committed (Podolny, 2009, p. 63). In sum, "Ethics, long buried in musty library tomes, is now fashionable" (Bunke, 1988, p. 2).

A result of these observations and outcries has been the creation and institution of "ethics" courses in the vast majority of academic institutions and existing corporations. The espoused belief of those instituting and promoting these programs is that ethics can be taught and ethical values can be instilled in both student and employee, respectively. This issue seeks to explore the "teachability" of ethics and the potential of ethics instruction to serve as a means of bettering ethical thinking and reasoning.

Verne E. Henderson opens this discussion by asserting that it is possible to teach ethics. One question he asks the detractors of ethics education to consider is: How well do other courses offered in a business curriculum stand up to the scrutiny given to business education? Of specific concern in this regard is the expectation that the "classroom formula will carry over into the reality of the marketplace" (p. 52).

Professor John Hooker teaches ethics, and his article outlines various arguments detractors employ to discount the value of ethics education. While Professor Hooker is a proponent of ethics education, he provides insight into the arguments made by observers and responds to their respective claims. The contrasting value of this particular article is to present the varied viewpoints and approaches that are used to diminish and question the value of ethics education as a tool for bettering ethical business practices and decision making. When reading this article, consider both the argument and the response and determine if you personally accept or reject Professor Hooker's position on this issue.

YES

Verne E. Henderson

Can Business Ethics Be Taught?

"Most of us have a child's notion of ethics and a graduate-school notion of finance, marketing, and management."

—Paul Thayer
(One-time CEO of LTV Corporation and former deputy defense secretary; sentenced to four years in prison for stock fraud.)

No one seems to question whether students have really learned macroeconomics, linear programming, or investment banking if they receive passing grades. But a passing grade in ethics doesn't mean much of anything.

Those who claim ethics can't be taught are really saying it can't be taught in such a way that everyone who has had a course in business ethics will from that day forth cease and desist from all unethical activity. What they want is a classroom formula that will carry over into the reality of the marketplace.

That's a tougher assignment than that given to other required courses in business schools. For example, is there any certainty that students will practice random-walk market theory when they become stockbrokers? Will all students be supply-side economists if they graduate from the University of Chicago? Of course not. Why, then, does business ethics evoke different expectations?

Many people don't look at ethics as the principles, policies, and value choices buried in every business decision. Instead they see ethics as a mysterious, ingrained character trait which must be implanted within the first five years of life.

If this infancy implantation is successful, they assume, it will provide such persons throughout their entire life with an unwavering determination to do the right thing. Unhappily, it is implied, this spiritualized intention to do good cannot be acquired through education at any later point in life.

But the reality of business ethics is that it's a never-ending process of refining, negotiating, and responding to multiple constituents with varying expectations.

Ethics is a social contract between us. We can talk about it, we can negotiate it. Once we've agreed on a particular ethic, it becomes binding. Moreover, any of us has the right and the obligation at any time to call the ethics of another person into question, based on this previous agreement to abide by certain ethical understandings. Ethics, like politics, is a public matter for open discussion by all.

Operating from this definition, it's easier to see the learning process that can take place. Ethical behavior is not always black and white. It's situational. Determining whether an act is ethical or not means looking at two important factors: Was the ethical violation intentional or inadvertent? Was it an act of omission or commission? Often people are not even aware of their intentions, but when violations of ethical contracts occur, determining the intentions behind the behavior helps in selecting appropriate punishments or retributions.

Looking at the consequences is also important. Has someone been hurt? Has the fabric of a relationship been irretrievably destroyed? Have lives been lost? Looking at the consequences of our decisions and behavior is usually the key ethical measurement. This dual emphasis on intentions and consequences requires us to look upon each ethical violation in its own context. Isn't this what business schools teach when it comes to manufacturing, financing, marketing? Everything is situational.

Make Ethics a Required Course

A business ethics course that is required of all M.B.A.s sends a powerful message: A top priority at this school is for all students to know and follow the generally accepted rules of business. Those rules are not clear, they are always changing, and different clients and constituents will have different ethical expectations. But the course will serve as a tacit pledge to negotiating acceptable standards.

The second reason ethics should be a required course is that we suffer from ethical naiveté. The marvels of technology surround us. Its experts have solved innumerable problems and produced one stunning achievement after another. What we know less well is how to satisfy the conflicting needs of citizen-customers who simultaneously require clean air and water as well as the products which destroy or pollute natural resources either before, during, or after their manufacture. A course in business ethics alerts future decision makers to the existence of these conflicts,

From *Management Review*, vol. 77, no. 8, August 1998, pp. 52–53. Copyright © 1998 by American Management Association. Reprinted by permission via Copyright Clearance Center.

reviews the stories of corporate successes and failures, and provides some helpful insights and suggestions.

Third, the business environment has changed as radically from an ethical perspective as it has in every other regard. The old principles of what's good and bad for our society, as well as the reasoning processes needed to make such decisions, are all immeasurably different. Medical science gives us some of the clearest examples of how the world has changed ethically. We have new medical technologies that permit us to sustain life far beyond the usefulness of that life either to the person or society at large. We never had to ask before whether we should use heroic methods to keep someone alive. We didn't have the extraordinary means to make some of our dimmest dreams come true.

From a comparable business point of view, it's only in recent decades that corporations responded to the opportunity of marketing in Third World countries an infant formula designed for Western culture. It is only in recent years that an American corporation calculated (or miscalculated) the advantages of setting up a huge pesticide plant in India. It is within just the last decade that computerized program trading on the stock market threatened its continued existence. There is no national or international congress that will set about resolving such issues.

Fourth, only business ethics really asks the long-term "what-if" questions. It seeks the greatest good for the greatest number for the greatest length of time. The long-range perspective has been sorely neglected in our corporate and national planning. There is tremendous pressure upon corporate executives to manage only to the quarterly bottom line. That's like jumping off a tall building and boasting half way down that "everything's all right so far."

The Right Teachers

Business ethics thrives under the leadership of a mature and knowledgeable facilitator. Participants need to talk, argue back, question, interrupt, fight with each other.

Strongly voiced political or religious views are taboo for effective discussion leaders, unless the group has been self-selected around a given issue. But if the purpose of the business ethics course is to encourage sensitive and reasoned anticipation or resolution of ethical dilemmas, you want a teacher, not a preacher.

I have reservations about seminars and workshops in business ethics that take the employee out of the context of work and peer relationships that will provide the greatest incentive for one decision rather than another. Too many of the ethical dilemmas posed by case studies and hypothetical dilemmas are just that, hypothetical. They're synonymous with Monday-morning quarterbacking.

In-house corporate seminars that reach through many divisions and departments, in contrast, represent a total commitment by the company to take business ethics seriously. Equally effective is assembling groups of people who work together regularly. They can not only share insights but develop some common understandings and commitments which help when unanticipated events occur.

Ethical dilemmas are not much different than any others. Incentives swing the answer in one direction or the other. This, I think, is the real reason many people are cynical about whether or not business ethics can be taught. We already know more ethical things than we're putting into practice.

Verne E. Henderson is professor of ethics and social issues at the Arthur D. Little Management Education Institute and lecturer at Northeastern and Boston Universities. Henderson holds a DB degree from the University of Chicago Divinity School and a MS degree from the Sloan School of Management of the Massachusetts Institute of Technology. Henderson is also president of Revehen Consultants, which specializes in business ethics, consensus development, conflict management, and career counseling, and publishes the quarterly newsletter *Business Ethics Resource*.

John Hooker  **NO**

The Case Against Business Ethics Education: A Study in Bad Arguments

Several popular arguments against teaching business ethics are examined: (a) the ethical duty of business people is to maximize profit within the law, whence the irrelevance of ethics courses (the Milton Friedman argument); (b) business people respond to economic and legal incentives, not to ethical sentiments, which means that teaching ethics will have no effect; (c) one cannot study ethics in any meaningful sense anyway, because it is a matter of personal preference and is unsusceptible to rational treatment; (d) moral character is formed in early childhood, not while sitting in ethics class; and (e) business students see no motivation to study ethics and will not take it seriously. The mistakes and confusion that underlie these arguments are exposed.

Introduction

The case for business ethics education is many-faceted, evolving, and difficult to summarize. A central mission of the present journal is to contribute to its development. But the case against teaching business ethics, or at least one that seems to be in wide circulation, yields to a simple characterization: it is utterly unconvincing. It rests on layers of mistakes and confusion. Perhaps it is fitting, in the inaugural issue of a journal dedicated to business ethics education, to root out some of these mistakes and expose them to the light of day.

Popular arguments against business ethics instruction might be organized as follows:

- The Milton Friedman argument. The ethical duty of business people is to maximize profit. This means they should study marketing, finance, and operations and should not waste time studying ethics.
- The argument from incentives. Even if there are duties beyond profit maximization, the only practical way to encourage ethical behavior is to install financial and legal incentives. Business people respond to these, not ethics lectures.
- The gut feeling argument. One cannot study ethics in any meaningful sense anyway, since it is something you feel, not something you think about.
- The moral development argument. Moral character is formed in early childhood, not while sitting in ethics class. By the time students enter business school, it is too late to change.
- The motivational argument. Even if there is reason to study ethics, business students see no motivation to study it and do not take the subject seriously.

This sort of skepticism is far from universal, as many acknowledge the relevance of ethics instruction and call on business schools to do a better job of it. Yet time and again I have detected such arguments lurking behind views expressed by students, colleagues, business people, and media commentators.

The Milton Friedman Argument

Economist Milton Friedman's (1970) essay, "The Social Responsibility of Business Is to Increase Its Profits," is a perennial favorite of my students. It argues that corporate officers have no obligation to support such social causes as hiring the chronically unemployed or reducing pollution beyond that mandated by law. Their sole task is to maximize profit for stockholders, subject to the limits of law and "rules of the game" that ensure "open and free competition without deception or fraud." It follows that the only kind of ethics instruction one needs for a business career is finance, marketing, and operations management, perhaps along with some business law to make sure that one knows the rules of the game.

Friedman does not rule out such pro bono activity as supporting the arts or sponsoring social service organizations. But it must always be justifiable on the grounds that it enhances the long-term profitability of the corporation, if only through image building or good public relations.

Friedman advances two main arguments for his position. First, corporate executives and directors are not qualified to do anything other than maximize profit. Business people are expert at making money, not at making social policy, and it is by making money that they contribute to human welfare. They lack the perspective and training to address complex social problems, which should be left to governments and social service agencies.

The second argument, which is rooted in Friedman's libertarian philosophy, maintains that corporate officers have no right to do anything other than maximize profit. If they invest company funds to train the chronically unemployed or reduce emissions below legal limits, they in effect levy a "tax" on the company's owners, employees and customers in order to accomplish a social purpose. But they have no right to spend other people's money on social welfare projects. At best, only elected representatives of the people have such authority. Sole proprietors can spend the company's money any way they want, since it is their money, but fiduciaries and hired managers have no such privilege. If they want to contribute to social causes, they are free to donate as much of their own money as they please.

These are beguiling arguments, and the first one contains an important element of truth. Business people may in fact make their greatest contribution when they efficiently marshal resources in a competitive environment to provide a vast array of products and services. Friedman's essay in fact says surprisingly little about this immensely positive side of business.

What Friedman does say in his first argument is fallacious, because it sets up a straw man. No one claims that managers must address social problems in the comprehensive way that government regulators or social agencies do. Theirs is the lesser task of evaluating their particular company's impact. Determining just how far they must go to meet this obligation is what business ethics is all about. Business ethics, rather than social ethics in general, is the required competency. Friedman gives us no reason to doubt that business people can acquire it.

Students generally concede this point but maintain that business ethics, once distinguished from ethics in general, simply collapses into the duty to maximize profit within the law. There are no other specifically business-related obligations than this, and no training beyond business law and the traditional managerial skills is necessary. Yet this claim is not only unsupported but highly implausible, particularly in an international context. The famous Nestlé infant formula case is useful for making this point (Buchholz 1997). Nestlé promoted its formula in developing countries by hiring nurses in local clinics to recommend formula over breast feeding. Since clean water was often unavailable to mix with the powdered formula, babies became ill. The company continued its marketing efforts despite worldwide protests and relented only after years of massive consumer boycotts of its products. Friedman's theory finds no fault with Nestlé's perfectly legal conduct so long as it maximized profits.

At this point students invariably insist that Nestlé's callousness actually hurt its long-run profitability, due to the public relations fallout, and it was therefore unethical by Friedman's criterion. It is a classic example of adjusting the facts to fit the theory, but I make a different point. I suggest that they are so insistent that Nestlé's behavior reduced profit, without really knowing this to be true, precisely because they know a priori that this behavior was wrong regardless of its financial or legal implications. Business ethics is therefore irreducible to law and profit maximization.

Friedman's second argument asserts that company officers overstep their authority as agents for the owners when they do anything other than maximize profit. Corporate law may sometimes limit their authority in this way, but it is unclear why such a limitation is implicit in an agent's role. On the contrary, it seems more plausible that the agent inherits the ethical duties of the owners, as suggested for instance by Kenneth Goodpaster (1991) in his critique of stakeholder analysis.

When I discuss Friedman's article in class, I sometimes make this point by way of a parable (which is based on an actual incident). A hurricane strikes and cuts off electricity as well as routes to the outside world. There is a desperate need for portable electric generators, and local sellers take the opportunity to charge an exorbitant price. Assuming this sort of price gouging is legal, a store manager has no right, on Friedman's view, to "tax" the owners by charging less than the market will bear. The dealer does, however, have a right to ask the buyer to pay more, since the purchase decision is voluntary.

I next ask the students to agree with me that it is wrong for an individual to exploit hurricane victims, for instance by demanding a high price for something they need. (If we cannot agree on this, I change the example.) Friedman admits that it is perfectly all right for a sole proprietor to give customers a break on the price. But if the owner turns the business over to professional managers, ethical obligation does not suddenly vanish. Can it be permissible to exploit victims of disaster through agents, when it is wrong to do it personally? One might as well say that an organized crime boss can avoid responsibility for murder by hiring a hit man. Agents who act ethically at company expense therefore do not usurp the authority of owners. On the contrary, they carry out duties that the owners are bound to observe, whether they run the business themselves or through agents.

This is not to say that managers must use company funds to advance any ethically defensible cause that may attract the owners, such as preserving the Amazonian rainforest or promoting peace in the Middle East. Again, it is a matter of distinguishing business ethics from social ethics. The owners have no obligation as business people to advance general environmental or foreign policy positions. Only business-related obligations, such as the duty not to price gouge or dump untreated waste, transfer to agents hired to run a business. Managers must somehow distinguish business-related from other obligations, but this is precisely one of the reasons they should study business ethics.

Friedman's appeal to libertarian principles is equally specious. He states that spending the owners' money in the service of ethics is coercion and therefore wrong, while raising prices is permissible because customers can choose not to buy. But price gouging "taxes" hurricane victims no less surely than lower prices "tax" the owners. It forces a choice between paying ridiculous prices and letting a warehouse full of food spoil. Both taxes are involuntary, and simply to state that one is legitimate and the other not is to beg the question.

In a final attempt to salvage Friedman's case, one might maintain that whatever may be the merits of single-mindedly maximizing profit, business people will in fact do so. It is human nature to respond to incentives. Since college instruction will not change human nature, business ethics courses are pointless. Yet this is not Friedman's argument. It is the argument from incentives, to which I now turn.

The Argument from Incentives

The argument begins with the familiar hypothesis that economic phenomena are best explained as resulting from the choices of utility-maximizing, self-interested individuals. Moral sentiments (to use Adam Smith's term) therefore play no significant role in economic life. If business people behave ethically, it is only because financial inducements and legal sanctions are properly calibrated, not because Kant or Aristotle inspired them to do the right thing. Such ethical lapses as the recent series of U.S. business scandals can only be addressed by such measures as regulatory reform, improved corporate governance, and removal of conflicts of interest. Ethics instruction has no place in this picture.

Many students (and faculty) believe strongly in this worldview, which has been part of Western intellectual furniture since the Scottish Enlightenment. Yet the seminal figure of that movement, Francis Hutcheson, had a very different outlook. He held that human actions are best explained as motivated by sympathy, not self-interest. His admiring student Adam Smith expressed a related view in his first book, *The Theory of Moral Sentiments*, where he maintains that we respond to and judge the actions of others out of empathy with their situation. The idea that self-interest motivates human beings was advanced by David Hume, Smith's Scottish contemporary. Hume's compelling case influenced Smith and many others, and Smith deals with it in his second book, *An Inquiry into the Nature and Causes of the Wealth of Nations*, the one we almost always quote today.

There is little doubt that mainstream Western thinking honors Hume more than Hutcheson. Yet Hutcheson's moral psychology may be closer to the truth: there is in fact a fair amount of evidence to support the thesis that humans are naturally altruistic. Common sense alone suggests that creatures who work for the good of the group would have a long-term survival advantage relative to selfish individuals. Martin Hoffman (2000) makes a comprehensive case that the human species in fact exhibits multiple and redundant layers of altruism, and his conclusions are corroborated by a number of investigators (Gibbs, 2003).

It is not necessary to make a case for altruism, however, to refute the argument from incentives. It suffices to show that financial incentives and legal penalties alone

cannot regulate business behavior. They cannot because economic behavior is radically dependent on preexisting cultural practices. Culture shapes our attitudes toward work, authority, commitment, negotiation, consumption, fairness, and obedience to rules, and these are the foundation of economic activity—the last one being particularly important in a market system.

The incentive system of the business world does not create these structures; it presupposes them.

At one level we are misled by a confusion of necessary and sufficient conditions. We see corrupt systems in which the incentives are all wrong, and we infer that if the incentives were right, the corruption would go away. But this does not follow. Even if proper economic and legal incentives are necessary for ethical behavior, they may be insufficient.

I illustrate the point in class by telling a (true) story. A colleague of mine attended a conference in a certain country that is known for its high crime rate. During the conference he took a day off to relax on the beach. When a boy suddenly appeared and made off [with] his beach bag, my colleague gave chase. On reaching a major avenue, he waved down a police cruiser and exclaimed, "Stop that boy! He stole my bag." The officer responded, "Did he get your money?" "No, thank God. It's hidden in my shoe." At this point the officer drew his revolver and said, "Hand it over."

The incentives are in place. Laws provide for the punishment of theft. Yet unless people are generally predisposed to live by the rules, the enforcers—those who are supposed [to] apply the incentives and sanctions—will be as corrupt as everyone else. Well-designed incentives and regulations are undeniably important in a market system. Yet the system can succeed only if cultural mechanisms inculcate norms and behavior patterns that allow it to operate under real-world conditions. Ethics instruction may well be one of these mechanisms.

The U.S. business scandals, for example, illustrate the insufficiency of sanctions and economic incentives no less than their necessity. They show how easy it is, in the U.S. business context, to violate the rules that do exist and get away with it. The system clearly relies on voluntary compliance by the vast majority of players, compliance that derives from underlying cultural values.

Culturally instilled values temper the profit motive as well. Corporations that ruthlessly exploit every profit opportunity are prominent in the news, but they are the exception. I invite the reader to make acquaintance with some local business people and observe how they operate. My own observation is that they balance profitability against a desire to behave decently, perhaps by dealing sympathetically with employees or being a good citizen of the community, whether or not these actions have bottom-line justification. They understand that business is not a game unto itself but an integral part of a larger society that makes business possible. They instinctively recognize the connection between business and culture. It is the balanced and socially responsible approach of these rank-and-file business people, not a single-minded imperative to maximize shareholder value, that allows the business system to work in the real world.

These arguments may yet fail to convince staunch believers in incentives. In their view, one need only look a little harder to find the inducements that explain everything. They have a ready response, for example, to my story of the corrupt police officers: the system failed because the police themselves were improperly incentivized. If officer salaries were adequate, if their supervisors received some reward for crime reduction, and so on with their bosses, the outcome would have been different. This brings us to a deeper appreciation of what is going on here. Incentives provide not so much an explanation of behavior as a regulative principle for explanation itself. Only explanations that are grounded in legal/economic rewards and penalties are allowed to count as explanations. We must therefore keep looking for an incentive-based rationale for the police officer's conduct until we find one that is more or less plausible, even if it is unverified. Obviously, once we make this sort of move, the argument from incentives is beyond refutation. (See Brockway, 1995, for a different critique of the incentive principle.)

This situation calls for an oblique maneuver. One tactic is to draw attention to the role of culture in business without explicitly broaching the issue of behavioral explanation. I do this at length elsewhere (Hooker, 2003), but in a classroom setting where there is limited time, I find it helpful to approach the matter through cross-cultural ethics. I describe how the business system in one culture may rest on entirely different norms and practices than in another. Cronyism and nepotism, for example, may reflect moral virtue in a high-context, relationship-based culture (to use the terminology of Edward T. Hall, 1966, 1983), whereas they may signal corruption in a low-context, rule-based culture. They undergird the system in one case and undermine it in the other. When students see the radical dependence of business on cultural support in another country, they may be more inclined to recognize it in their own. The discussion and refinement of ethical ideas may of course be one element of this cultural support.

The Gut Feeling Argument

If one has not studied ethical reasoning, it is hard to imagine what it could be like. Too often the conclusion is that ethics is not amenable to rational treatment. Different people simply have different values, much as some people like broccoli and some do not.

Even if ethics is a matter of taste, one might yet insist that education can refine tastes, an assumption that seems to underlie some art appreciation courses. But it is a curious view indeed that ethics has no intellectual content, when so many of history's most renowned intellectuals have contributed to the field.

The best antidote to ethical anti-intellectualism is to show ethical reasoning in action. Distinctions must be drawn, terms defined, and bad arguments distinguished from good ones. Ethics class is the ideal place for this. My own view is that ethical theories should be developed and applied as rigorously in ethics class as physics in engineering class, even if this may not be the current fashion. Taking ethical theory seriously does not imply that there is a single theory that explains everything, nor does it deny that ethical choice requires praxis as well as theoria—any more than applying Newton's laws to bridge building presupposes that they explain everything, or that good engineering design reduces to stress calculations. It simply recognizes that to treat ethics intellectually at all is, by virtue of the nature of reason, to commit oneself to making that treatment as complete and closely reasoned as human faculties allow. An added benefit of theoretical rigor is that when students find the subject as intellectually demanding as integral calculus, they are likely to take it more seriously.

The identification of ethics with gut feeling does not stem wholly from a lack of acquaintance with ethical reasoning, however. Another factor is popular psychology: a vague notion that cognitive development has little to do with moral development. Ethical judgment is seen as an essentially nonrational function that is tied to emotions and early childhood experience. One learns ethics from Mom and Dad, not from college professors. This view is perhaps warmed-over Freud, but it is very much alive today. It is integral to the moral development argument against ethics instruction, and I will deal with it in that context.

The Moral Development Argument

I now come to what may be the most prevalent and most insidious of the specious arguments against business ethics education. In its simplest expression it might go like this. Moral character is formed in childhood. By the time a young person reaches college age, it is too late to change. Ethics instruction therefore serves no practical purpose.

The premise of this argument, that character is fully formed in childhood, is neither true nor sufficient for the conclusion. I will first show the latter.

Let us assume, for the sake of argument, that moral character is fixed early in life. This does not imply that ethics instruction serves no useful purpose, since it can change behavior even if it does not change character.

It is generally acknowledged that college education can change behavior, irrespective of whether it changes character. Otherwise we ought to shut down business schools, indeed all professional schools. The opponent of ethics education presumably concedes that finance, marketing and operations courses change behavior, but insists that an ethics course does not. Yet this distinction is quite arbitrary. Where is the evidence? Why is ethics class, the one class that deals directly with how one should behave, incapable of changing behavior, when all the other classes in the building have practical effect?

There are a number of reasons to suspect that ethics instruction can affect conduct without going so far as to change character. It provides a language and conceptual framework with which one can talk and think about ethical issues. Its emphasis on case studies helps to make one aware of the potential consequences of one's actions. It presents ethical theories that help define what a valid ethical argument looks like. It teaches one to make distinctions and avoid fallacies that are so common when people make decisions. It gives one an opportunity to think through, at one's leisure, complex ethical issues that are likely to arise later, when there is no time to think. It introduces one to such specialized areas as product liability, employment, intellectual property, environmental protection, and cross-cultural management. It gives one practice at articulating an ethical position, which can help resist pressure to compromise. Perhaps none of this is of interest to the scoundrels in the class, but it can be quite useful to everyone else.

Now, what are the reasons to suspect that ethics instruction cannot influence behavior in the absence of character change? The moral development argument is silent on this point.

The argument's premise is questionable as well. It is far from clear that moral character is fixed in early childhood and cannot develop during college years. On the contrary, there is a good deal of evidence that moral and cognitive development are closely related and can continue throughout young adulthood and beyond.

The evidence is found in the developmental psychology literature, which has offered a major alternative to Freudian views since the 1930s. The field's founder, Jean Piaget, is best known for describing stages of cognitive development in early childhood, but he had broader interests. If Piaget stood for anything, he stood for the close relationship between the cognitive and other aspects of human development. Lawrence Kohlberg (1981) proposed stages of moral development that parallel the cognitive stages. Robert Kegan (1981) and James Fowler (1982) found further parallels with the development of meaning structures and spiritual values. William Perry (1968) and Sharon Parks (1986) focused on college-age development, and Gibbs (2003) provides a recent review of the field.

Descriptions of the developmental stages vary in the literature, but most accounts include a stage, normally attained in adolescence, that is marked by a striving for independence. Cognitively one learns how to think analytically and to criticize ideas that were passively accepted in earlier years. Morally this phase often begins with a thoroughgoing relativism, followed by doctrinaire adherence to a certain philosophy or ideology, such as Marxism, laissez-faire capitalism, or fundamentalist religion. Cognitive development therefore ushers in a new stage of moral development.

Business students in their twenties are typically somewhere in this stage of development or are perhaps beginning to move beyond it. From an ethical point of view, it is clearly inadequate for business leadership, as it cannot deal with the complexity and ambiguity of real-life situations. It too often relies on simplistic solutions, such as a doctrinaire insistence that a business person's sole duty is to maximize shareholder value.

There is a subsequent stage in which one learns to tolerate uncertainty and ambiguity. Cognitively, one accepts that there is merit on both sides of an argument and that an issue may never be completely resolved. One does not abandon critical analysis, but on the contrary perseveres in an effort to think systematically even while recognizing that no existing system is adequate to the complexity of life. This extends into the moral sphere, where one undertakes the lifelong task of working out a personal philosophy while respecting the nuance and unpredictability of real situations. If all goes well, this stage is reached in mature adulthood.

The relevant lesson here is that business education can and must assist with the cognitive development that enables movement toward ethical maturity. Sharon Parks (1993) indicates several ways in ethics instruction can play a role in this.

Developmental psychology has its critics, and the stages are not as clean cut as their descriptions may suggest. They may vary across cultures, and empirical work suggests that people often occupy two or three stages at once. Yet the essential point for present purposes is the interconnectedness of cognitive and moral growth. This basic thesis is not only consistent with a large body of evidence but is often confirmed in our personal experience. At any rate it cannot simply be dismissed with a wave of the hand, as is attempted by the moral development argument considered here.

The Motivational Argument

This final argument takes us into ethics class on the first day of the semester. Whatever may be the merits of teaching the material in the syllabus, the students in the room do not want to hear it. They see no relevance to their careers. They would much rather be in a finance or marketing course, or interviewing with some additional companies. Since as every good teacher knows, learning is 95% motivation, the students are not going to learn much in this class.

Actually a fair number of business students are keenly interested in ethical issues and want to hear them discussed. Yet others see ethics as a waste of time, and some are quite vocal about it, perhaps taking their complaints to school administrators.

Instructors have devised a number of strategies to overcome this recalcitrance. They convince students that ethical conduct is smart business, because they can "do well by doing good." They integrate discussion of ethical issues into courses students regard as legitimate, such as finance and marketing. They bring in seasoned executives to talk about how ethics is a constant factor in their decision making.

Motivational strategies must be developed—and discussed in a journal such as this one. Yet ethics class may attract more than its share of motivational problems due to a common misconception about the field.

The misconception is illustrated by a student comment I recently saw on an anonymous course evaluation form. "This course is a waste of time. It won't convince anyone to be ethical." The instructor discussed some ethical issues but never tried to convince students to be ethical. Why did the student assume otherwise? I think it is because of an underlying assumption about ethics: the only possible function of ethical discourse is to persuade one to be ethical. Financial discourse and marketing discourse are different, because they have an intellectual function, namely to clarify and explain the concepts underlying finance and marketing. Ethical discourse, by contrast, is necessarily homiletic. It can only exhort one to be ethical.

I could cite many more examples. Recently a student in my class pointed out that different ethical theories sometimes judge a given act differently. Does this not mean, he said, that clever individuals can simply choose the theory that justifies what they want to do? His concern was not that ethics fails because the theories contradict each other. It fails because it does not persuade one to be ethical.

The conception of ethical discourse as exclusively hortatory obviously reinforces the gut feeling argument. It supports the moral development argument as well, since that argument assumes that ethics courses cannot change behavior without changing character, even though finance and marketing courses can. This makes sense if one assumes that ethical discourse can do its work only by changing one's values, whereas finance and marketing can provide a richer knowledge base that enables one to realize pre-existing values.

Ethical discourse is perhaps viewed as it is because moral utterances in everyday life are almost always illocutionary acts, in John Austin's sense of the term. When Mom says that it is wrong to hit people, she is not expounding on a normative theory of violence but is admonishing her child not to hit. Ethical argument is almost always expected to induce action rather than to establish truth. It is no wonder that people fail to appreciate that ethics can be as much an intellectual endeavor as physics.

This may explain why many students object to ethics instruction with such animus. Ethics class is different from the others. The finance or marketing instructor enlightens them, but the ethics instructor preaches to them. There is, after all, nothing else one can do with ethical discourse. Yet students do not want to be preached to, and they react negatively.

I believe that breaking down this conception of ethics is an important step toward defusing the motivational argument. In my classes I use a direct approach. Practically my first words are, "I'm not here to convince you to be ethical." They are not going to hear a sermon from me, but theory and application, just as in finance class. I go on to explain that their finance instructors do not try to convince them to make money. They assume that students want to make money and tell them how. My role is analogous. I assume students want to be ethical and try to tell them how. In other words, I refuse to defend ethics. Rather than persuade students that they can do well by doing good, I suggest how they can do good by doing well: how they can use business as an instrument for making the positive contribution I know they want to make. Some students may see this as naive, but I remind them that I am in good company; I may even pass around a copy of *The Theory of Moral Sentiments*.

This approach takes me off the defensive. It presents ethics as a tool for realizing one's aspirations, rather than a rulebook of limits and admonitions. It invites students to begin thinking about how they might really make the world a little better.

References

Brockway, G. P. (1995), *The End of Economic Man*, 3rd ed., New York: W. W. Norton. Buchholz, E. (1997), "The Nestlé Corporation," in T. L. Beauchamp and N. E. Bowie (eds), Ethical.

Theory and Business, New York: Prentice-Hall.

Fowler, J. W. (1982), *Stages of Faith: The Psychology of Human Development and the Quest for Meaning*, New York: Harper and Row.

Friedman, M. (1970) , "The Social Responsibility of Business Is to Increase Its Profits," *New York Times Magazine* (September 13).

Gibbs, J. C. (2003), *Moral Development and Reality: Beyond the Theories of Kohlberg and Hoffman*, Thousand Oaks, CA: Sage Publications.

Goodpaster, K. E. (1991), "Business Ethics and Stakeholder Analysis," *Business Ethics Quarterly* 1(1).

Hall, Edward T. (1966), *The Hidden Dimension*, New York: Doubleday.

Hall, Edward T. (1983), *The Dance of Life*, New York: Doubleday.

Hoffman, M. L. (2000), *Empathy and Moral Development: Implications for Caring and Justice*, Cambridge, U.K.: Cambridge University Press.

Hooker, J. N. (2003), *Working Across Cultures*, New York: Stanford University Press.

Kegan, R. (1981), *The Evolving Self: Meaning and Process in Human Development*, Cambridge, MA: Harvard University Press.

Kohlberg, L. (1981), *The Philosophy of Moral Development: Moral Stages and the Idea of Justice*, New York: Harper and Row.

Parks, S. D. (1986), *The Critical Years: The Young Adult Search for a Faith to Live By*, New York: Harper and Row.

Parks, S. D. (1993), "Is It Too Late? Young Adults and the Formation of Professional Ethics," in T. R. Piper, M. C. Gentile and S. D. Parks, *Can Ethics Be Taught? Perspectives, Challenges and Approaches at Harvard Business School*, Cambridge, MA: Harvard University Press.

Perry, W. G. (1968), *Intellectual and Ethical Development in the College Years*, New York: Holt.

JOHN HOOKER is the T. Jerome Holleran professor of business ethics and social responsibility and a professor of operations research at the Tepper School of Business at Carnegie Mellon University. Hooker is the founding editor-in-chief of the *Journal of Business Ethics Education* and co-organized four conferences on international corporate responsibility. Hooker holds doctoral degrees in philosophy and operations research and joined the Tepper School in 1984 and has since held several visiting posts, most recently at the London School of Economics.

EXPLORING THE ISSUE

Can Ethical Malaise Be Remedied Through Ethics Education?

Critical Thinking and Reflection

1. What are ethics?
2. Are there universal or global ethics?
3. Should ethics be taught in schools and other organizations?
4. Who defines the content of an ethics course? Are there any problems with this arrangement?
5. Is instruction enough to change behavior?
6. How would you measure the success or failure of a course in ethics?

Is There Common Ground?

Both parties to this debate have powerful arguments to draw on and data to back their opposing positions. However, it does appear that the parties involved in this debate agree that ethics are lacking in the business environment and that there is concern that this present state will be ongoing based on business' past history. Additionally, both groups believe there is a need to do something to improve the practice of ethical and moral decision making. The outstanding debatable issue is What should be done? Given the current global economic, social, and political state and the notion that history is an indicator of the future, it is anticipated that this discussion and debate will continue.

Additional Resources

Bowden, P. and Smythe, V. (2008). "Theories on Teaching & Training in Ethics," *Electronic Journal of Business Ethics and Organization Studies*, 13(2), pp. 19–26.

Bunke, H.C. (1988). "Should We Teach Ethics?" *Business Horizons*, July/August, p. 2.

Christensen, L.J., Peirce, E., Hartman, L.P., Hoffman, W.M., and Carrier, J. (2007). "Ethics, CSR, and Sustainability Education in the *Financial Times*

Top 50 Global Business Schools: Baseline Data and Future Research Directions," *Journal of Business Ethics*, 73, pp. 347–368.

Ciulla, J.B. (2011). "Is Business Ethics Getting Better? A Historical Perspective," *Business Ethics Quarterly*, April, pp. 335–343.

Cloninger, P.A. and Selvarajan, T.T. (2010). "Can Ethics Education Improve Ethical Judgment? An Empirical Study," *SAM Advanced Management Journal*, Autumn, pp. 4–11.

Feeman, R.E., Steward, L., and Moriarty, B. (2009). "Teaching Business Ethics in the Age of Madoff," *Change*, November/December, pp. 37–42.

George, R.J. (1987). "Teaching Business Ethics: Is There a Gap Between Rhetoric and Reality?" *Journal of Business Ethics*, October, pp. 513–518.

Kaplan, D.A. (2009). "MBAs Get Schooled in Ethics," *Fortune*, October 29, p. 27.

Maltby, D.E. (1988). "The One-Minute Ethicist," *Christianity Today*, February 19, pp. 26–29.

Podolny, J.M. (2009). "Buck Stops (and Starts) at Business School," *Harvard Business Review*, June, p. 63.

Thornton, L.F. (2009). "Leadership Ethics Training: Why Is It So Hard to Get It Right," *T&D*, September, pp. 58–61.

Internet References . . .

Ethics Education in Business Schools

Association to Advance Collegiate Schools of Business International (AACSB) (2004). "Ethics Education in Business Schools."

www.aacsb.edu/publications/researchreports/ archives/ethics-education.pdf

Business Ethics in Undergraduate Education

Campbell, K.P. (2012). "Business Ethics in Undergraduate Education."

www.diversityweb.org/DiversityDemocracy/vol14no1/ report.cfm

The Hush-Hush Side of Business Ethics Education

Drozdowski, H. (2011). "The Hush-Hush Side of Business Ethics Education," June 22.

http://aacsbblogs.typepad.com/dataandresearch/ 2011/06/the-real-inside-job-of-business-ethics- education.html

How Can You Measure the Effectiveness of Ethics Education?

Nadler, J. (2010). "How Can You Measure the Effectiveness of Ethics Education?" November 18.

www.scu.edu/ethics-center/ethicsblog/herhonor .cfm?c=8648

"Water Cooler Ethics": A New Approach to Business Ethics Education

Ohreen, D. (2012). "'Water Cooler Ethics': A New Approach to Business Ethics Education," July 16.

http://business-ethics.com/2012/07/16/1645-water- cooler-ethics-a-new-approach-to-business-ethics- education/

Embedding Ethics in Business and Higher Education: From Leadership to Management Imperative

Soule, E. (2005). "Embedding Ethics in Business and Higher Education: From Leadership to Management Imperative," June.

www.bhef.com/publications/documents/ embedding_ethics_05.pdf

UNIT 2

UNIT

Human Resource Management

*A*ffirmative action has been with the law of the United States for several decades. There can be no question that it has helped in obtaining more and better opportunities for minorities and females during this time. However some critics question if affirmative action has become outdated or if it is still needed. Companies have the right to protect themselves and their employees from harm and to ensure a safe and drug-free workplace; however, employees also have a right to privacy. Given this conflict, policies such as drug testing, monitoring social media, and forbidding workplace romances are under scrutiny. In the late 1950s, women made about 40 percent less than did males. By 2008, the male–female wage gap had only shrunk to 23 percent. Is discrimination still responsible for this difference? This unit explores these and other important human resource management questions for managers.

Selected, Edited, and with Issue Framing Material by:
Kathleen J. Barnes, *East Stroudsburg University*
and
George E. Smith, *Albright College*

ISSUE

Does an Employer's Need to Monitor Workers Trump Employee Privacy Concerns?

YES: Laura Petrecca, from "More Employers Use Tech to Track Workers," *USA Today* (March 17, 2010), http://usatoday30.usatoday.com/money/workplace/2010-03-17-workplaceprivacy15_CV_N.htm

NO: National Workrights Institute, from *Privacy Under Siege: Electronic Monitoring in the Workplace* (2005), www.workrights.org/issue_electronic.html

Learning Outcomes
After reading this issue, you should be able to:
• Understand the positive and negative consequences of employee monitoring in the workplace.   • Understand how employee monitoring can be used as an effective workplace tool.   • Understand the policies that might be implemented concerning employee monitoring.   • Appreciate the legal implications of the use of employee monitoring in the workplace.

ISSUE SUMMARY

YES: Laura Petrecca provides insightful analysis on this issue while explaining how, when, and why monitoring can and should be used in the workplace to protect employers against lawsuits (e.g., sexual harassment, copyright infringement), to increase security, and to improve employee productivity.

NO: The National Workrights Institute acknowledges that monitoring is legal for most employers most of the time, but argues that more stringent laws should be enacted to provide greater protection of employee rights.

One of the oldest sources of workplace conflict arises from the need of managers to monitor and control employee behavior at work. The trouble is that employees feel they have legitimate rights to privacy and that these rights are violated when management monitors workplace behavior. Although this issue is not new, over the past couple of decades it has taken on increased importance as a result of advances in electronic technology that allow for much closer monitoring of a much wider range of employee behaviors. Consequently, employees, now more than ever, feel that their rights are being violated. Employers and shareholders respond that their property rights are frequently violated by employees at the workplace. Thus, it is not surprising that they view monitoring employee behavior as a legitimate method of protecting their property.

An important study by the American Management Association (AMA) in 2005 gives a good perspective on just how prevalent electronic monitoring in the workplace has become. The AMA study surveyed more than 500 U.S. businesses, the majority of which had more than 2,500 employees. The results revealed that wide-ranging electronic monitoring methods were employed as a means to "manage productivity and protect resources" (American Management Association, 2005). For example, 76 percent of surveyed firms monitor employee web-surfing activities, and 65 percent use software designed to block access to unauthorized Internet locations. Over one-third (36 percent) of the firms monitor employee computer keystrokes, and 50 percent reported storing and reviewing employee e-mails. Finally, over half (51 percent) reported using video surveillance to reduce theft and sabotage, while another 57 percent reported monitoring or restricting employee telephone behaviors, including the inappropriate use of voicemail.

To those supportive of employee monitoring policies, the results of the AMA survey are perfectly reasonable. Beyond the desire to reduce theft and to increase employee productivity, two additional arguments are frequently made in defense of employee monitoring. First is the fact that corporations can be held legally responsible for the behaviors of their employees at work. By way of example, consider an employee who causes an accident while under the influence of drugs at work. The employee not only causes property and human harm, but also puts the organization into a legal bind because the firm can be held legally responsible for the employee's actions. As noted in Issue 6 in this text, businesses react to this threat by monitoring employee behavior via workplace drug testing.

A second argument supporting an employer's right to monitor involves the issue of property rights. As noted earlier, shareholders have property rights in the organization and are legally allowed to defend and protect it. When an employee uses the organization's property (i.e., computers, telephones, etc.) improperly, the employee is not only violating his or her employment contract, but is also essentially stealing from the company. Thus, from the shareholders' perspective, monitoring employee behavior is simply a way of protecting their property.

On the other side of this debate are those who claim that employees have rights in the workplace. These rights include the right to privacy. Advocates of this perspective assert that monitoring all too often goes beyond tracking employee productivity and is used to gather personal information on employees. They point to numerous instances of management spying on employees with video cameras in restrooms and other non-work-related areas in the office. A second argument raised by supporters of employee rights is to note that many studies have shown little or no evidence that monitoring actually results in productivity gains, thereby undermining an important component of the pro-monitoring position. It should be noted, however, that despite the strong emotional appeal of the privacy rights position, it has not held up well in the courtroom. As noted in the "NO" article for this topic, "And yet there are few, if any, legal protections for employees."

YES ↵

Laura Petrecca

More Employers Use Tech to Track Workers

Almost every worker has done it: gotten in a little Facebook updating, personal e-mailing, YouTube watching and friend calling while on the clock.

Such indiscretions often went undetected by company management everywhere but the most secure and highly proprietary companies or governmental agencies. Not anymore.

METHODS: Employers use myriad ways to monitor workers
CORPORATE PULSE: Executive Suite front page
FOR ENTREPRENEURS: Small Business front page

Firms have become sharp-eyed, keenly eared watchdogs as they try to squeeze every penny's worth of their employees' salaries and to ensure they have the most professional and lawsuit-proof workplaces.

Managers use technological advances to capture workers' computer keystrokes, monitor the websites they frequent, even track their whereabouts through GPS-enabled cellphones. Some companies have gone as far as using webcams and minuscule video cameras to secretly record employees' movements.

"There are two trends driving the increase in monitoring," says Lewis Maltby, author of the workplace rights book *Can They Do That?* "One is financial pressure. Everyone is trying to get leaner and meaner, and monitoring is one way to do it. The other reason is that it's easier than ever. It used to be difficult and expensive to monitor employees, and now, it's easy and cheap."

Employers no longer have to hire a pricey private investigator to install a complicated video system or computer-use tracking devices. Now, they can easily buy machine-monitoring software and tiny worker-tracking cameras at a local electronics store or through Internet retailers.

Monitoring has expanded beyond expected, highly regulated industries such as pharmaceuticals and financial services. Employees at radio stations, ad agencies, media outlets, sports leagues, even thinly staffed mom-and-pop workplaces are tracked.

Smarsh, one of many firms that offers technology to monitor, archive and search employee communications on e-mail, IM, Twitter and text-messaging, services about 10,000 U.S. workplaces.

"Employees should assume that they are going to be watched," says CEO Stephen Marsh.

Keeping an Eye Out

Two-thirds of employers monitor workers' Internet use, according to an American Management Association/ePolicy Institute survey from 2007, the latest data available from those groups. Nearly half of employers said they track content, keystrokes and time spent at the keyboard.

They're seeking increased productivity but also are watching workers to make sure they're not spilling trade secrets, sending boss-slamming e-mails to bloggers who cover their particular industry, sexually harassing co-workers or posting discriminatory remarks on personal blogs.

Such monitoring has increasingly become part of the public debate in recent months because of several publicized events:

- Next month, the U.S. Supreme Court will hear oral arguments in a case examining the allowable scope of monitoring workers' use of a company-provided pager.

Ontario, Calif., police officer Jeff Quon sent personal, and sometimes sexually explicit, text messages to his wife and a co-worker using an employer-provided pager. His office had a written company policy stating it retained the right to monitor work activities such as e-mail and Internet use but didn't specify text messages. Quon says his rights were violated because the department had an informal practice of not reviewing messages when the employee paid for overage charges, which he had done.

Among the issues the Supreme Court will examine: "Does the employee have an expectation of privacy when using an employer-issued handheld device to transmit personal messages? . . . And whether his wife, who was not an employee, had a privacy expectation," says Wendy Lane, an attorney at Rutter Hobbs & Davidoff.

The decision in this case could be a "game changer" if Quon prevails, says Nancy Flynn, founder of training and consulting firm ePolicy Institute. "This could have implications for all (employer-supplied) electronic devices."

- The National Transportation Safety Board last month suggested using the "black box" cockpit recorders to routinely monitor pilots' conversations to make sure they are focused on work. The NTSB says this type of monitoring is a safety "essential" to make sure pilots are focused on flying—but pilots' unions say the practice would be intrusive.

- Japanese cellphone maker KDDI this month announced the creation of motion-sensing technology that can monitor even the smallest movements by employees, such as walking, climbing stairs and cleaning, according to a BBC report. If strapped to a cleaning worker's waist, a device with this technology can track actions such as scrubbing, sweeping and emptying garbage cans—and report the results back to managers.

Employer Advantage

In most cases, the employer has the upper hand.

"Federal law gives employers the legal right to monitor all computer activity," says Flynn. "The computer system is the property of the employer, and the employee has absolutely no reasonable expectations of privacy when using that system."

That means employers can track which websites workers visit, the instant messages they send to co-workers, even e-mails sent through personal accounts—such as Gmail—while employees are logged onto the company network or using company-owned equipment such as a laptop.

"A classic mistake is thinking that changing to your personal account buys you any privacy," says Maltby. "If you send an e-mail out, it goes through your company server. If they're monitoring e-mail, the personal e-mail gets monitored just like business e-mail." Often, employers have good reason to snoop. According to a 2009 AMA/ePolicy survey:

- 14% of employees admit to e-mailing confidential or proprietary information about a firm, its people, products and services to outside parties.
- 14% admit to sending third parties potentially embarrassing and confidential company e-mail that is intended strictly for internal readers.
- 89% of users admit to using the office system to send jokes, gossip, rumors or disparaging remarks to outsiders.
- 9% have used company e-mail to transmit sexual, romantic or pornographic text or images.

On the employer side, 1-in-10 say they've gone to court to fight lawsuits that were specifically triggered by employee e-mail. In addition, 2% of employers were ordered by courts or regulators to produce employee instant messages (IMs). That's twice the amount reported in 2006.

Seen as Intrusive

Maltby's book and a new report from the law firm Jackson Lewis list multiple examples of employees getting fired for something as innocuous-sounding as social-media use. But once employees step into dangerous areas such as

publicly criticizing their company, they are vulnerable to employer discipline.

Bosses can penalize employees for what they deem as "inappropriate" posts, videos and pictures on social-networking sites, even if a worker uses those sites during non-working hours.

Management at independent brokerage and investment banking firm J.P. Turner not only tracks e-mail, it also follows up on the personal Twitter and Facebook use of the approximately 100 employees at their Atlanta headquarters and the company's registered representatives at more than 180 U.S. offices.

J.P. Turner doesn't allow "unapproved, professional use of social-networking sites," and searches for company mentions on those sites—such as an employee listing the firm name on his or her personal Facebook biography. If a posting associated with the company doesn't reflect good judgment on behalf of the user, the firm notifies that worker's supervisor and asks to have the post removed, says Compliance Officer Michael Isaac.

Even as they make some seemingly harmless—and some not-so-harmless—infractions, employees are usually horrified when they realize they are being watched.

"Frankly, employees tend to resent monitoring," says Flynn.

And they are often surprised and embarrassed at the ramifications.

In 2001, Heather Armstrong launched the blog *Dooce.com* to write about topics such as pop culture and music. She also wrote about her co-workers at a small software company.

"I really, really thought that my employer was not ever going to find it," she says. But a fellow employee tipped off the company vice presidents, and Armstrong was fired.

"They just said it was unacceptable that I had done this," she says.

All of her belongings were boxed up, and she was escorted to her car. "I was humiliated," she says. "It was a dumb move on my part."

Her advice for would-be bloggers: Get company permission. "No matter who you don't want to read it—they'll find it," she says.

They Have Their Reasons

Many staffers don't realize that their employers have legal and ethical reasons behind their snooping. Workplaces with monitoring policies often don't let employees know they are trying to prevent serious issues such as sexual harassment cases.

"You can't expect an untrained workforce to be compliant," says Flynn. "If employers would just take the time to do some training and explain, 'Here's why we're doing the monitoring. We're not electronic voyeurs, we're not trying to dig into your personal life, that's not our concern,' then the whole monitoring scenario would go over much more successfully with employees."

Yet, even if a company is seemingly open about its monitoring, there is reason for workers to be concerned about what communications they receive from management.

A court precedent says that employees have no rights to privacy in e-mail, even if a company promises not to track it, Maltby says. Also, workers should never assume that if they don't get any memos on monitoring, that it isn't happening. "Just because your boss doesn't tell you he's monitoring, that doesn't mean it's not happening," he says.

Maltby and other workplace experts suggest a healthy dose of paranoia—as well as the purchase of a personal cell-phone and computer that are never used for work-related tasks—as the only safe way around the watchful boss.

"It's technically possible to monitor just about anything," says Marsh. And for those who really want to be safe, he suggests leaving the work building, going around the corner and "talking to someone face to face."

Laura Petrecca is a writer for *USA Today* newspaper.

National Workrights Institute

 **NO**

Privacy Under Siege: Electronic Monitoring in the Workplace

Introduction

Everyone in the office knew that Gail would change her clothes in her cubicle for the gym after the work day was done. When her employers installed a hidden camera to monitor the person in the neighboring cubicle's suspected illegal activities, her daily ritual was captured on film. The first few times could have been labeled as mistakes, but the filming of Gail changing her clothes over a five month period was inexcusable.

Electronic monitoring is a rapidly growing phenomenon in American businesses. Introduced in the early twentieth century for such limited uses as timing breaks and measuring hand-eye movements, systematic electronic monitoring has since grown into the very fabric of American business practice. As technologies become more powerful and easy and inexpensive to install and maintain, the rates of electronic monitoring in this country have skyrocketed. In 1999 the percentage of employers who electronically monitor their workers was 67%. Just two years later, in the year 2001 this number had increased to 78%. By 2003, 92% of employers were conducting some form of workplace monitoring. This rapid growth in monitoring has virtually destroyed any sense of privacy as we know it in the American workplace. Employers now conduct video surveillance, listen in on employee telephone calls, review employee computer use such as e-mail and the Internet and monitor their every move using GPS. But as legitimate work product is being monitored, so are the personal habits and lives of employees. As technology has proliferated in the workplace, it has become ever more penetrating and intrusive. And yet there are few, if any, legal protections for employees. There has been no attempt to balance employer demands with legitimate employee privacy concerns. Collection and use of personal information is a rampant byproduct of workplace monitoring and threatens the very freedoms that we cherish as Americans. Legislation is necessary to govern the practice of electronic monitoring in the workplace, protect employee privacy and return a sense of fundamental fairness and dignity to the American workplace.

Privacy and Intrusion Issues

While employers generally initiate electronic monitoring in response to legitimate business concerns, the results have been devastating to employee privacy. Virtually everything we do and say at work can be, and is, monitored by our employers. Our employers watch us on video cameras, read our e-mails, listen to our voice mail, review documents on our hard drives, and check every Web site we visit.

This would be bad enough if it involved only work related behavior and communication, but it doesn't. The advent of cell phones, pagers, and home computers is rapidly erasing the traditional wall between the home and the workplace. People now regularly receive communications from their employer at home. Maggie Jackson, former workplace correspondent for the Associated Press, estimates that the average professional or managerial employee now receives over 20 electronic messages from work every week. This new flexibility also means that personal communication increasingly occurs in the workplace. An employee who spent much of the weekend on a cell phone with her boss will not (and should not) consider it inappropriate to make a personal call from the office.

This means that employer monitoring systems frequently record personal communications. Often, this communication is not sensitive. But sometimes the messages are very personal. An employee who sends their spouse a romantic e-mail while eating lunch at his or her desk can find that their love letter has been read by their boss. Or a note to a psychiatrist stored in an employee's hard drive is disclosed.

Internet monitoring can be extremely invasive. People today turn to the Internet as their primary source of information, including sensitive subjects they would be uncomfortable communicating about on their office telephone or e-mail. In part, this is because of the efficiency of internet research. Even an untrained person can find information on the Web in minutes that would have taken hours or even days to find by traditional means (if they could find it at all). People also turn to the Internet for information because they can do so anonymously.

The result is that people turn to the Internet for information and help about the most sensitive subjects imaginable. Women who are victims of domestic abuse turn to the Internet for information about shelters and other forms of help. People also turn to the Web for information and help with drug and alcohol problems, financial difficulties, marital problems, and medical issues. Monitoring Web access gives an employer a picture window into employees' most sensitive personal problems.

Most invasive of all is video monitoring. Some cameras are appropriate. Security cameras in stairwells and parking garages make us all safer without intruding on privacy. But employers often install cameras in areas that are completely indefensible. Many employers have installed hidden video cameras in locker rooms and bathrooms, sometimes inside the stalls. No one should be subjected to sexual voyeurism on the job.

Such problems are made worse by the manner in which monitoring is often conducted. Most employers make no effort to avoid monitoring personal communications. The majority of employers install systems that make no distinction between business and personal messages, even when more discriminating systems are available.

In addition to official monitoring, IT employees often monitor their fellow employees for personal reasons. Most employers give such employees carte blanche access to employee communications. While it is possible to set up technical barriers to ensure that monitoring is confined to official programs, few employers use them. Many employers do not even have policies directing IT employees to restrict their monitoring to official programs. Even employers with such policies rarely have procedures to enforce them. As a result, employees involved in monitoring often read the messages of fellow employees for their own amusement.

The final indignity is that employees don't even know when they are being watched. While a majority of employers provide employees what is described as notice, still many do not and the information currently provided is generally useless. The standard employer notice states only that the company reserves the right to monitor anything at any time. Employees do not know whether it is their e-mail, voice mail, Web access, or hard drive that is monitored. They do not know whether the monitoring is continuous, random, or as needed. They do not even know whether they are being monitored at all. Such notice is almost worse than no notice at all.

As bad as the situation is today, it is likely to be far worse in the future. Many people today do work for their employer on their home computers. The most direct example of this is telecommuting. Approximately 20 million employees and independent contractors now work at home at least one day per month, and this number is growing rapidly. Millions more have linked their home computer to their office network so they can work from home informally on evenings and weekends.

When this occurs, people's home computers are subject to monitoring by their employer. Workplace computer monitoring systems monitor the entire network, including a home computer that is temporarily part of the network. This means that personal communications in our home computers will be revealed to our employers. Personal e-mail sent from or received by our home computers will be disclosed to our employers, along with personal letters, financial records, and any other personal information in our home computers. Not only is this possible, it is highly likely. When asked if they would be interested in having

personal information from employees' home computers, corporate attorneys responded positively.

Monitoring and Productivity

Employers generally conduct electronic monitoring in order to increase productivity. It is far from clear, however, that monitoring achieves this goal. In fact, too much monitoring can actually decrease productivity by increasing employee stress and decreasing morale.

In a study conducted for Bell Canada it was reported that 55% of all long distance and directory assistance operators experienced added stress due to some form of monitoring. Increased stress can often lead to physical symptoms. In a study by the Department of Industrial Engineering, University of Wisconsin-Madison, higher levels of stress in monitored employees resulted in an increase in somatic complaints, including a 27% increase in occurrences of pain or stiffness in shoulders, a 23% increase in occurrences of neck pressure and a 21% increase in back pain experienced by employees. Such stress and stress related symptoms can create medical expenses, lost time and absenteeism.

Studies have shown that the introduction of electronic monitoring into the workplace is likely to encourage employees to favor quantity of work produced over quality. Even employers who do not intend on placing production increases above quality may do so inadvertently, simply because quality is more difficult to monitor electronically. Pressure to increase productivity commonly has adverse effects on the quality of work produced. In two studies published in the National Productivity Review the authors found that "monitored employees were less willing to pursue complex customer inquiries than their unmonitored coworkers." Similar results were found in other productivity studies.

Trust between employee and employer is crucial to maintaining a high level of productivity and unnecessary and covert monitoring is harmful to this balance. A recent study conducted jointly by Microsoft and the London School of Economics found that "providing information in an environment of trust can greatly facilitate the coordination of work." Indeed "Mutual trust is not an added bonus of the mobile organization, it is an absolute core principle. . . Mistrust results in the perceived need to engage in activities only serving the purpose of demonstrating ability internally and not generating business value."

This does not mean that employers should never collect information about employees' work by electronic means. It does mean, however, that monitoring should not be employed based on a general idea that it will increase productivity. Before initiating any program of monitoring, employers should carefully consider:

1. Why they believe this specific monitoring program will increase efficiency.
2. The effect of the monitoring program on employee stress.

3. The effect of the program upon employee morale.
4. Whether the value of the increased efficiency outweighs the cost of increased stress and decreased morale.

As with any other important decision, employers should attempt to quantify these factors and conduct a cost-benefit analysis.

More Effective Solutions

Most employers are not voyeurs. More often than not, they would rather not know personal information about their employees that has no bearing on job performance. Yet there is rarely an attempt to be more discriminating in their practices or a balancing of employer needs with employee privacy concerns. There are a variety of ways that employers can address specific concerns without monitoring highly personal information. The following are a few suggestions.

- Businesses should properly train managers and supervisors to deal with employee issues and problems. Most businesses do not have managers that are properly trained to deal with sensitive employee subjects. These staffs need to be observant and reactive to employee needs. Properly trained managers are a company's best asset in terms of dealing directly with and correcting many of the concerns that prompt the adoption of electronic monitoring practices. Supervising staffs can set conduct guidelines, address concerns, mediate complaints, as well as monitor and deal individually with those employees that choose to abuse company resources.
- Businesses should always conduct an in-house assessment to identify whether electronic monitoring is even necessary. This seems like an obvious point, but many businesses adopt large scale monitoring programs on the assumption that they will add benefits to their workplace without identifying their own specific requirements and whether the adoption of an electronic monitoring program would meet those requirements.
- Before deciding to conduct monitoring, management should speak with employees about the productivity problem. Employees may suggest alternative ways of solving the problem. If monitoring is chosen, employees can participate in designing the monitoring program and its scope in a way that is acceptable to them.
- If monitoring is conducted, the scope should be as narrow as is consistent with achieving the desired objective. Employers should be especially careful to restrict the program to business related communications and avoid monitoring personal communications. Additionally they should utilize Web access software that eliminates the need for monitoring each individual Web site an employee visits.

- Consider monitoring on an "event basis." This involves conducting monitoring when it is known something inappropriate has occurred and confining the monitoring to dealing with that event.
- If a company does choose to adopt a program of electronic monitoring, proper notice should be given well in advance of any monitoring practices. This notice should explicitly state what would be monitored as well as when this monitoring would occur. The American Management Association has recommended that employers give notice of electronic monitoring since 1997.

The Numbers: Electronic Monitoring Has Become a Common Practice

Electronic monitoring in the American workplace has seen dramatic growth in recent years. Prior to 1980, electronic monitoring was virtually unknown. When the Congressional Office of Technology Assessment studied its use in 1987, only 7% of employees were affected. But in only 6 years, a MacWorld survey found that electronic monitoring had nearly tripled (to 20% of employees). In 2001, the American Management Association reported that the percentage of companies monitoring had risen to 78.4%. By 2003, 92% of employers were conducting workplace monitoring.

Even more troubling are the ways employers monitor:

- 75% of employers that monitor do so without individualized cause
- 50% of all employers that do have a monitoring policy do not train their employees about their monitoring policy
- 20% of employers do not have a written monitoring policy
- 25% of employers do not have in place any procedures or safeguards to ensure that the monitoring process is not abused

While the national debate over privacy rages, the unregulated growth of electronic monitoring in the American workplace shows no signs of abating.

Everyday People: Stories of Workplace Monitoring across America

California

At a Neiman-Marcus Store in Fashion Island Newport Beach, Kelly Pendleton, a two-time "employee of the year" discovered a hidden camera in the ceiling of the changing room used by female employees that was being monitored by male colleagues.

Employees of Consolidated Freightways were horrified to find that the company had installed hidden cameras in its restrooms—some cameras pointing directly at the urinals. Over a thousand hours of video records were made covering thousands of employees. "The guys were really shaken, and some of the women went home crying," says Joe Quilty, the dockworker who discovered the hidden cameras.

An AT&T employee received a formal reprimand for using the company e-mail system to send a love note to his wife, also an AT&T employee.

9th Circuit Court of Appeals Judges disabled computer monitoring software that had been installed by the Administrative Office of the U.S. Courts without notice or consent. Judge Alex Kozinski charged that the surveillance system was a needless invasion of privacy. Several members of Congress agreed, Rep. Howard Berman wrote "While it may be appropriate to monitor an employee's Internet use or e-mail in certain circumstances, I do not believe indiscriminate, systematic monitoring is appropriate. . . It is particularly inappropriate for the courts, which will inevitably be called on to rule in cases involving questions of employee privacy."

Alana Shoars was in charge of the Epson Torrance, California plant e-mail system. Ms. Shoars assured Epson employees that their e-mail was private. She discovered later that her supervisor was reading all employee e-mail in the Torrance plant.

Florida

An employee of Walt Disney World videotaped female employees in bathrooms and locker rooms. After several months, Disney security became aware of these activities, but did nothing to correct the situation for many months. Finally, Disney decided to conduct a sting operation by setting up its own video surveillance system. None of the female employees were informed so they could take measures to protect themselves and both the employees and the voyeur were videotaped hours in the dressing room area.

The general manager of the Apalachicola Times newspaper installed a hidden video camera in the employee bathroom and made 29 videotapes worth of recordings. Barbara Lynn Perry, one of several women who was regularly videotaped remarked "No one had my permission as far as surveillance. . . . I was never formally or informally asked for my permission. I had no idea there was a camera in the bathroom."

Georgia

Air force machinist Donald Thompson is placed under investigation by the Office of Special Counsel for forwarding an e-mail lampooning the president's qualifications. "To me, sending it was just an electronic version of water cooler chit chat" he said.

Female employees at a local plant in Pendergrass run by Atlas Cold Storage were regularly videotaped in the bathroom without their knowledge or consent. According to employees, the plant manager would regularly remind them that "there's not anywhere you can go where I can't see you."

Hawaii

Hawaiian airlines pilot Robert Konop sets up a personal, password protected website so that he and fellow pilots can have private discussions and freely criticize management. A Vice-President of the airline pressures a fellow pilot for the password and accesses the site.

Illinois

A technology professional was terminated after his boss listened in on a phone conversation he was having with his girlfriend after his shift ended.

An employee quits after his boss announces to the entire office the content of a personal e-mail that had been retrieved from the monitoring system.

Maryland

A 17-year-old woman, Jennifer Smith, testified before the Judiciary Committee of the Maryland House of Representatives that in her job as a lifeguard, she was videotaped changing into her bathing suit by her supervisor at the county swimming pool.

Massachusetts

At the Sheraton Boston Hotel hidden cameras were discovered in the employee changing room. Hours of tape of employees in different stages of undress were logged. One of the Sheraton workers, Jean L. Clement, stated that: "Learning about the secret videotaping made me very scared at work because I feel as though I'm being watched wherever I go, which is how I felt when I lived in Haiti."

Nebraska

Melissa Haines of Broken Bow, an employee of Mid-Nebraska Individual Services, discovered hidden monitors the employer had installed to record personal as well work related conversations. "My job has been awful. Is there anything I can do? What I say to a friend should be confidential," she remarked.

New Jersey

The City of Clinton Township, NJ installed GPS tracking devices behind the front grilles of patrol cars without notifying their officers.

A female employee logs onto an expectant mothers' Web site at her job during working hours. Just looking for information, the employee tells no one of her possible condition. Soon after, her immediate supervisor congratulates her on her pregnancy.

Heidi Arace and Norma Yetsko, two employees of the PNC Bank, were terminated after forwarding jokes on their company's e-mail. Such letters had been regularly sent in the past by fellow employees with the attention of the employer and they had previously never enforced any monitoring policies. As Arace puts it, "I was cold. I was frozen. It was like I lost everything in my life. You get a simple e-mail like this, you read it; you chuckle; forward it on, click. Done deal . . . everyone was doing it."

New York

Howard Boyle, president of a fire sprinkler installation company in Woodside, N.Y., presented his employees with cell phones to use without informing them that they were equipped with GPS. Mr. Boyle can find out where they are at all times including during breaks and while they are off duty. "They don't need to know," said Mr. Boyle. "I can call them and say, 'Where are you now?' while I'm looking at the screen and knowing exactly where they are."

Lourdes Rachel Arias and Louis J. Albero discovered that their employer, Mutual Central Alarm Service, was monitoring and recording all incoming and outgoing telephone calls including personal and private conversations without notice or consent.

Pennsylvania

Despite assurances from his employer that e-mail was confidential, that it would not be intercepted, and that it would not be used for the basis for discipline or discharge, Michael Smyth is terminated for sending an unprofessional message from his home over the company e-mail.

Tennessee

Joyce Carr and Bernice Christianson discovered that their employer, Northern Telecom, was secretly taping all incoming and outgoing private telephone conversations in a Nashville plant by means of hidden microphones. An investigation discovered systematic efforts by top management to wiretap public pay phones in the employee cafeteria and monitor conversations through microphones in the plant sprinkler system.

Texas

Microsoft, which had no monitoring policy at the time, opens the personal folders of employee Bill McLaren's office computer even though they are password protected.

Washington

At Washington's WJLA-TV station, tracking devices were installed in station vehicles supposedly to allow editors to know where the closest vehicle might be to a breaking story, but employees claimed that the devices had been used to monitor them. Employees recounted stories of managers phoning them to instruct them to drive slower or to question them about stopping at certain locations.

Electronic Monitoring of Employees a Lack of Legal Regulation
Federal Law

The only relevant federal legislation to protect employee privacy is the Omnibus Crime Control and Safe Streets Act of 1968, as amended by the Electronic Communications Privacy Act of 1986. The ECPA, with certain exceptions, prohibits the interception, disclosure, or use of a wire, oral or electronic communication. This protection applies to all businesses involved in interstate commerce and has also been interpreted to extend to most intrastate phone communications. It also applies to conversations between employees that employers may overhear because the employees are wearing headsets. The Act creates both criminal and civil causes of action. Civil remedies may include compensatory and punitive damages, as well as attorney's fees and other litigation costs.

There are three exceptions to this blanket prohibition. One exception allows wire and communications service providers (common carriers) to intercept communications if done for quality of service purposes. Under this exception, a telephone company can monitor its employees to ensure adequate job performance and supervise customer contacts.

A second exception allows interception when there is consent. A party to the communication may intercept the communication, or prior consent may be given by one of the parties to the communication. Generally, courts will not find implied consent. For instance, knowledge of the capability of monitoring alone will not substitute for actual consent. See *Watkins v. L.M. Berry & Co.,* 704 F. 2d 577 (11th Cir. 1983). Consent will be implied where the employee is aware of a general monitoring program and uses a business-only phone to make a personal call when other phones are provided for that purpose. See *Simmons v. Southwestern Bell Tel. Co.,* 452 F. Supp. 392 (W.D. Okla. 1978), aff'd., 611 F 2d 342 (10th Cir. 1979).

The third and primary exception allows for wire eavesdropping when done in the "ordinary course of business": context and content. Under a context analysis, emphasis is placed on the importance of the business policy served by the monitoring and extent to which the monitoring furthers that policy without unnecessarily interfering with employee privacy. Business units whose primary function involves customer contact via telephone have the strongest argument for the legitimacy of monitoring. The "unnecessary interference" element includes considerations of whether the monitoring was announced or covert and whether separate telephones were provided for personal calls. A content analysis focuses on whether the monitored call was personal or business in nature. Regardless of their chosen approach, the courts have consistently held that an employer violates the act when it continues to monitor a purely personal phone call after learning of its personal nature. See *U.S. v. Harpel,* 493 F. 2d 346 (10th Cir. 1974) and *U.S. v. Axselle,* 604 F. 2d 414 (5th Cir. 1980). The employer may be limited to a "reasonable" length of time to make this determination. Courts which have considered this question have defined "reasonable" as anywhere from 10 seconds to 5 minutes (See Watkins and Axselle).

ECPA does prohibit access to stored communications (Stored Communications Act) but this prohibition is also subject to severely weakening exceptions. There remain access exemptions for the person or entity providing a wire or electronic communications service and for the user of that service with respect to a communication of or intended for that user. Employers are likely to fall under one or both of such exceptions.

What limited protections ECPA does provide to employees have been greatly weakened because the statute has quickly become outdated. The ECPA does not apply to most common forms of monitoring technologies such as electronic mail monitoring, Internet monitoring and video surveillance. Since ECPA requires an "interception" of a communication, communications in a stored state are exempt. Additionally, as in the case of electronic mail, courts have so far found that company owned proprietary systems are exempt. See *Shoars v. Epson*, 90 SWC 112749 and 90 BC 7036 (Superior Court, Los Angeles County). Assurances by employers that monitored and stored employee e-mails are not reviewed by management is no guarantee that employers will not reprimand or terminate employees for the content of their e-mail messages. See *Smyth v. Pillsbury & Co.* 914 F. Supp. 97, 101 (E.D. Pa. 1996).

Additionally the ECPA does not require an employer to give notice of electronic monitoring practices, nor is there any other statute that requires an employer to give notice of monitoring practices, no matter how invasive the monitoring may be.

State Law

In addition to federal statute, employees sometimes also receive some privacy protection from various state constitutional, common law and statutory sources. Most states have a constitutional provision that reflects the proscriptions in the Fourth amendment regarding search and seizure. Some states have specific constitutional guarantees of privacy that extend beyond the Federal Constitution's privacy rights. Only California courts, however, have held that the state constitutional right of privacy applies with respect to both public and private employers. See *Porten v. University of San Francisco*, 134 Cal. Rptr. 839 (Cal Ct. App. 1976). In all other states, employees have successfully invoked the state constitutional right of privacy only after establishing the government as the employer. Some state courts, such as New Jersey and Alaska, have nevertheless determined that their state constitutions can form a basis for creating public policy arguments in favor of a private sector employee's right to privacy.

A majority of states do have statutes restricting the interception of wire communications by private individuals. These states, however, generally mirror the ECPA, and

contain similar exceptions and exemptions. Although some states have shown a willingness to legislate in the employee privacy area, the efforts have only been piecemeal. Within the past year California has added a section to its Labor Code that prohibits an employer from monitoring, without a court order, employees in restrooms, locker rooms or other places designated by the employer for changing clothes. Labor Code, Sec 435 (a) to (c). Additionally, Connecticut added a section to its labor code requiring employers to give employees written notice of the types of monitoring which may occur. Conn. Gen. Stat. Sec 31-48d. Nevertheless, state governments have not addressed the issue comprehensively or uniformly, and in most cases have not addressed it at all.

Finally, some limited protections exist in the common law of torts. The tort that most plaintiffs use to challenge employer monitoring and surveillance is the intrusion-on-seclusion tort. The classic conception of this tort, recognized in every state, is that it is used to punish highly offensive privacy invasions. There has been an attempt to apply the tort in the employment context to challenge workplace monitoring abuses. Under present law, however, formidable obstacles face the employee who wishes to bring such a privacy claim.

First, the intrusion-on-seclusion tort requires the employee to establish that the monitoring conduct is highly objectionable to a reasonable person. Because routine monitoring can appear harmless from some perspectives (especially that of a third party), and because the negative effects of such monitoring are often gradual and incremental, this standard frequently forecloses an employee claim. In particular, when the monitoring complained of has been arguably linked to work-related activities, those challenges have been unsuccessful. See *Barksdale v. IBM*, 620 F. Supp. 1380 (W.D.N.C. 1985). Additionally, courts have not been receptive to employee claims that their work environments contain sufficiently private spaces for an invasion of privacy to occur. See *Ulrich v. K-Mart Corp.*, 858 F. Supp. 1087 (D. Kan. 1994). For example, an employee's office, desk or locker may be held to be the employer's property, and therefore not private. The combination of these elements typically defeats an employee's tort claim in all but the most egregious of circumstances, which usually involve monitoring in areas such as bathrooms or locker rooms. Even in such highly private areas, state court decisions are mixed. See, for example, *Speer v. Department of Rehabilitation & Correction*, 646 N. E. 2d 273 (Ohio Ct. Cl. 1994).

Questions and Answers
Is there a Need for Workplace Privacy Legislation?

Yes. The explosion of workplace surveillance in recent years has stripped Americans of virtually all their privacy on the job. Nearly 80% of employers now use electronic surveillance. Soon it will be universal. Employer monitoring practices often go well beyond specific and even legitimate management concerns. They are rarely tailored to meet individual employer demands or balanced with employee privacy concerns. Current laws are outdated, vague or more often silent on this issue. A balance between the legitimate concerns of business and employee privacy must be created.

Should Employers Give Notice of Monitoring?

Yes. Employers may need to conduct monitoring for quality control and other business reasons, but they do not need to do it in secret. Indeed, the American Management Association and most corporate counsels recommend that employers provide notice of monitoring programs. Legitimate monitoring programs do not need to be carried out behind employees' backs. Secret monitoring is not only unnecessary, it is counterproductive. The purpose of monitoring is to ensure that employees are following company policy regarding the use of electronic communications technology. If employees know that the company monitors e-mail or Internet access, they will be more careful to follow the rules. Most important, secret monitoring is ethically wrong. People have a right to know when they are being watched. Reading someone else's messages without telling them is both deceptive and a profound violation of their privacy.

In What Situations Should Monitoring be Limited?

Employers have legitimate reasons for many monitoring programs. Company e-mail systems have sometimes been used to send inappropriate material that contributes to a hostile environment. The seemingly endless level of information on the Internet has led some employees to spend excessive time at work Web surfing. Employers need to respond to these concerns. But, without limitation, employers' efforts to prevent abuse can often lead to serious invasions of privacy. People are not robots. They discuss the weather, sports, their families, and many other matters unrelated to their jobs while at work. While many of these non-work related conversations are innocuous, some are highly personal. An employee might tell her best friend about problems with her husband or share concerns about family financial problems, or their fear that their child may have a drug problem. Most employers are not voyeurs. More often than not, they would rather not know personal information about their employees that has no bearing on job performance. Yet there is rarely an attempt to separate personal from business related communications. An employer is well equipped to run an efficient and productive business without monitoring the content of personal communications.

Clearly the most invasive workplace monitoring practice; video surveillance of highly private areas such as bathrooms and locker rooms, is never conducted in the ordinary course of business and is ripe for abuse. Employees have a heightened expectation of privacy and personal autonomy in such areas. Such monitoring destroys the very essence of human dignity, is highly degrading and such activity disproportionately involves the secret photography of women. The decision to breach such highly sensitive areas and to what degree, is a decision better suited to the reasoned judgment of a court of law.

Why Should the Government be Entitled to Dictate How Private Management Can Run Their Businesses?

The government at times must act to ensure that management treats its workers fairly and justly. In the past, Congress has passed numerous laws placing restrictions on private business activities. Such laws include actions prohibiting private businesses from hiring children, discriminating against women and minorities, and paying sub-minimum wages. In addition, legislation has been enacted to ensure employees' rights to organize unions, and to receive prior notice of expected plant closings. Today, in order to protect employees' right to privacy and dignity, restrictions on electronic monitoring by employers must be enacted.

Federal Legislative History

Congress has introduced two notable bills in the past fifteen years to protect employee privacy. These bills were endorsed by a variety of civil rights and labor organizations.

The Privacy for Consumers and Workers Act

On February 27, 1991, the late Senator Paul Simon and Representative Pat Williams introduced the PCWA. The bill would have required employers to clearly define their privacy policies and notify prospective employees of those practices that would affect them. It would have required that surveillance be limited to job related functions and would have prohibited such surveillance of personal communications. It would have prohibited video surveillance in highly personal places such as bathrooms (unless there was suspicion of illegal conduct) and would have required notification when telephone monitoring was taking place. Additionally, it would give employees access to records collected as a result of surveillance.

The Notice of Electronic Monitoring Act

A more limited version of PCWA was introduced by Senator Schumer on July 20, 2000. NEMA would have subjected an employer to liability for intentionally monitoring an employee without first having given the employee substantive notice that the employer was engaged in such a monitoring program. Notice fulfilling the requirements of the Act would include the type of monitoring taking place, the means, the type of information that would be gathered including non-work related information, the frequency of monitoring and how the information would be used. An exception to such notice was made if the employer had reasonable grounds to believe the employee was engaged in illegal conduct and surveillance would produce evidence of such. NEMA put no actual restrictions on an employer's ability to monitor as long as they complied with the notice provisions.

Workplace Privacy Act

A Bill

To amend title 18, United States Code, to authorize electronic monitoring conducted in the ordinary course of business, provide for the disclosure of electronic monitoring of employee communications and computer usage in the workplace and limit electronic monitoring in highly sensitive areas of the workplace.

Section 1. Short Title

This Act may be cited as the 'Workplace Privacy Act'

Section 2. Electronic Monitoring in the Workplace

(a) IN GENERAL—(1) Except as otherwise specifically provided in this section, an employer may, by any electronic means, read, listen to, or otherwise monitor any wire communication, oral communication, or electronic communication of an employee of the employer, or otherwise monitor the computer usage of an employee of the employer if the monitoring meets the requirements of sections (b) and (e) and—
(A) The monitoring is conducted at the employer's premises and
(B) The monitoring is conducted in the normal course of employment while the employee is engaged in any activity which is a necessary incident to the rendition of his service or to the protection of the rights or property of the employer.
(2) An employer who conducts monitoring in violation of this section shall be liable to the employee for relief as provided in subsection (f).

(b) IN GENERAL—(1) Except as provided in subsection (d), an employer who intentionally, by any electronic means, reads, listens to, or otherwise monitors any wire communication, oral communication, or electronic communication of an employee of the employer, or otherwise monitors the computer usage of an employee of the employer, without first having provided the employee notice meeting the requirements of subsection (b) shall be liable to the employee for relief as provided in subsection (f).

(2) Not later than one year after first providing notice of electronic monitoring under paragraph (1), and annually thereafter, an employer shall provide notice meeting the requirements of subsection (b) to all employees of the employer who are subject to such electronic monitoring.
(3) Before implementing a material change in an electronic monitoring practice described in paragraph (1), an employer shall provide notice meeting the requirements of subsection (b) to all employees of the employer who are subject to electronic monitoring covered by that paragraph as a result of the change.

(c) NOTICE—A notice meeting the requirements of this subsection is a clear and conspicuous notice, in a manner reasonably calculated to provide actual notice, describing—
(1) the form of communication or computer usage that will be monitored;
(2) the means by which such monitoring will be accomplished and the kinds of information that will be obtained through such monitoring, including whether communications or computer usage not related to the employer's business are likely to be monitored;
(3) the frequency of such monitoring; and
(4) how information obtained by such monitoring will be stored, used, or disclosed.

(d) EXCEPTION—An employer may conduct electronic monitoring described in subsection (a) without the notice required by subsection (b) if the employer has reasonable grounds to believe that—
(1) a particular employee of the employer is engaged in conduct that—
(A) violates the legal rights of the employer or another person; and
(B) involves significant harm to the employer or such other person; and
(2) the electronic monitoring will produce evidence of such conduct.

(e) IN GENERAL—(1) No employer or agent of an employer may engage in video or audio monitoring of an employee in bathrooms, dressing rooms, locker rooms, or other areas where employees change clothing unless—
(A) Such monitoring is authorized by court order.
(2) An employer who conducts monitoring in violation of this section shall be liable to the employee for relief as provided in subsection (f).

(f) CIVIL ACTION—(1) Any person aggrieved by any act in violation of this section may bring an action in a United States district court.
(2) a court in an action under this section may award—

(A) actual damages, but not less than liquidated damages in the amount of $5,000;

(B) punitive damages;

(C) reasonable attorneys' fees and other litigation costs reasonably incurred; and

(D) such other preliminary and equitable relief as the court determines to be appropriate.

(g) ENFORCEMENT ACTION BY SECRETARY

(1) IN GENERAL—Any employer who violates this section shall be liable to the United States for a civil money penalty in an amount not to exceed $10,000 for each violation, except that, if the violation is knowing, the penalty for the violation may be up to $25,000.

(b) Written Notice and Opportunity for Hearing— The Secretary of Labor shall assess a civil penalty under subsection (a) by an order made on the record after opportunity for a hearing provided in accordance with section 554 of title 5, United States Code. In connection with the hearing, the Secretary may issue subpoenas requiring the attendance and testimony of witnesses and the production of evidence that relates to the subject matter of the hearing.

(c) Determination of Amount of Civil Money Penalty—In determining the amount of a civil money penalty under subsection (a), the Secretary shall take into account—

(1) the nature, circumstances, extent, and gravity of the violation or violations; and

(2) with respect to the violator, the ability to pay, effect on ability to continue to do business, any history of prior violations, the degree of culpability, and such other matters as justice may require.

(h) WAIVER OF RIGHTS—(1) The rights provided by this Act may not be waived by contract or otherwise, unless such waiver is part of a written settlement to a pending action or complaint.

(i) PREEMPTION—(1) Nothing in this Act shall be construed to preempt, modify, or amend any State, county, or local law, ordinance, or regulation providing greater protection to the privacy of employees.

NATIONAL WORKRIGHTS INSTITUTE was founded in January 2000 by the former staff of the American Civil Liberties Union's National Taskforce on Civil Liberties in the Workplace. The Institute's creation grew from the belief that the workplace is a critical front in the fight for human rights and the belief that this effort required the creation of a new organization dedicated to human rights in the workplace. The Institute's mission is to be the one human rights organization which commits its entire effort to workplace issues. The Institute's goal is to improve the legal protection of human rights in the workplace.

EXPLORING THE ISSUE

Does an Employer's Need to Monitor Workers Trump Employee Privacy Concerns?

Critical Thinking and Reflection

1. Would clearer or stricter guidelines on employee monitoring mitigate potential legal challenges?
2. Would different employee monitoring systems change employees' behavior?
3. Can employee behavior be effectively monitored?
4. Should employers monitor employee behavior? Under what circumstances or in which situations?

Is There Common Ground?

The issue discussed here creates a difficult situation for managers: Don't monitor employees and run the risk of employee theft, low productivity, and corporate liability, or monitor the workplace and potentially create an atmosphere of stress, distrust, and low company loyalty among employees. While there has been no attempt to balance employer demands with legitimate employee privacy concerns, there is consensus that employee monitoring is a complex issue that will be debated for quite some time.

Additional Resources

Alder, G.S., Ambrose, M.L., and Noel, T.W. (2006). "The Effect of Formal Advance Notice and Justification on Internet Monitoring Fairness: Much About Nothing?" *Journal of Leadership and Organizational Studies*, 13(1), pp. 93–108.

Boehle, S. (2008). "They're Watching You, *Training*, September, pp. 23–29.

Ciochetti, C.A. (2011). "The Eavesdropping Employer: A Twenty-First Century Framework for Employee Monitoring," *American Business Law Journal*, Summer, pp. 285–369.

Curran, K., McIntyre, S., Meenan, H., McCloy, F., and Heaney, C. (2004). "Civil Liberties and Computer Monitoring," *American Journal of Applied Sciences*, 1(3), pp. 225–229.

Dupree, Jr, C.M. and Jude, R.K. (2006). "Who's Reading Your Email? Is That Legal?" *Strategic Finance*, April, 45–47.

Martin, K. and Freeman, E. (2003). "Some Problems with Employee Monitoring," *Journal of Business Ethics*, 43, pp. 353–361.

Zetter, K. (2007). "Is Your Boss Spying on You?" *The Reader's Digest*, September, pp. 170–177.

Internet References . . .

2005 Electronic Monitoring & Surveillance Survey: Many Companies Monitoring, Recording, Videotaping—and Firing—Employees

American Management Association. (2005). "2005 Electronic Monitoring & Surveillance Survey: Many Companies Monitoring, Recording, Videotaping—and Firing—Employees," *American Management Association News*.

http://www.amanet.org/training/articles/Electronic-Monitoring-Surveillane-12.aspx

Don't Be an Every Minute Manager

Ryan, L. (2005). "Don't Be an Every Minute Manager," *BusinessWeek* Online, September 15.

http://www.businessweek.com/stories/2005-09-14/dont-be-an-every-minute-manager

Selected, Edited, and with Issue Framing Material by:
Kathleen J. Barnes, *East Stroudsburg University*
and
George E. Smith, *Albright College*

ISSUE

Is Workplace Drug Testing a Wise Corporate Policy?

YES: Elaine Davis and Stacie Hueller, from "Strengthening the Case for Workplace Drug-Testing: The Growing Problem of Methamphetamines," *SAM Advanced Management Journal* (Summer 2006)

NO: Russ Belville, from "Drug Testing Does No Good," *The Oregon Herald* (April 20, 2005), www.oregonherald .com/n/radicalruss/20050420_workplace-drug-testing.html

---

Learning Outcomes

After reading this issue you should be able to:

- Understand the positive and negative consequences of drug testing in the workplace.
- Understand how drug testing can be used as an effective workplace tool.
- Understand what policies might be implemented concerning workplace drug testing.
- Appreciate the practical managerial implications of drug testing policies use in the workplace.

ISSUE SUMMARY

YES: Scholars Elaine Davis and Stacie Hueller provide an analysis on how and why businesses should address the growing use of methamphetamines in the workplace.

NO: Russ Belville cites results of several studies questioning the effectiveness of workplace drug testing. He further argues that given their expense, drug-testing policies are not sound strategic initiatives.

Substance abuse costs employers tens of millions of dollars every year as a result of the increased levels of absenteeism, work-related accidents, health care costs, and theft. The National Institute on Drug Abuse reports that 75 percent of illegal drug users are employed, and approximately 20 percent of 18- to 25-year-olds use drugs at the workplace. It's not surprising, then, that private employers across the country have adopted various types of drug-testing policies as a way of fighting back. The federal government is also involved in the battle, having entered with the passage of the Drug-free Workplace Act of 1988. This act requires all government agencies and firms with governmental contracts to take action toward eliminating drugs from the workplace.

Despite society's apparent acceptance of drug testing at work, there is considerable resistance to the policy of testing employees. Central to the opposition's position is the issue of employee privacy rights. Notwithstanding the indisputable fact that corporations have a right to protect themselves, critics of workplace drug testing fear that it infringes on employee privacy rights. Critics also

point to studies that call into question the degree to which employee productivity is truly affected by workplace drug use.

Responses to the employee privacy issue have generally fallen into one of three categories and can be thought of as comprising a continuum of viewpoints. At one end of this continuum are those who are against drug testing in the workplace under any and all circumstances. This group typically invokes a rights-based argument in contending that individual rights always trump organizational rights. America is a country founded on the belief in the supremacy of individual rights and because drug testing violates an individual's right to privacy, organizations should not be allowed to implement them under any condition.

At the opposite end of this continuum reside the protesting advocates. The view here is that organizations are actually a collection of individuals who share common ownership of the firm and have a right to protect themselves and their property. Inasmuch as they can be held accountable for the moral and legal violations committed by their employees, organizations should be allowed to exercise reasonable control over the workplace. Thus, when taking into account the tremendous damage drug abuse can inflict on an organization, workplace drug testing would appear to be a reasonable managerial policy.

Perhaps the most commonly espoused view, representing the midpoint of our continuum, is that corporations should maintain employee privacy as an important corporate principle. Testing can be done, but all efforts should be made to protect employee privacy throughout the process, and testing should be implemented only in cases where reasonable grounds for suspicion exist. Thus, the determination to test an employee or employees is made only when there is evidence that consumption of these substances results in undesirable behaviors such as lower productivity or increasing the likelihood of safety violations.

Before you read the following selections and develop your own opinion, some facts should be presented. It is important to know that the courts have consistently sided with the rights of corporations to test employees provided there is no evidence of discrimination in its implementation or unwarranted targeting of specific individuals for testing. Also, courts have been particularly supportive when the job in question is of a sensitive nature.

Indeed, the fact that workplace drug testing is legal is seemingly attributable to its widespread use and practice by employers. Recent surveys of major American corporations indicate that nearly 90 percent of the firms use some form of drug testing. Almost all firms surveyed use tests as part of the applicant process and eliminate from consideration those individuals who fail (Gray and Brown, 2002). Thus, workplace drug testing is both legal and widespread; nevertheless, the question remains, does that make it good corporate policy?

Supporting the view that workplace drug testing makes business sense are scholars Elaine Davis and Stacie Hueller. They focus attention on the growing problem of methamphetamine use both in society and in the workplace. After providing background on the drug and the threat it poses in the workplace, the authors detail appropriate steps

management can take to curb its use. Russ Belville disagrees with the practice of drug testing. Specifically, he cites results from several studies that suggest drug testing does not lead to either increases in employee productivity or to a decrease in the number of workplace accidents resulting from unsafe employee behaviors.

Beyond the right-to-privacy argument, drug-testing opponents have raised a host of concerns. Foremost among these is the accuracy of the tests themselves. Critics point out that the repercussions from inaccurate test scores can be devastating not only to the specific individuals involved, but also to the rest of the workforce. Employee confidence in management's neutrality as well as the appropriateness of testing can be severely eroded if innocent individuals are punished or guilty employees go undetected.

Testing also seems to send a message of distrust from management to employees regardless of whether such a perception is accurate. As Russ Belville notes in his selection, another important concern is the expense of testing. There is, not surprisingly, a cost/accuracy tradeoff: Cheap tests are notoriously undependable, and highly accurate tests are extremely expensive. Small firms may have little choice but to use inexpensive tests while large firms with thousands of employees might find the costs to be prohibitive. Finally, critics worry about the confidentiality and use of the information obtained from these tests. These critics fear that employers will use the information to target employees for dismissal on grounds that are completely unrelated to job performance.

Despite the valid points raised by the opposing side, supporters of drug testing policies note that, often, those individuals who have a reason to fear drug tests are the ones that are the most vocal against their use. By way of illustration of this point, consider the results of an interesting study: Human resource scholars found that students that had never used drugs were much more likely to support workplace drug testing programs than were students that had used drugs in the past (Murphy, Thornton, and Reynolds, 2002).

YES ⤶

Elaine Davis and Stacie Hueller

Strengthening the Case for Workplace Drug Testing: The Growing Problem of Methamphetamines

Introduction and Background

According to the National Institute on Drug Abuse (NIDA), an estimated 75% of illegal drug users are employed and one out of five workers in the 18–25 age bracket uses drugs at the worksite. Methamphetamine (meth) use, in particular, is causing growing alarm for employers across the U.S. In a 2004 summary report by Quest Diagnostics Inc. that analyzed all drug test results performed by the company, positive tests for meth increased 68% over a one-year period. The resulting negative workplace behaviors have caused many companies to increase drug screenings. According to Quest Diagnostics, the country's largest drug-testing company, the number of workers and applicants testing positive for meth has been rapidly increasing in the general workforce, led by southeastern states such as Georgia and Alabama. In addition, U.S. police raids of meth labs increased as much as 500%. Police nationwide rank methamphetamine the No. 1 drug they battle today: in a survey of 500 law-enforcement agencies in 45 states released in July of 2005 by the National Association of Counties, 58% said meth is their biggest drug problem. According to the World Health Organization, the drug is more abused worldwide than cocaine and heroin and is increasingly popular with workers in highly industrialized economies. Future projections indicate that meth use will surpass cocaine as the illegal stimulant of choice.

Implications for employers are great. The U.S. Department of Labor estimates annual workplace losses due to drug use of over $100 billion. Meth abuse losses are from accidents, health insurance and medical costs, absenteeism, tardiness, sick leave abuse, grievances, disability payments, lowered productivity, lowered co-worker morale, turnover, equipment damage, damage to public image, threats to public safety, worksite security and theft. According to the U.S. Center for Substance Abuse Prevention, National Clearinghouse for Alcohol and Drug Information (NCADI), drug users consume almost twice the employment benefits as nonusers, are absent 50% more often, and file more than twice as many workers' compensation claims.

The University of Arkansas Center for Business and Economic Research conducted an economic impact study in Benton County, Arkansas. According to the findings, meth use costs employers an estimated $42,000 per meth-using-worker each year. This number does not include treatment, law enforcement, or other drug related expenditures. The Center identified five categories in which meth use most notably affects the workplace. The first and largest impact is on employee absenteeism; employees who use meth are five times more likely to miss work than non-using co-workers. Second, meth users are less productive; it takes four meth users to do the job of three non-meth users. Third, employee theft is more likely. Fourth, health insurance premiums are higher with meth users in the workplace. Lastly, employers pay more in workers' compensation costs because meth users are more likely to file claims and the claim is typically more expensive.

Meth use has moved across socio-economic levels. Once exclusively the choice of low-income people, truckers, and bikers, it is now being used by overworked secretaries, stressed teachers, soldiers on long battle missions, attorneys in law firms, and workers in the medical profession, all in attempts to boost concentration, stamina, and deal with the increasing work pressure of longer hours and need for greater productivity. Furthermore, meth is different from other illegal drugs used in the workplace. It causes more damage to the employee's brain, is more likely to cause mental illness in those who are predisposed, including psychosis, and increases the propensity to aggressive behavior and violence.

Alarm over meth use has intensified in the workplace and organizations are struggling with ways to handle the significant risks of employee abuse. This has led many companies that previously did not have drug policies to implement them and those with policies to revisit and clarify them. A drug-free workplace with well thought out drug-testing procedures, supervisor and staff training, and establishment of an Employee Assistance Program are key elements for organizations to ward off meth's effects. Many companies whose drug problems cannot be remedied using drug-free policies alone have enlisted the help of local law enforcement, and some evidence shows this has helped scale back the problem in the workplace.

Methamphetamine Overview

The drug. Use of amphetamines and their methyl subgroup methamphetamines has been widely documented, as early as the first German synthesis in 1887. They were used to treat asthma, low blood pressure, weight loss, depression, and as a stimulant, but over-the-counter sales were banned in the 1970s due to increasing abuses. The more potent meth is a highly addictive synthetic drug that stimulates the central nervous system with effects similar to the drug "speed." Meth can be taken orally, smoked, injected, or snorted. Known by names such as "ice," "Tina," "glass," and "crystal," meth users experience a high immediately after taking the drug, which lasts for 8 to 14 hours. During this time, users exhibit high energy behavior and usually do not eat or sleep. Methamphetamines work by blocking the brain's ability to rid itself of the euphoria-causing neurotransmitter dopamine. Meth is very similar to cocaine, but cocaine is metabolized more quickly in the body. Thus, the high achieved from meth last hours, compared to a cocaine high which lasts only 30–45 minutes; users often identify the long high as its main attraction. The hours-long meth high is also more suitable to people punching time clocks than the 30-minute cocaine high. Workers can't be running to the bathroom every half hour to get high on cocaine; if an employee does meth in the morning, he or she is good until noon. Meth is also often referred to as the "poor man's cocaine."

Short-term effects of meth use include increased attention and decreased fatigue, increased activity, decreased appetite, euphoria or rush, increased respiration, and hyperthermia. While short-term effects are mostly physical, long-term effects are both physical and psychological and include dependence and addiction, psychosis (paranoia, hallucinations, and mood disturbances), stroke, and severe weight loss. Chronic use can result in inflammation of the heart lining, episodes of violent behavior, extreme paranoia, anxiety, confusion, insomnia, and lead poisoning. Acute lead poisoning occurs because production requires lead acetate as a reagent. Errors during production can lead to drug contamination, which inevitably can poison users.

Continued meth use can damage areas of the brain related to cognition and memory which may persist even years after discontinuation of use. Meth addiction causes long-term, sometimes irreversible behavioral, cognitive, and psychological problems that can continue throughout life. According to Paul Thompson, a brain-mapping expert at UCLA, regular meth users lose about 1% of their brain cells every year, which is comparable to the loss experienced by people with Alzheimer's disease, stroke, and epilepsy. The long-term effects of meth are unusually harsh compared with other drugs.

- **Meth crime.** Because meth is relatively easy to make, abusers eventually attempt to make it themselves. With the advent of the Internet, meth recipes and ingredients are very accessible. Labs are typically found in rural areas; close proximity to farms and distant neighbors make obtaining chemicals necessary for production easy and detection less likely. In Minnesota, the Department of Corrections (DOC) reports that compared to other criminal offenses (which tend to be concentrated in large urban areas) meth has been largely a rural phenomenon, with 72% of the meth offenders incarcerated outside metro counties. This rural overrepresentation is even greater for those imprisoned for the manufacture and sale of meth, with 87% of the offenders coming from rural Minnesota. The Minnesota DOC also reports that as of July 1, 2005, meth inmates constituted 49% of drug offenders in Minnesota prisons. Statistics from the Minnesota Department of Public Safety reveal that meth lab seizures rose more than 700 percent between 1998 and 2003. Minnesota's experience is not unlike that of neighboring states, with Iowa particularly hard hit. Missouri tops the list with more than 8,000 labs, equipment caches, and toxic dumps seized between 2002 and 2004.
- **Company culture.** Employees are being asked by their employers to do more, and meth seems to provide a good solution to busy work schedules and demanding bosses. Many occupations demand long hours of repetitive work, such as construction and manufacturing, and, as a result, these are the most common workplaces where employees use methamphetamines. However, methamphetamine is increasingly a white-collar drug as well; its use is growing in the entertainment, sales, retail, and legal professions. The California Bar Association revealed that one in four lawyers who are admitted voluntarily to drug rehabilitation are addicted to methamphetamines.

In pursuit of increased products and profits, it is easy for corporations and managers to remain unaware of methamphetamine abuse. Although the increasing us of meth consistently makes headlines, part of corporate America doesn't recognize it as a serious problem. Researchers, counselors, and government officials say employers have done little to address the erratic behavior, accidents, increased sick days, and health costs attributed to or associated with its use. According to former workers and addicts at a recreational vehicle manufacturing facility in South Bend, Indiana, their employer was aware of the prevalent meth use, but did nothing about it. According to these workers, employers benefit from allowing employees to use meth. It allows them to be more productive by working faster and avoiding accidents because of their increased state of alertness. This contradicts earlier statistics citing the heavy financial cost of meth use.

Further examples of complacent corporations are those with employees known as "maintenance users." Maintenance users are hard to recognize because "many of the drug's initial characteristics, increased concentration and the ability to work longer hours are traits valued by managers and unlikely to be seen as a problem." Initially, the drug does increase performance. In defense of corporations, some users can hide their methamphetamine use for a very long time and not have altered performance.

Prevention and Solutions: Creating a Drug Free Workplace

According to the Department of Labor and the Department of Health and Human Services Drug Free Workplace Guidelines, a drug-free workplace adheres to a program of policies and activities that discourage alcohol and drug abuse and encourages treatment, recovery, and return to work. The Substance Abuse and Mental Health Services Administration (SAMHSA), a division of the Department of Health and Human Services, advocates six components for a drug-free workplace program: assessment, policy, education and training, EAPs, and drug testing. . . .

Needs assessment involves assessing the current state of drug addiction in your workplace, determining areas needing focused attention and the means by which to evaluate any newly implemented programs. Quantifiable measures of success could include lower absenteeism, reduced turnover, and fewer accidents and workers' compensation claims.

Policy development is the foundation of a drug-free workplace. A written policy tells employees the organization's position on drug abuse and explains what will happen if the policy is violated. Consultation with an attorney is warranted to ensure compliance with state and federal law, particularly with nonregulated industries outside the scope of the Drug-Free Workplace Act of 1988, which mandates a drug-free workplace for recipients of federal contracts and grants. Because each state's laws governing drug testing in the workplace are different, establishing a well-written policy will help companies comply with state and federal laws and meet legal challenges.

Employers should determine which types of drugs they will be testing for, since different tests target specific drugs. Employers' policies should also state what will happen to employees or new hires if they test positive for drug use, such as termination or the chance to enter a company-sponsored drug treatment program. Some states mandate rehabilitation and do not allow dismissal. Employers in states without such mandates must decide what they are willing to pay for, since meth treatment can last as long as a year and is very costly. In addition, the policy should set limits on when employees are eligible for rehire after drug-related termination. A drug-free policy must be clear to employees and must be applied consistently from executives to entry-level employees. It is also important for U.S. companies that conduct business internationally to have a standard drug testing policy, because other countries are also feeling the effect of methamphetamines in the workplace. . . .

Employee education is vital and must be more than sending an e-mail to all employees outlining the policy and requiring their adherence. Essential education includes the policy, how to get assistance and referrals, how employee performance problems will be evaluated, appeal provisions, procedures of drug testing if testing is included, confidentiality, and other employee protections in the policy. Companies that proactively advertise a drug-free workplace and offer education to employees, can help deter substance abuse in the workplace. Not only does education help employees understand the effects of substance abuse on their company, it also helps employees identify the common signs of abuse. Corporations who sponsor programs for a drug-free workplace will also display goodwill towards their communities in helping the fight against methamphetamines.

Supervisor training is essential so they know the signs and symptoms of meth abuse and know company policy so they can explain it to other employees. They also need to understand their role, which is not to diagnose addiction but to rate employee performance. The quickest way to spot potential problems is to know your employee's performance. If it starts to decline, steps should be taken to find out why. Supervisors should have comprehensive detailed training about the specifics of the policy. They should learn how to assess situations appropriately and act in the event employees violate the policy. The mandatory training should be documented to prove that supervisors attended and the policy was covered in detail.

Employee Assistance Programs (EAP) offer help to employees and their families with drug and alcohol abuse problems, in addition to personal and work-related problems such as health, finances, and marital and social issues. As part of these programs it is important to address the needs of employees who are not abusers themselves but may face these problems due to a loved one's addiction. EAP enrollment has increased steadily over the past 10 years. EAP play a key role in the fight against meth abuse, providing necessary counseling to employees.

Drug testing serves as a deterrent to continued use of illicit substances and provides a means to detect and identify employees or job applicants who are using meth. Through detection and identification, employers may be able to assist employees in recognizing and admitting their abuse problems so that they may obtain necessary treatment. The American Management Association reports that 60% of employers test employees and new hires.

According to the Joseph Rowntree Foundation, the four fundamental reasons for employing drug testing in the workplace are safety, organizational efficiency, reputation risk, and employee welfare. Employees under the influence of meth at work pose a risk to themselves and others, and employers have a duty to their employees to maintain a safe working environment. Drug testing allows organizations to remain efficient by "weeding out" users who are unproductive, have high rates of absenteeism, and cause high turnover rates. Furthermore, some companies drug test solely because they are concerned about potential damage to their reputations by drug users.

Four common programs are used by companies to test current and prospective employees for drug abuse: random testing, reasonable suspicion testing, post-accident testing, and return-to-work testing. Many states discourage or restrict random testing. Employers have the right to test based on reasonable suspicion, but must have documentation supporting their suspicions. They must provide transportation to and from the testing facility to keep the suspected user from driving under the influence. Post-accident testing is common in many workplaces when human error may be the cause of accidents. A positive post-accident test may prevent employees from collecting workers' compensation or unemployment benefits.

Return-to-work testing is often a stipulation for employees after participating in a drug treatment program. Employees often sign "contracts" with their employers outlining the procedures they must follow to return to work. Elements of the contract often include ongoing rehabilitation programs, passing drug tests upon returning to work, and submitting to unannounced, repeated drug testing. The contracts also state that if the employee fails to follow any of the procedures, employment will be terminated.

While urine and blood testing are the most prevalent, they are also the easiest methods for which users can submit fraudulent specimens. Hair, sweat, and saliva cannot be tampered with as easily; however, a simple Web search for "drug testing" lists numerous Web sites touting advice and selling kits to help drug users pass any type of drug screenings. Recent arrests of some high-profile athletes and movie actors have focused attention on The Whizzinator, a product worn inside pants to conceal a tampered urine sample. As companies get more aggressive in their drug testing and enforcement, more products will be marketed to beat the tests.

Examples of companies who are successfully dealing with meth are numerous. Creative Memories, a large scrapbook manufacturer in St. Cloud, Minnesota, became aggressive with drug testing, policy enforcement, and creating a rehabilitation culture that encourages employees to seek help. The company has seen positive results. HR Director Cindy Mason-Sebastian has been so impressed with the results that she now takes one of her employees, formerly addicted to meth, with her to make team presentations to other organizations on how to control meth in the workplace. One employee tells groups that "getting caught by Creative Memories was the best thing that ever happened to me." Matson Navigation Co., a shipping company in Hawaii, added an educational film to their training lineup. It had been made specifically for the shipping industry and showed maritime workers using meth, which is particularly dangerous in that industry. The impact on employees of seeing co-workers on screen was profound.

Alternatives. Although drug testing and drug-free workplace policies are the two most common methods of handling drug use, there are other alternatives. For most companies, policies that include drug testing, education,

and training will be comprehensive enough to curtail most of employee drug use. However, some companies find they need stronger measures. A harsher measure for drug prevention is establishing an undercover operation in conjunction with local law enforcement. Such operations are being undertaken by more organizations with systemic meth problems. Although time intensive (nearly 15 months at a plant in Baltimore), undercover operations are often successful, especially when meth use is widespread or sales are occurring on site. An undercover officer applies for a position, typically a janitor or position that allows mobility throughout the workplace, and then infiltrates a group of users or dealers. After building trust and sometimes simulating drug use with the offenders, the officer collects data that eventually lead to arrests. To maintain confidentiality at the company, only corporate security and Human Resource executives are aware of the investigation until completion. At a GM plant in Baltimore, undercover agents worked for 15 months to collect evidence that led to the arrest of 24 people.

Conclusion

Methamphetamine abuse is a growing problem across the United States and has grave implications for companies, especially major employers in rural areas. Employers see their labor pool shrink as potential employees are passed over due to a positive drug test, or existing employees begin using and are fired for excessive absences, low productivity, or other costly behaviors. Employers have been forced to spend thousands of dollars to implement drug testing to maintain a safe environment. Meth abuse brings a multitude of problems to corporations, and their Human Resources departments may the frontlines of this dilemma.

Meth use may continue, but employers, communities, and law enforcement can work collaboratively at least to stop continued growth in usage. To control this increasing problem, companies need to develop a drug-free policy, educate employees, train supervisors, perform drug tests regularly, and assist employees who need help with abuse. Developing a comprehensive drug-free workplace is a huge undertaking, but the costs of not doing so are even greater. Companies cannot afford to be complacent.

ELAINE DAVIS is St. Cloud State University's G. R. Herberger Distinguished Professor of Business and has published over 40 journal articles on human resources topics.

STACIE HUELLER is an accounting instructor at Minneapolis Business College and a certified public accountant.

Russ Belville   **→ NO**

Drug Testing Does No Good

Recently, an RV manufacturing plant in Goshen, Indiana, made headlines because they had drug tested all 120 of their employees and found that nearly a third of them tested positive for some illicit substance.

What caused the company to drug test all of their employees? Was there a rash of accidents? Had productivity dropped significantly? Were there increasing incidents of absenteeism and illness? Did a supervisor notice any drug use occurring at the plant, or notice an employee obviously under the influence of drugs?

No. The only reason the plant spent the time, effort, and money to test their employees was due to a police tip that there was a drug problem at the plant. In other words, there was no reason for the company to believe they had a drug problem.

You would think that running a manufacturing plant with one third of your employees working under the influence would lead to some obvious problems. You'd be right. The problem is that a positive drug test does not indicate that a person is under the influence of drugs. It only indicates that a person has done drugs in the past.

The methods of drug testing have evolved over the past decade. Once, businesses, schools, and government could only test a person's urine. These tests were so easily defeated that the tests only detect whether you're too dumb to fool the test. But new methods of testing the blood, saliva, and hair have made fooling a drug test much harder.

With the urine test, evidence of past use of cocaine, amphetamines, and other hard drugs can be detected for 72 hours after use. Thus, a worker testing positive for these drugs could have ingested these substances on a Friday evening and be completely sober for work on Monday. Likewise, a person seeking a new job need only abstain from these substances for three days.

Ironically, the one drug with the lowest potential for abuse and harm, marijuana, remains detectable in a person's urine for 30 to 45 days. It is odd to consider that for two employees passing a urine test, one may have been abstaining from smoking pot last month while the other may have been smoking crack all of last month up until three days ago.

The newer testing does a better job of detecting drug use; some tests can indicate the use of any illicit substance for up to three months prior to the test. However, all that means is that problem drug users who wish to go straight

and re-enter the workforce have a longer wait before they can apply for work. Without gainful employment, how much harder is it for a recovering addict to stay sober?

There must be a good reason for American businesses spending up to $1 billion per year on drug testing. One of the usual reasons for this expenditure is workforce productivity.

However, when independent researchers analyzed the statistics on drug testing and productivity, they found some surprising results. According to The Committee on Drug Use in the Workplace (CDUW) assembled by the government's own National Institute of Drug Abuse, "The empirical results suggest that drug testing programs do not succeed in improving productivity. Surprisingly, companies adopting drug testing programs are found to exhibit lower levels of productivity than their counterparts that do not."

How could a company actually lose productivity by drug testing workers? CDUW suggests four possible reasons:

1. Drug testing is expensive. Tests cost around $50 per worker. A congressional committee estimated that the cost of each positive result in government testing was $77,000 because the positive rate was only 0.5%. Then there's the costs of administration, medical review, follow-up tests for positive results, treatment or discipline for the worker, or searching, hiring, and training a new worker.
2. Drug testing lowers employee morale. An overwhelming majority of workers find drug testing to be an invasion of privacy. They consider drug testing unfair when it is only detecting prior use, not current impairment. They find it profoundly unfair that these tests do not consider the abuse of alcohol, which is a more significant factor in workplace safety and productivity. The lowered morale causes employees to show less loyalty to a company, not work as hard, and good workers may seek other jobs with non-drug testing firms.
3. Drug use may actually increase productivity for some people. The CDUW found that moderate use of drugs or alcohol had either a positive effect or no effect on worker productivity. Numerous studies have found that moderate marijuana use actually increased productivity. Furthermore, marijuana users who are treating pain, cancer, AIDS, multiple sclerosis, glaucoma,

Updated version of essay originally published at www.RadicalRuss.com and seen in *The Oregon Herald,* April 20, 2005. Copyright © 2009 by Au Gratin Productions, Inc. Reprinted by permission of Russ Belville, NORML Outreach Coordinator. http://www.oregonherald.com/n/radicalruss/ 20050420_workplace-drug-testing.html arthritis, migraines, or even depression are much more productive than they would be without treatment.

4. Drug testing may lead marijuana smokers (by far the largest segment of the drug using population) to using harder drugs. Since most workplaces still choose the cheaper urine testing over the other tests, marijuana smokers may instead use harder drugs or alcohol, all of which are flushed quickly from the system. Marijuana's low addictiveness allows a casual user to remain healthy and productive, while the high addictiveness of the harder drugs make it more likely for the person to slip from casual use to the severe abuse that causes the illness, absenteeism, safety risks, and low productivity the drug tests were meant to alleviate in the first place.

Another excuse offered for drug testing is workplace safety. We don't want to have drug-impaired workers operating heavy machinery, public transportation, or any other industry where safety is of paramount concern. Of course, this reasoning falls flat when we recall that drug testing does not detect impairment. But perhaps one could assume that someone who has used drugs in the past may be more likely to use them on the job and endanger fellow employees and the public.

Unfortunately, the data do not support that assumption. Many companies use some form of impairment testing, a system that does not test for drugs, but rather hand-eye coordination, concentration, and reaction times. Those companies that have used these systems have found that severe fatigue and illness, not drug or alcohol use, are the most common causes of workplace accidents.

One added advantage of these tests is that they do reduce the level of workplace accidents. Also, workers are much more accepting of impairment tests, as they do not violate privacy and are perceived to be fairer than drug testing. Also, the impairment tests are much cheaper to administer and they actually detect the problem that drug testing does not—worker impairment.

The final nail in the coffin of any workplace drug testing argument is the fact that casual drug users (once per week or less) are just as likely to find employment and hold down a job as their non-drug using counterparts. Our drug testing regime has not kept casual drug users out of the workplace at all, and those users are not adversely affecting productivity, safety, or their own career goals.

Businesses and government aren't the only entities routinely testing for drugs. Our schools are now testing our children for evidence of illicit drug use. In a series of controversial rulings, the Supreme Court has steadily added to the number of our children being drug tested.

First they allowed students to be tested for cause; if a student was suspected of using or possessing drugs on campus, he or she could be tested. Next they ruled that students involved with extracurricular athletics could be tested randomly, citing the need for safety in potentially dangerous sports activities.

Most recently, the justices have decided that students in any extracurricular activity, from band to chess club, could be tested randomly. Justice Clarence Thomas expressed the opinion of the slim 5-4 majority stating that children involved in after-school activities voluntarily give up some of their rights to privacy.

Many of the same issues of safety and productivity are raised in support of drug testing students, and they are met with the same evidence found in the workplace. No significant differences in accidents or performance are found between schools that drug test and those that do not, nor between students who pass drug tests and those who fail.

However, with the student population there are other arguments that are stated: we need to send a message to students that drug use will not be tolerated and we need to provide disincentives for students to stop using drugs.

This argument also falls flat when confronted with the evidence. A federally funded study in 2003 of over 76,000 students in almost 900 schools found no correlation between drug testing and student drug use. Kids were just as likely to use drugs at the drug testing schools as the non-drug testing schools.

Moreover, just as workplace drug testing has the unintended consequence of lowering morale and productivity, school drug testing has its unintended consequences. Kids who might be falling in with the wrong crowd are discouraged from joining the after-school sports or clubs that would provide a healthier environment. Kids already enrolled in extra-curricular activities must sacrifice their privacy and discover that their word and their achievements are not trusted.

Of course, like workplace drug testing, there's the added expense of operating such a program, a cost that weighs heavily against chronically insufficient school budgets. The cost of one positive drug test result could have bought new instruments for the band, computers for the classroom, or equipment for the team.

Further compounding the futility of all drug testing is the fact that there is no perfect drug test. Every test gives a significant amount of false-positives and false-negatives. Many common over-the-counter medications can show up as an illicit drug. Cold tablets containing pseudoephedrine may be detected as amphetamines (speed). Cold remedies with dextromethorphan can register positive for opiates (heroin). Naproxen/ibuprofen-based pain relievers give positives for cannabis (marijuana). Nasal sprays sometimes indicate for MDMA (ecstasy).

Even some common foods can cause a failed drug test. Poppy seeds that you ingest from muffins or bagels can register as heroin. Large amounts of riboflavin (vitamin B-2) and perfectly legal (and incredibly healthy) hemp seed oil can register as marijuana.

Then of course there are many prescription drugs that can lead to a false positive. Amoxicillin, the antibiotic most prescribed for those allergic to penicillin, can show up as cocaine. Many asthma medications register as ecstasy or amphetamines. Even in the absence of these pharmaceuticals, some medical conditions can register a false positive. Kidney infection, liver disease, and diabetes can all lead to false positives for cocaine, ecstasy, opiates, or amphetamines.

Worst of all, you may fail a drug test through no fault of your own. A small fraction of people excrete larger amounts of certain enzymes in their urine that may produce a false positive. One researcher hypothesizes that the higher levels of melanin (the pigment producing cell) found in darker-skinned people may lead to positives for marijuana, because melanin and THC metabolites share a similar molecular structure.

For every false positive there is a person who has suffered the indignity of the accusation, the suspicion of family, co-workers, and friends, the threat of job loss or school suspension, and the burden of proving themselves innocent of a crime they did not commit. For every false negative there is the time, money, and effort wasted failing to discover someone who is actually using drugs.

But beyond the obvious futility and waste involved, there is one superseding argument against drug testing: it is un-American.

Our Founding Fathers laid out our basic liberties in the Bill of Rights. Drug testing violates at least two of our most sacred liberties.

Our 5th Amendment lays out two basic legal concepts: that we cannot be compelled to testify against ourselves and that we are innocent until proven guilty. Drug testing assumes that you are guilty until your body proves you to be innocent. Being compelled to provide urine, hair, saliva, or blood is a testimony against yourself. The Founders were clearly against compelling the citizenry toward self-incrimination; they had seen the results of tyrants using these techniques throughout history. It's a shame our courts haven't been as wise.

Our 4th Amendment is the basis for our right to privacy and freedom from government investigations and seizures without warrant and probable cause. Drug testing is certainly an invasion of privacy; it's hard to imagine how a stranger watching you urinate isn't an invasion of privacy. If there is no probable cause to believe you have committed a crime, there is no good reason to seize your bodily fluids.

Sadly, courts have decided that going to work or school is a voluntary activity, that you exchange some of your expectation to privacy in getting a job or an education, and that employers and educators are not the police or government. It's hard for me to imagine how work or education is truly voluntary; I guess that homelessness and ignorance are a viable choice in their minds; a choice I think would lead to more drug abuse, not less.

For many people, there is no choice but to swallow their pride, surrender their rights, face the embarrassment, risk the false positive, and take the drug test. Almost half of all employers perform some sort of drug testing. The farther down the socio-economic scale, the more likely a worker will face a pre-employment drug test. Around 36% of financial, business, and professional services test their new hires, compared to more than three-fourths of manufacturing and more than 60% of wholesale, retail, and other services. Yet rates of illicit drug use remain fairly constant among all segments of society.

The cash-strapped schools are less likely to be testing for drugs. In 2003, some 19% of schools had drug testing for cause, only 5% tested student-athletes, and only 4% tested participants in all extra-curricular activities. But for the student at these schools, unlike the worker, attendance is compulsory and there aren't many other options available. Their choices are to either avoid all extracurricular activities (which can be determining factors in college selection and future career) or suffer the same risks and indignities as their parents in the workforce.

Drug testing is but one of the many failures in our government's war on casual drug users, and its failure to achieve its stated goals is one of the easiest to prove. Fortunately, many companies are coming to recognize this fact—rates of workplace and school drug testing have declined steadily since 1990. But there remains a federal government with a strong inclination toward abrogating the rights of citizens to look "tough on crime," and many industries that stand to gain from increased drug testing.

Personally, I just try to imagine what possible argument could have convinced hemp farmers Thomas Jefferson and George Washington to pee in a cup in order to get a job.

Russ Belville has been a journalist and radio show host. He currently lives outside of Portland, Oregon.

EXPLORING THE ISSUE

Is Workplace Drug Testing a Wise Corporate Policy?

Critical Thinking and Reflection

1. Would guidelines on drug testing mitigate potential legal challenges?
2. Would different drug testing methods change employees' behavior?
3. Will a drug testing policy spur other ways for employees to use drugs?
4. Can organizations truly monitor and control employee behavior in this arena?
5. What are the ethical issues and limitations of workplace drug testing?
6. Can employees' drug use on their personal time be effectively contained?

Is There Common Ground?

One reason the issue of workplace drug testing is so contentious is that both sides can easily cite data in support of their position. Even an issue as black and white as determining whether an employee should be administered a drug test in the workplace can be difficult. While finding common ground on even basic aspects of this important management topic is difficult, there is consensus that workplace drug testing is a highly charged topic that will be debated for quite some time.

Additional Resources

Dressler, G. (2008). *Human Resource Management*, 11th ed., Pearson Prentice-Hall.

George Gray, Darrel Brown (2002). *Perspectives in Business Ethics*, 2nd ed., Laura P. Hartman, ed., New York: McGraw-Hill, p. 433.

Mathis, R.L. and Jackson, J.H. (2007). *Human Resource Management*, 11th ed., New York: Thompson South-Western.

Murphy, Thornton, and Reynolds (2002). *Perspectives in Business Ethics*, 2nd ed., Laura P. Hartman, ed., New York: McGraw-Hill Irwin.

Tunnell, K.D. (2004). "Pissing on Demand: Workplace Drug-Testing and the Rise of the Detox Industry," New York: NYU Press.

Internet References . . .

Second Federal Court in Two Weeks Halts Suspicionless Drug Testing of Teachers

American Civil Liberties Union. (2009). "Second Federal Court in Two Weeks Halts Suspicionless Drug Testing of Teachers," *American Civil Liberties Union.*

www.aclu.org/drugpolicy/testing/38356prs20090115 .html

Establishing a Drug-Free Workplace

Klein, K.E. (2007). "Establishing a Drug-Free Workplace," *BusinessWeek*, September 1.

www.businessweek.com/smallbiz/content/aug2007/ sb2007081_883800.htm

National Institute on Drug Abuse

www. NIDA.nih.gov

Reasons for Drug-Testing

U.S. Department of Health and Human Services (USHHS) and Substance Abuse and Mental Health Services Administration (SAMHSA). (2005). "Reasons for Drug-Testing," USDHH, SAMHSA Division of Workplace Programs.

http://workplace.samhsa.gov/DrugTesting/pdf/ Reasons%20for%20Drug%20Testing%20-% 20February%202005.pdf

Selected, Edited, and with Issue Framing Material by:
Kathleen J. Barnes, *East Stroudsburg University*
and
George E. Smith, *Albright College*

ISSUE

Is Social Media a Tool of Expression or Trouble for Businesses?

YES: Christopher E. Parker, from "The Rising Tide of Social Media," *The Federal Lawyer* (May 2011, pp. 14–16)

NO: David L. Barron, from "Social Media: Frontier for Employee Disputes," *Baseline* (January 2012, p. 14)

Learning Outcomes

After reading this issue, you should be able to:

- Understand the positive and negative consequences of social media in the workplace.
- Understand how social media can be used as an effective workplace tool.
- Understand why organizations might implement policies concerning social media.
- Appreciate the legal implications of social media use in the workplace.

ISSUE SUMMARY

YES: Christopher Parker argues that the prevalence of social media is quite clear and a useful tool for business. Many employers now routinely use social networking sites in advertising, marketing, communication, and decision making, and to conduct research about the backgrounds of job candidates.

NO: David Barron argues that employees are increasingly making complaints to human resources departments and management over offensive or harassing statements made online. With the rise of cyber-bullying and "textual harassment," employees must be made to understand that company policies extend into cyberspace and social media forums, and these policies must be followed.

"**S**ocial media" is a broad term that generally includes various electronic and web-based means of disseminating or sharing information. Social media includes Facebook, LinkedIn, Twitter, MySpace, YouTube, blogs, chat rooms, wikis, photo-sharing sites, and more. The use of social media is becoming not only increasingly prevalent in the daily lives of people from all walks of life, but also a greater presence in the daily business of many employers.

With employees using social media more frequently in both their private lives and at their jobs, the lines between appropriate and inappropriate uses of this technology are easily blurred. The utility of social media is not limited to the private lives of individuals as a form of self-expression. Businesses are increasingly using social media in advertising, marketing, communication, and decision making related to employment issues.

There are various social media situations that may create headaches for employers. For example, a supervisor who "friends" subordinates in a discriminatory fashion (e.g., only members of the same race or ethnic group) is running the risk of being perceived as unfair or, even worse, a racist. Managers who hack into or gain access to employees' social media sites in violation of security protections or permissions are doing so at the risk of violating employee privacy. Similarly, texts, tweets, and electronic communications can become the subject of a workplace investigation if a complaint is made. Finally, some postings on social media sites have been deemed by the National Labor Relations Board (NLRB) to be protected activity.

With new technology and communications avenues come new obligations and challenges to police and regulate those avenues in the workplace. Although each workplace is different and there is no one-size-fits-all approach to social media, it is critical for employers to recognize the risks and, at a minimum, provide some reasonable guideposts for employee conduct.

To mitigate potential issues surrounding social media, companies should strongly consider establishing clear policies regarding the following work-related issues:

- use of the company's hardware, software, and computer systems;
- harassment, including via social media;
- trade secrets of the businesses;
- need for confidentiality, non-compete, and non-solicitation;
- use of social media and electronic communication during nonworking hours; and
- social networking and the Federal Communication Commission's (FCC) requirements.

Our two authors examine the issue of social media in the workplace from different perspectives. Christopher Parker argues that the prevalence of social media is quite clear and a potentially useful tool for business. Many employers now routinely use social networking sites in advertising, marketing, communication, and decision making, and to conduct research about the backgrounds of job candidates. David Barron, on the other hand, argues that employees are increasingly making complaints to human resources departments and management over offensive or harassing statements made online. With the rise of cyber-bullying and "textual harassment," employees must be made to understand that company policies extend into cyberspace and social media forums, and these policies must be followed. Both authors do agree that social media in the workplace is in the midst of a state of growth and flux and employers should thoughtfully identify and implement guidelines needed to avoid potentially costly and damaging lawsuits.

YES ↩   Christopher E. Parker

The Rising Tide of Social Media

Guess what? The manner in which employees communicate, both within and outside the workplace, has changed. It's not just e-mails and text messaging anymore, but a broad category of platforms collectively referred to as "social media." These media are now beginning to influence the workplace—the same workplace where we spend many of our waking hours before adjourning to discuss how this time was spent with our friends, family, and connections in cyberspace (known and unknown). Increased communication brings increased opportunity to offend and breach confidences in ways that may have a significant impact on a business. As with all things new, the courts and administrative agencies are hustling to respond and develop the legal landscape involved in using social media.

"Social media" is a broad term that generally includes various electronic and web-based means of disseminating or sharing information, including Facebook®, LinkedIn®, Twitter®, MySpace®, YouTube®, blogs, chat rooms, wikis, photo-sharing sites, and more. The use of social media is becoming not only increasingly prevalent in the daily lives of people from all walks of life but also a greater presence in the daily business of many employers.

With employees using social media more frequently in both their private life and at their jobs, the lines between the uses are easily blurred. Are an employee's after-hours comments on a workplace incident subject to regulation or discipline? Where does one draw the line when the screen name or identity of the individual posting the message is unknown or difficult to decipher? Does it make a difference if the employee clearly identifies himself or herself with the message? Is there a difference in what is considered an appropriate response to a comment about a co-worker as compared to company management? Some of the answers to these potential dilemmas are seemingly obvious; others are not. Legal issues and challenges concerning social media in the workplace are currently winding their way through the court systems, and the legal outcomes are as uncertain as the myriad of fact patterns that may be presented.

The Use of Social Media

The prevalence of social media is quite clear. Facebook claims to have 500 million active users (www.facebook.com/press/info.php?statistics) and, even though the estimate is impossible to verify, there are over 70 million blogs, with almost 1.5 million being added each day. The utility of social media is not limited to the private lives of individuals. Businesses are increasingly using social media in advertising, marketing, communication, and decision-making related to employment issues.

Many employers now routinely use social-networking sites to conduct research about the backgrounds of job candidates. The information runs the gauntlet of potentially delicate information that is assembled about an applicant as part of the hiring process: alcohol use, social groups, religion, age, sexual preference, and the list goes on and on. To further complicate the issue, employees (or applicants) may feel a false sense of privacy or anonymity about the information they are sharing over the Internet, leading them to share too much information about themselves with their employer or too much information about their employer with others. The informality of social networking undoubtedly contributes to piece-meal bites (or perhaps "bytes") of information that may lead to inaccurate and unfortunate conclusions. Claims of invasion of privacy or unlawful discrimination abound.

Potential Effects of Social Media on the Relationship Between the Employer and the Employee

The terrain for potential claims relating to social media and its impact on the workplace is still in the development stage. The gut-level reaction most frequently observed from employees who learn that their employer has checked them out online is a claim of invasion of privacy. These claims, despite their naïveté when it comes to the Internet, can be (legally) frustrated by an employer's well-drafted policy advising applicants and employees of exactly how publicly accessible information may be used as part of the decision-making process in the workplace. A simple declaration that public sources of information, including social media portals, may be considered in the determination or evaluation of the applicant or employee may help dispel any expectation of privacy on the part of an employee.

Privacy claims are not the only landmine with which employers need to contend. The Stored Communications Act, 18 U.S.C. 2701, protects the privacy of stored Internet communications. Although the protections do not apply to communications "readily accessible to the general public," the main issue in the context of workplace disputes is how the employer gained access to the information. A case heard by the Fourth Circuit Court of Appeals—*Van Alstyne v. Electronic Scriptorium Ltd.*, 560 F.3d 199 (4th Cir. 2009)—involved an employer who was accused of violating the Stored Communications Act by improperly accessing an employee's personal e-mail account. The employee discovered the e-mail "break-in" only when the employer tried to present the e-mails as evidence against the employee in a sexual harassment claim she had filed. In another case, the New Jersey District Court found that employers had violated the Stored Communications Act—but not the employee's common law right to privacy—by gaining access to the employee's chat group on MySpace without the employee's authorization. The employer gained access to the chat group only after coercing another employee to provide the password. *Pietrylo v. Hillside Restaurant Group*, No. 06-5754 (FSH), 2009 WL 3128420 (D.N.J. Sept. 25, 2009). In both cases, the employer was found to have overstepped legal boundaries by gaining access to information that had been subject to security efforts without proper permission.

The Fair Credit Reporting Act requires the consent of an applicant or an employee before an employer can ask a "consumer reporting agency" or another third party to conduct a background check and produce a "consumer report" or other written report of its findings. Even though employers may use consumer reports that contain information from social-networking sites, they must disclose to their employees that such information was the basis for any adverse actions that may have been taken. The Fair Credit Reporting Act does *not* prevent employers from reviewing social-networking sites themselves; however, the act leaves a loophole for employers to do background checks.

The Electronic Communications Privacy Act makes it unlawful to listen to or observe the contents of a private communication without the permission of at least one party to the communication. In addition, the act prohibits parties from intentional interception, access, disclosure, or use of another party's electronic communications. This law has been interpreted to include e-mail communications and may provide some protections for employees' privacy. There are, however, exceptions that the employer may find helpful.

Potential Discrimination Claims Against the Employer

Even though the possibility of an unfiltered look at a job candidate may be tempting, the employer faces serious risks when using the Internet to investigate employees and job applicants. These risks include the potential of discovering information that the employer is not allowed to ask in person or use in the selection or disciplinary process. Using Facebook as an example, many people have listed information for their personal profile that reveals their race, political affiliation, age, sexual orientation, national origin, and more. Status updates, tweets, and blogs may also reveal a person's potential disabilities, past medical conditions, or the medical conditions of family members.

Potential Implications of Employees' Postings and Social Media Content on the Employer

Employers must beware of confidential information to which employees have access through their jobs becoming public knowledge through employees' use of social media, even in the apparent context of the employee's role as a private individual. Not only can employees leak confidential information about their companies, they may knowingly or unknowingly publish confidential information about their employers' clients or business associates. For example, if an employee works for a health care provider and later "tweets" about a patient at work, that employee could be disseminating information protected by the Health Insurance Portability and Accountability Act (HIPAA) creating serious liabilities for the employer. Other communications by employees may implicate federal copyright or trademark laws. Although many of these types of communications would be unexpected and subject to monitoring if they occurred within the workplace, the user's theoretical anonymity when using the Internet and social media outlets can lead to unexpected consequences.

Guidelines issued by the Federal Trade Commission regarding endorsements and testimonials in advertising may have serious implications for an employee's online activity. The guidelines require all endorsers, including employees, to disclose "material connections" between the endorser and the product or company about which they comment. Because material connections include employment relationships, if a company's employee enjoys contributing to websites dedicated to product reviews, for example, and discusses a product produced by his or her employer, the employee may be considered an endorser and must then abide by the Federal Trade Commission's guidelines. An employer can be held accountable for an employee's actions every time the employee tweets or changes his or her Facebook status regarding a new product at work. A company may then face liability for any unsubstantiated or false claims made by employees, even if they are not authorized to make such comments.

This example further highlights the importance of having thoughtful technology use and confidentiality policies in place for both on-duty and off-duty use.

Training employees about the potential consequences of their actions and the way to best use—or not to use—social media, even on their own time, may be just as important as properly disseminating a written policy. However, policies governing the use of a company's technology, which include off-duty activities, cannot simply ban social media use in its entirety. As discussed below, overbroad policies dealing with use of technology can create liabilities of their own for employers.

Protected Speech and Activity

When dealing with an employee who is using social media in a way the employer does not like or with which the employer does not want to be associated, many employers would simply prefer to terminate the employee who is using social media in that way. Although termination would often seem to be the ideal resolution for the employer in situations like this, employers must be careful when making this decision. Even though the First Amendment does not protect an employee of a private employer from termination or adverse action because of the content of online postings, the content of the postings and information may invoke other kinds of protection, such as Title VII of the Civil Rights Act of 1964. Depending on the content of the online communication, whistle-blower protections under state and federal laws may also be triggered.

Recently, the National Labor Relations Board (NLRB) issued a complaint after an employee was fired from American Medical Response of Connecticut for posting negative comments about her supervisor on her Facebook page. The employer had a policy prohibiting employees from making disparaging remarks about the company or supervisors and from discussing the company "in any way" over the Internet, including via social networks, without advance permission. The NLRB argued that policies restricting an employee's right to criticize working conditions, including the right to publish such criticisms to co-workers, violates the National Labor Relations Act. Faced with further litigation with the NLRB, the case was settled in early February 2011, with the employer agreeing to refrain from limiting the rights of its employees to communicate on work-related issues away from the workplace.

What Should an Employer Do?

The legal arena surrounding the use of social media in the workplace is in the midst of what may be a lengthy evolution. Employers have to balance their own needs to protect their assets against the legal rights of their employees.

Companies should strongly consider establishing clear policies regarding several work-related issues:

- use of the company's hardware, software, and computer systems;
- harassment, including via social media;
- trade secrets of the business;
- need for confidentiality, non-compete, and non-solicitation;
- use of social media and electronic communication during nonworking hours; and
- social networking and the Federal Communication Commission's requirements.

Employers' policies should prohibit employees from discussing, including through social media, company information that is confidential or proprietary; clients', partners', vendors', and suppliers' information that is confidential or proprietary; and information that has been embargoed, such as product launch dates or release dates; and pending organizations. At the same time, employers need to recognize that across-the-board restrictions on communications are subject to challenge. Policies related to use of technology and electronic communication should cover use of the company's intellectual property; sexual references; obscenity; reference to illegal drugs; disparagement of any race, religion, gender, age, sexual orientation, disability, or national origin; and the disparagement of the company's or competitors' products, services, executive leadership, employees, strategy, and business prospects.

One cautionary note must be made: The information provided in this column is intended to apply primarily to employment in the private sector. Employers in the public sector face additional limitations on the potential restraints that can be imposed based on the Constitution. As with all such issues, employment policies and decisions related to new issues raised by the widespread use of social media should be discussed with legal counsel, because the landscape is in a state of growth and rapid change.

CHRISTOPHER E. PARKER is a member in the Atlanta, Georgia office of Miller & Martin PILC and serves as the vice-chair for the firm's labor and employment law practice. He is a former chair of the FBA Labor and Employment Law Section and a past president of the Atlanta Chapter of the FBA. Parker received BS and JD degrees from the Ohio State University.

David L. Barron

 **NO**

Social Media: Frontier for Employee Disputes

Ten years ago, employers struggled to adapt their policies to the Internet and email. Today, the new frontier is social media.

With new technology and communication avenues come new obligations to police and regulate those same avenues in the workplace. Although each workplace is different and there is no one-size-fits-all approach to social media, it is critical for employers to recognize the risks and, at a minimum, provide some reasonable guideposts for employee conduct.

Textual Harassment

No employer wants to be the "Facebook police," but employees are increasingly making complaints to human resources departments and management over offensive or harassing statements made online. With the rise of cyberbullying and "textual harassment," employees must be made to understand that company policies extend into cyberspace and social media forums, and these policies must be followed.

If an employee makes a complaint about online activity, it should be investigated just like any other complaint of harassment or discrimination. That said, an investigation can often be hampered by the lack of access to social media sites.

Suggestions to work around this problem include requesting that witnesses provide screen shots or copies of offending text messages. The employer can also request that an accused employee provide access to his or her Facebook page for the limited purpose of verifying whether the allegations are true. If such access is refused, consider taking statements from employees who may have seen the relevant statements made on a social media site.

Facebook Perils

It has become clear that real liability issues are associated with managers "friending" subordinates. It's unlawful for a manager to inquire in the workplace about certain personal information that's displayed on social media sites. For example, a manager who discovers on Facebook that an employee has a serious illness may later be accused of unlawful discrimination.

In addition, a supervisor who friends subordinates in a discriminatory fashion (e.g., only members of the same race or ethnic group) is running the risk of being perceived as unfair or, even worse, a racist. Since friending some supervised employees but not others is a risky proposition that could lead to hurt feelings or lawsuits, many companies have advised supervisors to refrain from friending workers who are in a direct line of supervision.

Employee Privacy

It should go without saying that management must never hack into or gain access to employees' social media sites in violation of security protections or permissions. If a site is viewable by the public, however, an employee has no right to privacy, and no permission is required.

Gray areas arise where a worker who has access to another worker's site brings information to management without the other employee's permission. Most courts agree that employees allow access to their Facebook page at their own peril. If someone shares that information with an employer, that is a risk assumed by the employee who granted the access. Simply put, an employer need not ignore evidence of misconduct because it comes through an indirect source.

Similarly, texts, tweets and electronic communications can become the subject of a workplace investigation if a complaint is made. One thing to keep in mind is that an employer can lawfully search employee-owned cell phones only if the employer provides notice in its policies that employees have no expectation of privacy for information stored on these devices. As long as such notice is provided, an employer has the right to search a cell phone, just as it would to search a vehicle or purse if a violation of policy is suspected.

Other Headaches

There are a number of emerging legal issues that have created headaches for employers. First, some postings on social media sites have been deemed by the National Labor Relations Board to be protected activity.

Firing an employee over an online social media complaint about wages, a "jerk" boss or employment conditions, for example, can lead to a lawsuit. Some states also have laws protecting employees from discipline for lawful offduty conduct. Thus far, it is unclear whether these laws will apply to social media activity.

Also, employers should exercise caution in setting up their own social media pages and allowing nonexempt employees to monitor and update those pages. Blogging, tweeting or posting company-related information online is considered work, and hourly employees must be compensated for this time, including any applicable overtime.

In summary, having a social media policy is no longer relevant only for high-tech companies and large corpora-tions. Employers of all sizes and industries are facing substantial legal risks, and they should review this emerging area to identify what guidelines need to be implemented to avoid lawsuits.

DAVID L. BARRON is a labor and employment attorney at Cozen O'Connor's Houston office.

EXPLORING THE ISSUE

Is Social Media a Tool of Expression or Trouble for Businesses?

Critical Thinking and Reflection

1. Would workplace guidelines on social media mitigate potential legal issues for an employer?
2. Would workplace guidelines on social media affect employee behavior?
3. Will a social media control policy spur attempts to find other ways to obtain information on co-workers and colleagues?
4. Should employers be allowed to prevent employee expression via social media?

Is There Common Ground?

There appears to be a consensus that social media in the workplace is in the midst of a state of growth, evolution, and rapid change. Many employers now routinely use social networking sites in advertising, marketing, communication, and decision making, and to conduct research about the backgrounds of job candidates. Employees are also increasingly making complaints to human resources departments and management over offensive or harassing statements made online. Both authors agree that social media in the workplace are in the midst of a state of growth and rapid change and that organizations should thoughtfully identify and develop guidelines to potentially head off and avoid potential lawsuits and liability.

Additional Resources

Farley, A. (2011). "Building a Social Media Policy," *ABA Bank Marketing*, October, pp. 18–22.

McCarthy, M.P. and Krishna, S. (2011). "Social Media: Time for a Governance Framework," *NACD Directorship*, September, p. 88.

Segal, J. (2012). "Widening Web of Social Media," *HR Magazine*, June, pp. 117–120.

Internet References . . .

Tool or Trouble?

Bednar, J. (2011). "Tool or Trouble?" December 19, pp. 33–36.

http://businesswest.com/

Why You Need a Social Media Policy

Henricks, M. (2011). "Why You Need a Social Media Policy," January 6.

www.entrepreneur.com/article/217813

820,000 Reasons to Have a Social Media Policy

Hyman, J. (2012). "820,000 Reasons to Have a Social Media Policy."

www.workforce.com/article/20120719/ BLOGS07/120719931/820-000-reasons-to- have-a-social-media-policy

UNIT 3

UNIT

Strategic Management

*M*ost investors and executives do their utmost to help their firms grow and to increase profits. It seems obvious: Successful firms are growing firms. So why would highly knowledgeable and respected business scholars and observers argue that growth is not necessary for a firm to be successful? Speaking of growth, consider the issue of mergers and acquisitions. Would you be surprised to learn that, frequently, firms that engage in these behaviors actually experience a loss in corporate value? So why are mergers and acquisitions (M&As) so popular? With continued pressure on businesses for profitability, outsourcing and reshoring/insourcing are attractive options for businesses. For answers to these and other emotionally charged questions, dive into the four topics comprising this unit.

Selected, Edited, and with Issue Framing Material by:
Kathleen J. Barnes, *East Stroudsburg University*
and
George E. Smith, *Albright College*

ISSUE

Is Growth Always an Inherent Corporate Value?

YES: **Clayton M. Christensen** and **Michael E. Raynor,** from *The Innovator's Solution* (Harvard Business School Press, 2003)

NO: **Jim Mackey** and **Liisa Välikangas,** from "The Myth of Unbounded Growth," *MIT Sloan Management Review* (Winter 2004)

Learning Outcomes

After reading this issue you should be able to:

- Understand the positive and negative consequences of growth strategy on American corporations.
- Understand how growth can be used as an effective corporate strategy.
- Understand what policies might be implemented to support an effective growth corporate strategy.
- Appreciate the practical implications of corporate growth strategy use in the workplace.

ISSUE SUMMARY

YES: Clayton M. Christensen and Michael E. Raynor argue that firms are subject to pressures to continually grow from sources both inside and outside of the organization.

NO: Business scholars Jim Mackey and Liisa Välikangas cite many interesting statistics to support the view that lasting growth is elusive and unrealistic and, thus, not necessary to define a firm as successful.

Open any business periodical today and you might expect to see headlines like these from recent editions of the *Wall Street Journal*:

- "Caterpillar Gets Bugs Out of Old Equipment; Growing Remanufacturing Division Is Central to Earnings-Stabilization Plan" (July 5, 2006, p. A.16)
- "Changing the Light Bulb; No Joke: LED Technology Fuels Fast Growth in the Once-Staid Industry" (June 8, 2006, p. B.1)
- "Churchill Downs Searches for Growth" (May 24, 2006, p. B.3A)
- "To Clorox CEO, U.S. Is Bright Spot for Growth" (June 26, 2012, http://online.wsj.com/article/SB100014 240527023044586045774907617561 57228.html)

What do these headlines have in common? If you noticed each assumes that corporate growth is a good and necessary strategy, kudos to you. Without a doubt, growth can be beneficial for both corporations and society at large. Indeed, Caterpillar found that growth in remanufacturing

was beneficial even when the economy was down, and the lighting industry is brightening up because of growth in the light-emitting diodes (LED) market.

On the other hand, it is also true that sustained growth is a difficult and elusive goal. For instance, consider these *Wall Street Journal* headlines:

- "Cadbury Schwepps PLC: Margin-Growth Target Stifled by Rising Energy Costs" (June 8, 2006, p. n/a)
- "Telenor's Messy Excursion in Russia Shows Pitfalls of Hunting for Growth" (July 7, 2006, p. C.1)

Both of these selections detail problems resulting from strategic decisions driven by the need for growth. In fact, many business observers suggest that such predicaments seem to be the rule rather than the exception for companies attempting a growth strategy. This leaves us with the current debate where we ask—Must firms constantly grow to be considered successful?

Clayton M. Christensen and Michael E. Raynor argue that pressures to meet this "growth imperative" come from both within and without the organization. Externally, the perpetuation of this imperative is largely fueled by shareholders who expect to see value created through growth. These expectations for growth are built into the stock market's valuation of a company's stock. Indeed, if a firm fails to meet its expectations for growth—typically reflected in lower than anticipated earnings—the company will take a beating in the stock market. Moreover, if a company does meet its expectations for growth, it is often rewarded with even higher growth expectations for the future.

Although a company's main demand for growth may be from its shareholders, this is certainly not the only source of pressure the company needs to recognize. Typically, in a growing company, employees will expect that they will have opportunities to move up and gain better positions for themselves. In this manner, employees also demand growth. Thus, it is not surprising that most top-level executives consider growth as the dominant, underlying goal of the organization.

But what about the other side of the debate? Isn't it possible that the continuous, unbounded growth companies and investors hope for is really just a "myth" for most firms? This is the claim of the selection by Jim Mackey and Liisa Välikangas. They cite many interesting statistics to support the view that lasting growth is elusive and unrealistic. Further, they argue, such growth is not only elusive, but can be very costly, particularly if the firm is currently not in a growth phase. To illustrate their point, Mackey and Välikangas state, "When stalled companies make massive investments in an attempt to return to double-digit growth, it seems analogous to spending life savings on a lottery ticket" (p. 90). Furthermore, although the company may experience resistance from investors and other stakeholders interested in corporate growth, there are other nongrowth options available that firms should consider as legitimate, realistic alternative business behaviors. Nevertheless, Mackey and Välikangas concede that the attitude in today's environment is toward propagating growth and warn investors, CEOs, and employees alike to be wary of potential pitfalls that may accompany a growth strategy. Their advice is wise, and we recommend it to you next time you pick up a business journal, read a headline about a company failing to meet its growth expectations, and conclude that the firm is failing.

Jim Mackey and
Liisa Välikangas

➡ **NO**

The Myth of Unbounded Growth

Growth is not perpetual and its continued pursuit can be a death knell, especially for large, mature companies.

Imagine the CEO of a growth company telling its shareholders, "Henceforth we will be pursuing no risky new research, acquisitions or new business ventures. We will concentrate on being stewards of our existing business and will simply pay all profits as dividends." This is an unlikely scenario, to say the least. The reality is that markets expect growth. There is a deeply held assumption that neither a company nor its management is viable unless it is able to grow. Growth gives investors a feeling that management is doing its job. Growth is typically perceived as a proactive (rather than a defensive) strategy. Or maybe, as the Red Queen says in Lewis Carroll's *Through the Looking Glass,* "Here it takes all the running you can do to keep in the same place. If you want to get somewhere else, you must run at least twice as fast as that!"

"The only way managers can deliver a return to shareholders that exceeds the market average," Clayton Christensen and Michael Raynor wrote in *The Innovator's Solution,* "is to grow *faster* than shareholders expect," however irrational that may be.[1] Indeed, a recent CSFB HOLT study found that 50% of the valuation of the 20 most valuable companies was based on expected cash flows from future investments.[2] Nevertheless, it has become almost a national sport to suggest that there is a set of visionary, great or otherwise noteworthy companies that can grow indefinitely—only to have those companies, almost invariably, fall from grace shortly thereafter. "The golden company that continually performs better than the markets has never existed. It is a myth," wrote Richard Foster and Sarah Kaplan in *Creative Destruction.*[3] Indeed, of the companies on the original *Forbes* 100 list in 1917, only 18 remained in the top 100 by 1987 and 61 had ceased to exist. Of these highly respected survivors, Foster and Kaplan point to only two companies—General Electric Co. and Eastman Kodak Co.—which outperformed the 7.5% average return on the S&P 500 during this 70-year period, and they beat the average by only 0.3%.

The truth is, companies are successful until they are not.[4] The consistent pattern of stalled or halted growth among the largest U.S. corporations over the last 50 years is eye-opening. Research by the Corporate Strategy Board (CSB) in 1998[5] suggested that there is a "cloud layer" at which growth starts to stall, beginning in the $30 billion range (CPI-adjusted 1996 dollars).[6] Of the 172 companies that have made it to the *Fortune* 50 from 1954 to 1995,[7] only 5% were able to sustain a growth rate above the GDP (and half of those have stalled since the study).[8] In addition, once stalled, no U.S. company larger than $15 billion has been able to restart growth that exceeded that of the GDP. In *How To Grow When the Markets Don't,*[9] Adrian Slywotzky, Richard Wise and Karl Weber call this "the Great Divide, moving from a past of strong growth . . . into a future of low or no growth." The authors say that many companies did so without fully recognizing the change, thereby exacerbating the problem, sometimes fatally. Companies often see a stall as a temporary blip, soon to be overcome with investment and execution of their growth strategy, but in their book *Permanently Failing Organizations,*[10] Marshall Meyer and Lynn Zucker write that many of these companies are merely lingering in a state of decay before they ultimately fail.

As companies increase in size, the variability in growth rate decreases (that is, growth slows down).[11] The classical model of growth—assuming a log-normal distribution of company sizes in a population of companies[12]—fails to explain this phenomenon.[13] Strictly from a numerical perspective, sustaining rapid growth is a massive challenge for a *Fortune* 50 company. For example, to sustain its current 17% growth rate, Merck & Co. Inc. (the 17th largest with revenue of $52 billion) must add $9 billion in revenue this year, $11 billion next year and so on. In five years, Merck's revenues would need to be $114 billion—more than double its current number.

The Cost of the Growth Chase

For a large company, not only are the odds of consistently achieving this kind of growth quite long, but the pursuit of that growth can also be very costly. To pursue billion dollar growth targets quickly, executives feel they must invest billions in the quest.[14] The result is falling profitability often accompanied by huge restructuring charges. Whereas the market cap decline may begin before or after the stall, the eventual fall is dramatic. The CSB study found that 28% of stalled firms lost over 75% of market cap relative to the Dow Jones Industrial Average (DJIA), and 69% lost at least 50%; the average valuation fell by 61%.[15] When this happens, a once great company begins to search for its lost formula, often until the very viability of the company is eventually questioned, as was the case for Sears, Roebuck and Co., IBM Corp., Digital Equipment

Corp., Xerox Corp., Motorola Inc., Lucent Technologies and many others. Employees suffer as well. In 53% of the stalls, head count was reduced by over 20%, and morale declined noticeably.

Kodak, as noted, outperformed the S&P 500 for 70 years—from 1917 to 1987—but today it is the poster child for stalled companies. Its revenue stopped growing faster than the GDP in 1980 when it was No. 29 on the *Fortune* 50 list. Its recent *nominal* market cap is 41% below its 1980 level. When benchmarked against the 10-fold increase in the DJIA since 1980, Kodak's relative market cap has fallen a whopping 94%. Cutting more than 70% of its semiannual dividend, Kodak now seeks to migrate from film[16] and plans to invest $3 billion in digital photography, in which it has been investing since 1972. Kodak also recently announced its $250 million acquisition of Scitex Corp.'s Digital Printing to bolster its entry into the inkjet printer market. Yet film still accounts for about 50% of Kodak's profits.[17] Thus the odds that Kodak can reignite growth are not judged to be good. Kodak's long-term debt is rated triple-B-minus, one notch above speculative, by Standard & Poor's. In an unprecedented revolt, "investors have lost confidence" in Kodak's growth investments and now seek "radically different strategies to maximize shareholder value."[18]

Given the dismal track record that stalled growth companies have when attempting to return to double-digit internal growth, the massive (and often belated) investments they make in that regard seem analogous to spending the company's life savings on a lottery ticket. The reality for many shareholders is that unless the company is sold while still healthy, the promised payoff never comes, due to low valuation in the sale of nonperforming assets, restructuring charge write-offs, goodwill depreciation and pension- or product-related liabilities. The hard-earned equity evaporates, and assets are sold at near book value in fire sales or in bankruptcy to creditors. *Fortune* 50 bankruptcies are relatively rare,[19] but Enron, WorldCom, PG&E, United AirLines, Kmart, Bethlehem Steel and LTV are recent examples. Others like Lucent, Xerox, Fleming, AMR and Goodyear hover on the brink. Still others are sold for a fraction of their earlier value or at a slight premium to a long-stagnant stock price—for example, Digital, Compaq, Beatrice Foods, Firestone, Uniroyal, American Motors, Armour Food, Gulf Oil, RCA and Union Carbide.

What's a CEO To Do?

It is clear that many strong forces—ranging from natural limitations and managerial complexity to stakeholder harmony and antitrust concerns—make continuous growth very difficult for already-large companies. Rather than continue to seek growth at any cost, the solution is to seek alternatives to the dilemma—in a sense, to fool the natural limits to growth that large companies face. There are three logical alternatives: Break up the company, create a new corporate form, or make a graceful growth-to-value transition.

Breaking up the company IBM spun off Lexmark, HP gave birth to Agilent, AT&T divested itself of Lucent, GM launched Delco, Sears separated from Allstate, and 3M broke off Imation. Such spinoffs generally enhance stockholder value both at the time of the announcement and by about 20% in the subsequent 18 months.[20] J.P. Morgan discovered that smaller breakups performed better.[21] It is important, though, that the post-breakup units be small enough (less than $10 billion) to have significant room for growth. Although not all breakups create successful new companies, they do help bring focus to the parent company. J.P. Morgan also found that "the remaining, slimmer parent does materially better than the market following separation."[22]

Nevertheless there is significant resistance to divestiture because it seems "like a tacit admission of failure, evidence of poor management, or in some corporate cultures even . . . treason."[23] The myth of unbounded growth further perpetuates resistance to this seemingly reasonable solution. Indeed, "of the 50 largest divestitures . . . more than three-quarters were completed under pressure, most only after long delays when problems became so obvious that action was unavoidable."[24]

Experimenting with a new corporate form Whereas attempts at internal independence, including tracking stocks and partial spinoffs, may prove not to offer lasting solutions, evolving new organizational forms and management practices over time can afford a company greater scale and scope.[25] Just as the divisional organization (supported by innovations including the telephone and railroads) extended the management capability beyond that of the functional organization in the early 1900s, perhaps an even more decentralized organization (supported by innovations including the Internet and e-commerce) will enable the next growth leap. Also, business models that foster competition between different parts of the organization (for example, GM's Chevrolet vs. Pontiac or HP's Inkjet vs. Laserjet) may offer growth advantages. In addition, internal markets for ideas and talent (such as Shell's GameChanger innovation program) that are open to anyone within the organization with a worthwhile contribution to make may provide new routes to growth.[26]

Take Visa, for example, with an estimated 2003 sales volume of $2.7 trillion. It is technically not a company nor does it appear in the *Fortune* rankings. Yet it has a powerful brand, a strategy for growth, and an integrated business system composed of hundreds of card-issuing financial institutions battling for customers.[27] Similarly, electronics firms today outsource manufacturing, integrate supplier design, engage in software alliances, participate in standards' bodies and contribute to and benefit from open-source movements.[28] They are integrated ecosystems that compete for ideas, innovation, people and investment. Here the corporation may no longer be the relevant unit of competitive analysis; the new corporate form is a boundaryless organization.

Making a transition from growth to value Using reduced investment to grow earnings can help a company make a graceful transition from a high P/E growth stock to a moderate P/E value stock. Market cap may decline (relative to the DJIA), but this strategy can help avoid the dramatic poststall crash or near bankruptcy that can occur when former growth companies begin delivering neither growth nor profit and are assessed at breakup value. Specific tactics may include increasing earnings stability, balance-sheet strengthening, boosting dividend payout, cost and asset reduction, reductions in marketing and R&D, portfolio adjustments (especially divestitures and spinoffs), and stock repurchase (only if P/E is in single digits). Most companies that survive their growth stall eventually make this transition. It is often delayed, however, due to persistent attempts to recapture growth (for example, IBM in the mid-1980s and early 1990s), or forced after being acquired by a value-oriented firm (for example, Allied Signal's acquisition of Honeywell in 1999). GE, however, shifted focus from growth to profit in the 1950s and transitioned without a crisis. Microsoft's recent decision to begin paying dividends may imply an early recognition of the growth-to-value transition.

This strategy—which requires a shift in corporate culture and investor expectations—may be unpopular because it marks a radical departure from the past. It is thus difficult for any leader to achieve unless precipitated by a crisis. Even when there is a perceived crisis, preliminary case studies indicate that such a transition will take from five to eight years.[29] Denial and short-term incentives create additional barriers because management tends to want to believe they can win the lottery to recapture unbounded growth.

Facing the Liability of Corporate Size

In evaluating their options, the CEO and the board should consider where their company is in its life cycle—growth, stall or poststall. Growth stalls can be anticipated by assessing the natural limits of the company's dominant growth strategy and its pattern of financial performance. Senior managers and board members also have to realistically assess their company's capabilities in innovation and new business creation in order to decide whether their capital and talent would be better spent on core business development than on an increasingly fruitless pursuit of mega-growth. These are not easy decisions to make, especially given the almost unquestioned culture of growth that continues to exist in today's environment. The biggest challenge and first step toward making those decisions, however, is to overcome denial and acknowledge that unbounded growth is indeed a myth.

References

1. C.M. Christensen and M. Raynor, "The Innovator's Solution: Creating and Sustaining Successful Growth" (Boston: Harvard Business School Press, 2003).

2. M.J. Mauboussin and K. Bartholdson, "The Pyramid of Numbers," The Consilient Observer (Credit Suisse First Boston Newsletter) 2, no. 17 (Sept. 23, 2003): 5. See also Christensen and Raynor, "The Innovator's Solution," 22, note 7, regarding methodology.

3. S. Kaplan and R. Foster, "Creative Destruction: Why Companies That Are Built To Last Underperform the Market—and How To Successfully Transform Them" (New York: Doubleday/Currency, 2001).

4. G. Hamel and L. Välikangas, "The Quest for Resilience," Harvard Business Review 81 (September 2003): 52–63. See also Kaplan and Foster, "Creative Destruction," 11, 14. Kaplan and Foster note that the turnover rate among Fortune 500 companies has accelerated—reaching nearly 10% in 1998—implying that no more than one-third of today's major corporations will survive in an economically important way over the next 25 years. Further, according to unpublished research done by the Woodside Institute in 2003, the number of S&P 500 companies that have suffered a five-year earnings decline has more than doubled in the last 30 years, suggesting a severe lack of strategic resilience.

5. Corporate Strategy Board, "Stall Points: Barriers to Growth for the Large Corporate Enterprise" (Washington, D.C.: Corporate Executive Board, 1998).

6. The stall range had increased over time slightly faster than inflation (pp. 20–21).

7. This is also true for service companies of equivalent scale.

8. See Corporate Strategy Board, "Stall Points," 13. Wal-Mart, American International Group, Target, and United Parcel Service are still growing; 3M, Hewlett-Packard, PepsiCo and Procter & Gamble now appear to have stalled. In addition, this study by the Corporate Strategy Board cites six companies that stalled but then restarted growth to 1% over GDP. Of those, Chase, Coca-Cola, Fleming and Motorola appear to have stalled again. Only Johnson & Johnson and Merck are still growing. Thus only six out of 172 Fortune 50 (3.5%) are still growing relative to the economy.

9. A.J. Slywotzky, R. Wise and K. Weber, "How To Grow When the Markets Don't" (New York: Warner Books, 2003), 14–15.

10. M.W. Meyer and L.G. Zucker, "Permanently Failing Organizations" (Thousand Oaks, California: Sage Publications, 1989).

11. M.H.R. Stanley, L.A.N. Amaral, S.V. Buldyrev, S. Havlin, H. Leschhorn, P. Maass, M.A. Salinger and H.E. Stanley, "Scaling Behaviour in the Growth of Companies," Nature 379 (Feb. 29, 1996): 804–806.

12. R. Gibrat, "Les Inégalités Economiques" (Paris: Sirey, 1933).

13. G. Carroll and M. Hannan, "The Demography of Corporations and Industries" (Princeton, New Jersey: Princeton University Press, 1999). See also Mauboussin and Bartholdson, "The Pyramid of Numbers," which describes mathematical distributions called power laws and their abundance in nature and social systems.

14. Christensen and Raynor, "The Innovator's Solution," 236–243. In this passage, including the section titled

"The Death Spiral From Inadequate Growth," the authors state that large targets and large investments paradoxically are "likely to condemn innovators to a death march" and that "capital becomes a poison for growth ventures."

15. Market cap changes are measured relative to the Dow Jones Industrial Average from peak to trough within 10 years of stall.

16. J. Bandler, "Kodak Cuts Dividend by 72% To Finance Digital Shift," Wall Street Journal Europe, Sept. 26, 2003, A4.

17. S. London, "Kodak Aims To Become a Model of Reinvention," Financial Times, Sept. 27, 2003, 8.

18. W.C. Symonds, "Commentary: The Kodak Revolt Is Short-Sighted," BusinessWeek, Nov. 3, 2003, 38.

19. Kaplan and Foster, "Creative Destruction," 3. However, of the 20 largest U.S. bankruptcies in the past two decades, 10 occurred in the last two years; see Hamel and Välikangas, "The Quest for Resilience."

20. D. Sadtler, A. Campbell and R. Koch, "Breakup! How Companies Use Spin-Offs To Gain Focus and Grow Strong" (New York: Free Press, 1997), 4, 27–31.

21. Ibid., p. 30.

22. J.P. Morgan, "J.P. Morgan's Spinoff Study" (New York: J.P. Morgan, June 6, 1995, updated August 20, 1997 and July 23, 1999); P.A. Gaughan, "Mergers, Acquisitions and Corporate Restructurings," 3rd ed. (New York: John Wiley & Sons, 1997), 414–417; G.L. Hite and J.E. Owers, "Security Price Reactions Around Corporate Spin-Off Announcements," Journal of Financial Economics 12, no. 4 (1983): 409–436; K. Schipper and A. Smith, "Effects of Recontracting on Shareholder Wealth: The Case of Voluntary Spin-Offs," Journal of Financial Economics 12, no. 4 (1983): 437–467; and J.A. Miles and J.D. Rosenfeld, "The Effect of Voluntary Spin-Off Announcements on Shareholder Wealth," Journal of Finance 38, no. 5 (1983): 1597–1606. Each study documents a mean abnormal spin-off announcement return of approximately 3%.

23. L. Dranikoff, T. Koller and A. Schneider, "Divesting Proactively," McKinsey on Finance, summer 2002, 1, www.corporatefinance.mckinsey.com_downloads/knowledge/mof/2002_no4/divesting.pdf.

24. Ibid. Also see L. Dranikoff, T. Koller and A. Schneider, "Divestiture: Strategy's Missing Link," Harvard Business Review 80 (May 2002): 74–83; and D.J. Ravenscraft and F.M. Scherer, "Mergers, Sell-Offs and Economic Efficiency" (Washington, D.C.: Brookings Institution Press, 1987), 167.

25. A.D. Chandler, Jr., and T. Hikino, "Scale and Scope: The Dynamics of Industrial Capitalism" (Cambridge, Massachusetts: Belknap Press, 1990).

26. For a description of the GameChanger program, see G. Hamel, "Bringing Silicon Valley Inside," Harvard Business Review 77 (September-October 1999): 70–84.

27. M.M. Waldrop, "The Trillion Dollar Vision of Dee Hock," Fast Company, October 1996, 75; and D.W. Hock, "Birth of the Chaordic Age" (San Francisco: Berrett-Koehler, 2000).

28. G. von Krogh, "Open-Source Software Development," MIT Sloan Management Review 44, no. 3 (spring 2003): 14–18.

29. Refers to ongoing studies of Fortune 50 companies conducted by the Billion Dollar Growth Network. The work goes beyond the 50 growth-stall case studies developed jointly with the Corporate Strategy Board in 1997–1998, focusing instead on what happened after the stall—how the companies managed their transition to a lower growth value model. The studies generally examine companies over the past 20-year period, relying on annual reports, Compustat data, secondary sources and follow-up interviews.

JIM MACKEY is the managing director at the Billion Dollar Growth Network, a research consortium focused on large-company growth and innovation.

LIISA VÄLIKANGAS is a professor of innovation management at the Helsinki School of Economics, president and cofounder of Innovation Democracy, Inc., a nonprofit company supporting local innovation and entrepreneurship in countries important to world stability (e.g., Afghanistan).

PLEASE NOTE: To access the "YES" selection, please refer to "The Innovator's Solution: Creating and Sustaining Successful Growth," by Clayton M. Christensen and Michael E. Raynor immediately following this issue.

EXPLORING THE ISSUE

Is Growth Always an Inherent Corporate Value?

Critical Thinking and Reflection

1. What might be the tactics of a corporate growth strategy?
2. What might be the costs to consumers, corporations, and the nation of corporations following an unmitigated corporate growth strategy?
3. What is the likelihood that an enacted corporate growth strategy will lead to anticipated outcomes?
4. What does the future hold for corporations following corporate growth strategies?
5. Is it realistic for corporations, employees, shareholders and society to expect continuous corporate growth?

Is There Common Ground?

One reason the issue of corporate growth strategy is so contentious is that both sides of this debate can access data in support of their position. While finding common ground and agreement on basic aspects of this important management topic is difficult, there is consensus that corporate growth as a corporate strategy is an important topic that will continue to be debated.

Additional Resources

Christensen, C. (1997). *The Innovators Dilemma: When New Technologies Cause Great Firms to Fail,* Harvard Business School Press.

Christensen, C.M. and Raynor, M. (2003). *The Innovators Solution: Creating and Sustaining Successful Growth,* Harvard Business School Press.

Collins, J. (2001). *Good to Great,* HarperBusiness.

Hamel, G. and Välikangas, L. (2003). "The Quest for Resilience," *Harvard Business Review,* 81, pp. 52–63.

Kaplan, S. and Foster, R. (2001). *Creative Destruction: Why Companies That Are Built to Last Underperform the Market—And How to Successfully Transform Them,* Doubleday/Currency.

Zook, C. and Allen, J. (2001). *Profit from the Core,* Harvard Business School Press.

Internet References . . .

How to Develop a Business Growth Strategy

Dahl, D. (2010). "How to Develop a Business Growth Strategy," *Inc.*, February 25.

www.inc.com/guides/small-business-growth-strategies.html

Three Strategies for Achieving and Sustaining Growth

Liabotis, B. (2007). "Three Strategies for Achieving and Sustaining Growth," *Strategy*, July/August.

www.iveybusinessjournal.com/topics/strategy/three-strategies-for-achieving-and-sustaining-growth#

HARVARD
BUSINESS
SCHOOL
PRESS

The Growth Imperative

EXCERPTED FROM

The Innovator's Solution:
Creating and Sustaining Successful Growth

BY

Clayton M. Christensen and Michael E. Raynor

Harvard Business School Press
Boston, Massachusetts

ISBN-13: 978-1-4221-1535-0
1535BC

CHAPTER ONE

THE GROWTH IMPERATIVE

Financial markets relentlessly pressure executives to grow and keep growing faster and faster. Is it possible to succeed with this mandate? Don't the innovations that can satisfy investors' demands for growth require taking risks that are unacceptable to those same investors? Is there a way out of this dilemma?

This is a book about how to create new growth in business. Growth is important because companies create shareholder value through profitable growth. Yet there is powerful evidence that once a company's core business has matured, the pursuit of new platforms for growth entails daunting risk. Roughly one company in ten is able to sustain the kind of growth that translates into an above-average increase in shareholder returns over more than a few years.[1] Too often the very attempt to grow causes the entire corporation to crash. Consequently, most executives are in a no-win situation: equity markets demand that they grow, but it's hard to know *how* to grow. Pursuing growth the wrong way can be worse than no growth at all.

Consider AT&T. In the wake of the government-mandated divestiture of its local telephony services in 1984, AT&T became primarily a long distance telecommunications services provider. The break-up agreement freed the company to invest in new businesses, so management almost immediately began seeking avenues for growth and the shareholder value that growth creates.

The first such attempt arose from a widely shared view that computer systems and telephone networks were going to converge. AT&T first tried to build its own computer division in order to position itself at that intersection, but was able to do no better than annual losses of $200 million. Rather than retreat from a business that had proved to be unassailable from the outside, the company decided in 1991 to bet bigger still, acquiring NCR, at the time the world's fifth-largest computer maker, for $7.4 billion. That proved only to be a down payment: AT&T lost another $2 billion trying to make the acquisition work. AT&T finally abandoned this growth vision in 1996, selling NCR for $3.4 billion, about a third of what it had invested in the opportunity.

But the company *had* to grow. So even as the NCR acquisition was failing, AT&T was seeking growth opportunities in technologies closer to its core. In light of the success of the wireless services that several of its spun-off local telephone companies had achieved, in 1994 the company bought McCaw Cellular, at the time the largest national wireless carrier in the United States, for $11.6 billion, eventually spending $15 billion in total on its own wireless business. When Wall Street analysts subsequently complained that they were unable to properly value the combined higher-growth wireless business within the lower-growth wireline company, AT&T decided to create a separately traded stock for the wireless business in 2000. This valued the business at $10.6 billion, about two-thirds of the investment AT&T had made in the venture.

But that move left the AT&T wireline stock right where it had started, and the company *had* to grow. So in 1998 it embarked upon a strategy to enter and reinvent the local telephony business with broadband technology. Acquiring TCI and MediaOne for a combined price of $112 billion made AT&T Broadband the largest cable operator in the United States. Then, more quickly than anyone could have foreseen, the difficulties in implementation and integration proved insurmountable. In 2000, AT&T agreed to sell its cable assets to Comcast for $72 billion.[2]

In the space of a little over ten years, AT&T had wasted about $50 billion and destroyed even more in shareholder value—all in the hope of *creating* shareholder value through growth.

The bad news is that AT&T is not a special case. Consider Cabot Corporation, the world's major producer of carbon black, a compound that imparts to products such as tires many of their most important properties. This business has long been very strong, but the core markets haven't grown rapidly. To create the growth that builds shareholder value, Cabot's executives in the early 1980s launched several aggressive growth initiatives in advanced materials, acquiring a set of promising specialty metals and high-tech ceramics businesses. These constituted operating platforms into which the company would infuse new process and materials technology that was emerging from its own research laboratories and work it had sponsored at MIT.

Wall Street greeted these investments to accelerate Cabot's growth trajectory with enthusiasm and drove the company's share price to triple the level at which it had languished prior to these initiatives. But as the losses created by Cabot's investments in these businesses began to drag the entire corporation's earnings down, Wall Street hammered the stock. While the overall market appreciated at a robust rate between 1988 and 1991, Cabot's shares dropped by more than half. In the early 1990s, feeling pressure to boost earnings, Cabot's board brought in new management whose mandate was to shut down the new businesses and refocus on the core. As Cabot's profitability rebounded, Wall Street enthusiastically doubled the company's share price. The problem, of course, was that this turnaround left the new management team no better off than their predecessors: desperately seeking growth opportunities for mature businesses with limited prospects.[3]

We could cite many cases of companies' similar attempts to create new-growth platforms after the core business had matured. They follow an all-too-similar pattern. When the core business approaches maturity and investors demand new growth, executives develop seemingly sensible strategies to generate it. Although they invest aggressively, their plans fail to create the needed growth fast enough; investors hammer the stock; management is sacked; and Wall Street rewards the new executive team for simply restoring the *status quo ante*: a profitable but low-growth core business.[4]

Even expanding firms face a variant of the growth imperative. No matter how fast the growth treadmill is going, it is not fast enough. The reason: Investors have a pesky tendency to discount into the *present* value of a company's stock price whatever rate of growth they *foresee* the company achieving. Thus, even if a company's core business is growing vigorously, the only way its managers can deliver a rate of return to shareholders in the future that exceeds the risk-adjusted market average is to grow *faster* than shareholders expect. Changes in stock prices are driven not by simply the *direction* of growth, but largely by *unexpected* changes in the *rate of change* in a company's earnings and cash flows. Hence, one company that is projected to grow at 5 percent and in fact keeps growing at 5 percent and another company that is projected to grow at 25 percent and delivers 25 percent growth will both produce for future investors a market-average risk-adjusted rate of return in the future.[5] A company must deliver the rate of growth that the market is projecting just to keep its stock price from falling. It must *exceed* the consensus forecast rate of growth in order to boost its share price. This is a heavy, omnipresent burden on every executive who is sensitive to enhancing shareholder value.[6]

It's actually even harder than this. That canny horde of investors not only discounts the expected rate of growth of a company's *existing* businesses into the present value of its stock price, but also discounts the growth from new, yet-to-be-established lines of business that they expect the management team to be able to create in the future. The magnitude of the market's bet on growth from unknown sources is, in general, based on the company's track record. If the market has been impressed with a company's historical ability to leverage its strengths to generate new lines of business, then the component of its stock price based on growth from unknown sources will be large. If a company's past efforts to create new-growth businesses have not borne fruit, then its market valuation will be dominated by the projected cash flow from known, established businesses.

Table 1-1 presents one consulting firm's analysis of the share prices of a select number of *Fortune* 500 companies, showing the proportion of each firm's share price on August 21, 2002, that was attributable to cash generated by existing assets, versus cash that investors expected to be generated by new investments.[7] Of this sample, the company that was on the hook at that time to generate the largest percentage of its total growth from future investments was Dell Computer. Only 22 percent of its share price of $28.05 was justified by cash thrown off by the company's present assets, whereas 78 percent of Dell's valuation reflected investors' confidence that the company would be able to invest in new assets that would generate whopping amounts of cash. Sixty-six percent of Johnson & Johnson's market valuation and 37 percent of Home Depot's valuation were grounded in expectations of growth from yet-to-be-made investments. These companies were on the hook for *big* numbers. On the other hand, only 5 percent of General Motors's stock price on that date was predicated on future investments. Although that's a chilling reflection of the track record of GM's former management in creating new-growth businesses, it means that if the present management team does a better job, the company's share price could respond handsomely.

Probably the most daunting challenge in delivering growth is that if you fail once to deliver it, the odds that you ever will be able to deliver in the future are very low. This is the conclusion of a remarkable study, *Stall Points,* that the Corporate Strategy Board published in 1998.[8] It examined the 172 companies that had spent time on *Fortune*'s list of the 50 largest companies between 1955 and 1995. Only 5 percent of these companies were able to sustain a real, inflation-adjusted growth rate of more than 6 percent across their entire tenure in this group. The other 95 percent reached a point at which their growth simply stalled, to rates at or below the rate of growth of the gross national product (GNP). Stalling is understandable, given our expectations that all growth markets become saturated and mature. What is scary is that of all these companies whose growth had stalled, only 4 percent were able to successfully reignite their growth even to a rate of 1 percent above GNP growth. Once growth had stalled, in other words, it proved nearly impossible to restart it.

The equity markets brutally punished those companies that allowed their growth to stall. Twenty-eight percent of them lost more than 75 percent of their market capitalization. Forty-one percent of the companies saw their market value drop by between 50 and 75 percent when they stalled, and 26 percent of the firms lost between 25

TABLE 1-1

Portion of Selected Firms' Market Value That Was Based on Expected Returns from New Investments on August 21, 2002

Fortune 500 rank	Company Name	Share Price	Percent of Valuation That Was Based on:	
			New Investments	Existing Assets
53	Dell Computer	$28.05	78%	22%
47	Johnson & Johnson	$56.20	66%	34%
35	Procter & Gamble	$90.76	62%	38%
6	General Electric	$32.80	60%	40%
77	Lockheed Martin	$62.16	59%	41%
1	Wal-Mart Stores	$53.88	50%	50%
65	Intel	$19.15	49%	51%
49	Pfizer	$34.92	48%	52%
9	IBM	$81.93	46%	54%
24	Merck	$53.80	44%	56%
92	Cisco Systems	$15.00	42%	58%
18	Home Depot	$33.86	37%	63%
16	Boeing	$28.36	30%	70%
11	Verizon	$31.80	21%	79%
22	Kroger	$22.20	13%	87%
32	Sears Roebuck	$36.94	8%	92%
37	AOL Time Warner	$35.00	8%	92%
3	General Motors	$49.40	5%	95%
81	Phillips Petroleum	$35.00	3%	97%

Source: CSFB/HOLT; Deloitte Consuting analysis.

and 50 percent of their value. The remaining 5 percent lost less than 25 percent of their market capitalization. This, of course, increased pressure on management to regenerate growth, and to do so quickly—which made it all the more difficult to succeed. Managers cannot escape the mandate to grow.[9] Yet the odds of success, if history is any guide, are frighteningly low.

Is Innovation a Black Box?

Why is achieving and sustaining growth so hard? One popular answer is to blame managers for failing to generate new growth—implying that more capable and prescient people could have succeeded. The solve-the-problem-by-finding-a-better-manager approach might have credence if failures to restart growth were isolated events. Study after study, however, concludes that about 90 percent of all publicly traded companies have proved themselves unable to sustain for more than a few years a growth trajectory that creates above-average shareholder returns.[10] Unless we believe that the pool of management talent in established firms is like some perverse Lake Wobegon, where 90 percent of managers are below average, there has to be a more fundamental explanation for why the vast majority of good managers has not been able to crack the problem of sustaining growth.

A second common explanation for once-thriving companies' inability to sustain growth is that their managers become risk averse. But the facts refute this explanation, too. Corporate executives often bet the future of billion-dollar enterprises on an innovation. IBM bet its farm on the System 360 mainframe computer, and won. DuPont spent $400 million on a plant to make Kevlar tire cord, and lost. Corning put billions on the line to build its optical fiber business, and won big. More recently it sold off many of its other businesses in order to invest more in optical telecommunications, and has been bludgeoned. *Many* of the executives who have been unable to create sustained corporate growth have evidenced a strong stomach for risk.

There is a third, widely accepted explanation for why growth seems so hard to achieve repeatedly and well, which we also believe does not hold water: Creating new-growth businesses is simply unpredictable.

8 | THE INNOVATOR'S SOLUTION

Many believe that the odds of success are just that—odds—and that they are low. Many of the most insightful management thinkers have accepted the assumption that creating growth is risky and unpredictable, and have therefore used their talents to help executives manage this unpredictability. Recommendations about letting a thousand flowers bloom, bringing Silicon Valley inside, failing fast, and accelerating selection pressures are all ways to deal with the allegedly irreducible unpredictability of successful innovation.[11] The structure of the venture capital industry is in fact a testament to the pervasive belief that we cannot predict which new-growth businesses will succeed. The industry maxim says that for every ten investments—all made in the belief they would succeed—two will fail outright, six will survive as the walking wounded, and two will hit the home runs on which the success of the entire portfolio turns. Because of this belief that the process of business creation is unfathomable, few have sought to pry open the black box to study the *process* by which new-growth businesses are created.

We do not accept that most companies' growth stalls because the odds of success for the next growth business they launch are impossibly low. The historical results may indeed seem random, but we believe it is because the process for creating new-growth businesses has not yet been well understood. In this book we intend to pry open the black box and study the processes that lead to success or failure in new-growth businesses.

To illustrate why it is important to understand the processes that create those results, consider these strings of numbers:

1, 2, 3, 4, 5, 6
75, 28, 41, 26, 38, 64

Which of these would you say is random, and which is predictable? The first string looks predictable: The next two numbers should be 7 and 8. But what if we told you that it was actually the winning numbers for a lottery, drawn from a drum of tumbling balls, whereas the second is the sequence of state and county roads one would follow on a scenic tour of the northern rim of Michigan's Upper Peninsula on the way from Sault Ste. Marie, Ontario to Saxon, Wisconsin?

Given the route implied by the first six roads, you can reliably predict the next two numbers—2 and 122—from a map. The lesson: You cannot say, just by looking at the result of the process, whether the process that created those results is capable of generating predictable output. You must understand the process itself.

The Forces That Shape Innovation

What can make the process of innovation more predictable? It does *not* entail learning to predict what *individuals* might do. Rather, it comes from understanding the *forces* that act upon the individuals involved in building businesses—forces that powerfully influence what managers choose and cannot choose to do.

Rarely does an idea for a new-growth business emerge fully formed from an innovative employee's head. No matter how well articulated a concept or insight might be, it must be shaped and modified, often significantly, as it gets fleshed out into a business plan that can win funding from the corporation. Along the way, it encounters a number of highly predictable forces. Managers as individuals might indeed be idiosyncratic and unpredictable, but they all face forces that are similar in their mechanism of action, their timing, and their impact on the character of the product and business plan that the company ultimately attempts to implement.[12] Understanding and managing these forces can make innovation more predictable.

The action and impact of these forces in shaping ideas into business plans is illustrated in a case study of the Big Idea Group (BIG), a company that identifies, develops, and markets ideas for new toys.[13] After quoting a senior executive of a multibillion-dollar toy company who complained that there have been no exciting new toy ideas for years, the case then chronicles how BIG attacks this problem—or rather, this opportunity.

BIG invites mothers, children, tinkerers, and retirees who have ideas for new toys to attend "Big Idea Hunts," which it convenes in locations across the country. These guests present their ideas to a panel of experts whose intuition BIG executives have come to trust. When the panel sees a good idea, BIG licenses it from the inventor and over the next several

10 | THE INNOVATOR'S SOLUTION

months shapes the idea into a business plan with a working prototype that they believe will sell. BIG then licenses the product to a toy company, which produces and markets it through its own channels. The company has been extraordinarily successful at finding, developing, and deploying into the market a sequence of truly exciting growth products.

How can there be such a flowering of high-potential new product opportunities in BIG's system, and such a dearth of opportunities in the large toy company? In discussing the case, students often suggest that the product developers in the toy company just aren't as creative, or that the executives of the major company are just too risk averse. If these diagnoses were true, the company would simply need to find more creative managers who could think outside the box. But a parade of people has cycled through the toy company, and none has been able to crack the apparent lack of exciting toy ideas. Why?

The answer lies in the process by which the ideas get shaped. Midlevel managers play a crucial role in *every* company's innovation process, as they shepherd partially formed ideas into fully fledged business plans in an effort to win funding from senior management. It is the middle managers who must decide which of the ideas that come bubbling in or up to them they will support and carry to upper management for approval, and which ideas they will simply allow to languish. This is a key reason why companies employ middle managers in the first place. Their job is to sift the good ideas from the bad and to make good ideas so much better that they readily secure funding from senior management.

How do they sift and shape? Middle managers typically hesitate to throw their weight behind new product concepts whose market is not assured. If a market fails to materialize, the company will have wasted millions of dollars. The system therefore mandates that midlevel managers support their proposals with credible data on the size and growth potential of the markets that each idea targets. Opinions and feedback from significant customers add immeasurably to the credibility of claims that an idea has potential. Where does this evidence come from, given that the product hasn't yet been fully developed? It typically comes from existing customers and markets for similar products that have been successful in the past.

Personal factors are at work in this shaping process, too. Managers who back ideas that flop often find their prospects for promotion effectively truncated. In fact, ambitious managers hesitate even to propose ideas that senior managers are not likely to approve. If they favor an idea that their superiors subsequently judge to be weak, their reputation for good judgment can be tarnished among the very executives they hope to impress. Furthermore, companies' management development programs rarely leave their most talented middle managers in a position for longer than a few years—they move them to new assignments to broaden their skills and experience. What this means, however, is that middle managers who want a reputation for delivering results will be inclined to promote only those new-growth ideas that will pay off within the time that they reside in that particular job.

The process of sorting through and packaging ideas into plans that can win funding, in other words, shapes those ideas to resemble the ideas that were approved and became successful in the past. The processes have in fact evolved to weed out business proposals that target markets where demand might be small. The problem for growth-seeking managers, of course, is that the exciting growth markets of tomorrow are small today.

This is why the senior managers at the major toy company and at BIG can live in the same world and yet see such different things. In every sizable company, not just in the toy business, the set of ideas that has been processed and packaged for top management approval is *very* different from the population of ideas that is bubbling at the bottom.

A dearth of good ideas is rarely the core problem in a company that struggles to launch exciting new-growth businesses. The problem is in the shaping process. Potentially innovative new ideas seem inexorably to be recast into attempts to make existing customers still happier. We believe that many of the ideas that emerge from this packaging and shaping process as me-too innovations could just as readily be shaped into business plans that create truly disruptive growth. Managers who understand these forces and learn to harness them in making key decisions will develop successful new-growth businesses much more consistently than historically has seemed possible.[14]

Where Predictability Comes From: Good Theory

The quest for predictability in an endeavor as complex as innovation is not quixotic. What brings predictability to any field is a body of well-researched *theory*—contingent statements of what causes what and why. Executives often discount the value of management theory because it is associated with the word *theoretical,* which connotes *impractical.* But theory is consummately practical. The law of gravity, for example, actually is a theory—and it is useful. It allows us to predict that if we step off a cliff, we will fall.[15]

Even though most managers don't think of themselves as being theory driven, they are in reality voracious consumers of theory. Every time managers make plans or take action, it is based on a mental model in the back of their heads that leads them to believe that the action being taken will lead to the desired result.[16] The problem is that managers are rarely aware of the theories they are using—and they often use the wrong theories for the situation they are in. It is the absence of conscious, trustworthy theories of cause and effect that makes success in building new businesses seem random.

To help executives to know whether and when they can trust the recommendations from management books or articles (including this one!) that they read for guidance as they build their businesses, we describe in the following sections a model of how good theories are built and used. We will repeatedly return to this model to illustrate how bad theory has caused growth builders to stumble in the past, and how the use of sound theory can remove many of the causes of failure.[17]

How Theories Are Built

The process of building solid theory has been researched in several disciplines, and scholars seem to agree that it proceeds in three stages. It begins by describing the phenomenon that we wish to understand. In physics, the phenomenon might be the behavior of high-energy particles. In the building of new businesses, the phenomena of interest are the things that innovators do in their efforts to succeed, and what the results of those actions are. Bad management theory results when researchers impatiently observe one or two success stories and then assume that they have seen enough.

After the phenomenon has been thoroughly characterized, researchers can then begin the second stage, which is to classify the phenomenon into categories. Juvenile-onset versus adult-onset diabetes is an example from medicine. Vertical and horizontal integration are categories of corporate diversification. Researchers need to categorize in order to highlight the most meaningful differences in the complex array of phenomena.

In the third stage, researchers articulate a theory that asserts what causes the phenomenon to occur, and why. The theory must also show whether and why the same causal mechanism might result in different outcomes, depending on the category or situation. The process of theory building is iterative, as researchers and managers keep cycling through these three steps, refining their ability to predict what actions will cause what results, under what circumstances.[18]

Getting the Categories Right

The middle stage in this cycle—getting the categories right—is the key to developing useful theory. To see why, imagine going to your medical doctor seeking treatment for a particular set of symptoms, and before you have a chance to describe what ails you, the physician hands you a prescription and tells you to "take two of these and call me in the morning."

"But how do you know this will help me?" you ask. "I haven't told you what's wrong."

"Why wouldn't it work?" comes the reply. "It cured my previous two patients just fine."

No sane patient would accept medicine like this. But academics, consultants, and managers *routinely* dispense and accept remedies to management problems in this manner. When something has worked for a few "excellent" companies, they readily advise all other companies that taking the same medicine will be good for them as well. One reason why the outcomes of innovation appear to be random is that many who write about strategy and management ignore categorization. They observe a few successful companies and then write a book recommending that other managers do the same things to be successful too—without regard for the possibility that there might be some circumstances in which their favorite solution is a bad idea.[19]

For example, thirty years ago many writers asserted that vertical integration was the key to IBM's extraordinary success. But in the late 1990s we read that *non*-integration explained the triumph of outsourcing titans such as Cisco and Dell. The authors of "best practices" gospels such as these are no better than the doctor we introduced previously. The critical question that these researchers need to resolve is, "What are the *circumstances* in which being integrated is competitively critical, and when is a strategy of partnering and outsourcing more likely to lead to success?"

Because theory-building scholars struggle to define the right and relevant categorization of circumstances, they rarely can define the circumstances immediately. Early studies almost always sort researchers' observations into categories defined by the *attributes* of the phenomena themselves. Their assertions about the actions or events that lead to the results at this point can only be statements about *correlation* between attributes and results, not about causality. This is the best they can do in early theory-building cycles.

Consider, for illustration, the history of man's attempts to fly. Early researchers observed strong correlations between being able to fly and having feathers and wings. Possessing these attributes had a high *correlation* with the ability to fly, but when humans attempted to follow the "best practices" of the most successful flyers by strapping feathered wings onto their arms, jumping off cliffs, and flapping hard, they were not successful—because as strong as the correlations were, the would-be aviators had not understood the fundamental causal mechanism that enabled certain animals to fly. It was not until Bernoulli's study of fluid mechanics helped him articulate the mechanism through which airfoils create lift that human flight began to be *possible*. But understanding the mechanism itself still wasn't enough to make the ability to fly perfectly *predictable*. Further research, entailing careful experimentation and measurement under various conditions, was needed to identify the *circumstances* in which that mechanism did and did not yield the desired result.

When the mechanism did not result in successful flight, researchers had to carefully decipher *why*—what it was about the circumstances in which the unexpected result occurred that led to failure. Once categories could be stated in terms of the different types of circumstances in which aviators might find themselves, then aviators could predict the conditions in which flight was and was not possible. They could develop technologies and techniques for successfully flying in those circumstances where flight was viable. And they could teach aviators how to recognize when the circumstances were changing, so that they could change their methods appropriately. Understanding the mechanism (what causes what, and why) made flight possible; understanding the categories of circumstances made flight predictable.[20]

How did aviation researchers know what the salient boundaries were between these categories of circumstance? As long as a change in conditions did not require change in the way the pilot flew the plane, the boundary between those conditions didn't matter. The circumstance boundaries that mattered were those that mandated a fundamental change in piloting techniques in order to keep the plane flying successfully.

Similar breakthroughs in management research increase the predictability of creating new-growth businesses. Getting beyond correlative assertions such as "Big companies are slow to innovate," or "In our sample of successful companies, each was run by a CEO who had been promoted from within," the breakthrough researcher first discovers the fundamental *causal* mechanism behind the phenomena of success. This allows those who are looking for "an answer" to get beyond the wings-and-feathers mind-set of copying the attributes of successful companies. The foundation for predictability only begins to be built when the researcher sees the same causal mechanism create a *different* outcome from what he or she expected—an anomaly. This prompts the researcher to define what it was about the circumstance or circumstances in which the anomaly occurred that caused the identical mechanism to result in a different outcome.

How can we tell what the right categorization is? As in aviation, a boundary between circumstances is salient only when executives need to use fundamentally different management techniques to succeed in the different circumstances defined by that boundary. If the same statement of cause and effect leads to the same outcome in two circumstances, then the distinction between those circumstances is not meaningful for the purposes of predictability.

To know for certain what circumstances they are in, managers also must know what circumstances they are *not* in. When collectively exhaustive and mutually exclusive *categories of circumstances* are defined, things get predictable: We can state what will cause what and why, and can predict how that statement of causality might vary by circumstance. Theories built on categories of circumstances become easy for companies to employ, because managers live and work in circumstances, not in attributes.[21]

When managers ask questions such as "Does this apply to my industry?" or "Does it apply to service businesses as well as product businesses?" they really are probing to understand the circumstances. In our studies, we have observed that industry-based or product/service-based categorization schemes almost never constitute a useful foundation for reliable theory. *The Innovator's Dilemma,* for example, described how the same mechanism that enabled entrant companies to up-end the leading established firms in disk drives and computers also toppled the leading companies in mechanical excavators, steel, retailing, motorcycles, accounting software, and motor controls.[22] The circumstances that mattered were not what industry you were in. Rather, there was a mechanism—the resource allocation process—that caused the established leaders to win the competitive fights when an innovation was financially attractive to their business model. The same mechanism disabled the established leaders when they were attacked by disruptive innovators—whose products, profit models, and customers were not attractive.

We can trust a theory only when its statement of what actions will lead to success describe how this will vary as a company's circumstances change.[23] This is a major reason why the outcomes of innovation efforts have seemed quite random: Shoddy categorization has led to one-size-fits-all recommendations that in turn have led to the wrong results in many circumstances.[24] It is the ability to begin thinking and acting in a circumstance-contingent way that brings predictability to our lives.

We often admire the intuition that successful entrepreneurs seem to have for building growth businesses. When they exercise their intuition about what actions will lead to the desired results, they really are employing theories that give them a sense of the right thing to do in various circumstances. These theories were not there at birth: They were learned through a set of experiences and mentors earlier in life.

If some people have learned the theories that we call intuition, then it is our hope that these theories also can be taught to others. This is our aspiration for this book. We hope to help managers who are trying to create new-growth businesses use the best research we have been able to assemble to learn how to match their actions to the circumstances in order to get the results they need. As our readers use these ways of thinking over and over, we hope that the thought processes inherent in these theories can become part of their intuition as well.

We have written this book from the perspective of senior managers in established companies who have been charged to maintain the health and vitality of their firms. We believe, however, that our ideas will be just as valuable to independent entrepreneurs, start-up companies, and venture capital investors. Simply for purposes of brevity, we will use the term *product* in this book when we describe what a company makes or provides. We mean, however, for this to encompass product *and* service businesses, because the concepts in the book apply just as readily to both.

The Outline of This Book

The Innovator's Dilemma summarized a theory that explains how, under certain circumstances, the mechanism of profit-maximizing resource allocation causes well-run companies to get killed. *The Innovator's Solution*, in contrast, summarizes a set of theories that can guide managers who need to grow new businesses with predictable success—to become the disruptors rather than the disruptees—and ultimately kill the well-run, established competitors. To succeed predictably, disruptors must be good theorists. As they shape their growth business to be disruptive, they must align every critical process and decision to fit the disruptive circumstance.

Because building successful growth businesses is such a vast topic, this book focuses on nine of the most important decisions that all managers must make in creating growth—decisions that represent key actions that drive success inside the black box of innovation. Each chapter offers a specific theory that managers can use to make one of these decisions in a way that greatly improves their probability of success. Some of this theory has emerged from our own studies, but we are indebted to many other scholars for much of what follows. Those whose work we draw upon have contributed to improving the predictability of business building because their assertions of causality have been built upon circumstance-based categories. It is because of their careful work that we believe that managers can begin using these theories explicitly as they make these decisions, trusting that their predictions will be applicable and reliable, given the circumstances that they are in.

The following list summarizes the questions we address.

- *Chapter 2:* How can we beat our most powerful competitors? What strategies will result in the competitors killing us, and what courses of action could actually give us the upper hand?
- *Chapter 3:* What products should we develop? Which improvements over previous products will customers enthusiastically reward with premium prices, and which will they greet with indifference?
- *Chapter 4:* Which initial customers will constitute the most viable foundation upon which to build a successful business?
- *Chapter 5:* Which activities required to design, produce, sell, and distribute our product should our company do internally, and which should we rely upon our partners and suppliers to provide?
- *Chapter 6:* How can we be sure that we maintain strong competitive advantages that yield attractive profits? How can we tell when commoditization is going to occur, and what can we do to keep earning attractive returns?

- *Chapter 7:* What is the best organizational structure for this venture? What organizational unit(s) and which managers should contribute to and be responsible for its success?
- *Chapter 8:* How do we get the details of a winning strategy right? When is flexibility important, and when will flexibility cause us to fail?
- *Chapter 9:* Whose investment capital will help us succeed, and whose capital might be the kiss of death? What sources of money will help us most at different stages of our development?
- *Chapter 10:* What role should the CEO play in sustaining the growth of the business? When should CEOs keep their hands off the new business, and when should they become involved?

The issues that we tackle in these chapters are critical, but they cannot constitute an exhaustive list of the questions that should be relevant to launching a new-growth business. We can simply hope that we have addressed the most important ones, so that although we cannot make the creation of new-growth businesses perfectly risk free, we *can* help managers take major steps in that direction.

Notes

1. Although we have not performed a true meta-analysis, there are four recently published studies that seem to converge on this estimate that roughly one company in ten succeeds at sustaining growth. Chris Zook and James Allen found in their 2001 study *Profit from the Core* (Boston: Harvard Business School Press) that only 13 percent of their sample of 1,854 companies were able to grow consistently over a ten-year period. Richard Foster and Sarah Kaplan published a study that same year, *Creative Destruction* (New York: Currency/Doubleday), in which they followed 1,008 companies from 1962 to 1998. They learned that only 160, or about 16 percent of these firms, were able merely to survive this time frame, and concluded that the perennially outperforming company is a chimera, something that has never existed at all. Jim Collins also published his *Good to Great* (New York: HarperBusiness) in 2001, in which he examined a universe of 1,435 companies over thirty years (1965–1995). Collins found only 126, or about 9 percent, that had managed to outperform equity market averages for a decade or more. The Corporate Strategy Board's findings in *Stall Points*

(Washington, DC: Corporate Strategy Board, 1988), which are summarized in detail in the text, show that 5 percent of companies in the *Fortune 50* successfully maintained their growth, and another 4 percent were able to reignite some degree of growth after they had stalled. The studies all support our assertion that a 10 percent probability of succeeding in a quest for sustained growth is, if anything, a generous estimate.

2. Because all of these transactions included stock, "true" measures of the value of the different deals are ambiguous. Although when a deal actually closes, a definitive value can be fixed, the implied value of the transaction at the time a deal is announced can be useful: It signals what the relevant parties were willing to pay and accept at a point in time. Stock price changes subsequent to the deal's announcement are often a function of other, exogenous events having little to do with the deal itself. Where possible, we have used the value of the deals at announcement, rather than upon closing. Sources of data on these various transactions include the following:

NCR

"Fatal Attraction (AT&T's Failed Merger with NCR)," *The Economist*, 23 March 1996.

"NCR Spinoff Completes AT&T Restructure Plan," *Bloomberg Business News*, 1 January 1997.

McCaw and AT&T Wireless Sale

The Wall Street Journal, 21 September 1994.

"AT&T Splits Off AT&T Wireless," AT&T news release, 9 July 2001.

AT&T, TCI, and MediaOne

"AT&T Plans Mailing to Sell TCI Customers Phone, Web Services," The *Wall Street Journal*, 10 March 1999.

"The AT&T-Mediaone Deal: What the FCC Missed," *Business Week*, 19 June 2000.

"AT&T Broadband to Merge with Comcast Corporation in $72 Billion Transaction," AT&T news release, 19 December 2001.

"Consumer Groups Still Questioning Comcast-AT&T Cable Merger," Associated Press Newswires, 21 October 2002.

3. Cabot's stock price outperformed the market between 1991 and 1995 as it refocused on its core business, for two reasons. On one side of the equation, demand for carbon black increased in Asia and North America as car sales surged, thereby increasing the demand for tires. On the supply side, two other American-based producers of carbon black exited the industry because

they were unwilling to make the requisite investment in environmental controls, thereby increasing Cabot's pricing power. Increased demand and reduced supply translated into a tremendous increase in the profitability of Cabot's traditional carbon black operations, which was reflected in the company's stock price. Between 1996 and 2000, however, its stock price deteriorated again, reflecting the dearth of growth prospects.

4. An important study of companies' tendency to make investments that fail to create growth was done by Professor Michael C. Jensen: "The Modern Industrial Revolution, Exit, and the Failure of Internal Control Systems," *Journal of Finance* (July 1993): 831–880. Professor Jensen also delivered this paper as his presidential address to the American Finance Association. Interestingly, many of the firms that Jensen cites as having productively reaped growth from their investments were disruptive innovators—a key concept in this book.

   Our unit of analysis in this book, as in Jensen's work, is the individual firm, not the larger system of growth creation made manifest in a free market, capitalist economy. Works such as Joseph Schumpeter's *Theory of Economic Development* (Cambridge, MA: Harvard University Press, 1934) and *Capitalism, Socialism, and Democracy* (New York: London, Harper & Brothers, 1942) are seminal, landmark works that address the environment in which firms function. Our assertion here is that whatever the track record of free market economies in generating growth at the macro level, the track record of individual firms is quite poor. It is the performance of firms within a competitive market to which we hope to contribute.

5. This simple story is complicated somewhat by the market's apparent incorporation of an expected "fade" in any company's growth rate. Empirical analysis suggests that the market does not expect any company to grow, or even survive, forever. It therefore seems to incorporate into current prices a foreseen decline in growth rates from current levels and the eventual dissolution of the firm. This is the reason for the importance of terminal values in most valuation models. This fade period is estimated using regression analysis, and estimates vary widely. So, strictly speaking, if a company is expected to grow at 5 percent with a fade period of forty years, and five years into that forty-year period it is still growing at 5 percent, the stock price would rise at rates that generated economic returns for shareholders, because the forty-year fade period would start over. However, because this qualification applies to companies growing at 5 percent as well as those growing at 25 percent, it does not change the point we wish to make; that is, that the market is a harsh taskmaster, and merely meeting expectations does not generate meaningful reward.

6. On average over their long histories, of course, faster-growing firms yield higher returns. However, the faster-growing firm will have produced higher

returns than the slower-growing firm only for investors in the past. If markets discount efficiently, then the investors who reap above-average returns are those who were fortunate enough to have bought shares in the past when the future growth rate had not been fully discounted into the price of the stock. Those who bought when the future growth potential already had been discounted into the share price would not receive an above-market return. An excellent reference for this argument can be found in Alfred Rappaport and Michael J. Mauboussin, *Expectations Investing: Reading Stock Prices for Better Returns* (Boston: Harvard Business School Press, 2001). Rappaport and Mauboussin guide investors in methods to detect when a market's expectations for a company's growth might be incorrect.

7. These were the closing market prices for these companies' common shares on August 21, 2002. There is no significance to that particular date: It is simply the time when the analysis was done. HOLT Associates, a unit of Credit Suisse First Boston (CSFB), performed these calculations using proprietary methodology applied to publicly available financial data. The percent future is a measure of how much a company's current stock price can be attributed to current cash flows and how much is due to investors' expectations of future growth and performance. As CSFB/HOLT defines it,

> *The percent future is the percentage of the total market value that the market assigns to the company's expected future investment. Percent future begins with the total market value (debt plus equity) less that portion attributed to the present value of existing assets and investments and divides this by the total market value of debt and equity.*

CSFB/Holt calculates the present value of existing assets as the present value of the cash flows associated with the assets' wind down and the release of the associated nondepreciating working capital. The HOLT CFROI valuation methodology includes a forty-year fade of returns equal to the total market's average returns.

Percent Future = [Total Debt and Equity (market) – Present Value Existing Assets]/[Total Debt and Equity (market)]

The companies listed in table 1-1 are not a sequential ranking of *Fortune* 500 companies, because some of the data required to perform these calculations were not available for some companies. The companies listed in this table were chosen only for illustrative purposes, and were not chosen in any way to suggest that any company's share price is likely to increase or decline. For more information on the methodology that HOLT used, see <http://www.holtvalue.com>.

8. See *Stall Points* (Washington, DC: Corporate Strategy Board, 1998).

9. In the text we have focused only on the pressure that equity markets impose on companies to grow, but there are many other sources of intense pressure. We'll mention just a couple here. First, when a company is growing, there are increased opportunities for employees to be promoted into new management positions that are opening up above them. Hence, the potential for growth in managerial responsibility and capability is much greater in a growing firm than in a stagnant one. When growth slows, managers sense that their possibilities for advancement will be constrained not by their personal talent and performance, but rather by how many years must pass before the more senior managers above them will retire. When this happens, many of the most capable employees tend to leave the company, affecting the company's abilities to regenerate growth.

    Investment in new technologies also becomes difficult. When a growing firm runs out of capacity and must build a new plant or store, it is easy to employ the latest technology. When a company has stopped growing and has excess manufacturing capacity, proposals to invest in new technology typically do not fare well, since the full capital cost and the average manufacturing cost of producing with the new technology are compared against the marginal cost of producing in a fully depreciated plant. As a result, growing firms typically have a technology edge over slow-growth competitors. But that advantage is not rooted so much in the visionary wisdom of the managers as it is in the difference in the circumstances of growth versus no growth.

10. Detailed support for this estimate is provided in note 1.

11. For example, see James Brian Quinn, *Strategies for Change: Logical Incrementalism* (Homewood, IL: R.D. Irwin, 1980). Quinn suggests that the first step that corporate executives need to take in building new businesses is to "let a thousand flowers bloom," then tend the most promising and let the rest wither. In this view, the key to successful innovation lies in choosing the right flowers to tend—and that decision must rely on complex intuitive feelings, calibrated by experience.

    More recent work by Tom Peters (*Thriving on Chaos: Handbook for a Management Revolution* [New York: Knopf/Random House, 1987]) urges innovating managers to "fail fast"—to pursue new business ideas on a small scale and in a way that generates quick feedback about whether an idea is viable. Advocates of this approach urge corporate executives not to punish failures because it is only through repeated attempts that successful new businesses will emerge.

Others draw on analogies with biological evolution, where mutations arise in what appear to be random ways. Evolutionary theory posits that whether a mutant organism thrives or dies depends on its fit with the "selection environment"—the conditions within which it must compete against other organisms for the resources required to thrive. Hence, believing that good and bad innovations pop up randomly, these researchers advise corporate executives to focus on creating a "selection environment" in which viable new business ideas are culled from the bad as quickly as possible. Gary Hamel, for example, advocates creating "Silicon Valley inside"—an environment in which existing structures are constantly dismantled, recombined in novel ways, and tested, in order to stumble over something that actually works. (See Gary Hamel, *Leading the Revolution* [Boston: Harvard Business School Press, 2001].)

We are not critical of these books. They can be very helpful, given the present state of understanding, because if the processes that create innovations were indeed random, then a context within which managers could accelerate the creation and testing of ideas would indeed help. But if the process is *not* intrinsically random, as we assert, then addressing only the context is treating the symptom, not the source of the problem.

To see why, consider the studies of 3M's celebrated ability to create a stream of growth-generating innovations. A persistent highlight of these studies is 3M's "15 percent rule": At 3M, many employees are given 15 percent of their time to devote to developing their own ideas for new-growth businesses. This "slack" in how people spend their time is supported by a broadly dispersed capital budget that employees can tap in order to fund their would-be growth engines on a trial basis.

But what guidance does this policy give to a bench engineer at 3M? She is given 15 percent "slack" time to dedicate to creating new-growth businesses. She is also told that whatever she comes up with will be subject first to internal market selection pressures, then external market selection pressures. All this is helpful information. But none of it helps that engineer create a new idea, or decide which of the several ideas she might create are worth pursuing further. This plight generalizes to managers and executives at all levels in an organization. From bench engineer to middle manager to business unit head to CEO, it is not enough to occupy oneself only with creating a context for innovation that sorts the fruits of that context. Ultimately, every manager must create something of substance, and the success of that creation lies in the decisions managers must make.

All of these approaches create an "infinite regress." By bringing the market "inside," we have simply backed up the problem: How can managers decide which ideas will be developed to the point at which they can be subjected to the selection pressures of their internal market? Bringing the market still deeper inside simply creates the same conundrum. Ultimately, innovators must judge what they will work on and how they will do it —and what they should consider when making those decisions is what is in the black box. The acceptance of randomness in innovation, then, is not a stepping-stone on the way to greater understanding; it is a barrier.

Dr. Gary Hamel was one of the first scholars of this problem to raise with Professor Christensen the possibility that the management of innovation actually has the potential to yield predictable results. We express our thanks to him for his helpful thoughts.

12. The scholars who introduced us to these forces are Professor Joseph Bower of the Harvard Business School and Professor Robert Burgelman of the Stanford Business School. We owe a deep intellectual debt to them. See Joseph L. Bower, *Managing the Resource Allocation Process* (Homewood, IL: Richard D. Irwin, 1970); Robert Burgelman and Leonard Sayles, *Inside Corporate Innovation* (New York: Free Press, 1986); and Robert Burgelman, *Strategy Is Destiny* (New York: Free Press, 2002).

13. Clayton M. Christensen and Scott D. Anthony, "What's the BIG Idea?" Case 9-602-105 (Boston: Harvard Business School, 2001).

14. We have consciously chosen phrases such as "increase the probability of success" because business building is unlikely ever to become perfectly predictable, for at least three reasons. The first lies in the nature of competitive marketplaces. Companies whose actions were perfectly predictable would be relatively easy to defeat. Every company therefore has an interest in behaving in deeply unpredictable ways. A second reason is the computational challenge associated with any system with a large number of possible outcomes. Chess, for example, is a fully determined game: After White's first move, Black should always simply resign. But the number of possible games is so great, and the computational challenge so overwhelming, that the outcomes of games even between supercomputers remain unpredictable. A third reason is suggested by complexity theory, which holds that even fully determined systems that do not outstrip our computational abilities can still generate deeply random outcomes. Assessing the extent to which the outcomes of innovation can be predicted, and the significance of any residual uncertainty or unpredictability, remains a profound theoretical challenge with important practical implications.

15. The challenge of improving predictability has been addressed somewhat successfully in certain of the natural sciences. Many fields of science appear today to be cut and dried—predictable, governed by clear laws of cause and effect, for example. But it was not always so: Many happenings in the natural world seemed very random and unfathomably complex to the ancients and to early scientists. Research that adhered carefully to the scientific

method brought the predictability upon which so much progress has been built. Even when our most advanced theories have convinced scientists that the world is not deterministic, at least the phenomena are predictably random.

Infectious diseases, for example, at one point just seemed to strike at random. People didn't understand what caused them. Who survived and who did not seemed unpredictable. Although the outcome seemed random, however, the process that led to the results was not random—it just was not sufficiently understood. With many cancers today, as in the venture capitalists' world, patients' probabilities for survival can only be articulated in percentages. This is not because the outcomes are unpredictable, however. We just do not yet understand the process.

16. Peter Senge calls theories *mental models* (see Peter Senge, *The Fifth Discipline* [New York: Bantam Doubleday Dell, 1990]). We considered using the term *model* in this book, but opted instead to use the term *theory*. We have done this to be provocative, to inspire practitioners to value something that is indeed of value.

17. A full description of the process of theory building and of the ways in which business writers and academics ignore and violate the fundamental principles of this process is available in a paper that is presently under review, "The Process of Theory Building," by Clayton Christensen, Paul Carlile, and David Sundahl. Paper or electronic copies are available from Professor Christensen's office, cchristensen@hbs.edu. The scholars we have relied upon in synthesizing the model of theory building presented in this paper (and only very briefly summarized in this book) are, in alphabetical order, E. H. Carr, *What Is History?* (New York: Vintage Books, 1961); K. M. Eisenhardt, "Building Theories from Case Study Research," *Academy of Management Review* 14, no. 4 (1989): 532–550; B. Glaser and A. Straus, *The Discovery of Grounded Theory: Strategies of Qualitative Research* (London: Wiedenfeld and Nicholson, 1967); A. Kaplan, *The Conduct of Inquiry: Methodology for Behavioral Research* (Scranton, PA: Chandler, 1964); R. Kaplan, "The Role for Empirical Research in Management Accounting," *Accounting, Organizations and Society* 4, no. 5 (1986): 429–452; T. Kuhn, *The Structure of Scientific Revolutions* (Chicago: University of Chicago Press, 1962); M. Poole and A. Van de Ven, "Using Paradox to Build Management and Organization Theories," *Academy of Management Review* 14, no. 4 (1989): 562–578; K. Popper, *The Logic of Scientific Discovery* (New York: Basic Books, 1959); F. Roethlisberger, *The Elusive Phenomena* (Boston: Harvard Business School Division of Research, 1977); Arthur Stinchcombe, "The Logic of Scientific Inference," chapter 2 in *Constructing Social Theories* (New York: Harcourt,

Brace & World, 1968); Andrew Van de Ven, "Professional Science for a Professional School," in *Breaking the Code of Change*, eds. Michael Beer and Nitin Nohria (Boston: Harvard Business School Press, 2000); Karl E. Weick, "Theory Construction as Disciplined Imagination," *Academy of Management Review* 14, no. 4, (1989): 516–531; and R. Yin, *Case Study Research* (Beverly Hills, CA: Sage Publications, 1984).

18. What we are saying is that the success of a theory should be measured by the accuracy with which it can predict outcomes across the entire range of situations in which managers find themselves. Consequently, we are not seeking "truth" in any absolute, Platonic sense; our standard is practicality and usefulness. If we enable managers to achieve the results they seek, then we will have been successful. Measuring the success of theories based on their usefulness is a respected tradition in the philosophy of science, articulated most fully in the school of logical positivism. For example, see R. Carnap, *Empiricism, Semantics and Ontology* (Chicago: University of Chicago Press, 1956); W. V. O. Quine, *Two Dogmas of Empiricism* (Cambridge, MA: Harvard University Press, 1961); and W. V. O. Quine, *Epistemology Naturalized.* (New York: Columbia University Press, 1969).

19. This is a serious deficiency of much management research. Econometricians call this practice "sampling on the dependent variable." Many writers, and many who think of themselves as serious academics, are so eager to prove the worth of their theories that they studiously avoid the discovery of anomalies. In case study research, this is done by carefully selecting examples that support the theory. In more formal academic research, it is done by calling points of data that don't fit the model "outliers" and finding a justification for excluding them from the statistical analysis. Both practices seriously limit the usefulness of what is written. It actually is the discovery of phenomena that the existing theory cannot explain that enables researchers to build better theory that is built upon a better classification scheme. We need to do *anomaly-seeking* research, not anomaly-avoiding research.

     We have urged doctoral students who are seeking potentially productive research questions for their thesis research to simply ask when a "fad" theory won't work—for example, "When is process reengineering a bad idea?" Or, "Might you ever want to outsource something that *is* your core competence, and do internally something that is *not* your core competence?" Asking questions like this almost always improves the validity of the original theory. This opportunity to improve our understanding often exists even for very well done, highly regarded pieces of research. For example, an important conclusion in Jim Collins's extraordinary book *From Good to Great* (New York: HarperBusiness, 2001) is that the executives of these successful

28 | THE INNOVATOR'S SOLUTION

companies weren't charismatic, flashy men and women. They were humble people who respected the opinions of others. A good opportunity to extend the validity of Collins's research is to ask a question such as, "Are there circumstances in which you actually *don't* want a humble, noncharismatic CEO?" We suspect that there are—and defining the different circumstances in which charisma and humility are virtues and vices could do a great service to boards of directors.

20. We thank Matthew Christensen of the Boston Consulting Group for suggesting this illustration from the world of aviation as a way of explaining how getting the categories right is the foundation for bringing predictability to an endeavor. Note how important it was for researchers to discover the circumstances in which the mechanisms of lift and stabilization did *not* result in successful flight. It was the very search for failures that made success consistently possible. Unfortunately, many of those engaged in management research seem anxious *not* to spotlight instances their theory did not accurately predict. They engage in anomaly-avoiding, rather than anomaly-seeking, research and as a result contribute to the perpetuation of unpredictability. Hence, we lay much responsibility for the perceived unpredictability of business building at the feet of the very people whose business it is to study and write about these problems. We may, on occasion, succumb to the same problem. We can state that in developing and refining the theories summarized in this book, we have truly sought to discover exceptions or anomalies that the theory would not have predicted; in so doing, we have improved the theories considerably. But anomalies remain. Where we are aware of these, we have tried to note them in the text or notes of this book. If any of our readers are familiar with anomalies that these theories cannot yet explain, we invite them to teach us about them, so that together we can work to improve the predictability of business building further.

21. In studies of how companies deal with technological change, for example, early researchers suggested attribute-based categories such as incremental versus radical change and product versus process change. Each categorization supported a theory, based on correlation, about how entrant and established companies were likely to be affected by the change, and each represented an improvement in predictive power over earlier categorization schemes. At this stage of the process there rarely is a best-by-consensus theory, because there are so many attributes of the phenomena. Scholars of this process have broadly observed that this confusion is an important but unavoidable stage in building theory. See Thomas Kuhn, *The Structure of Scientific Revolutions* (Chicago: University of Chicago Press, 1962). Kuhn chronicles at length the energies expended by advocates of various competing theories at this stage, prior to the advent of a paradigm.

In addition, one of the most influential handbooks for management and social science research was written by Barney G. Glaser and Anselm L. Strauss (*The Discovery of Grounded Theory: Strategies of Qualitative Research* [London: Wiedenfeld and Nicholson, 1967]). Although they name their key concept "grounded theory," the book really is about categorization, because that process is so central to the building of valid theory. Their term "substantive theory" is similar to our term "attribute-based categories." They describe how a knowledge-building community of researchers ultimately succeeds in transforming their understanding into "formal theory," which we term "circumstance-based categories."

22. Clayton M. Christensen, *The Innovator's Dilemma: When New Technologies Cause Great Firms to Fail* (Boston: Harvard Business School Press, 1997).

23. Managers need to know if a theory applies in their situation, if they are to trust it. A very useful book on this topic is Robert K. Yin's *Case Study Research: Design and Methods* (Beverly Hills, CA: Sage Publications, 1984). Building on Yin's concept, we would say that the breadth of applicability of a theory, which Yin calls its *external validity,* is established by the soundness of its categorization scheme. There is no other way to gauge where theory applies and where it does not. To see why, consider the disruptive innovation model that emerged from the study of the disk drive industry in the early chapters of *The Innovator's Dilemma.* The concern that readers of the disk drive study raised, of course, was whether the theory applied to other industries as well. *The Innovator's Dilemma* tried to address these concerns by showing how the same theory that explained who succeeded and failed in disk drives also explained what happened in mechanical excavators, steel, retailing, motorcycles, accounting software, motor controls, diabetes care, and computers. The variety was chosen to establish the breadth of the theory's applicability. But this didn't put concerns to rest. Readers continued to ask whether the theory applied to chemicals, to database software, and so on.

Applying any theory to industry after industry cannot prove its applicability because it will always leave managers wondering if there is something different about their current circumstances that renders the theory untrustworthy. A theory can confidently be employed in prediction only when the categories that define its contingencies are clear. Some academic researchers, in a well-intentioned effort not to overstep the validity of what they can defensibly claim and not claim, go to great pains to articulate the "boundary conditions" within which their findings can be trusted. This is all well and good. But unless they concern themselves with defining what the other circumstances are that lie beyond the "boundary conditions" of their own study, they circumscribe what they can contribute to a body of useful theory.

24. An illustration of how important it is to get the categories right can be seen in the fascinating juxtaposition of two recent, solidly researched books by very smart students of management and competition that make compelling cases for diametrically opposite solutions to a problem. Each team of researchers addresses the same underlying problem—the challenge of delivering persistent, profitable growth. In *Creative Destruction* (New York: Currency/Doubleday, 2001), Richard Foster and Sarah Kaplan argue that if firms hope to create wealth sustainably and at a rate comparable to the broader market, they must be willing to explore radically new business models and visit upon themselves the tumult that characterizes the capital markets. At the same time, another well-executed study, *Profit from the Core* (Boston: Harvard Business School Press, 2001), by Bain consultants Chris Zook and James Allen, drew upon the same phenomenological evidence—that only a tiny minority of companies are able to sustain above-market returns for a significant time. But *their* book encourages companies to focus on and improve their established businesses rather than attempt to anticipate or even respond to the vagaries of equity investors by seeking to create new growth in less-related markets. Whereas Foster and Kaplan motivate their findings in terms of the historical suitability of incrementalism in a context of competitive continuity and argue for more radical change in light of today's exigencies, Zook and Allen hold that focus is timeless and remains the key to success. Their prescriptions are mutually exclusive. Whose advice should we follow? At present, managers grappling with their own growth problems have no choice but to pick a camp based on the reputations of the authors and the endorsements on the dust jacket. The answer is that there is a great opportunity for circumstance-focused researchers to build on the valuable groundwork that both sets of authors have established. The question that now needs answering is: What are the circumstances in which focusing on or near the core will yield sustained profit and growth, and what are the circumstances in which broader, Fosteresque creative destruction is the approach that will succeed?

Selected, Edited, and with Issue Framing Material by:
Kathleen J. Barnes, *East Stroudsburg University*
and
George E. Smith, *Albright College*

ISSUE

Is Outsourcing a Wise Corporate Strategy?

YES: BusinessWeek, from "The Future of Outsourcing: How It's Transforming Whole Industries and Changing the Way We Work," *Bloomberg BusinessWeek* Special Report: Outsourcing (January 30, 2006), www.businessweek.com/magazine/content/06_05/b3969401.htm

NO: Ephraim Schwartz, from "Painful Lessons from IT Outsourcing Gone Bad," InfoWorld.com (August 25, 2008), www.infoworld.com/d/adventures-in-it/painful-lessons-it-outsourcing-gone-bad-032

Learning Outcomes
After reading this issue you should be able to:
• Describe the positive and negative consequences of outsourcing as a corporate strategy.
• Discuss how outsourcing can be used as an effective corporate strategy.
• Understand what tactics might be used to implement outsourcing as an effective corporate strategy.
• Appreciate the practical implications of outsourcing as a corporate strategy.

ISSUE SUMMARY

YES: *BusinessWeek* writers argue that outsourcing is likely to become even more important to corporate America in the near future. Indeed, they suggest that it has the potential to transform whole industries.

NO: *InfoWorld* columnist Ephraim Schwartz explores the often-overlooked costs associated with failed outsourcing initiatives. His analysis consists of four brief case studies of outsourcing initiatives that turned out badly.

Based on the past presidential elections, it would appear that one of the most contentious issues in American society is the outsourcing question. In 2004, the Democratic nominee, John Kerry, repeatedly expressed his disdain for U.S. firms that "sent jobs overseas" and promised, if elected, to punish those businesses that engaged in outsourcing. In 2008, while on the campaign trail, then-Democratic presidential nominee Barack Obama said, "Unlike John McCain, I will stop giving tax breaks to corporations that ship jobs overseas, and I will start giving them to companies that create good jobs right here in America." (Griswold, 2009). Speaking in front of a joint session of Congress on February 24, 2009, President Obama made this statement: "We will restore a sense of fairness and balance to our tax code by finally ending the tax breaks for corporations that ship our jobs overseas." (Ikenson, 2009).

As Eduardo Porter notes, the political rhetoric noted in the previous paragraph is a ploy taken "from a [political] playbook used repeatedly by politicians of the right and left over the last two decades" ("The Folly of Attacking

Outsourcing," *New York Times*, August 8, 2012, B1. Porter continues by noting some of the recent history of this debate in political circles:

> In 1992, Ross Perot ran for president on the strength of the "giant sucking sound" of jobs going to Mexico. Four years later, Pat Buchanan tried to gain the Republican nomination by promising to repeal the North American Free Trade Agreement and withdraw from the World Trade Organization. In 2004, John Kerry accused George W. Bush of providing tax breaks to outsourcers.

Perhaps part of the reason this topic is so controversial is because it overlaps and is related to several other contentious issues. Some critics claim that outsourcing encourages the development of sweatshops in Third World countries. Proponents of outsourcing often claim that increased competition from globalization virtually requires outsourcing as a business strategy. Depending on which side of the protectionism issue is being considered, outsourcing is presented as either pro- or anti-American. Given the antagonism that exists in the minds of many toward outsourcing, one might reasonably question whether outsourcing is a wise course of action for a firm to follow.

Proponents of outsourcing have strong points on their side of the issue. The call to end outsourcing is, in their view, merely protectionism in disguise, a concept entirely at odds with traditional American political and economic principles. American capitalism and prosperity were built on free trade; forcing American firms to forego cheap overseas labor in the name of patriotism will ultimately cause U.S. firms, and society, to suffer. In terms of the exploitation of foreign labor argument, supporters respond that it is not exploitation at all.: Edwin Locke, Dean's Professor of Leadership and Motivation at the University of Maryland and a contributing author to the Ayn Rand Institute, an influential think tank, addresses

the claim that multinational companies [e.g., American firms] exploit workers in poor countries by paying lower wages than they would pay in their home countries. Well, what is the alternative? It is: no wages! The comparative advantage of poorer countries is precisely that their wages are low, thus reducing the costs of production. If multinational corporations had to pay the same wages as in their home countries, they would not bother to invest in poorer countries at all and millions of people would lose their livelihoods.

Supporters also point out that the United States has the second highest corporate tax rate in the world, thus incentivizing firms to both make investments and move operations overseas.

On the other hand, those who argue that outsourcing is bad business generally rely on several lines of attack. The first and most obvious argument is that outsourcing moves jobs out of America and into foreign countries. Make no mistake, this is no small trend: Millions of jobs have left American shores in recent years, and many millions more are vulnerable. Critics also point to the growth of outsourcing in the service sector as an alarming trend. The historical justification for outsourcing was built on the belief that jobs lost in manufacturing would be replaced by jobs in the service sector as the United States shifted from an industrial to a service-based economy. Because the current outsourcing wave is primarily service based, the concern is that outsourcing will accelerate further as we continue to move toward a service-oriented society. Finally, consistent with our comments earlier about the sweatshop issue, many charge that outsourcing is nothing more than American firms exploiting cheaper labor in other countries to increase profits.

In the selections that follow, both sides of this interesting topic will be discussed. In the first selection, *BusinessWeek* writers argue that outsourcing is likely to become even more important to corporate America in the near future. In contrast to this position, *InfoWorld* columnist Ephraim Schwartz explores the often-overlooked costs associated with failed outsourcing initiatives by analyzing four brief case studies of outsourcing initiatives that turned out badly.

YES ↵

BusinessWeek

The Future of Outsourcing: How It's Transforming Whole Industries and Changing the Way We Work

Globalization has been brutal to midwestern manufacturers like the Paper Converting Machine Co. For decades, PCMC's Green Bay (Wis.) factory, its oiled wooden factory floors worn smooth by work boots, thrived by making ever-more-complex equipment to weave, fold, and print packaging for everything from potato chips to baby wipes.

But PCMC has fallen on hard times. First came the 2001 recession. Then, two years ago, one of the company's biggest customers told it to slash its machinery prices by 40% and urged it to move production to China. Last year, a St. Louis holding company, Barry-Wehmiller Cos., acquired the manufacturer and promptly cut workers and nonunion pay. In five years sales have plunged by 40%, to $170 million, and the workforce has shrunk from 2,000 to 1,100. Employees have been traumatized, says operations manager Craig Compton, a muscular former hockey player. "All you hear about is China and all these companies closing or taking their operations overseas."

But now, Compton says, he is "probably the most optimistic I've been in five years." Hope is coming from an unusual source. As part of its turnaround strategy, Barry-Wehmiller plans to shift some design work to its 160-engineer center in Chennai, India. By having U.S. and Indian designers collaborate 24/7, explains Vasant Bennett, president of Barry-Wehmiller's engineering services unit, PCMC hopes to slash development costs and time, win orders it often missed due to engineering constraints—and keep production in Green Bay. Barry-Wehmiller says the strategy already has boosted profits at some of the 32 other midsize U.S. machinery makers it has bought. "We can compete and create great American jobs," vows CEO Robert Chapman. "But not without offshoring."

Come again? Ever since the offshore shift of skilled work sparked widespread debate and a political firestorm three years ago, it has been portrayed as the killer of good-paying American jobs. "Benedict Arnold CEOs" hire software engineers, computer help staff, and credit-card bill collectors to exploit the low wages of poor nations. U.S. workers suddenly face a grave new threat, with even highly educated tech and service professionals having to compete against legions of hungry college grads in India, China, and the Philippines willing to work twice as hard for one-fifth the pay.

Workers' fears have some grounding in fact. The prime motive of most corporate bean counters jumping on the offshoring bandwagon has been to take advantage of such "labor arbitrage"—the huge wage gap between industrialized and developing nations. And without doubt, big layoffs often accompany big outsourcing deals.

The changes can be harsh and deep. But a more enlightened, strategic view of global sourcing is starting to emerge as managers get a better fix on its potential. The new buzzword is "transformational outsourcing." Many executives are discovering offshoring is really about corporate growth, making better use of skilled U.S. staff, and even job creation in the U.S., not just cheap wages abroad. True, the labor savings from global sourcing can still be substantial. But it's peanuts compared to the enormous gains in efficiency, productivity, quality, and revenues that can be achieved by fully leveraging offshore talent.

Thus entrepreneurs such as Chapman see a chance to turn around dying businesses, speed up their pace of innovation, or fund development projects that otherwise would have been unaffordable. More aggressive outsourcers are aiming to create radical business models that can give them an edge and change the game in their industries. Old-line multinationals see offshoring as a catalyst for a broader plan to overhaul outdated office operations and prepare for new competitive battles. And while some want to downsize, others are keen to liberate expensive analysts, engineers, and salesmen from routine tasks so they can spend more time innovating and dealing with customers. "This isn't about labor cost," says Daniel Marovitz, technology managing director for Deutsche Bank's global businesses (DB). "The issue is that if you don't do it, you won't survive."

The new attitude is emerging in corporations across the U.S. and Europe in virtually every industry. Ask executives at Penske Truck Leasing why the company outsources dozens of business processes to Mexico and India, and they cite greater efficiency and customer service. Ask managers at U.S.-Dutch professional publishing giant Wolters Kluwer (**WTKWY**) why they're racing to shift software development and editorial work to India and the Philippines, and they will say it's about being able to pump out a greater variety of books, journals, and Web-based content more rapidly. Ask Wachovia Corp. (**WB**), the Charlotte

(N.C.)-based bank, why it just inked a $1.1 billion deal with India's Genpact to outsource finance and accounting jobs and why it handed over administration of its human-resources programs to Lincolnshire (Ill.)-based Hewitt Associates (**HEW**). It's "what we need to do to become a great customer-relationship company," says Director of Corporate Development Peter J. Sidebottom. Wachovia aims to reinvest up to 40% of the $600 million to $1 billion it hopes to take out in costs over three years into branches, ATMs, and personnel to boost its core business.

Here's what such transformations typically entail: Genpact, Accenture (**ACN**), IBM Services, or another big outsourcing specialist dispatches teams to meticulously dissect the workflow of an entire human resources, finance, or info tech department. The team then helps build a new IT platform, redesigns all processes, and administers programs, acting as a virtual subsidiary. The contractor then disperses work among global networks of staff ranging from the U.S. to Asia to Eastern Europe.

In recent years, Procter & Gamble (**PG**), DuPont (**DD**), Cisco Systems (**CSCO**), ABN Amro (**ABN**), Unilever, Rockwell Collins (**COL**), and Marriott (**MAR**) were among those that signed such megadeals, worth billions.

In 2004, for example, drugmaker Wyeth Pharmaceuticals transferred its entire clinical-testing operation to Accenture Ltd. "Boards of directors of virtually every big company now are insisting on very articulated outsourcing strategies," says Peter Allen, global services managing director of TPI, a consulting firm that advised on 15 major outsourcing contracts last year worth $14 billion. "Many CEOs are saying, 'Don't tell me how much I can save. Show me how we can grow by 40% without increasing our capacity in the U.S.,'" says Atul Vashistha, CEO of outsourcing consultant neoIT and co-author of the book *The Offshore Nation*.

Some observers even believe Big Business is on the cusp of a new burst of productivity growth, ignited in part by offshore outsourcing as a catalyst. "Once this transformation is done," predicts Arthur H. Harper, former CEO of General Electric Co.'s equipment management businesses, "I think we will end up with companies that deliver products faster at lower costs, and are better able to compete against anyone in the world." As executives shed more operations, they also are spurring new debate about how the future corporation will look. Some management pundits theorize about the "totally disaggregated corporation," wherein every function not regarded as crucial is stripped away.

Processes, Now on Sale

In theory, it is becoming possible to buy, off the shelf, practically any function you need to run a company. Want to start a budget airline but don't want to invest in a huge back office? Accenture's Navitaire unit can manage reservations, plan routes, assign crew, and calculate optimal prices for each seat.

Have a cool new telecom or medical device but lack market researchers? For about $5,000, analytics outfits such as New Delhi-based Evalueserve Inc. will, within a day, assemble a team of Indian patent attorneys, engineers, and business analysts, start mining global databases, and call dozens of U.S. experts and wholesalers to provide an independent appraisal.

Want to market quickly a new mutual fund or insurance policy? IT services providers such as India's Tata Consultancy Services Ltd. are building software platforms that furnish every business process needed and secure all regulatory approvals. A sister company, Tata Technologies, boasts 2,000 Indian engineers and recently bought 700-employee Novi (Mich.) auto- and aerospace-engineering firm Incat International PLC. Tata Technologies can now handle everything from turning a conceptual design into detailed specs for interiors, chassis, and electrical systems to designing the tooling and factory-floor layout. "If you map out the entire vehicle-development process, we have the capability to supply every piece of it," says Chief Operating Officer Jeffrey D. Sage, an IBM and General Motors Corp. (**GM**) veteran. Tata is designing all doors for a future truck, for example, and the power train for a U.S. sedan. The company is hiring 100 experienced U.S. engineers at salaries of $100,000 and up.

Few big companies have tried all these options yet. But some, like Procter & Gamble, are showing that the ideas are not far-fetched. Over the past three years the $57 billion consumer-products company has outsourced everything from IT infrastructure and human resources to management of its offices from Cincinnati to Moscow. CEO Alan G. Lafley also has announced he wants half of all new P&G products to come from outside by 2010, vs. 20% [in 2006]. In the near future, some analysts predict, Detroit and European carmakers will go the way of the PC industry, relying on outsiders to develop new models bearing their brand names. BMW has done just that with a sport-utility vehicle. And Big Pharma will bring blockbuster drugs to market at a fraction of the current $1 billion average cost by allying with partners in India, China, and Russia in molecular research and clinical testing.

Of course, corporations have been outsourcing management of IT systems to the likes of Electronic Data Systems (**EDS**), IBM (**IBM**), and Accenture for more than a decade, while Detroit has long given engineering jobs to outside design firms. Futurists have envisioned "hollow" and "virtual" corporations since the 1980s.

It hasn't happened yet. Reengineering a company may make sense on paper, but it's extremely expensive and entails big risks if executed poorly. Corporations can't simply be snapped apart and reconfigured like LEGO sets, after all. They are complex, living organisms that can be thrown into convulsions if a transplant operation is botched. Valued employees send out their résumés, customers are outraged at deteriorating service, a brand name can be damaged. In consultant surveys, what's more, many U.S. managers complain about the quality of off-shored work and unexpected costs.

But as companies work out such kinks, the rise of the offshore option is dramatically changing the economics of reengineering. With millions of low-cost engineers, financial analysts, consumer marketers, and architects now readily available via the Web, CEOs can see a quicker payoff. "It used to be that companies struggled for a few years to show a 5% or 10% increase in productivity from outsourcing," says Pramod Bhasin, CEO of Genpact, the 19,000-employee back-office-processing unit spun off by GE last year. "But by offshoring work, they can see savings of 30% to 40% in the first year" in labor costs. Then the efficiency gains kick in. A $10 billion company might initially only shave a few million dollars in wages after transferring back-office procurement or bill collection overseas. But better management of these processes could free up hundreds of millions in cash flow annually.

Those savings, in turn, help underwrite far broader corporate restructuring that can be truly transformational. DuPont has long wanted to fix its unwieldy system for administering records, payroll, and benefits for its 60,000 employees in 70 nations, with data scattered among different software platforms and global business units. By awarding a long-term contract to Cincinnati-based Convergys Corp., the world's biggest call-center operator, to redesign and administer its human resources programs, it expects to cut costs 20% in the first year and 30% a year afterward. To get corporate backing for the move, "it certainly helps a lot to have savings from the outset," says DuPont Senior Human Resources Vice-President James C. Borel.

Creative new companies can exploit the possibilities of offshoring even faster than established players. Crimson Consulting Group is a good example. The Los Altos (Calif.) firm, which performs global market research on everything from routers to software for clients including Cisco, HP, and Microsoft (MSFT), has only 14 full-time employees. But it farms out research to India's Evalueserve and some 5,000 other independent experts from Silicon Valley to China, the Czech Republic, and South Africa. "This allows a small firm like us to compete with McKinsey and Bain on a very global basis with very low costs," says CEO Glenn Gow. Former GE exec Harper is on the same wavelength. Like Barry-Wehmiller, his new five-partner private-equity firm plans to buy struggling midsize manufacturers and use offshore outsourcing to help revitalize them. Harper's NexGen Capital Partners also plans to farm out most of its own office work. "The people who understand this will start from Day One and never build a back room," Harper says. "They will outsource everything they can."

Some aggressive outsourcers are using their low-cost, superefficient business models to challenge incumbents. Pasadena, (Calif.)-based IndyMac Bancorp Inc. (NDE), founded in 1985, illustrates the new breed of financial services company. In three years, IndyMac has risen from 22nd-largest U.S. mortgage issuer to No. 9, while its 18% return on equity in 2004 outpaced most rivals. The thrift's initial edge was its technology to process, price, and approve loan applications in less than a minute.

But IndyMac also credits its aggressive offshore outsourcing strategy, which Consumer Banking CEO Ashwin Adarkar says has helped make it "more productive, cost-efficient, and flexible than our competitors, with better customer service." IndyMac is using 250 mostly Indian staff from New York-based Cognizant Technology Solutions Corp. (CTSH) to help build a next-generation software platform and applications that, it expects, will boost efficiency at least 20% by 2008. IndyMac has also begun shifting tasks, ranging from bill collection to "welcome calls" that help U.S. borrowers make their first mortgage payments on time, to India's Exlservice Holdings Inc. and its 5,000-strong staff. In all, Exlservice and other Indian providers handle 33 back-office processes offshore. Yet rather than losing any American jobs, IndyMac has doubled its U.S. workforce to nearly 6,000 in four years—and is still hiring.

Superior Service

Smart use of offshoring can juice the performance of established players, too. Five years ago, Penske Truck Leasing, a joint venture between GE and Penske Corp., paid $768 million for trucker Rollins Truck Leasing Corp.—just in time for the recession. Customer service, spread among four U.S. call centers, was inconsistent. "I realized our business needed a transformation," says CFO Frank Cocuzza. He began by shifting a few dozen data-processing jobs to GE's huge Mexican and Indian call centers, now called Genpact. He then hired Genpact to help restructure most of his back office. That relationship now spans 30 processes involved in leasing 216,000 trucks and providing logistical services for customers.

Now, if a Penske truck is held up at a weigh station because it lacks a certain permit, for example, the driver calls an 800 number. Genpact staff in India obtains the document over the Web. The weigh station is notified electronically, and the truck is back on the road within 30 minutes. Before, Penske thought it did well if it accomplished that in two hours. And when a driver finishes his job, his entire log, including records of mileage, tolls, and fuel purchases, is shipped to Mexico, punched into computers, and processed in Hyderabad. In all, 60% of the 1,000 workers handling Penske back-office process are in India or Mexico, and Penske is still ramping up. Under a new program, when a manufacturer asks Penske to arrange for a delivery to a buyer, Indian staff helps with the scheduling, billing, and invoices. The $15 million in direct labor-cost savings are small compared with the gains in efficiency and customer service, Cocuzza says.

Big Pharma is pursuing huge boosts in efficiency as well. Eli Lilly & Co.'s (LLY) labs are more productive than most, having released eight major drugs in the past five years. But for each new drug, Lilly estimates it invests a hefty $1.1 billion. That could reach $1.5 billion in four years. "Those kinds of costs are fundamentally unsustainable," says Steven M. Paul, Lilly's science and tech executive vice-president. Outsourcing figures heavily in Lilly's strategy to lower that cost to $800 million. The drugmaker now does 20% of its chemistry work in China for one-quarter the U.S. cost and helped fund a startup lab, Shanghai's Chem-Explorer Co., with 230 chemists. Lilly now is trying to slash the costs of clinical trials on human patients, which range from $50 million to $300 million per drug, and is expanding such efforts in Brazil, Russia, China, and India.

Other manufacturers and tech companies are learning to capitalize on global talent pools to rush products to market sooner at lower costs. OnStor Inc., a Los Gatos (Calif.) developer of storage systems, says its tie-up with Bangalore engineering-services outfit HCL Technologies Ltd. enables it to get customized products to clients twice as fast as its major rivals. "If we want to recruit a great engineer in Silicon Valley, our lead time is three months," says CEO Bob Miller. "With HCL, we can pick up the phone and get somebody in two or three days."

Such strategies offer a glimpse into the productive uses of global outsourcing. But most experts remain cautious. The McKinsey Global Institute estimates $18.4 billion in global IT work and $11.4 billion in business-process services have been shifted abroad so far—just one-tenth of the potential offshore market. One reason is that executives still have a lot to learn about using offshore talent to boost productivity. Professor Mohanbir Sawhney of Northwestern University's Kellogg School of Management, a self-proclaimed "big believer in total disaggregation," says: "One of our tasks in business schools is to train people to manage the virtual, globally distributed corporation. How do you manage employees you can't even see?"

The management challenges will grow more urgent as rising global salaries dissipate the easy cost gains from offshore outsourcing. The winning companies of the future will be those most adept at leveraging global talent to transform themselves and their industries, creating better jobs for everyone.

BusinessWeek is a weekly business magazine currently headquartered in New York City.

Ephraim Schwartz

 **NO**

Painful Lessons from IT Outsourcing Gone Bad

As companies look to economize in a weak economy worsened by rising energy costs, it may be more tempting than ever to consider outsourcing your IT—whether to a cloud-based provider, to a shop in your town, or to a provider in some far-off land. Certainly, outsourcing has worked well for many companies, but it can also lead to business-damaging nightmares, says Larry Harding, founder and president of High Street Partners, a global consultancy that advises company on how to expand overseas. After all, if outsourcers fail, you're left holding the bag without the resources to fix the problem.

In his consulting, Harding has seen many outsourcing horror stories, from corrupt general managers "with all sorts of conflicts of interest" (such as service providers getting kickbacks from landlords on the leased space) to projects torn apart by huge turnover rates. "You end up with project teams that are hugely inconsistent. You might have a good team in place, but a month later, three-quarters of the team has transitioned," Harding says.

"Only when executed well can it pull out hundreds of millions in cost and transform organizations," says Brian Keane, CEO of Dextrys, an outsourcing service provider that focuses mainly on China.

In the sometimes panicked desire to save money—especially with the powerful lure of "half-price" workers in places like India, China, and the Philippines—good execution flies out the window. And that's where the problems flock in. Outsourcing is not for the faint-hearted or the ill-prepared. It just doesn't "happen."

That's why understanding what can go wrong before you jump into outsourcing is a great way to reduce your risk because then you can approach outsourcing with eyes wide open, Harding notes. The companies who've lived through outsourcing horrors have two things in common: lack of preparedness going into a new relationship and lack of communication once the projects gets under way. Other factors can make these worse, of course.

Outsourcing's Biggest Horror Show

In the pantheon of outsourcing horror stories, the $4 billion deal between the U.S. Navy and global services provider EDS stands out as one of the most horrific. It started back in 2003 when the Plano, Texas, vendor beat out the likes of IBM and Accenture for the contract. The deal was to manage voice, video, networking, training, and desktops for 350,000 Navy and Marine Corps users. But just one year later, EDS was writing off close to $350 million due to its inability to come even close to fulfilling its obligations.

The reasons behind the failure are complex, but suffice it to say that one of the major causes behind the debacle was that EDS, perhaps anxious to win the prize, never realized that the Navy and Marine Corps had tens of thousands of legacy and custom applications for which it was expected to either integrate or rip and replace. An EDS spokesperson said at the time the company's goal was to get the number of legacy apps down to a mere 10,000 to 12,000.

While there was plenty of blame to go around at EDS, the Navy took its share of blame as well. One of the major issues with the Navy was that the buck stopped nowhere. There was no single person or entity that could help EDS determine what legacy applications were needed and what applications could be excised. EDS, for example, found 11 different label-making applications, but there was no one who could say which 10 to eliminate.

Most companies will never face outsourcing problems on the scale of the Navy and EDS. But many will face their own horrors on systems and projects just as critical. Consider these four modern examples and what lessons the companies painfully learned.

Horror No. 1: A Medical Firm's Configuration Management Surprise

When Fran Schmidt, now a configuration engineer with Orasi Consulting, was told at her previous job in the medical industry to head up a team to outsource the existing in-house development and quality assurance IT departments, she faced the usual problems.

"There was one Indian fellow no one could understand over the phone. It took us months to figure out what he was saying," Schmidt recalls with a smile.

That was expected. But what the medical firm didn't count on was that its existing configuration management tool, Microsoft Visual SourceSafe, which worked fine locally, would be a total bust when used collaboratively between two groups 8,000 miles apart. It took the remote teams in India an average of 13 hours to get updates on source code. And with a time difference of about 11 hours, the outsourcers were behind a full day's work.

"When we hit the [Send] button, there was no code done by the previous shift the entire time they were at work," recalls Schmidt. Not having immediate access to what was previously done the day before caused major problems for in-house developers. "All our progress schedules were behind. It's a domino effect with everyone playing catch-up." And the firm's customers paid the price: They were upset because they were not getting the same level of care that they expected.

The medical firm ultimately switched its configuration management tool to AccuRev, cutting the transoceanic updating from 13 hours to about an hour and a half. All told, it took around six months to recover from the disaster, Schmidt recalls.

The obvious lesson was the need to test your infrastructure before going live in an offshoring scenario. But the medical firm also learned another hard lesson: The desire to save big bucks so blinded the executives that they didn't realize they were replacing a group of people experienced with using a product to a group of people who were looking at it for the first time. "We underestimated the loss of knowledge that would take place during the transition," Schmidt says.

Horror No. 2: Manufacturing Efficiency Doesn't Extend to Marketing

Executives in charge of a small consumer product group at Hewlett-Packard were under the gun. They were told in no uncertain terms to cut all costs related to getting the product into the big-box stores such as Best Buy and Circuit City, recalls Margaret McDonald, then marketing manager for the HP department and now president of her own company, McDonald Wordsmith Communications. (McDonald would not name the product and would only say that it is sold today at places such as Best Buy.)

"We were trying to get as much work as possible over to the Taiwan manufacturer with the goal to get the cost for these products down as low as possible," McDonald recalls. The Taiwanese outsourcer had a great deal of experience in getting the bill-of-materials costs lower, and HP was seeing that benefit. So managers started pushing for more savings elsewhere, insisting that the entire project be handed over to Taiwan—everything from manufacture to writing the instruction manuals to all the marketing materials.

"These execs were being evaluated on cost, not on the quality of the brand," says McDonald. When she tried to tell her managers that what they wanted was unreasonable for an outsourced manufacturer to deliver, they accused her of just trying to hold on to her job.

As she predicted, the project turned out to be a disaster. Take this example of the Taiwan-produced marketing materials: "This glamour of new product will perfectly fit to your daily life from any of locations!" Of course, non-native English prose like that never saw the light of day, but it wasted six months until the higher-ups finally realized what was happening.

McDonald isn't sure her managers learned a lesson. She sees the failure not due to the offshore firm hired or even the miscommunication between the US and Taiwan firms. Instead, she sees the problems as a failure within HP, between its own internal organizations. "The main [HP] branding people had no idea was going on." And the local managers reacted to the extreme cost pressures in a vacuum, with no concern for protecting the brand, McDonald says. The fact that the job was outsourced simply created the right circumstances for these internal flaws to finally become evident.

Horror No. 3: Giant Telecom Stumbles in Transition to Offshore

Steve Martin, a consultant and partner at Pace Harmon, a company that is often called in to help fix outsourcing deals gone bad, recalls the giant telecommunications company headed for disaster: It never considered the fact that although its new offshore provider was good at coding, it did not understand the business side of telecommunications.

The outsourcing project was divided into two phases. In phase one, all the internally managed operations were moved to an outsourced service provider (in this case, based in the United States). The idea was to test and stabilize the outsourcing approach with a local provider first, before taking the riskier step of moving the application development offshore.

The first phase went fairly well, so the telecom initiated phase two, shifting the effort to India. That didn't proceed so smoothly. The Indian provider simply didn't understand the telecom business, so lost in the transition halfway across the globe was all the telecom's inherent knowledge of the business applications—what it is supposed to do and why. "All of that knowledge got left in the US," Martin recalls.

Because the Indian firm didn't understand what it was coding, it took much longer to develop the applications. And they didn't work well, resulting in even more time and effort to figure out where they went wrong and fix them. It got so bad that the telecom canceled the offshoring midway and brought the effort back home.

Of course, there were lingering problems to resolve, such as how to handle the disputes over tens of millions of dollars in service credits the telecom believed it was due from the Indian outsourcer, which argued that it delivered what it had been asked to do. "An amazingly large amount of costs had to be reconciled," Martin notes. The two companies eschewed a legal battle to avoid the bad publicity, ultimately settling the dispute privately.

What the telecom company learned the hard way was that there is more to a deal than signing the contract. In the original deal, pricing took precedence over every other consideration because the executives wanted to show that they saved millions of dollars. Shortchanged in the process were the details of the transition, the development processes, and the governance. Adequate thought was not given to the obligations of the people who were responsible for executing the transition.

"The contract was executed from a business perspective, where it looked great, but not enough thought was given to how to programmatically move to the new environment," Martin says.

Horror No. 4: Service Provider Blacks Out the Client

James Hills, president of marketing firm MarketingHelp-Net, probably had one of the most terrifying offshore experiences of all. When a dispute between his new company and the Web site developers grew heated, he came into the office one day—only to discover the developers had shut his client's site down.

"I came in and checked e-mail. No e-mail, no Web site. They had simply turned it off. It was all gone," Hills recalls. While he was shocked to discover this, in some ways, he was not surprised. After all, the relationship with the offshore provider had been troubled from the start.

It started when Hills took on an assignment from a major client. Rather than trying to develop Web design skills needed to complete the client's project, Hills decided to farm that part of the job out to an offshore provider in the Philippines, at a savings of half of the cost of working with a local Web site designer, says Hills.

As soon as the offshore provider began sending back completed work, Hills knew there was trouble: "Functionality and community features didn't mesh properly, and the design wasn't what we were looking for." On top of that, the offshore provider continually missed deadlines.

Becoming increasingly frustrated, Hills didn't make the final payment. The result, of course, was a panicked wake-up call from his client telling him there was no e-mail and no Web site.

Looking back, Hills says that if had he to do it over, he would have been more diligent in checking references. He did only a perfunctory check of references, unfortunately taking it for granted that the offshore design firm actually created the Web sites they claimed.

Time differences also played a key role in the soured relationship. "We weren't able to communicate directly, only through IM," Hills says. And as a small startup at the time, he couldn't support multiple shifts at home to get overlap with India, nor ask his staff to work 20 hours a day to cover both time zones. And sending a manager to the Philippines was out of the question, Hills says.

Hills doubts he'll ever outsource again, but if he did, he would insist that the job be done with a US-based company that puts its offshore staff onto the company's payroll. "No contract workers," Hills says tersely.

EPHRAIM SCHWARTZ is an editor-at-large at InfoWorld.com. He also writes the Reality Check blog at www.inforworld.com/blogs/ephraim-schwarz.

EXPLORING THE ISSUE

Is Outsourcing a Wise Corporate Strategy?

Critical Thinking and Reflection

1. What might be the tactics of an outsourcing strategy?
2. How might an outsourcing strategy be implemented in a corporation?
3. What might be the costs to consumers, corporations, and the nation of corporations committed to an outsourcing strategy?
4. What is the likelihood that an enacted outsourcing strategy will lead to anticipated outcomes?
5. What does the future hold for companies following outsourcing strategies?

Is There Common Ground?

One reason the issue of outsourcing policies is so contentious is that both sides can easily cite data in support of their position.

While finding common ground on basic aspects of this important management topic is difficult, there is consensus that outsourcing policies are an important topic that will be debated for quite some time, especially in certain industries.

Additional Resources

Insinga, R.C. and Werle, M.J. (2000). "Linking Outsourcing to Business Strategy," *The Academy of Management Executive*, November, pp. 58–70.

Kakabadse, A. and Kakabadse, N. (2005). "Outsourcing: Current and Future Trends," *Thunderbird International Business Review*, March/April, pp. 183–204.

Lankford, W. and Parsa, F. (1999). "Outsourcing a Primer," *Management Decision*, pp. 310–316.

Internet References . . .

Customer Disservice? Critics Say the Promised Savings from Offshoring Come at Too Steep a Price, While Companies Say Very Little at All

Alster, N. (2005). "Customer Disservice? Critics Say the Promised Savings from Offshoring Come at Too Steep a Price, While Companies Say Very Little at All," *CFO Magazine, CFO IT*, Fall.

www.cfo.com/article.cfm/4390954

TARP Relief Law Might Discriminate Against Off-Shore Call Centers

Bierce, W.B. (2009). "TARP Relief Law Might Discriminate Against Off-Shore Call Centers," Outsourcing-law .com, January 24.

http://blog.outsourcing-law.com/2009/01/tarp-relief-law-might-discriminate.html

Anti-Outsourcing Campaign Renewed by Lou Dobbs

Boyd, R. (2005). "Anti-Outsourcing Campaign Renewed by Lou Dobbs," *The New York Sun*, February 2.

www.nysun.com/business/anti-outsourcing-campaign-renewed-by-lou-dobbs/8635/

Outsource, Outsource, and Outsource Some More

Griswold, D.T. (2004). "Outsource, Outsource, and Outsource Some More," Center for Trade Policy Studies, The Cato Institute, May 3.

www.freetrade.org/pubs/articles/dg-05-03-04.html

Shipping Jobs Overseas or Reaching New Customers? Why Congress Should Not Tax Reinvested Earnings Abroad

Griswold, D.T. (2009). "Shipping Jobs Overseas or Reaching New Customers? Why Congress Should Not Tax Reinvested Earnings Abroad," *Center for Trade Policy Studies*, Free Trade Bulletin, January 13.

www.freetrade.org/node/926

The Outsourcing Canard

Ikenson, D. (2009). "The Outsourcing Canard," Cato at Liberty.org, February 25.

http://www.cato.org/blog/outsourcing-canard

On May Day Celebrate Capitalism

Locke, E.A. (2003). "On May Day Celebrate Capitalism," The Ayn Rand Institute, April 24

www.aynrand.org/site/
News2?page=NewsArticle&id=7449

The Folly of Attacking Outsourcing

Porter, E. (2012). "The Folly of Attacking Outsourcing," *New York Times*, August 7.

www.nytimes.com/2012/08/08/business/economy/in-outsourcing-attacks-tired-rhetoric-and-no-political-leadership-economic-scene.html?_r=0

Selected, Edited, and with Issue Framing Material by:
Kathleen J. Barnes, *East Stroudsburg University*
and
George E. Smith, *Albright College*

ISSUE

Will the Use of Reshoring/Insourcing by Corporations Increase?

YES: Andrew Sikula, Sr., Chong W. Kim, Charles K. Braun, and John Sikula, from "Insourcing: Reversing American Outsourcing in the New World Economy," *Supervision* (vol. 71, no. 8, 2010, pp. 5–9)

NO: David J. Lynch, from "'Reshoring' of Jobs Looks Meager," *Bloomberg BusinessWeek* (2012), www.businessweek.com/articles/2012-07-05/reshoring-of-jobs-looks-meager

---

Learning Outcomes

After reading this issue, you should be able to:

- Describe the positive and negative consequences of reshoring/insourcing as a corporate strategy.
- Understand what tactics might be used to implement reshoring/insourcing as an effective corporate strategy.
- Appreciate the practical implications of reshoring/insourcing as a corporate strategy.
- Understand what factors are driving insourcing/reshoring.
- Understand whether insourcing/reshoring a fad or a trend that is here to stay.
- Know whether all businesses look to insource/reshore.
- Understand strategically, what are the benefits of insourcing/reshoring versus outsourcing.

ISSUE SUMMARY

YES: Andrew Sikula and colleagues discuss reasons why a movement to insourcing is currently occurring. The authors conclude that this movement is going to expand during the next several years in the United States.

NO: David Lynch observes that many of the jobs a nation (e.g., China) is losing are heading to other low-cost Asian nations. In addition, he observes that while some jobs have returned to the United States other jobs are still being shipped out of the country.

"Insourcing" is when an organization uses internal labor and personnel and other resources to supply the operational needs of its enterprise. Insourcing is a management decision made to maintain control of critical production processes or competencies. Insourcing is the opposite of outsourcing which is the process where firms shift work outside of its borders.

In recent decades of our increasingly global environment and marketplace, insourcing has taken on an expanded definition. It now often means letting work go outside the organization yet keeping it within national boundaries, rather than subcontracting to suppliers overseas. Outsourcing today often is synonymous with "offshoring" or moving work offshore to another country typically overseas. When the insourcing definition is expanded in this manner, it is an extension of a company's workplace without transferring the project management and decision-making control to an external provider.

There are many reasons why the resourcing pendulum has begun to significantly swing back toward insourcing and away from outsourcing within the United States and elsewhere. The eight factors or determinants of insourcing include (1) communication, (2) employee morale/loyalty, (3) control, (4) security, (5) transportation, (6) innovation, (7) customer satisfaction, and (8) speed to market.

Offshoring is defined as the movement of a business process done at a company in one country to the same or another company in another, different country. Often the work is moved because of a lower cost of operations in the new location, access to qualified personnel abroad, in particular in technical professions, and increasing speed to market. Outsourcing is the movement of internal business processes to an external organizational unit and refers to the process by which an organization gives part of its work to another firm/organization and makes it responsible for most of the applications as well as the design of the enterprise business process. "Reshoring," sometimes called "backshoring," is when jobs that were offshored are brought back onshore.

In the selections that follow, both sides of this interesting topic will be discussed. In the first article, Andrew Sikula and colleagues discuss reasons why a movement to insourcing is currently occurring. The authors conclude that this movement is going to expand during the next several years in the United States. In contrast to this position, David Lynch observes that many of the jobs a nation such as China is losing are heading to other low-cost Asian nations. In addition, he observes that while some jobs have returned to the United States, other jobs are still being shipped out of the country.

YES ⟵

Andrew Sikula, Sr., Chong W. Kim,
Charles K. Braun, and John Sikula

Insourcing: Reversing American Outsourcing in the New World Economy

Pendulum Swings and Globality

Politics and economics swing like a pendulum. So do life, health and human emotions. What is a popular belief and value during one period of time may not be in another. Even deep-seated religion is subject to fluctuation. These flows of nature and humankind apply to the marketplace as well. Abundances and shortages of supply and demand come and go for all goods and services. This phenomenon as it applies to the insourcing vs. outsourcing issue is the subject of this commentary and analysis.

We now live in a new world economy of global interaction and wholeness. Events in any part of the earth can and do almost instantaneously affect all other parts of the globe. High speed digital electronic communications have greatly helped to speed up this interactivity.

For decades now, economists have convinced us that we live in one international marketplace in which global laws of supply and demand determine consumer behavior. Also, increasingly recognized is the fact that politics, culture, ethics and science are now global as well. Mankind, morality, nature and the weather follow certain absolute laws and set patterns. They may be displayed differently in various locations at any point in time, but they are all universals with some common principles. The talk over the last many decades on relationism, situationalism and human specialty and uniqueness has been overdone. In truth, human beings have more in common than they have differences, and different lands and cultures are more alike than disparate.

Having said this about human and geographical similarity, we still need to recognize the pendulum swing between extremes within common production and manufacturing life cycles. This article discusses the human resource pendulum swing between insourcing and outsourcing work effort and accomplishment.

Insourcing Definition

Insourcing is when an organization uses especially internal labor and personnel, but other resources as well, to supply the operational needs of its enterprise. Insourcing is a management decision made to maintain control of critical production or competencies. Insourcing is the opposite of outsourcing which is the process of firms shifting work outside of its borders.

In recent decades in our increasingly global environment and marketplace, insourcing has taken on an expanded definition. It now often means letting work go outside yet keeping it within national boundaries rather than subcontracting to suppliers overseas. Outsourcing today often is synonymous with offshoring or moving work offshore to another country typically overseas. When the insourcing definition is expanded in this manner, it is an extension of a company's workplace and workforce without transferring the project management and decision-making control to an external provider.

Insourcing is akin to the "promotion from within" concept. Labor and personnel still constitute the bulk of both core competencies and operational expenses for most organizations. Keeping employees trained, developed, motivated and happy at work are pivotal characteristics of well-run, successful enterprises. This is often best achieved when workers are given internal opportunities for professional growth and personal advancement. Promotion from within is the manner in which this becomes possible. In-housing promotions and advancements usually make the majority happy. The outside hiring of personnel, especially into key, well-paid organizational positions, often demoralizes loyal staff members who have often waited years for a chance to advance themselves within their current employment structure. Inside promotions usually result in a chain of internal other promotions from within which spread new life, enthusiasm and additional vigor among many dedicated and aspiring current coworkers and colleagues. As an example, Ashland University in Ohio within the last three years has gone inside for most of its key position openings including University President, Seminary President, Provost, Graduate School Dean, Education Dean, Business Vice President and Facilities Vice President.

Insourcing Evolution

Insourcing vs. outsourcing as resource decisions have always been under close examination. However, the last three decades have seen a great expansion of the outsourcing phenomenon. In the early 1980s, organizations in the United States and elsewhere began delegating their

From *Supervision,* 71(8): 3–9. Copyright © by Andrew Sikula Sr., Chong W. Kim, Charles K. Braun, and John Sikula Reprinted by permission of the authors.

non-core functions to external organizations which specialized in providing a particular product, service or function. Initially, outsourcing was done in an attempt to save on labor costs as many unionized companies found it cheaper to produce their products in non-unionized, underdeveloped countries, even though other raw material transportation costs might increase. This first started for unskilled labor jobs but quickly spread to technical labor, white collar positions, and then to professional services. Eventually, sometimes even entire departmental work units were shifted overseas. Areas of organizational operation once thought to be almost sacred, or at least extremely critical, began to appear in India, Indonesia, Japan, Vietnam, the Dominican Republic and elsewhere. Examples include accounts payable, billing, training, engineering, manufacturing, customer service, technical support, sales/ordering, and others. Clothing companies such as Levi Strauss and shoe companies such as Nike and Reebok often have manufacturing, marketing and distribution all done on foreign soil. International call centers now often perform air travel, hotel reservations and tele-marketing. Outsourcing overseas has even spread to highly specialized medical fields including clinical records, disease diagnosis and the reading of x-rays. In the minds of many, the idea that anything and everything can be outsourced became a possibility.

This all began to change around the turn of the millennium and as we entered the 21st Century. Unhappy customers, especially in regard to foreign-based call centers, started the outsourcing reversal. Overseas scandals, global economic recession and terrorism fueled the embers. A lack of control both in terms of company operations and national security strengthened a turn to insourcing. "Speed to market" became a much more important competitive sales advantage as long distances and transportation costs increasingly offset lower labor expense. Also, in the United States, we are beginning to see a resurgence of national pride, an increased concern for safety, and a desire to return to older traditional work patterns and ways of accomplishing tasks. All of these factors have resulted in a new wave of insourcing and a decline in the popularity and practice of outsourcing. Outsourcing is still a robust theme and practice, but it has lost its momentum.

Insourcing Determinants

There are many reasons why the resourcing pendulum has begun to significantly swing back toward insourcing and away from outsourcing within America and elsewhere. We will briefly mention eight determinants below. They are easy to understand and do not need prolonged elaboration. The eight insourcing factors or determinants roughly in order of importance include (1) communication; (2) employee morale/loyalty; (3) control; (4) security; (5) transportation; (6) innovation; (7) customer satisfaction; and (8) speed to market.

Communication

It is obviously easier to communicate with someone who is nearby rather than far away. Although computers and digital electronics have made it much easier to communicate with distant colleagues and partners, distance still is a significant barrier to communication. Time differences and various time zones are part and parcel of the communication distance problem. Insourcing reduces or eliminates this obstacle. Considerable time saving is achieved when resource supply chain components are local or internal. Since time is money, expenses can be minimized and profits maximized more readily with neighboring or nearby resources. Communicating is a human interaction, and although it can be aided by computers and electronics, most communication is initiated, received and acted upon by human beings. People communicate more efficiently and effectively when geographical space is lessened.

Employee Morale/Loyalty

Worker motivation and dedication are enhanced when employees know that their work efforts are appreciated and rewarded. Keeping work and promotions inside an organization reduces employee turnover and lowers employee training and management development expenses. Promotion from within costs much less than outsourcing in terms of advertising costs, travel expenses for interviewees, and especially in terms of negotiated salaries. People who know that they will have a chance to move ahead professionally and get promotions over time within their own organization can be life-long, productive assets to an organization. On the other hand, letting work that was formally done inside now go outside of company walls almost always will lead to unhappy employees who start to feel that their work careers may be in jeopardy. The fear of losing one's job and economic insecurity result when companies outsource management employment opportunities.

Control

Control is exercising restraint, direction and command over people and resources. Holding things in check and supervision are easiest to achieve and maintain when production and distribution factors or inputs are nearby. Work products or services need to be regulated and quality checked, and insourcing makes such requirements easier to achieve than does outsourcing. Administration and guidance can be better accomplished and more economically implemented, especially in regard to human oversight, if managers are local instead of regional, national and/or international.

Security

Security is an extension and expansion of control. Security involves safety and freedom from danger and risk. Security eliminates doubt and anxiety and brings about protection and confidence. Security involves precautions taken to guard against crime, theft, attack, sabotage and/or espionage. Security enhances assurance and attempts to guarantee against loss. Security is vital at the personal, corporate and national levels. Insourcing helps bring about security to societal levels and becomes more difficult as resource supply chains are outsourced. Security is becoming more important at all social strata, as we now live in an increasingly insecure world, where violent terrorist attacks are daily events throughout the world. Homeland security is currently viewed as the number one priority for our national government by most Americans.

Transportation

Goods and services must be delivered to customers. With goods, and with services to a lesser degree, physical distance separates where a product is made from where it is consumed. This space interval may be thousands of miles, especially when offshoring is involved. Even domestic conveyance of items may involve long transport. For example, the average distance a food item purchased in the USA travels between production and consumption is 1,500 miles. The transfer of items across seas can be extremely expensive, and now foreign piracy has become an additional expense and concern. Insourcing can significantly reduce product transportation delivery problems and costs.

Innovation

Innovation is the introduction of new products, services and methods. Innovation involves novel conception, design, creation and invention. It was once thought that this research and development (R&D) requirement for sustained business advantage could best be achieved using an array of employed international professionals. Some evidence suggests otherwise. Today, most business experts believe that insourcing R&D produces better results than outsourcing same. The United States has always been the leader in introducing new products and services to the world, and this is still the case. Although foreign countries may more cheaply copy, produce and improve American invented products, the USA still retains an edge in innovation and creating new things.

Customer Satisfaction

U. S. employers sometimes have had to learn the hard way that happy customers are often more concerned about quality rather than the price of goods and services. This is especially true of services, but it applies to products or goods as well. For example, many companies have seen a big increase in unhappy customers as a result of outsourcing technical services, often to India. Especially in regard to call centers, such corporations have underestimated the negative impact that customer dissatisfaction can have on the bottom line. Also, there is a movement to "Buy American" products, and this movement has both formal organizational bodies as well as unorganized individuals supporting the "made in the USA" purchasing philosophy.

Speed to Market

Price and quality are not the only factors affecting buying decisions. Increasingly important is speed to market or how quickly one might have a purchased good or service in hand. In many cases, speed to market is more important than price and/or quality. Common examples are pharmaceutical purchases. However, sometimes even very big ticket items are involved. Immediate occupancy can affect a home purchase, and the delivery date of a new car often determines who gets the sale. We live in an egocentric world where immediate gratification and current pleasure are important considerations for many overeager consumers. Insourcing enhances the speed to market consumption criterion because it helps eliminate delivery delays.

Outsourcing Weights

There are, of course, also reasons why companies have used outsourcing in the past and will continue to utilize it. We will next list the eight main determinants of outsourcing decisions, again in an estimated descending order of importance. These are easy to comprehend and they do not need individual commentary. Eight outsourcing factors or determinants are (1) labor cost; (2) management delegation; (3) simplicity; (4) expertise; (5) competition; (6) quality; (7) adaptability; and (8) tax advantages.

A few general comments about these eight variables should suffice. Both management delegation and simplicity involve the belief that some unskilled and other professional personnel labor can be performed more economically by workers in undeveloped or underdeveloped countries where wages and salaries are considerably lower than in the United States. There is also the belief, which is erroneous, that this delegation of work elsewhere will make domestic operational matters easier or simpler to manage. Combine these considerations with the often mistaken idea that increased competition will result in hiring the most expert resource suppliers who will produce a better product and service—and presto, you have a rationale for outsourcing. And if things do not go well, you can change the whole thing or arrangement tomorrow or next year (the adaptability advantage). Also, there are both legitimate tax advantages for outsourcing as well as (many believe) other hidden or illegal monetary gains to be had when offshoring activities are involved. . . .

In reality, insourcing vs. outsourcing is neither an either/or nor a black/white decision. It is not necessary to do only one or the other. An organization can insource and outsource at the same time. By insourcing and outsourcing simultaneously, an enterprise can have the best of what both offer in an attempt to obtain a sustainable competitive advantage. We might appropriately label this combination of insourcing and outsourcing as "rightsourcing". However, it is nonetheless true that organizations collectively are seeing a trend away from outsourcing and back to insourcing as the resource supply pendulum shifts to the other direction from where it has been for the last three decades.

Insourcing Examples

Americans and others are experiencing a return to the insourcing of supply chain resources. Internal suppliers of goods and services have come about, especially during the last eight years plus, because of declining economic conditions worldwide and a growing concern for homeland security caused by terrorism throughout the world. We will give some examples of enhanced resource insourcing at the personal-individual, professional-institutional, and governmental-national levels.

Personal-Individual

In an effort to reduce spending, Americans are doing a lot more for themselves now rather than relying so much on outside service providers. More child and elder care is being done by family members and/or close friends rather than by day care and nursing home agencies. Since Wal-Mart has doubled the cost of an oil/filter change from $15 to $30, many men today are now doing this chore of maintenance on family automobiles. Netflix is booming as people watch more movies at home and fewer in theatres. Fancy restaurant dinners have been cut back as family members eat more meals at home. Haircuts, exercising and alcoholic consumption at home are recently more commonplace. Home elder care is up and hospice residences now typically involve only the last couple days of life. Much of this has been made possible by the high unemployment rate with many people no longer having regular work to occupy their time.

Professional-Institutional

Even professional work is now being performed by regular folk trying to save a buck. Paying a plumber $75 an hour has incentivized many men and women to fix their own leaky faucets and toilets. Home remodeling is often now done by residents rather than by skilled construction tradesmen. Turbo Tax has enabled many households to prepare their own tax returns rather than rely on outside experts to do the work. Legal Zoom has enabled anyone and everyone to now prepare their own wills, trust, advance directives, power of attorney, and other legal documents without the exorbitant fees of an attorney.

Not just individuals but institutions have also turned to insourcing rather than outsourcing to save money. For example, within healthcare, the hospitalist movement is replacing the need for external physicians to make so many in-hospital patient rounds. Doctors and hospitals now hire other doctors who work full time within a hospital to make patient calls converting former travel time to patient care oversight involvement. Universities are using

overtime, graduate assistants, adjuncts, full-time temps, term contracts, electronic course delivery, and interims to fill faculty and staff position more as tenured and tenure-track faculty positions decline appreciably in number. Hourly billing by lawyers and accountants is used less today and may become a relic of history as legal insourcing takes hold. Prepaid legal service providers are available today for both individuals and institutions.

Governmental-National

At the national level as well, there is evidence of a move away from outsourcing and toward insourcing. Much of this movement is related to U. S. over-reliance on foreign crude oil produced by countries that are anti-American. The American expansion of natural gas capacity and usage is one such happening. So is the whole Going Green movement as solar, wind and water power are being harnessed more. Recycling is a form of insourcing. Using the National Guard for border patrol and emergency response are governmental-national insourcing examples. Using prison inmates to clean up road sides and fight fires are other government insourcing examples. AmeriCorps and its various internal service projects illustrate national insourcing. And indeed, the whole movement toward more volunteerism and service assistance to those in need is becoming increasingly organized today and is now supplementing our traditional national and governmental insourcing assistance organizations such as the Red Cross, Salvation Army, Goodwill, Meals on Wheels, veteran service organizations, homeless shelters, et al.

The Future of Insourcing

Insourcing is going to expand during the next several years in America, especially at the governmental-national level. In fact, in the minds of many, an overabundance of insourcing at the governmental-national level will cause more problems than it will solve because of high debt financing and the loss of individual freedom issues. Whether or not this will happen remains to be seen, but we are moving in this direction.

Uncle Sam is the biggest employer in the United States. There are 1.8 million federal employees. If you add in military and civilian Department of Defense employees, the number jumps to 4.8 million. During years of Republican rule, there was an effort to move many government jobs to the private sector. This is changing rapidly under President Obama. This past July, the Director of the Office of Management and Budget issued a memo to all Executive Branch departments strongly suggesting that it would be better to have more federal employees and fewer private contract workers. Accordingly, the Department of Defense is planning to reduce outside contractors and boost internal personnel by 33,400 civilian employees. Intelligence agencies have insourced thousands of contractor jobs already. The Department of Defense is planning to insource 3,200 formerly contracted positions.

Some have said that the government, and especially the military in recent years, has had a research supply chain management mentality of "just in case," while the private sector believes in and practices a "just in time" philosophy. Clearly, politicians of both parties have committed us and our offspring to more government than we can afford. With President Obama's call for public service and the current economic downturn, there has never been a better time to attract people into federal work positions. However, a rush to insource thousands of positions while trying to take on more and more government programs can end in disaster. Government control of banking, the auto industry, insurance, education and health care is moving forward. Government agencies should approach insourcing with a clear plan of action focusing on inherently governmental positions (such as defense), key mission critical roles (such as economic stability), and core competencies (such as leadership). It must be remembered and should be practiced that government can best go about the people's business by largely staying out of it. The dilemma is obvious. Yes, there is a reversing trend toward more insourcing and less outsourcing, and this is a good movement in the right direction. But it is a move that should predominantly be featured within our culture at the personal-individual and professional-institutional levels and not at the governmental-national one. Otherwise, the uniqueness and promise of our great experience and investment in democracy will be at risk.

ANDREW SIKULA, SR., is a professor at Marshall University.

CHONG W. KIM is a professor at Marshall University.

CHARLES K. BRAUN is a professor at Marshall University.

JOHN SIKULA is vice president for Regional Centers and Outreach at Ashland University.

David J. Lynch

→ **NO**

'Reshoring' of Jobs Looks Meager

This spring, President Obama said he had "good news" to report: Lost American jobs are returning to the U.S. "For a lot of businesses," the president told a crowd in Albany, N.Y., on May 8, "it's now starting to make sense to bring jobs back home." In trumpeting this "reshoring" of jobs from abroad, the administration points to employers, including General Electric (GE) and Caterpillar (CAT), that have shifted some manufacturing to the U.S. The president also cited an April online survey by Boston Consulting Group showing that 37 percent of manufacturers with sales of more than $1 billion and almost half of those with more than $10 billion "plan to or are actively considering bringing back production from China to the U.S."

Yet there's little data to back up claims of a reshoring rush. For every company Obama praises for coming back home, there are others still shipping jobs out of the country. Honeywell International (HON) in Acton, Mass., plans to eliminate 23 positions by yearend when manufacturing of the company's stainless steel products moves to Nanjing, China. Boston Scientific (BSX) let go about 1,100 workers when the company moved production of its medical stents from Miami to Costa Rica.

The net effect of this two-way traffic on the labor market has been "zero," says Michael Janssen of the Hackett Group (HCKT), a business consulting firm that released a contrarian report on reshoring in May. "Some of these jobs that are coming back get a lot of press," he says. "There are just as many that get no press coverage still going offshore."

The White House stresses that manufacturers have added 495,000 jobs since January 2010, when factory employment bottomed out at almost 6 million below the 2000 level. Nearly 40 percent of those jobs were lost to other countries, either directly or because consumers chose imports over American-made products, says Robert Scott of the Economic Policy Institute in Washington. Now, a combination of rising wages for Chinese workers, a strengthening Chinese currency, and a new appreciation of the virtues of domestic production—including low-cost natural gas—has sparked a return to U.S. manufacturing, the administration says.

No one knows how many of the manufacturing jobs created since 2010 actually made a round trip from the U.S. to a foreign address and back. And if jobs are returning, they're doing so slowly. At the current pace of recovery, it will take 25 years for the U.S. to regain all the factory jobs lost since 2000.

China's cost advantage is gradually eroding. In 2005 production in China was 31 percent cheaper than in advanced nations, according to the Hackett Group's calculations. By 2013 the gap will be down to 16 percent, small enough for U.S. production to make sense in some cases, says the study. Likewise, Hal Sirkin, who wrote a 2011 Boston Consulting Group report that's optimistic about a U.S. manufacturing comeback, estimates that over the next eight years 2 million to 3 million jobs could result from improved U.S. competitiveness. "A significant chunk will be jobs that went to other countries and came back," he says.

So far, many of the jobs China is losing aren't heading to the U.S. but to other low-cost Asian nations. Rising wages in China led Coach (COH) to start looking for alternate places to make its wallets and handbags. By 2015 the company aims to reduce China's share of its production to about 50 percent from almost 80 percent today. New orders will be sent to factories in Vietnam, Indonesia, Thailand, and the Philippines. Reshoring to somebody else's shores will be more common in coming years than jobs returning to the U.S., says Tim Leunig, who teaches economic history at the London School of Economics: "The next president of the United States, whoever he is, will end his term with fewer Americans working in manufacturing than he inherited."

The bottom line: *Though manufacturers have created 495,000 jobs since 2010, there's little evidence it's because of a reshoring surge.*

DAVID J. LYNCH *is a reporter for Bloomburg News in Washington, DC.*

EXPLORING THE ISSUE

Will the Use of Reshoring/Insourcing by Corporations Increase?

Critical Thinking and Reflection

1. What might be the tactics of a reshoring/insourcing strategy?
2. How might a reshoring/insourcing strategy be implemented in a corporation?
3. What might be the costs to consumers, corporations, and the nation of corporations committed to a reshoring/insourcing strategy?
4. What is the likelihood that an enacted reshoring/insourcing strategy will lead to anticipated outcomes?
5. What does the future hold for companies following reshoring/insourcing strategies?

Is There Common Ground?

One reason the issue of reshoring/insourcing is so contentious is that both sides of this issue can cite data and provide examples in support of their position. For example, during times of high unemployment in a nation or region, society would seek opportunities for employment by reshoring or insourcing work back to that nation or region. In contrast, the argument can be made that the costs of operation and production might be lower when offshoring or outsourcing policies and practices are utilized. Thus, these practices may have either positive and/or negative effects on a corporation's bottom line or both. While finding common ground on basic aspects of this important management topic is difficult, there is consensus that reshoring/insourcing policies are an important topic that will be debated for quite some time.

Additional Resources

Cable, C. (2010). "Making the Case for Made in America," *Industry Week*, April, p. 56.

Cancino, A. and Jackson, C.V. (2012). "More Manufacuring Work Returns to U.S. Shores, *Chicago Tribune*, March 27.

DePass, D. (2012). "For Some Companies, 'Reshoring' Jobs Gains Appeal," *The Dallas Morning News*, August 11.

Free, M. (2012). "Is the Re-shoring of Manufacturing a Trend or a Trickle?" *Forbes*, June 27.

Kettl, D. F. (2012). "Insourcing Jobs Can Only Happen with States' Help," *Governing*, April.

Moser, H.C. (2012). "U.S. Manufacturing: Forgotten Wisdom from 1791," *Manufacturing Engineering*, March, p. 176.

Murphy, T. (2003). "Insourcing," *WARD'S AutoWorld*, May, pp. 44–48.

Quinn, J.B. and Hilmer, F.B. (1994). "Strategic Outsourcing," *Sloan Management Review*, Summer, pp. 43–55.

Internet References . . .

A New Chinese Export—Jobs

Knowledge@Wharton. (2012). "A New Chinese Export— Jobs."

http://business.time.com/2012/04/12/a-new-chinese-export-jobs/

Re-Shoring: Manufacturers Make a U-Turn

Morris, C. (2012). "Re-Shoring: Manufacturers Make a U-Turn."

http://www.cnbc.com/id/47535355//

Selected, Edited, and with Issue Framing Material by:
Kathleen J. Barnes, *East Stroudsburg University*
and
George E. Smith, *Albright College*

ISSUE

Does Expanding via Mergers and Acquisitions Make for Sound Corporate Strategy?

YES: Don de Camara and Punit Renjen, from "The Secrets of Successful Mergers: Dispatches from the Front Lines," *The Journal of Business Strategy* (vol. 25, no. 3, 2004, pp. 10–14)

NO: Anand Sanwal, from "M&A's Losing Hand," *BusinessFinance* Magazine (November 18, 2008), http://businessfinancemag.com/article/mas-losing-hand-1118

Learning Outcomes

After reading this issue, you should be able to:

- Define mergers and acquisitions.
- Explain both positive and negative consequences of corporate mergers and acquisitions.
- Discuss the potential risks of mergers and acquisitions.
- List the known "best practices" for mergers and acquisitions.

ISSUE SUMMARY

YES: Don de Camara and Punit Renjen note in their article that merger activity is a part of the contemporary business environment. They observe that despite the many prescriptions for merging, each merger is unique and has its own challenges. They contend that mergers can be successful, but the process requires close and careful attention.

NO: Anand Sanwal examines 33 large merger and acquisition (M&A) transactions from Europe, Canada, and the United States. The evidence is that a great number of these M&A transactions have actually destroyed value. He also contends that in many of the transactions that did fare well, luck was often a large factor.

Banks, cars, pharmaceuticals, phones, and beer—what do all these have in common? If you said "abundant merger and acquisition (M&A) activity in their industries," you are absolutely correct. Keep in mind that these are by no means the only industries to experience M&A transactions. For example, when looking in current business periodicals it doesn't take long to learn about the latest M&A transactions and deals. Indeed, mergers (two firms joining together to become one) and acquisitions (one firm buying another) are common means of expansion for many firms. They're also common means of expansion across industries, particularly when firms are looking to move into new business areas.

Firms undertake M&As for many, varied reasons. Among other things, the mergers and acquirers feel that they can increase revenues or cut costs through marketing activities such as cross-selling or bundling products together from the two firms. These companies may also believe that they can share various administrative duties, thus reducing costs further. Other firms undertake M&As as a means of obtaining valuable technology or critical skills that the target may possess. Still others try to diversify business activities to help control their exposure to risk. Sometimes activity is even triggered by other M&A activity, almost as if companies simply don't want to be left behind when an M&A wave is happening. Regardless of the reasons driving M&As, one thing seems evident, M&A transactions are not going away. All of this activity, however, hides an important, seldom-asked question: In reality, do M&As actually generate the value that is expected?

Contrary to those advocates that view M&A activity as a good expansion vehicle, many people argue that past M&A activity has actually destroyed value—so much so, in fact, that it suggests that it may not be sound corporate strategy. Although actual failure rates for M&A transactions depend upon a variety of variables (e.g., timeframe examined, measures used, etc.), it is not uncommon to see estimates stating poor performance or failure for M&As in the range of one-half to two-thirds of all such activity (Vaughn, 2008). Reasons for failures can be numerous. They range from not being able to integrate opposing corporate cultures to failing to capture the synergies that were expected to emerge from the combined entities. Not surprisingly, given these risks, internally generated growth initiatives are often advocated over attempting M&As. Author John Cummings notes that this may be particularly salient given current market conditions: "With debt financing likely scarce for the foreseeable future, the only way forward for most growth-minded organizations is via internally generated profitable revenue expansion—the organic route" (Cummings, 2008, pp. 12–17).

In the "YES" side selection, authors Don de Camara and Punit Renjen present data from two large successful mergers: Hewlett-Packard (HP)/Compaq and AmeriSource Health Corporation/Bergen Brunswig Corporation. While the authors acknowledge that roughly half of all mergers fail to create value, these particular cases represent mergers that resulted in substantial value creation. In their article, de Camara and Renjen are interested in exploring the lessons that can be learned from these large, successful mergers

as the companies attempted to apply "best practice" to their respective mergers. The article's primary "data" are based on interviews with Barbara Braun, the vice president for merger integration at HP, and Terrance P. Haas, senior vice president for operations at AmeriSourceBergen. One important caveat that de Camara and Renjen add at the conclusion of their article is that "best practice" may not always be enough as each merger situation is unique and presents its own challenges as well as its own opportunities.

The "NO" side of this debate is presented in Anand Sanwal's article where he provides evidence suggesting that a great number of recent large transactions have actually destroyed value. Additionally, he contends that many transactions that did fare well were often successful because of luck, rather than skill in managing the transaction. Although Sanwal discusses some factors that may increase the success of large M&As, he qualifies this discussion by noting that ". . . . all the research in the world won't change the fact that people like headlines and deals are going to happen." As you read through the selections, ask yourself if these M&A deals are the result of corporate executives chasing headlines or if they represent strategically sound corporate transactions.

YES ↵

Don de Camara and Punit Renjen

The Secrets of Successful Mergers: Dispatches from the Front Lines

Studies by academics, consulting firms, and the business press confirm that mergers are just as likely to destroy as to create shareholder value. Despite this track record, merger activity may be poised for a rebound. The increase in the first half of 2003 in US equity prices, which have tended to move in tandem with merger activity over the last decade, suggests that the pace of deal-making is likely to pick up once again. A single day in October 2003 witnessed four deals valued at more than $70 billion, the largest wave of activity since the 1990s bull market.

How can companies entering a merger, especially those planning the largest, most complex mergers, improve their likelihood of success? The list of merger best practices is familiar: concentrate on synergies; integrate quickly; maintain a focus on customers and revenue growth; communicate continuously; and address human and cultural issues.

Despite these well-known prescriptions, roughly half of mergers fail to create value, demonstrating how difficult it is to execute these tasks. How have successful mergers worked? And what lessons can be learned by firms that are contemplating acquisitions?

To gain a first-person perspective on what makes for merger success, we interviewed senior executives responsible for integration in two recent mega-mergers: Hewlett-Packard with Compaq and AmeriSource Health Corporation with Bergen Brunswig Corporation.

Hewlett-Packard/Compaq—Hewlett-Packard (HP) acquired Compaq in May 2002 for approximately $19 billion, in one of the largest and most heavily publicized mergers in history. Although the new firm set an objective of $2.4 billion in cost reductions by November 2003, the combined firm achieved $3.7 billion in annualized savings within one year of closing the deal. The company has also picked up new business in such areas as basic servers and computer services. Integration has proceeded so smoothly that the firm announced that it plans to wrap up the merger integration process in 2003, one year ahead of the original schedule. To understand the process behind the merger, we interviewed Barbara Braun, vice president for merger integration at HP.

AmeriSource Health Corporation/Bergen Brunswig Corporation—AmerisourceBergen was created in August 2001 from the merger of the third and fourth largest distributors of pharmaceuticals and related healthcare products and solutions in the USA. The merger, valued at approximately $3.8 billion, created the largest US drug wholesaler by revenue, with annual revenues in excess of $35 billion. The merger substantially increased the buying power of the combined firm and offered significant opportunities to increase efficiency through economies of scale. AmerisourceBergen is ahead of schedule in achieving its targeted $150 million in cost savings by the end of fiscal 2004. We interviewed Terrance P. Haas, senior vice president for operations at AmerisourceBergen, who played a central role in managing the integration of the two firms.

Here's how these two companies successfully turned merger best practices into reality.

Identifying Synergies

Successful mergers start with a clear understanding of the synergies they hope to capture. Not only does senior management need to understand the merger strategy, but they need to communicate it to the executives engaged in pre-merger planning and in post-merger integration. While cost reductions are usually one factor, most successful mergers are motivated by a vision of how the combined company will be better able to increase revenues and gain market share than either company could on its own.

Gaining increased capabilities was an important rationale for the HP merger with Compaq. In addition to cost reductions, the merger was designed to enhance HP's ability to serve the needs of both business and public sector customers and improve overall profitability. "Our goal in the merger was to blend HP and Compaq together holistically to create a company that would be stronger than the two companies were on their own," said Barbara Braun.

The principal motivations in the AmerisourceBergen merger were to expand the reach of the combined firm while achieving economies of scale. "AmeriSource had a strong distribution network and market penetration on the East Coast, while Bergen was strong on the West Coast," explained Terrance Haas. "By bringing together the two organizations, we increased our market share and created substantial opportunities to lower fixed costs and eliminate overhead."

Accelerating Integration

In mergers, speed is critical. While it is important to integrate well, it is just as important to integrate quickly. Firms that can burst from the starting gate are most likely to succeed. Some of the key factors that allowed these two firms to rapidly integrate their acquisitions included:

Early, Detailed Planning

At HP, a detailed integration plan was developed long before the merger closed. "The HP-Compaq plan was incredibly detailed and comprehensive," recalled Braun. "We asked ourselves: What would the new organization structure be, overall and in all its details? What would the product lines be? Who would manage the largest accounts for the new company? What would the top management structure be? Which business processes would be used? Which IT systems? The result was a detailed roadmap laying out what needed to be accomplished in every area of the company, who was responsible, and when it had to be completed. Since the merger closed, we have been executing this roadmap like clockwork."

While speed is important, Terrence Haas of AmerisourceBergen stressed that proper timing of integration is essential. "You certainly need to have the senior management in place as soon as possible. However, if you appoint executives below the management level before having an integration plan, they will be making decisions without knowing [the] firm's future operating model and may accidentally delay capturing the full value of the merger. Once the future operating model has been defined, executives at lower levels can be named and start executing against it."

Consider Clean Teams

Mergers of major firms that compete in the same markets face an additional barrier since antitrust rules in the USA, the European Union, and many other locations prohibit companies from sharing confidential information about their business practices until a lengthy regulatory review process has been completed. This can make it difficult or impossible to develop integration plans until regulatory approval has been secured.

To develop an integration plan despite the restrictions, HP created a "clean team" of employees of both organizations who shared confidential information about the two firms. "We created a clean team of people who were legally isolated in the pre-merger state from the rest of the two companies. Senior leaders were literally taken out of their day jobs and assigned to the clean team to plan the new company," said Braun. "We kept the clean team relatively small since its members would have been contaminated by insider information and could have potentially lost their jobs if the merger had not gone through." The use of a clean team allowed HP to complete detailed integration plans before the merger close.

Direct Senior Management Involvement

Active senior management commitment has proven critical to rapid merger integration. "There was a strong, unwavering commitment from senior management, including the CEOs of both companies, to plan and drive the merger forward as quickly as possible," said Braun. "HP's head of sales and marketing for business accounts and Compaq's CFO were each pulled out of their usual job to focus on merger integration."

Senior management played a critical role in the AmerisourceBergen meger. "Right from the beginning, we had our executive team in place and they were of one mind on where the merged company needed to go. We had a steering committee composed of the CEO, COO, CFO, president of our drug company, president of our specialty group, and the heads of human resources from both firms. This steering committee of senior management was closely involved throughout the merger in approving overall strategy and the vision for the merged company."

Adopt-and-Go

Both mergers illustrate the benefits of choosing the best aspects of the two organizations when integrating, rather than spending time in an attempt to design the perfect business process or system. HP calls this approach "adopt-and-go." "When it came to the IT systems, business processes, and product lines of the two companies, we didn't look to meld them into a brand new system," explained Braun. "Theoretically, this could have captured the best elements of each company's approach, but in reality it was a prescription for delay. Instead, the HP-Compaq teams analyzed each company's approach to determine which one was superior. Then we simply adopted the better approach as the new standard for the merged company and proceeded quickly to implementation."

At AmerisourceBergen, functional teams were responsible for comparing both the productivity and the operating costs of each business process. "The goal was to choose the most productive processes and then place them in locations that allowed the lowest per-unit cost," explained Haas. "If a team decided that the Bergen process was more productive, but the AmeriSource per-unit rate was lower, then we made the decision to adopt the Bergen process but place it in the AmeriSource location."

Central to this approach is resisting the tendency to choose IT systems or products based on tradition, politics, or personalities. "HP worked to make the decisions more objective and less subject to emotions and consensus," said Braun. "If we had something from HP and something from Compaq, we asked: Which one is objectively the best? For example, who is the market leader or has the most features?"

Serving Customers Despite a Merger

The fundamental organizational changes created by a major merger create the risk that customer satisfaction and sales will suffer. Employees tend to focus inwardly on integrating business processes, IT systems, and product lines rather than on serving customers and driving revenue growth.

"We had an integration office that handled merger strategy, supported by a program office that managed day-to-day implementation. These groups did all the 'heavy lifting' in bringing the two companies together, allowing managers to continue to focus on our customers," Haas said. One measure of the success of this approach is that AmerisourceBergen was rated as the number one national pharmaceutical distributor in September 2002 by Goldman, Sachs & Co. for the third year in a row.

HP maintained its focus on customers by keeping sales and support professionals deployed in the field, rather than by calling on them to plan and execute the merger. A few senior sales management executives developed integration plans for all selling activities, leaving the large majority of customer-facing employees available to serve customers and channel partners.

Communicating the Vision

Running throughout successful mergers, from strategy through implementation, is the need for ongoing communication. Successful mergers communicate early and often to customers, employees, partners, investors, and the media.

At AmerisourceBergen, communications were managed centrally by the integration office. "Our communications plan identified the key messages, the internal and external targets, the media we would use, and the timing of communications," said Haas. "All communications were either developed or approved by our integration office to ensure that there was consistency in the messages that we were communicating to our employees, to customers, and to investors."

The effort at HP indicates the enormity of the task. According to Braun, "Before the merger closed, we trained the top 1,000 leaders across the company around the world. Then employees were trained in both customer-facing and internal activities so that everyone was ready on day one to answer any questions that arose from customers. Finally, we held 17,000 team meetings across the world to present the new organization, roles, and responsibilities."

To be effective, communications need to be based on a realistic assessment of the facts, rather than being overly optimistic. This is especially critical with employees who are concerned about their jobs.

Getting a Handle on Culture

While most firms recognize the critical importance of human and cultural issues in a merger, these issues are especially hard to analyze and quantify. The first step is to maintain morale by addressing employee concerns about benefits. Unless care is taken, employees can spend more time worrying about their jobs and benefits than about sales and customer satisfaction.

Successful mergers also need to take into account the business culture of the new entity. Firms need to conceive the desired end state, the ideal culture they are looking to create for the new entity.

AmerisourceBergen faced the challenge of bringing together two companies with disparate approaches. "AmeriSource ran an extremely lean organization, with little corporate hierarchy, and was organized by region," said Haas. "On the other hand, Bergen had a deeper corporate infrastructure and was aligned centrally by function. After interviewing executives in both firms to identify what was working well and what could be improved, we decided to adopt a decentralized model that pushed decision-making and accountability as close to the customer as possible to increase responsiveness, while maintaining a low-cost operating philosophy. Our chief executive officer and chief operating officer have played central roles in instilling this culture throughout the new organization."

Integrating the Lessons

The experience of HP and AmerisourceBergen illustrates the practical realities of implementing merger best practices. "Adopt-and-go" planning, clean teams, direct management of integration by senior executives, and the 80/20 rule to ensure that executives remain focused on meeting customer needs are a few of the specific strategies that proved successful in these two mega-mergers. While each situation is unique, firms contemplating acquisitions can draw lessons from the hands-on experience of HP and AmerisourceBergen in successfully managing large, complex mergers where so many others have failed.

***

Don de Camara leads Deloitte's enterprise cost reduction service area. He formerly led Deloitte's merger integration service line and has extensive experience with acquisition and divestiture strategy, target screening, and integration planning. In addition, he assisted numerous enterprises in redefining their strategies and restructuring operations.

Punit Renjen is the primary architect of Deloitte's merger & acquisition (M&A) service line. He directs Deloitte's research into M&A and oversees the development of a methodology for creating value through M&A. He has assisted clients on engagements encompassing the entire M&A life cycle and led the development of a comprehensive, structured methodology for all phases of M&A activity with an emphasis on merger integration capabilities.

Anand Sanwal   → **NO**

M&A's Losing Hand

It's been an absolutely ugly October in global financial markets, and all indications point to continued uncertainty and volatility for the foreseeable future. Most CEOs and CFOs of public companies are looking dejectedly at company share prices that are a fraction of what they were just a year ago. For companies that are weathering the current storm, the question that progressive CEOs and CFOs will soon begin to consider, as they should, is where do we need to take our business in order to begin delivering shareholder value and returns once again?

Considering this question will require the crafting of a compelling narrative and strategy that these senior leaders can communicate to their employees, customers, and shareholders about what's next—i.e., where is the company's future profitable growth going to come from?

One of the often-used vehicles to achieve growth, in theory, has been mergers and acquisitions (M&A); however, current market conditions make M&A a dicey or even impractical option. The unavailability of credit and increasingly expensive short-term refinancing rates, coupled with the economic downturn and depressed equity prices, have all served to make M&A difficult to accomplish. This has resulted in a spate of dead deals in recent weeks.

According to Deal Logic, the first 13 days of October witnessed 49 deals valued at $57.6 billion pulled, after $62.8 billion worth of deals were pulled in September. Acquirers that were hit by M&A travails include the BG Group, Waste Management, Bristol-Myers Squibb, HSBC Holdings, Dubai World, Xstrata, and Walgreen, to name a few. From this list, it is obvious that the M&A downturn is hitting companies in a diverse array of sectors, industries, and geographies.

How should CEOs, CFOs, and shareholders react to the M&A malaise? Contrary to popular belief, and especially so for those considering a large M&A transaction, they should pop open a bottle of champagne and celebrate. Why? Because according to our research, "megadeals"—those in which the target's value exceeds $10 billion—more often than not destroy shareholder value.

This is the underlying conclusion of our study in which we evaluated all megadeals from 2002 to 2007. We examined 33 M&A megadeals from Europe, Canada, and the USA in which the acquirers were strategic buyers—not financial or private equity concerns. (Please note that because some data were unavailable, in some instances our results do not reflect all 33 deals; see the [box] to get a list of the evaluated deals.)

In what was arguably one of the greatest bull markets we've ever seen, we observed that megadeals actually destroyed value over 60 percent of the time. On average, transactions resulted in negative cumulative excess beta returns (−4.03 percent) in the year after their announcement. (See the sidebar for insights into the research methodology.)

Even among the handful of deals that generated positive returns, we found that success was more often than not attributable to macroeconomic factors beyond the control of the acquirer. So it seems that it is often better to be "lucky than good" or "in the right place at the right time" when undertaking large M&A transactions. Furthermore, the data show that many of the deals, whether successful or not, increased the beta of the acquirer. Higher-risk profiles resulted in a higher cost of capital for the company post-acquisition, making such deals "costlier" in ways that can be very damaging to the larger entity over the longer term.

Following the quantitative analysis of all of the megadeals, we also sought to determine what lessons we could take away from the good, the bad, and the ugly so that future M&A megadeals can avoid past pitfalls and replicate elements of the few successful ones. However, before we do so, it is important to reiterate that our research showed few to no valid reasons to engage in megadeal M&A unless the desire is to redistribute shareholder money to needy investment bankers and lawyers. This being said, all the research in the world won't change the fact that people like headlines, and deals are going to happen. Armed with this level of pragmatism, we developed a set of dimensions that should be considered when engaging in megadeal M&A.

Peeling Back the Findings

Regarding measures that you can control, here are some observations about how you can increase a deal's chances of success:

- **It's important not to overpay.** This is straight from the "master of the obvious" file, but it's clear that disciplined buyers outperform loose spenders. Evidence suggested that premium and performance are inversely correlated, meaning that the greater the premium, the worse the performance. By way of example, Boston Scientific's acquisition of Guidant involved a bidding war with Johnson & Johnson that resulted in Boston Scientific paying a handsome $80 per share as opposed to their original offer of $72. In the case of the Sprint Nextel deal, Nextel took advantage of Sprint's insecurity regarding its ability to compete against other carriers and as a result secured an excellent exit price. Both of these deals resulted in miserable excess returns.

In other cases such as Bank of New York's acquisition of Mellon Financial Corp., a very low premium was involved, as was the case in the CVS-Caremark and Manulife–John Hancock deals, which both did well. Price is not the only consideration, of course, but higher premiums generally make it more difficult for buyers to achieve high returns. The challenge ultimately is that when an acquirer pays a high premium, its shareholders get diluted or it uses cash to prevent dilution. The only way ultimately for the firm to get that cash back is to reengineer expenses out of the combined company. The synergies needed to pay for premium and the excess premium make this impossible. Moreover, the need to significantly reduce expenses can mean cutting muscle, not just fat, resulting in weakened competency and poor morale.

- **Acquiring a faster-growth target is looked upon favorably.** When companies acquire targets with higher growth expectations than their own, it appears that the market supports the acquisition. In contrast, when companies acquire targets that are underperforming and whose growth expectations are lower than their own, acquisitions tend to fail. In cases where both companies underperform and a transaction occurs, postdeal performance tends to be quite lackluster, as such an M&A is used as a poor replacement for an inability to generate organic growth. Unfortunately, combining two cubic zirconias rarely results in a real diamond.
- **Mergers of Equals outperform outright acquisitions.** To determine the effect that the relative size of the buyer to the target has on M&A performance, we found that in general, acquisitions that fell in the Merger of Equals category performed better than those that fell into the outright Acquisitions category. Originally, this seemed slightly counterintuitive; however, a closer look at some of the best-in-class examples shows that in Mergers of Equals, both companies tend to have a fair amount of interest in deal success and thus are more collaborative. In Mergers of Equals, both companies often bring different strengths to the table and thus allow the whole to be greater than the sum of the parts. For example, when Manulife Financial Corporation acquired John Hancock Financial Services, the former provided strong

brand recognition, while the latter offered strong access to capital markets, and both presented distinct distribution channels.

M&A Megadeal Success

Through research tied to individual transactions, we determined that high-performing deals considered the following dimensions and questions.

Practical Considerations

- **Macroeconomic and industry factors.** Am I appropriately considering macroeconomic factors on the upside and downside that could impact the industry and/or competitive landscape? Are my expectations for future growth of the target reasonable, and is the deal worthwhile even in a worst-case scenario?
- **Timing.** Are there internal concerns that should take managerial priority?
- **Price.** Am I being disciplined in my determination of the price?
- **Cost savings and revenue synergies.** Am I comfortable that the deal is attractive even if estimated cost savings or opportunities for revenue from the combined company are less than I expect?

Strategic Considerations:

- **Branding, distribution, and scale.** Does the deal provide the potential combined company with greater economies of scale, increased distribution channels, or stronger branding?
- **Organic growth.** Does the deal hamper the potential combined company's potential for organic growth?
- **Integration.** Have we properly accounted for managerial, technological, and cultural integration issues?
- **Geographic and product expansion.** Is there significant overlap between the potential combined companies' geographic and product markets, and will the deal provide an opportunity for expansion?

Our findings suggest in no uncertain terms that firms should be wary of undertaking M&A megadeals. If shareholders who are reeling from the last several months of performance can take solace in one fact, it is that the ability to do M&A may be hampered, at least in the short to medium term, by the economy and credit conditions.

However, these types of exogenous pressures on M&A will ultimately subside, and when this occurs, investment bankers and a host of others will come running back with suggestions for large M&A deals. They will also come equipped with facts and figures showing extensive strategic benefits and magnificent projections about cost and revenue synergies.

A CLOSER LOOK: RESEARCH METHODOLOGY

For each of the megadeal transactions evaluated (all of which took place between 2002 and 2007), data were collected and analyzed as follows:

- Data were collected from 60 business days prior to announcement until two years after close.
- Most of the analysis was conducted on data from 60 days prior to announcement until 265 days after announcement (slightly over a year) in order to put all of the deals on the same time scale. This was a sufficient time span because on average the deals closed within 121 days and most companies' excess returns displayed discernible patterns by the end of this time period.
- **Excess beta return was used as the primary metric for financial success** because it measures how much the individual stock's excess return varies in comparison with the market as a whole. The cumulative excess beta return was calculated by zeroing out the returns at the day before announcement (day −1) and then aggregating the returns for each successive day while holding day −1 as the base.
- **Each acquirer's returns were also compared to the company's specific sector index,** in order to account for macroeconomic factors or market trends that may have affected individual segments.
- **Each deal was analyzed on an individual basis** using financial data, company reports and presentations, and media reports and news surrounding each deal.

About the Deals Analyzed

- **The deals spanned all nine of the S&P 500 sectors.**
- **The Financials sector was particularly well represented,** owing to the fact that several financial institutions were engaging in aggressive geographic and market expansion during the time span covered.
- **Deals were categorized as either a "Merger of Equals" or as an "Acquisition."** For the purposes of this study, a "Merger of Equals" was defined as a deal in which the market capitalization of the buyer was less than or equal to 1.5 times the market capitalization of the target at 60 days prior to announcement. All others were considered "Acquisitions."
- **The majority of the deals were from the United States and Canada** simply because of the greater amount of information that was available; however, a few European deals were also included.

M&A Megadeals Evaluated

Acquirer	Target
Capital One	North Fork Bank
Wachovia	South Trust
Regions Financial	AmSouth Bancorp
General Growth Properties	Rouse Company
Wachovia	Golden West Financial
Bank of America	MBNA
JPMorgan Chase	Bank One
Manulife Financial	John Hancock Financial Services
Bank of America	FleetBoston Financial Group
Travelers Companies	Travelers Property Casualty
National Grid	Lattice Group
Harrah's Entertainment	Caesar's Entertainment
Sears Holdings	Sears Roebuck
SUPERVALU	Albertsons
P&G	Gillette
Anadarko Petroleum	Kerr-McGee
ConocoPhillips	Burlington Resources
Chevron	Unocal
Duke Energy	Cinergy
AstraZeneca	Medimmune
CVS	Caremark Rx
J&J	Pfizer Consumer Healthcare
Thermo Fisher Scientific	Fisher Scientific International
Boston Scientific	Guidant
Pfizer	Pharmacia
Symantec	Veritas Software
Sprint Nextel	Nextel Communications
Freeport-McMoRan	Phelps Dodge
Barrick Gold	Placer Dome

Oftentimes, they will paint a picture of market leadership, industry transformation, a bold new vision for the combined entity, and amazing shareholder returns. When this time comes, CEOs and CFOs must resist many elements of these "compelling" narratives, which we readily admit have a seemingly magnetic pull.

Instead, if—as stewards of shareholder money—they take a dispassionate view of the transaction in question, remember the abysmal historical track record of large M&A deals in the past, and also recognize the outsized role that luck plays in successful deals, the decision to say "no deal" should be quite easy.

ANAND SANWAL is a managing director at Brilliont, a firm specializing in corporate portfolio management, innovation, and reengineering. He is the former vice-president, corporate portfolio management and strategic business analysis at American Express.

EXPLORING THE ISSUE

Does Expanding via Mergers and Acquisitions Make for Sound Corporate Strategy?

Critical Thinking and Reflection

1. What can be done to protect the interests of customers and other stakeholders during mergers and acquisitions?
2. How quickly will or should the success (or failure) of a merger or acquisition be known or shown?
3. How might global mergers and acquisitions differ from mergers and acquisitions conducted in a single nation?
4. How would you measure the success or failure of a merger or acquisition?
5. Why do firms merge or acquire one another?
6. What role, if any, does corporate culture play in the merger and acquisition process?

Is There Common Ground?

The common ground that exists in this issue is that there is risk involved in the merger and acquisition process. This observation is made by the authors on both sides of this issue in their respective articles. However, despite the inherent risk, corporations have decided to continue to pursue a course of economic behavior and practice that includes mergers and acquisitions. The debate that exists here is whether or not the risk is worth the potential payoff. Given the documented high rate of failure and frequent inability of mergers and acquisitions to consistently return anticipated gains and expected benefits means that this issue is one that will continue to be discussed and receive additional scrutiny by corporate practitioners and observers for many years to come.

Additional Resources

Brouthers, K.D., van Hastenburg, P., and van den Ven, J. (1998). "If Most Mergers Fail Why Are They So Popular," *Long Range Planning*, June, pp. 347–353.

Cummings, J. (2008). "Why Organic Is Better," *Business Finance*, 14(12), December, pp. 12–17.

Epstein, M.J. (2005). "The Determinants and Evaluation of Merger Success," *Business Horizons*, January–February, pp. 37–46

Gadiesh, O. and Ormiston, C. (2002). "Six Rationales to Guide Merger Success," *Strategy & Leadership*, 30, pp. 38–40.

Goldberg, S. and Godwin, J.H. (2001). "Your Merger: Will It Really Add Value?" *The Journal of Corporate Accounting & Finance*, January/February, pp. 27–35.

Jackson, S.E. (2007). "Creating Value Through Acquisitions," *The Journal of Business Strategy*, 28(6), pp. 40, 41.

Kroll, K. (2008). "Deals in the Downturn," *Business Finance*, 14(5), May, pp. 20, 22, 24, 25.

Marks, M.L. (2000). "Mixed Signals," *Across the Board*, May, pp. 21–26.

Marks, M.L. and Mirvis, P.H. (2011). "Merge Ahead: A Research Agenda to Increase Merger and Acquisition Success," *Journal of Business Psychology*, 26, pp. 161–168.

Ruquet, M.E. (2008). "Cultural Fit Helps Drive Merger Success," *National Underwriter*, P&C, 112(33), pp. 19, 25, 26.

Sinkin, J. and Putney, T. (2009). "Keeping It Together," *Journal of Accountancy*, 207(4), pp. 24–28.

Trautwein, F. (1990). "Merger Motives and Merger Prescriptions," *Strategic Management Journal*, May/June, pp. 283–295.

Vaughn, R. (2008). "Navigating a Successful Merger," *Risk Management*, 55(1), pp. 36–38, 40, 41.

Internet References . . .

Does Your M&A Add Value?

Capron, L. and Kaiser, K. (2009). "Does Your M&A Add Value?" February 5.

www.ft.com/intl/cms/s/0/7bfb1e10-f256-11dd-9678-0000779fd2ac.html#axzz2EjgAxm20

UNIT 4

UNIT

Environmental Issues

*W*ith intensified pressure to protect the environment, governments of many countries are enacting protectionist economic policies and companies are seeking ways to be sustainable. This unit looks at whether it is possible for companies to create sustainable businesses and whether corporate sustainability reporting is a valuable corporate reporting tool. Finally, the newsworthy and important issues of whether corporations should adopt environmentally friendly policies of corporate social responsibility (CSR) and sustainable development and whether cap and trade policies work will be examined.

Selected, Edited, and with Issue Framing Material by:
Kathleen J. Barnes, *East Stroudsburg University*
and
George E. Smith, *Albright College*

ISSUE

Should Corporations Adopt Environmentally Friendly Policies of Corporate Social Responsibility (CSR) and Sustainable Development?

YES: **Sierra Club**, from "From the Current Articles of Incorporation & Bylaws, June 20, 1981" (July 13, 2006), www.sierraclub.org/policy/downloads/goals.pdf

NO: **Paul Driessen**, from *Roots of Eco-Imperialism* (Free Enterprise Press, 2004)

Learning Outcomes

After reading this issue you should be able to:

- Understand the positive and negative consequences of environmentally friendly corporate social responsibility and sustainable development policies.
- Understand how environmentally friendly corporate social responsibility and sustainable development policies can be used as effective marketing tools.
- Understand and identify policies that might be implemented concerning environmentally friendly corporate social responsibility and sustainable development.
- Appreciate the ethical and legal implications of environmentally friendly corporate social responsibility and sustainable development.

ISSUE SUMMARY

YES: The Sierra Club is a leading environmentalist organization and has consistently advocated for the implementation of CSR policies in the workplace. The selection presented here provides insight into their philosophy and expectations as they relate to corporate behavior and its impact on the natural environment.

NO: Paul Driessen, trained in environmental science and a major advocate for the world's poor, writes a blistering attack on CSR and its constituent policies. He argues that these policies bring misery and death to the world's poor and act as camouflage for the environmentalist's anticapitalism, pro-statism agenda.

Virtually every introductory-level management textbook includes a chapter examining the impact corporate business activities have on the earth's environment. Usually the discussion blames business for much of the damage done to the environment. For example, a typical comment: "For years, businesses conducted their operations with little concern about environmental consequences . . . [businesses were] responsible for consuming significant amounts of materials and energy and causing waste accumulation and resource degradation . . . Businesses would look the other way . . ." (Carroll and Buchholtz, 2009).

Generally, these texts prescribe the adoption of corporate social responsibility (CSR) initiatives to ensure greater acceptance of the needs of the natural environment. Beyond the ubiquitous advocacy of CSR, an increasing number of textbooks—reflecting not just the views of business academia but those of social commentators, environmental nongovernment organization (NGO) activists, and government leaders across the globe—argue that corporations need to adopt policies of "sustainable development," a concept that emphasizes restricting economic growth to levels that won't outstrip the replenishment rate of our natural resources (Carroll and Buchholtz, 2009).

Interestingly, both the concept of CSR and the birth of the modern environmentalism movement were products of the 1960s. Many scholars and social historians argue that the development of CSR was primarily due to the environmental activism of the 1960s successfully raising social awareness of the negative impact of corporate activity on the earth's environment (Horner, 2007). Thus, it is not surprising that the strongest force advocating CSR today is the environmentalism movement itself.

From an environmental perspective, the way to understand CSR is to view it as an umbrella concept under which a collection of related ideas fulfill specific roles in promoting responsible corporate behavior. *Stakeholder theory*, widely accepted in corporate America and the default approach for almost all business schools, argues that the traditional corporate concern for the creation of shareholder wealth first and foremost is misguided. A CSR/stakeholder approach suggests that all parties with a stake in a company's existence are entitled to input in determining the firm's activities, including the allocation of its revenues and profits. At present, amid the political and social atmosphere, it is the environmental stakeholder that is receiving increased attention and pressure in the corporate boardroom.

Sustainable development (SD) is another CSR-related, environmentally driven concept. SD came to prominence in the 1980s and has been very successful in raising awareness of the impact of corporate activity on the finite natural resources of the planet. As noted earlier, the key aspect of SD is concern for the natural resource needs of future generations. To this end, corporations should develop and implement business plans only after accounting for their potential long-term impact on the earth's natural resource base. The *precautionary principle* (PP) is frequently invoked by environmentalists as a means of alerting the public to possible environmental harm, primarily from the implementation of new technology. As the name suggests, it represents a defensive, assume-the-worst-until-proven-otherwise posture. In a very real sense, it is a guide for regulation.

The last three decades have seen the emergence of *socially responsible investing* (SRI) around the world. The idea behind SRI is to promote social acceptance of the environmentalist agenda by encouraging investment in firms or financial products that specifically reinforce pro-environmental corporate conduct. Taken together, the four concepts discussed here comprise the environmentalist's CSR agenda.

Here then, is your chance to examine this issue from both sides, as we ask you to decide whether or not

corporations should adopt enviro-friendly CSR policies. Those who are adamantly against these enviro-friendly CSR policies, as illustrated in Paul Driessen's pointed attack on environmentalism-driven CSR, reject blind acceptance of ideas such as the precautionary principle. Driessen maintains that acceptance and practice of these ideas can be just as damaging as the corporate actions the ideas are designed to restrain. The PP, for example, has dominated public discussion since its adoption by the environmentalists and has played a large role in the numerous laws and regulations that affect virtually every aspect of corporate behavior, not to mention personal lives. However, as Driessen and a rapidly growing number of critics have pointed out, in many instances, this view is much worse than a carelessly optimistic belief that there are no environmental problems at all.

Consider the case of the corporate average fuel economy (CAFÉ) ratings for automobiles. To address smog pollution and the widely accepted perception that worldwide oil supplies were running out, the federal government passed a law in 1975 establishing fuel-efficiency requirements for all cars. The problem is that, over time, these standards have forced automakers to make smaller, lighter, less safe cars. How unsafe? Two reputable studies (i.e., 1989 Harvard University and Brookings Institution study; 2001 National Academy of Sciences) concluded that the CAFÉ standards result in 1,200–3,900 additional deaths every year (Bidinotto, 2004, p. 4). "In the trade-off between saving gasoline and saving lives, the government rules willingly sacrifice lives" (Bidinotto, 2004, p. 4).

Given this finding, it is no surprise that large, safe SUVs are popular with the public; nor is it surprising that SUVs are viewed by environmentalists as a major factor to the depletion of fossil fuels and to global warming. The point of this example is that it is just as dangerous to err on the side of extreme pessimism about the environment as it is to be in a state of unfounded optimism. Further, business executives would be wise to refrain from engaging in unquestioned acceptance of CSR policies, particularly given the increasingly skeptical attitude of both the scientific community and the general public regarding the veracity of the man-made global warming position.

YES ↵

From the Current Articles of Incorporation & Bylaws, June 20, 1981

The purposes of the Sierra Club are to explore, enjoy, and protect the wild places of the earth; to practice and promote the responsible use of the Earth's ecosystems and resources; to educate and enlist humanity to protect and restore the quality of the natural and human environment; and to use all lawful means to carry out these objectives.

Beliefs about Environment and Society—Developed by Planning Committee and Printed in Sierra Club Goals Pamphlet, 1985–1989, with Board Knowledge, but Not Formally Adopted by It

Humans have evolved as an interdependent part of nature. Humankind has a powerful place in the environment, which may range from steward to destroyer. We must share the Earth's finite resources with other living things and respect all life-enabling processes. Thus, we must control human population numbers and seek a balance that serves all life forms.

Complex and diversified ecosystems provide stability for the Earth's life support processes. Development and other human activities can simplify ecosystems, undermine their dynamic stability, and threaten these processes. Wildness itself has a value serving all species, with too few remaining. We have more to fear from too little wildness than from too much.

Genetic diversity is the product of evolution acting on wildness, and is important because it is biological capital for future evolution. We must preserve genetic diversity in wild tracts and gene pools. No species should be hastened into extinction by human intervention.

The needs of all creatures must be respected, their destinies viewed as separate from human desires, their existence not simply for human benefit. All species have a right to perpetuation of the habitat necessary and required for survival. All creatures should have freedom from needless predation, persecution, and cruel or unduly confining captivity. We must seek moral restraints on human power to affect the well-being of so many species.

Humans must exercise stewardship of the Earth's resources to assure enough for other creatures and for the future. Thus, resources should be renewed indefinitely wherever possible, and resource depletion limited. Resources should be used as long as possible and shared, avoiding waste and needless consumption. We must act knowledgeably and take precautions to avoid initiating irreversible trends. Good stewardship implies a shared moral and social responsibility to take positive action on behalf of conservation.

The enjoyment of the natural environment and the Earth's wild places is a fundamental purpose of the Club, and an end in itself.

Ideal Goals (Summary)—for Environment and Society

- To sustain natural life-support systems, avoid impairing them, and avoid irreversible damage to them.

- To facilitate species survival; to maintain genetic diversity; to avoid hastened extinction of species; to protect prime natural habitat.

- To establish and protect natural reserves, including representative natural areas, wilderness areas in each biome, displays of natural phenomena, and habitats for rare and endangered species.

- To control human population growth and impacts; to limit human population numbers and habitat needs within Earth's carrying capacity; to avoid needless human consumption of resources; to plan and control land use, with environmental impact assessment and safeguards, and rehabilitation of damaged sites.

- To learn more about the facts, interrelationships, and principles of the Earth's ecosystems, and the place and impact of humans in them; to understand the consequences of human activities within the biosphere.

- To develop responsible and appropriate technology matched to end-uses; to introduce sophisticated technology gradually after careful assessment and with precautionary monitoring.

- To control pollution of the biosphere; to minimize waste residuals with special care of hazardous materials; to use the best available control technology at sources; and to recycle wastes.

To manage resources soundly; to avoid waste with long-term plans; to sustain the yield of living resources and maintain their productivity and breeding stocks; to prolong availability of nonliving resources such as fossil fuels, minerals, and water.

To impart a sense of social responsibility among consumers, developers, and public authorities concerning environmental protection; to regulate threats to public health; to avoid private degradation of public resources; to minimize impacts on innocent parties and future generations.

For The Sierra Club Organization

To acquire the knowledge, skills, resources, and energy to accomplish the Club's goals for environment and society.

To render service through ability to promote societal well-being; through improving environmental conditions and maintaining environmental quality; through equipping members with understanding, training, and motivation to be effective in improving environmental quality; to advance public education; to foster appreciation of outdoor experience and responsible outdoor behavior.

To have the following characteristics: to be energetic, actively moving projects to completion, catalyzing action, and using the most modern and efficient tools available; to be effective, able to achieve results in a knowledgeable and responsible manner; to possess a breadth of interest and vision encompassing any problem of the physical environment; to be willing to take risks; to be persistent in pursuit of Club causes; to see the Club itself as making history, and thus take a long view; to be cooperative with all who are working toward the same ends; to reflect excellence in Club publications; to be innovative in exploring new means toward Club goals.

To be constituted to reflect a carefully balanced and integrated variety of approaches—democratic, grassroots, decentralized—yet with a strong central core; to foster flexibility, initiative, and collaboration within a central framework of cohesiveness; to respect expertise of its various entities; to consult broadly among its entities and decide consensually but promptly, with decisions reflecting thorough and serious deliberation; while being basically a membership organization of volunteers, to work closely with professional and support staff; to define the roles of volunteers and staff clearly; to enhance effectiveness through enjoyment of social interaction between volunteers and staff; to be modern while retaining traditions and a sense of the past; to provide an example of good conduct and high standards for the Club and society.

To assure that the public perceives the Club as "the guardian of the environment"; as a leading force in key struggles for the environment in every area; as a powerful force which energizes campaigns and achieves its goals; and as a constructive force with a positive sense for meeting society's needs.

To obtain the necessary and sufficient resources to fulfill the Club's purposes, including:

1. To have a membership large enough to fulfill the Club's purposes and be credible in comparison with other organizations which aspire to be social forces, and large enough to be taken seriously by leaders in national political life; to develop wide-ranging competence among its members on issues; to generate a leadership capable of acting effectively on a great many issues; to produce annual revenues and net worth sufficient to meet its goals; to have geographical distribution of members; to have member representation in political units in the United States and Canada; to have members of varied ages, interests, and backgrounds; to have members who can provide expertise to address diverse issues, with widely varied professional and technical backgrounds and experience.
2. To have a staff large enough and with sufficient professional capacity to provide services to support member operations, and undertake specific staff programs such as lobbying, publications, and outings; staff should share the Club's basic values and assist volunteers in the pursuit of Club goals.
3. To have financial resources to finance the Club's operations at all levels; to have income from diverse sources; to build a net worth sufficient to allow financing of annual operations without borrowing, and ultimately representing at least half the annual operating budget.
4. To have the best possible information resources and systems available to guide and support Club actions; to have information which is sophisticated, current, accurate, in context, and accessible; to have a mix of news, intelligence, fundamental knowledge, theory, and plans; to maintain the institutions necessary to collect and disseminate this information, including a library, newsletters, various communications mechanisms, and links to existing information networks.

Vision Statement for the Sierra Club's Second Century, Board of Directors, September 16–17, 1989

The Challenge

We are facing a global environmental crisis that grows more urgent every day. Threats that were once inconceivable—such as massive oil spill disasters, global climate change, and the poisoning of our air, land, and water—are becoming common events. Species are being annihilated and wilderness is being destroyed at an alarming and accelerating rate.

We live each day knowing that in a few generations—unless humankind takes drastic steps to protect our planet—it is possible that the Earth will hurtle around the Sun devoid of life as we know it.

There is no priority more urgent than saving the Earth.

Our Vision

For nearly 100 years, Sierra Club members have shared a vision of humanity living in harmony with the Earth.

We envision a world where wilderness areas and open spaces are protected habitats sustaining all species . . . a world where oceans and streams are clean and the air is pure . . . a world where a healthy biosphere and a non-toxic environment are inalienable rights. In short, we envision a world saved from the threat of unalterable planetary disaster.

To save our planet, we must change the world—

Priorities must change: People must learn to live in ways that preserve and protect our precious resources.

Policies must change: Our institutions must abandon practices that recklessly endanger the environment.

Values must change: Progress must be measured by its long-term value to living systems and creatures rather than its short-term value to special interests or the economy.

To achieve this vision, people across the nation and around the world must speak out with a powerful voice that cannot be ignored. Aggressive grassroots action on an unprecedented scale is essential to protect our environment and our species. There is no other choice. It will require leadership that is visionary, experienced, and strong.

Our Role

The Sierra Club is uniquely qualified to lead this grass-roots action to save the Earth. We are America's largest and most effective grassroots environmental organization—an experienced, respected, and committed fellowship of citizen activists. Within our ranks lie the expertise, wisdom, and vitality to find the new directions needed to meet the challenges of the future.

We offer proven ability to influence public policy and empower individuals to confront local, national, and global problems. From town halls to our nation's capital to global institutions, Sierra Club activists are scoring enormous victories for the environment through personal action, education, litigation, lobbying, and participation in the political process.

As the Sierra Club prepares for its second century, we offer to America and the world our vision of humanity living in harmony with nature. We dedicate ourselves to achieving this vision as we reaffirm our passionate commitment to explore, enjoy, and protect the Earth.

Statement of Purposes, Development by the Planning Committee in 1985; amended by the Board of Directors, May 5–6, 1990

For purposes of planning, the Sierra Club's purpose, thus, is to preserve, protect, and enhance the natural environment.

The mission of the Sierra Club is to influence public, private, and corporate policies and actions through Club programs at the local, state, national, and international levels.

The strategy of the Sierra Club is to activate appropriate portions of a network of staff, members, and other concerned citizens, using legislative, administrative, electoral, and legal approaches, and to develop supporting public opinion.

Strategic Goals, Board of Directors, May 1–2, 1993

The following goals guide the Club's work:

I. Enhance public perception of "environment" (overcome the perception of limits):

A. Develop pressure by consumers for green products.
B. Educate public that strong environmental protection creates jobs.
C. Reduce consumption levels in the United States through increasing efficiency, recycling, producing more durable goods, and by making waste and nonessential products and packaging socially unacceptable.

II. Build upon and develop new forms of political leverage:

A. Mobilize market incentives to induce corporate environmental change.
B. Develop hybrid or "coordinated campaigns," targeting multiple levels of decision making.
C. Work to make existing institutions more responsive and accountable to community and environmental needs.
D. Create new vehicles for responsive institutions of government.
E. Develop unconventional alliances to overcome legislative obstacles.

III. Integrate concerns for environmental protection and social justice to strengthen the environmental movement:

A. Develop more effective means for communicating through race, class, age, and cultural barriers.
B. Re-position the Sierra Club as more visibly concerned about threats to community and workplace environments.
C. Encourage more extensive coalition work between local Sierra Club entities and environmental justice groups.

D. Develop a stronger capacity to influence state and local regulatory and land-use actions (particularly as these relate to pollution threats to vulnerable groups in our society and land uses they find unacceptable).

IV. Enhance the Club's position of leadership within the environmental movement:

A. Continue to develop programs to cultivate and train new leaders.

B. Nurture a culture within the Club that encourages cooperation and collaboration, and that rewards innovative ideas and contributions.

C. Significantly enhance our ability for "quick responses" to issues and challenges.

D. Strengthen the Club's public affairs capacity for "telling our story."

Sierra Club Promise, Board of Directors, November 20–21, 1993

As a Sierra Club member you are empowered to help save the Earth and enjoy the natural world around you.

JOIN OUR CRUSADE

Get involved

Help resolve . . . critical community, national and global environmental challenges.

Philosophy of Service and Stewardship, Board of Directors, September 16–17, 1995

To achieve its mission, the Sierra Club has organized persons of shared environmental concerns into a powerful and effective force for protecting the natural environment. As a grassroots-based organization, we rely on individuals for our resources, talent, and energy. Our members are our most important assets.

We are the Sierra Club. We are members helping other members. We trust and respect members and acknowledge their full range of contributions.

Good Stewardship is:

- providing members with a supportive environment that allows them to determine their relationship with the Club.
- facilitating each member's involvement in the organization at the level the member desires.
- entailing the wise and careful use of the member's time, energy, and resources.
- providing Club members with the materials, information, expertise, and other resources that will strengthen their relationship with the organization.
- creating the foundation that makes it possible for the Club to fulfill its mission now—and in the future.

Sierra Club "Premise" Poster, presented to the Board November 13–14, 1999, by the Communication & Education GovCom

This is not about getting back to nature. It is about understanding we've never left.

We are deep in our nature every day. We're up to our ears in it. It is under our feet, it is in our lungs, it runs through our veins. We are not visitors here. We weren't set down to enjoy the view. We were born here and we're part of it—like any ant, fish, rock, or blade of grass.

This connection is as personal as it is fundamental. It can't be proved with theorems and diagrams. You either feel it or you don't.

Sierra Club members feel it.

Maybe it came to you on a mountain trail, or on a river bank, or at a windowsill watching a spider's unthinking intelligence unfold. Simply put, it's the sudden conviction that there is something out there, something wonderful. And it is much, much bigger than you.

A revelation like this could easily overwhelm a person. We choose to let it inspire us. Nature, vastly complex and infinitely subtle, is our perfect metaphor. Related to everything, signifying everything, it is the spring where we go to renew our spirit. And it, in turn, asks something of us. It compels us to take responsibility and then to take action.

Look, there is nothing inevitable about the future of our environment. A poisoned stream can get worse, stay the same, or get better. It depends largely on what we choose to do. That simple belief, backed by 100 years of effort and result, is what drives the Sierra Club.

So, forget the grim cliché of the selfless environmentalist. When you accept your connection to nature, suddenly you can't look at the world without seeing something very personal in it. You are part of it, and you work for the planet because it gives you joy to do so.

You work for the planet because you belong to it.

Organizational and Issues Goals, Board of Directors, November 19–20, 2005

Organizational

In order to build grassroots power in our communities for achieving the Club's objectives related to our conservation initiatives, the Board of Directors adopts the following capacity-building priorities for 2006–2010. The Board asks all Club entities to contribute to the development of these capacities, not exclusively, but as top priorities identified through the Summit Direction Setting Process. The Board further directs staff and Governance Committees to work with grassroots activists to develop appropriate tools and support to:

1. *Seek new allies and build coalitions* to bring different perspectives together around common interests, and build political and community momentum around shared concerns and values.
2. *Create media visibility* through reporters, editors, and news coverage, visibility events, advertising, and other media access and outlets that put our point of view in the public eye and public debate.
3. *Organize people in our communities to take action together* in their neighborhoods and homes, through local networking, groups, and gatherings that build our activist numbers, strength, and diversity.
4. *Enlist public support with messages framed around solutions.* Take our message out to people in our communities with materials, presentations, and public education framed around solutions that the public can understand, relate to, and act on.

The Board of Directors affirms its commitment to the proposition that a key way the Sierra Club can fulfill its national purpose at this point in time is to invest its financial, staff, and moral resources in developing the capacity of its leaders, enhancing its organizational capacity, and conducting programs of effective local action—rekindling the movement that the Sierra Club played such a key role in launching. We affirm that development of the Club's volunteer leadership and the chapters and groups they lead is a critical investment in the strength of the organization as a whole and the environmental movement more broadly.

In order to build grassroots power for achieving the Club's objectives related to our Conservation Initiatives, the Board of Directors identifies four groups of priority decision-makers for 2006–2010. We wish to grow our capacity to influence (1) voters, (2) state officials, and (3) local officials, and maintain our present capacity to influence (4) federal officials.

Issues

The Board of Directors adopts three long-term National Conservation Initiatives for 2006–2010. They are: (1) Smart Energy Solutions, (2) Safe and Healthy Communities, and (3) America's Wild Legacy.

These three Conservation Initiatives will be the centerpieces of our national conservation agenda for the next five years. The single most important goal of this agenda will be to advance a smart, safe, clean energy future in the next decade.

To maximize success, the Conservation Governance Committee and the staff should seek out and give preference to projects and programs that overlap and provide synergy between these three initiatives.

These Conservation Initiatives represent the national conservation agenda that the Sierra Club Board has chosen for focused work over the next five years. They were selected after reviewing the Sierra Summit and pre-Summit

direction setting process results from the grassroots leadership and the Summit delegates.

Each initiative will eventually have specific goals, values, action objectives, and public policy outcomes selected to implement them. All Governance Committees and national staff are encouraged to work together to implement these Conservation Initiatives.

Clarification of Conservation Initiatives and their Emphases for 2006–2010, Board of Directors, March 4–5, 2006

The Sierra Club's 114-year history reflects a rich blend of activism and unifying campaigns. Over the last decades, periods of mobilization and focus have represented some of the Club's finest moments, and yielded some of our proudest victories: the Alaska Lands Act, Wild Forest campaign, the replacement of James Watt, the Superfund battle of 1986, California Desert Protection Campaign, the defeat of Newt Gingrich's Contract with America, and our 26-year long defense of the Arctic Refuge.

Now, we have the opportunity to distinguish ourselves again and to lead once more.

2006–2010 Conservation Initiatives

In November 2005, the Board of Directors adopted three long-term conservation initiatives for the Sierra Club—Smart Energy Solutions, America's Wild Legacy, and Safe and Healthy Communities.

Two of these three—America's Wild Legacy and Safe and Healthy Communities—have been part of the Sierra Club's priority conservation work for decades. In adopting them as Conservation Initiatives for 2006–2010, the Board declared its commitment to our continued leadership in these areas.

In contrast, the Sierra Club has not historically made broad energy policy a national priority campaign. Energy, historically, has been a less central and more episodic Club focus. But the times demand that we meet the challenge to move beyond a fossil fuel world and that the Club lead society through one of the largest transformational moments in American history.

The Club's leadership role in confronting global warming and transforming our energy economy advances not only the Club's Smart Energy vision, but our work for America's Wild Legacy and Safe and Healthy Communities as well. The Club must lead America in this moment; there is no other organization with the history, vision, and presence at the community level to play that role.

At the same time, the Club's highest priority for the next decade as an institution is to build its capacity and focus on Smart Energy Solutions. This is the Conservation Initiative where our existing capacities and abilities are least well developed. As a result, we want to identify those opportunities that address the threats from climate change and can contribute to effective solutions where our members live. In building support for this priority, we want to be promoting Smart Energy Solutions in our trainings, communications channels, fundraising, political work, activist outings, and other available opportunities. We ask and encourage all to participate in an early opportunity around Earth Day 2006. It will be our first opportunity to showcase, for example, our Cool Cities program around the country.

Engaging Our Members and Programs in Our Conservation Initiatives

The Board of Directors reaffirms the importance of all three Conservation Initiatives, and the need for the Club to provide support for volunteers and staff working on the Areas of National Concern in all three of these initiatives.

The Board, therefore, requests its Governance Committees, their sub-entities, all programs, and chapters and groups to assess and enhance their readiness to meet our new challenges, especially that of Smart Energy Solutions. The Board further encourages these same entities, as well as members, to join us at this critical time to build public sentiment to achieve all of our conservation initiatives.

In going forward, we are requesting staff and volunteer leaders at all levels to make available the Club's time, expertise, and resources in a way that supports the successful implementation of our Smart Energy Initiative as a truly powerful, effective, and fully integrated campaign, while retaining the Sierra Club's engagement and involvement across the full range of our Conservation Initiatives.

SIERRA CLUB is America's largest and most influential grassroots environmental organization.

Paul Driessen   **NO**

Roots of Eco-Imperialism

Like a mad scientist's experiment gone terribly awry, corporate social responsibility has mutated into a creature radically different from what its original designers envisioned. It now threatens to cause a moral meltdown, to spawn a system in which the most farfetched worries of healthy, well-fed First World activists routinely dominate business, economic, technological, scientific and health debates—and override critical concerns of sick, malnourished people in poor Third World countries.

This mutant version of corporate social responsibility demands that businesses and nations conduct their affairs in accord with new "ethical" codes that derive from several intertwined doctrines of social and environmental radicalism.

- **Stakeholder participation** theory asserts that any group that has an interest in, or could arguably be affected by, a corporate decision or the outcome of a public policy debate has a right to pressure the decision makers until they accede to the activists' demands.
- **Sustainable development** (SD) says companies must minimize the extraction and use of natural resources, because corporate activities must "meet the needs and aspirations of the present without compromising the ability of future generations to meet their needs."
- **The precautionary principle** (PP) holds that companies should halt any activities that might threaten "human health or the environment," even if no clear cause-and-effect relationship has been established, and even if the potential threat is largely (or entirely) theoretical.
- **Socially responsible investing** (SRI) insists that pension funds and individual investors should purchase shares in companies that have pledged to conform their corporate policies and actions to sustainability, precautionary and responsibility ideologies.

There is a certain allure to these doctrines—reinforced by news stories and reports extolling the concepts and asserting their widespread acceptance. However, neither the terminology nor its constant repetition represents a groundswell of actual public support or obviates fundamental problems with these precepts. The language might sound clear at first blush. But it is highly elastic and can easily be stretched and molded to fit a wide variety of activist claims, causes and agendas.

As a consequence, the doctrines are the subject of deep concern and passionate debate, as thoughtful people struggle to assess the risks posed for corporations, investors, employees, creditors, and customers—for scientific, economic, and technological advancement—and for people whose hope for a better future depends on ensuring plentiful supplies of affordable electricity, conquering disease and malnutrition, and having unencumbered access to modern technology and greater economic opportunity. As the debate rages, it is becoming increasingly obvious that the doctrines solve few problems and, instead, create a vast multitude of new difficulties.

⁕

At their root is the fact that these intertwined CSR doctrines primarily reflect the concerns, preferences, and gloomy worldview of a small cadre of politicians, bureaucrats, academics, multinational NGOs, and wealthy foundations in affluent developed countries. These self-appointed guardians of the public weal have little understanding of (and often harbor a deep distaste for) business, capitalism, market economies, technology, global trade, and the vital role of profits in generating innovation and progress.

Yet, it is they who proclaim and implement the criteria by which businesses are to be judged, decide which of society's goals are important, determine whether those goals are being met, and insist that countervailing needs, viewpoints, and concerns be relegated to secondary or irrelevant status. In so doing, they seek to impose their worldview and change society in ways, and to degrees, that they have not been able to achieve through popular votes, legislation, treaty, or even judicial decisions.

Inherent in the doctrines are several false, pessimistic premises that are at the core of ideological environmentalism. Eco activists erroneously believe, for example, that energy and mineral resources are finite, and are rapidly being exhausted. That activities conducted by corporations, especially large multinational companies, inevitably result in resource depletion, environmental degradation, impaired human and societal health, social harm, and imminent planetary disaster. And that it is primarily profits, not societal or consumer needs and desires—and certainly not a desire to serve humanity—that drive corporate decision-making.

In a nutshell, CSR doctrines are rooted too much in animosity toward business and profits, too much in conjectural problems and theoretical needs of future generations—and too little in real, immediate, life-and-death needs of present generations, especially billions of poor rural people in developing countries. The mutant doctrines give radical activists unprecedented leverage to impose the loftiest of developed world standards on companies, communities, and nations, while ignoring the needs, priorities, and aspirations of people who struggle daily just to survive.

Actually implementing the doctrines requires significant centralized control of land and energy use, economic production and consumption, corporate innovation and initiative, markets, transportation, labor, trade, housing, policy making processes, and people's daily lives. Under the activists' agenda, control would be monitored and enforced through United Nations, European Union, U.S., and other government agencies. All this is the antithesis of the private property rights, capitalism, and freedom of nations, communities, companies, and individuals to make their own decisions, in accord with their own cultural preferences and personal or societal needs—and thereby generate innovation, prosperity, human health, and environmental quality.

The ideological version of corporate social responsibility thus stands in direct opposition to the systems that have generated the greatest wealth, opportunities, technological advancements, and health and environmental improvements in history. Its real effect is to cede decision-making to a few; reduce competition, innovation, trade, investment, and economic vitality; and thereby impair future social, health, and environmental improvements.

According to activist theology, adherence to CSR concepts generates a "triple bottom line" (economic, social, and environmental) that companies should meet in judging "true" profitability and citizenship, David Henderson notes in *Misguided Virtue: False Notions of Corporate Responsibility*. Only by measuring their costs, benefits, and profits against all three standards can businesses meet "society's expectations," earn their "license to operate," and "give capitalism a human face," claim the activists.

But CSR's supposedly equal emphasis on all three components of the triple bottom line is typically skewed so that environmental considerations trump all others. This happens even where people's lives are put at risk, as in the case of strident activist opposition to pesticides despite widespread malaria, or to biotechnology despite rampant malnutrition and starvation.

Mutant CSR also enables countries to impose "legal" barriers to keep foreign goods out and protect domestic businesses and interests—typically through the use of malleable precautionary and sustainability rules that make it easy to cite far-fetched, unproven health or environmental risks, so as to justify heavy-handed actions.

Stakeholder dialogue, according to the World Business Council for Sustainable Development, is "the essence of corporate social responsibility." However, many of the "stakeholders" who seek "dialogues" are actually well-funded activist groups that assert a "right" to participate in corporate and government decision-making, simply because they have a passionate devotion to their cause.

Some stakeholders are "shareholder activists," who own substantial shares in a company—or just enough to qualify them to introduce resolutions at annual meetings, demanding that a company adopt their positions and agendas on sustainable development, global warming, the precautionary principle, or "human rights." Others may be politicians, bureaucrats, and other elites in developing countries, whose personal careers and interests are advanced substantially by being aligned with these causes. That the lives of poor people in these countries might thereby be put at greater risk is often only a secondary consideration.

According to the *Boston Globe, Sacramento Bee*, Capital Research Center, and others, the U.S. environmental movement alone has annual revenues of some $4 billion, primarily as a result of contributions from foundations, corporations, unions, trial lawyers, and taxpayer-funded government agencies. The international green movement's budget has been estimated to be well in excess of $8 billion a year.

As a result, well-organized, media-savvy pressure groups have unprecedented power to promote their agendas, define "society's expectations," and influence public perceptions, corporate decisions, and legislative and regulatory initiatives.

In the international arena, they frequently play a prominent role in negotiations, equal to or more dominant than many multinational companies and even some countries, especially Third World nations. Not surprisingly, the NGOs' agendas frequently conflict with and override the most pressing needs and concerns of people who are struggling to overcome widespread poverty and malnutrition, devastating epidemics, and a virtual absence of electricity and economic opportunity.

Corporate social responsibility, argues Gary Johns, can easily become "an assault on the interests and rights of 'real' stakeholders, those who have invested in or are creditors of corporations. It occurs when managers bow to pressure from interests that have no contract with the corporation, whether by way of employment, or supply of goods or services, or through ownership.

"CSR is also an assault on the interests of the electorate. It occurs by undermining the formal democratic consensus as to what constitutes reasonable business behavior. It also occurs when governments grant NGOs such status that it enables them to set themselves up as judges of corporate behavior," or of national decisions on critical health, economic, and environmental concerns.

In many cases, the activist groups' cumulative membership might be less than 0.01 percent of a community's or country's population. No one elected them as stakeholders. No plebiscite was held to make their narrow definitions and agendas the arbiter of what is moral or in the broader public interest. No election, adjudication, or even United Nations resolution gave them the authority to exclude other stakeholders from debates and decision-making processes—including entire nations and billions of destitute people, who are being denied the benefits of global trade, economic development, abundant affordable energy, and informed use of resources, pesticides, and biotechnology.

And yet, the activists define what is responsible, sustainable, or sufficiently cautious, often in a way that blocks any development which conflicts with their agendas. That other people might be adversely affected—or the world's most destitute citizens might remain mired in chronic hunger, poverty, disease, and despair—enters only superficially into their calculations.

In asserting their demands, they downplay the complex needs and circumstances that confront companies, communities and nations. They ignore the science-based regulatory systems that already protect citizens from actual risks, and raise public fears of far-fetched risks to justify endless delays or outright bans.

Businesses, elected officials, and citizens should take a leadership position on these issues, contest the demands of anti-business activists, challenge their motives, and dispute their underlying premises. As Johns suggests, they need to "make the NGOs prove their bona fides." They need to "question the extent to which [the activists] represent anyone or anything; question the size of their membership; question the source of their funds; and question their expertise. In other words, question their standing and their legitimacy."

Instead, too many businesses, community leaders, and citizens pursue a strategy of appeasement and accommodation, ceding moral authority to unelected NGOs, bureaucrats, "ethical" investor groups, and other activists. Some have actually endorsed the activists' demands and collaborated closely with them, despite serious adverse impacts on the world's poor.

♦♦♦

As a result, says University of Houston economics professor Thomas DeGregori, developed country activists are often able to co-opt local movements, hijacking them to radical agendas, brushing aside legitimate local concerns, and leaving the indigenous people worse off than before.

When India's impoverished Chipko people initiated a movement to build a road and gain access to Himalayan forest resources, to create a small wood products industry, First World environmentalists took it over. The voices of real local stakeholders were all but silenced, says

Australian professor Dr. Haripriya Ragan, and their struggle for resources and development were sacrificed to global environmental concerns. Leading the assault were radical anti-technology activist Vandana Shiva and groups that "tacitly support coercive conservation tactics that weaken local claims to resource access for sustaining livelihoods."

In other cases, "stakeholder involvement" becomes a form of extortion, in which "corporate greed" is replaced by "agenda greed." In 1995, Shell Oil was preparing to sink its Brent Spar offshore oil storage platform in the deep Atlantic, under a permit granted by the UK Environment Ministry. However, Greenpeace launched a vicious and sophisticated $2-million public relations assault that falsely accused the company of planning to dump tons of oil, toxic waste, and radioactive material in the ocean. Shell's timid and unimaginative response to the ensuing media nightmare got the company nothing but a bigger black eye, and it was forced to spend a fortune dismantling the platform onshore.

A year later, Greenpeace issued a written apology, effectively admitting that the entire campaign had been a fraud. There had been no oil or wastes on the structure. Of course, the admission got buried in the business pages or obituaries. Flush from their victory, the Rainbow Warriors went on to shake down other companies and promote bogus claims about chemicals, wood products, and genetically modified "Frankenfood."

Embarrassed by its stinging defeat, Shell tried to refurbish its reputation and learn from its mistakes. Apparently, the company's execs never actually graduated from the School of Hard Knocks. A few years later, when complaints alone failed to garner enough media attention to embarrass Shell over its alleged "failure to protect Nigeria's Ogoni people," Oxfam and Amnesty International hooked up with radical greens, to hammer the company for complicity in an "environmental catastrophe."

It turned out the catastrophe was caused by tribesmen sabotaging oil pipelines, says Dr. Roger Bate, a visiting fellow with the American Enterprise Insitute, to get gullible journalists to write stories that enabled Ogoni leaders to extort huge monetary settlements from the company. But Shell paid up anyway, in hopes that the problem would go away. Meanwhile, the rights groups and media ignored the racketeering, effectively aiding and abetting the tribal leaders, and setting the stage for future blackmail.

♦♦♦

Sustainable development, as defined by environmental activists, focuses too little on fostering sustained economic development, and too much on *restricting* development—typically in the name of protecting the environment. It also reflects their erroneous doctrine that we are rapidly depleting our natural resources and destroying the planet. The putative welfare of "fragile ecosystems" again trumps even the most obvious welfare of people, frequently leading desperate people to wreak havoc on the very eco-systems the activists claim to be protecting.

Leon Louw, executive director of South Africa's Free Market Foundation, refers to sustainable development as "voodoo science." It never asks "sustainable for how long: 10, 200, 1000, a million years? For whom? Advanced people with unknowable future technology, needs and resources? For how long must we conserve so-called 'non-renewables'? Must our descendants, by the same twisted logic, do likewise? Forever?"

Not one person alive at the dawn of the twentieth century could have envisioned the amazing technological feats of that era, its changing raw material needs, or its increasing ability to control pollution. In 1900, coal and wood provided heat. Air pollution and diseases we no longer even hear about killed millions. Telephones, cars and electricity were novelties for the rich. Common folk and freight alike were hauled by horses, which left behind 900,000 tons of manure a year in New York City alone. The Wright brothers still made bicycles. Air conditioners, radios, televisions, plastics, antibiotics, organ transplants and computers could not even be imagined.

Today, the pace of change is exponentially faster than 100 or even 50 years ago. To define sustainability under these conditions is impossible. To suppose that anyone could predict what technologies will exist, what pollutants will be a problem, what fuels and minerals we will need—in what quantities—is to engage in sheer science fiction. Or in the most deceitful public policy scam.

In short, the fundamental problem with "sustainable development," says Oxford University economist Dr. Wilfred Beckerman, is its demand that radical prescriptions be followed to achieve narrowly defined ends, determine which trade-offs should be emphasized, and decide which trade-offs are to be ignored. Here the concept has nothing to add. "Indeed, it subtracts from the objective of maximizing human welfare, because the slogan of sustainable development seems to provide a blanket justification for almost any policy designed to promote almost any ingredient of human welfare, irrespective of its cost and hence irrespective of the other ingredients of welfare."

❧

Precautionary theories likewise promote agendas set by eco-centric activists in developed countries. They ignore countervailing interests and needs of developing nations, such as: creating economic opportunity, ensuring adequate and reliable supplies of affordable energy, alleviating poverty, malnutrition and disease—and ultimately improving environmental quality and ensuring more sustainable practices. It gives CSR, SD, and PP precepts credit for any potential public health and environmental risks they might reduce, public policy analyst Indur Goklany points out, but imposes no "discredit" for risks, injuries, or deaths that they might generate.

Precautionary doctrines hold that, if anyone raises doubts about the safety of a technology, the technology should be severely restricted, if not banned outright, until it is proven to be absolutely safe. But improved safety resulting from introducing the new technology is typically ignored or given short shrift. The precautionary principle also holds that the more serious the theoretical damages, the more society should spend on precautionary measures, or be willing to sacrifice in opportunities foregone. Moreover, say its proponents, the inability to prove how much society might gain or lose from taking those measures should not stand in the way of extreme caution.

The net result is that the precautionary principle repeatedly stifles risk-taking, innovation, economic growth, scientific and technological progress, freedom of choice, and human betterment. Had it governed scientific and technological progress in past centuries, numerous historic achievements would have been limited or prevented, according to 40 internationally renowned scientists who were surveyed by the techno-whiz-kids at *Spiked*, in advance of its May 2003 London conference, "Panic Attack: Interrogating Our Obsession with Risk."

The experts listed modern marvels from A to Z that the precautionary principle would have stopped dead in their tracks: airplanes, antibiotics, aspirin, and automobiles; biotechnology, blood transfusions, CAT scans, and the contraceptive pill; electricity, hybrid crops, and the Green Revolution; microwaves, open heart surgery, and organ transplants; pesticides, radar, and refrigeration; telephones, televisions, water purification, and x-rays—to name but a few.

Imagine what our lives would be without these technological miracles. As Adam Finn, professor of pediatrics at Bristol University's Institute of Child Health observed, "pretty much everything" would have been prevented or limited under this stifling principle, because "there is nothing we do that has no theoretical risk, and nearly everything carries some risk."

Had today's technophobic zealots been in charge in previous centuries, we would have to roll human progress back to the Middle Ages—and beyond, since even fire, the wheel, and organic farming pose risks, and none would have passed the "absolute safety" test the zealots now demand. Putting them in charge now would mean an end to progress in the developed world, and perpetual deprivation and misery for inhabitants of developing nations.

❧

Socially responsible investing (SRI) has become another major driving force behind today's CSR movement, courtesy of a growing coterie of activist pension funds and "ethical" investor advisory firms. They claim to represent people who "want to retire into a clean, civil, and safe world." On this basis, pension fund directors pressure CEOs and shareholders to meet "acceptable standards" of precaution, sustainable development, social responsibility, and societal expectations.

Now, prevailing notions of corporate social responsibility may bring about a cleaner, safer, more civil world for the activists and pensioners, at least in the short run. But what about for the poorest citizens of Africa, Asia, and Latin America? Or even the poorest citizens of the United States, Europe, Canada, Australia, and Japan?

As to "societal expectations"—don't African and Asian societies have a right to expect that they will be protected against malaria, malnutrition, and dysentery? That they will not be told by rich First World foundations, government agencies, and pressure groups how they may or may not respond to lethal threats, including those the developed countries have already eliminated?

To suggest that "socially responsible investors" should have free rein to ignore the conditions and needs of desperate people in the Third World is incomprehensible. But that is often the effect of CSR and SRI policies, as the following chapters demonstrate.

⋅◈⋅

Corporate social responsibility may, as its advocates constantly assert, be based on a noble quest to improve society and safeguard humanity's and our Earth's future. This is a fundamental justification for modern ideological environmentalism. Of course, similar claims were made on behalf of other coercive, central-authority "isms" of the twentieth century.

However, debates over corporate social responsibility, stakeholder involvement, sustainable development, the precautionary principle, and socially responsible investing have in far too many instances allowed science and logic to be replaced by pressure tactics, political expediency, and a new form of tyranny. In the process, they have left many urgent questions unanswered.

- Are the asserted risks real? Do the benefits outweigh the risks? Will the radical policy proposals improve poor people's lives—or result in more poverty, misery, disease, and death for those most severely and directly affected by the decisions?
- Why have other stakeholders—such as the rural poor in developing countries—had only a limited role or voice in this process? Why are *their* interests not reflected in CSR and precautionary definitions or applications?
- Why have some companies, foundations, and nations collaborated so closely with NGO and government activists in promoting these mutant concepts?
- What is the source of the activists' supposed moral and legal authority for determining what is "ethical" or "socially responsible" or in accordance with "society's expectations"? Who elected them "stakeholders," to sit in judgment over what is or is not an "acceptable risk," or what costs, benefits, and health or economic priorities must be considered (or ignored) in making this determination?

James Shikwati, director of Kenya's Inter-Regional Economic Network, raises additional questions that weigh heavily on the minds of people in his part of the world.

- "Why do Europe's developed countries impose their environmental ethics on poor countries that are simply trying to pass through a stage they themselves went through?
- "After taking numerous risks to reach their current economic and technological status, why do they tell poor countries to use no energy, and no agricultural or pest-control technologies that might pose some conceivable risk of environmental harm?
- "Why do they tell poor countries to follow sustainable development doctrines that really mean little or no energy or economic development?"

Most of these questions might be unanswerable. But they certainly merit careful reflection. For in its most insidious role, corporate social responsibility—as currently defined and applied—ignores the legitimate aspirations and needs of people who have not yet shared the dreams and successes of even lower and middle income people in the developed world. It should come as no surprise that the poor people in developing countries increasingly view CSR, not as a mechanism to improve their lives, but as a virulent kind of neo-colonialism that many call eco-imperialism.

As corporate executives are frequently reminded, nobody cares how much you know, until they know how much you care. It might be appropriate to suggest that ideological environmentalism should devote as much attention to Third World babies, as it does to adorable harp seal pups.

Television, email, websites, satellite transmissions, and even old-fashioned newspapers have enabled well-financed activists to concoct, exaggerate, and spread public anxiety over a seemingly endless parade of theoretical risks. Even for Americans—who live in the safest nation on earth and are unfazed by traffic and numerous other dangers that pose far greater risks than those trumpeted by precautionary propagandists—the constant drumbeat of doom is hard to ignore.

To suggest that the mutant version of corporate social responsibility doctrines represent progress, "environmental justice," or ethical behavior stretches the meaning of those terms beyond the breaking point. In the end, what is truly not sustainable are the human and ecological tolls exacted by the callous policies of radical environmentalism.

Perhaps nowhere is that more apparent than in the arenas of energy, malaria control, malnutrition, and trade.

PAUL DRIESSEN is senior policy adviser for the Committee for a Constructive Tomorrow (CFACT), which is sponsoring the All Pain No Gain petition against global-warming hype. Driessen is also a senior policy adviser to the Congress of Racial Equality and author of *Eco-Imperialism: Green Power, Black Death.*

EXPLORING THE ISSUE

Should Corporations Adopt Environmentally Friendly Policies of Corporate Social Responsibility (CSR) and Sustainable Development?

Critical Thinking and Reflection

1. Would guidelines on corporate social responsible and sustainable development policies mitigate potential shareholder legal challenges?
2. Would different corporate social responsible and sustainable development programs change shareholders' view of a company?
3. Can a company's corporate social responsibility and sustainable development's effectiveness be effectively measured?
4. Should a company's corporate social responsibility and sustainable development be measured?
5. What role does a corporation's board of directors play in determining a corporation's level/commitment to social responsible practices?

Is There Common Ground?

Both sides of this debate have powerful arguments to draw on. Should the only purpose of an organization be to maximize profit, or do other stakeholders have a legitimate claim on the fruits of the organizations' success? It's a difficult situation for managers: Don't act in a socially responsible manner and run the risk of community alienation or act in a socially responsible manner and potentially create an atmosphere of stress, distrust, and alienation from shareholders. While there has been no attempt to balance shareholder and environmental demands, there is consensus that corporate social responsibility and sustainable development is a complex issue that will continue to be discussed for many years.

Additional Resources

Bidinotto, R.J. (2004). "Death by Environmentalism," *The Navigator*, The Objectivist Center, March, p. 4.

Carroll, A.B. and Buchholtz, A.K. (2009). *Business and Society: Ethics and Stakeholder Management*, South-Western Cengage.

Horner, C. (2007). *The Politically Incorrect Guide to Global Warming and Environmentalism*, Regnery Publishing.

Milloy, S. (2009). *Green Hell: How Environmentalists Plan to Control Your Life and What You Can Do to Stop Them*, Regnery Publishing.

Spencer, R. (2008). *Climate Confusion: How Global Warming Hysteria Leads to Bad Science, Pandering Politicians and Misguided Policies That Hurt the Poor*, Encounter Books.

Internet References . . .

Why Our Economy Is Killing the Planet and What We Can Do About It

New Scientist. (2008). "Why Our Economy Is Killing the Planet and What We Can Do About It," *New Scientist Special Report*, October 16.

http://business.highbeam.com/137753/article-1G1-188584009/why-our-economy-killing-planet-and-we-can-do

Danger in the Nursery: Impact of Tar Sands Oil Development in Canada's Boreal on Birds

Wells, J., Casey-Lefkowitz, S., and Chavarria, G. (2008). "Danger in the Nursery: Impact of Tar Sands Oil Development in Canada's Boreal on Birds," Natural Resources Defense Council, November.

www.nrdc.org/wildlife/borealbirds.asp

Selected, Edited, and with Issue Framing Material by:
Kathleen J. Barnes, *East Stroudsburg University*
and
George E. Smith, *Albright College*

ISSUE

Is Corporate Sustainability Reporting a Valuable Corporate Reporting Tool?

YES: Brian Ballou, Dan L. Heitger, and Charles E. Landes, from "The Future of Corporate Sustainability Reporting," *Journal of Accountancy* (vol. 202, no. 6, 2006, pp. 65–74)

NO: S. Prakash Sethi, from "Corporate Sustainability Reporting: Tackling Credibility and Conflicts of Interest," *Ethical Corporation* (January 29, 2010), www.ethicalcorp.com/communications-reporting/corporate-sustainability-reporting-tackling-credibility-and-conflicts-inter

---

Learning Outcomes

After reading this issue, you should be able to:

- Understand what corporate sustainability reporting is.
- Explain why corporations choose to report on their sustainability.
- Describe the reported limitations and strengths of contemporary sustainability reporting.
- Understand and explain the monitoring and audit process of corporate sustainability reporting and reports.

ISSUE SUMMARY

YES: Brian Ballou, Dan Heitger, and Charles Landes note that corporations have come to the realization that there is value to reporting on sustainability issues and note that this trend is increasing the number of reports published annually. The article also discusses some steps for improving the existing processes that are focused on the G3 Reporting Initiative and auditing.

NO: S. Prakash Sethi's article addresses a number of concerns tied to the sustainability reporting process. Notable among these are the fact that present standards grant corporations total control over the information disclosed and that there is little, if any, independent assessment of reports.

Much has been written about the need for and benefits and use of corporate social responsibility (CSR) reporting. An apparent impetus for the concerted interest in CSR reporting is the notion that "corporate social reporting has established itself as a key element in the movement for making corporations more socially responsible" (Hess, 2008, p. 447). One outcome of the present emphasis on making companies more socially responsible has been an increase in the overall level of reporting in the past decade as many corporations have voluntarily begun to provide data indicating an awareness of and responsibility for social and environmental obligations and impacts (Kolk, 2004b).

Concurrent with the increased interest in and attention to CSR and CSR-related activities has been the evolution and development of a potpourri of standards and guidelines affecting both the format and substance of CSR reporting and measurement. The ideologies and strategies underlying the various approaches have been spurred on by nongovernmental organizations (NGOs), academics, accounting professionals, and government. These efforts have spanned national and international boundaries. The increased attention and proliferation of standards and guidelines have led at least one observer to proclaim that "social reporting is on the verge of becoming a mainstream phenomenon" (Hess, 2008, p. 447).

When CSR reporting is effectively undertaken, CSR reporting "describes quantitatively what the company has done and is currently doing to address stakeholder concerns, while also highlighting the company's objectives for the future and how it will achieve them" (MacLean & Rebernak, 2007, p. 6). The envisioned end state of these reporting efforts for CSR proponents is that the reporting process will lead to "increased corporate accountability, greater stakeholder democracy, and ultimately corporate practices that are more consistent with sustainable development" (Hess, 2008, p. 447).

In this issue, Ballou, Heitger, and Landes explore the future of corporate sustainability reporting. Among their observations is the belief that pressure from internal and external stakeholders is pushing more organizations to report on their social and environmental performance. Additionally they note that some organizations have realized that there are potential comparative advantages to disclosing goals related to not only financial performance, but also nonfinancial performance. These authors anticipate continued growth in reporting and make the case for where and how the accounting profession can benefit and legitimize the reporting process.

Professor Sethi explores flaws in the reporting process. A noted concern regarding these reports is the credibility of the content of the reports. He notes that in his analysis of these reports "companies have largely misused this opportunity by loading their reports with generally non-substantive information" As a result, it is his sense that the reports do more to "exacerbate public distrust and skepticism" than to minimize these conditions.

YES ↵

Brian Ballou, Dan L. Heitger, and Charles E. Landes

The Future of Corporate Sustainability Reporting: A Rapidly Growing Assurance Opportunity

Faced with increased pressure from internal and external stakeholders, more organizations are measuring and reporting on their social and environmental performance as well as the usual financial reporting measures. Stakeholders have been pressing companies to publicly report this information either in annual financial reports to shareholders or in voluntary corporate performance reports. The worldwide growth of socially responsible investment funds, investment rating systems such as the Dow Jones Sustainability Index and investment policy disclosure requirements also have put financial pressures on companies to make these kinds of nonfinancial disclosures.

As this trend grows, so, too, will the role of accountants and auditors. CPAs within organizations will play a key role by providing and measuring the social and environmental information, using their skills to improve its quality and facilitate its use to make sound business decisions in areas such as investment appraisal, budgeting and strategic planning. Auditors also will have a significant role in verifying the accuracy of the reported information as well as the systems and practices from which it is derived. This article provides all CPAs with an overview of corporate sustainability reporting and the role it may play in businesses worldwide.

Beyond the Bottom Line

Organizations have come to realize that meeting stakeholder expectations is as necessary a condition for sustainability as the need to achieve overall strategic business objectives. While maximizing shareholder value continues to be an overriding concern, companies will not be able to do that over the long term if they don't meet other key stakeholder interests. According to a Pricewaterhouse-Coopers report, *The Value Reporting Revolution: Moving Beyond the Earnings Game,* "to create long-term economic value for society—shareholders and other stakeholders alike—sustainability says that companies must also create social and environmental value." To create transparent reports that provide accurate and reliable data, as well as a fair picture of overall performance, many companies are now reporting results across the "triple bottom line" of economic, environmental and social performance.

Triple-bottom-line reporting, also known as corporate sustainability reporting (CSR), involves reporting nonfinancial and financial information to a broader set of stakeholders than just shareholders (see exhibit 1). The reports inform stakeholder groups of the reporting organization's ability to manage key risks. Because these interests vary, the type of information varies; however, much of it has to do with the company's economic, operational, social, philanthropic and environmental objectives.

A number of companies—DuPont, Mobil, Allstate, Gap Inc. and British Petroleum-Amoco among them—recognize the potential comparative advantages of publicly disclosing their goals related to nonfinancial and financial performance measures and then reporting on how well they achieve them. To better understand the pressure to be transparent about a broad number of issues, consider that Wal-Mart's annual revenues exceed the gross domestic product (GDP) of Austria; Exxon-Mobil's revenue is greater than the GDP of Argentina or Turkey; and General Motors' revenue is more than the combined GDP of Columbia and the Philippines. All of them are among the world's 50 largest countries.

Criteria for Preparing Sustainability Reports

Reports on corporate sustainability generally are prepared based on reporting criteria established by an outside organization or the company's internal guidelines. The most dominant reporting regulations are those of the Global Reporting Initiative (GRI). Launched in 1997 with the goal of "enhancing the quality, rigor, and utility of sustainability reporting," the GRI began to develop criteria that could eventually serve as the basis for generally accepted reporting standards. The GRI has received active support and input from numerous groups—including businesses, not-for-profit organizations, accounting regulatory bodies (including the AICPA), investor organizations and trade unions—to build reporting guidelines that are accepted worldwide. In October 2006 it released its

From *Journal of Accountancy*, vol. 202, no. 6, 2006, pp. 65–74. Copyright © 2006 by American Institute of Certified Public Accountants. Reprinted by permission via the Copyright Clearance Center.

Exhibit 1

TYPICAL STAKEHOLDERS FOR U.S. PUBLICLY OWNED ORGANIZATIONS

Financial stakeholders

- Shareholders (institutions, hedge funds, employees and individuals)
- Bond holders
- Banking institutions
- Employees (including unions)
- Other sources of capital (venture capitalists)

Supply chain stakeholders

- Customers
- Alliance partners
- Direct suppliers
- Upstream suppliers
- Contractors

Regulatory stakeholders

- Securities and Exchange Commission
- Internal Revenue Service
- Occupational Health and Safety Administration
- Food and Drug Administration
- Environmental Protection Agency
- Accounting standard setters (FASB, IASB, PCAOB)
- Federal Communications Commission

Political stakeholders

- Federal government (lawmaking and court decisions, for example)
- State governments
- International governments
- United Nations
- European Union
- OPEC
- NATO

Social stakeholders

- Local communities
- General public
- Academia
- Charitable organizations funded by companies
- Environmental and social organizations

second comprehensive set of reporting guidelines—called the G3 Reporting Framework.

The rapid increase in the number of companies around the world adopting GRI standards and issuing corporate sustainability reports, along with the fact that the GRI works closely with the United Nations, gives its reporting criteria the credibility necessary to be considered generally accepted. Overall, the number of organizations reporting under GRI guidelines has grown exponentially since 2000. As of October 2006, nearly 1,000 international companies from more than 60 countries had registered with the GRI and were issuing corporate sustainability

reports using some or all of its standards. (See exhibit 2 for a list of the 100 U.S. companies.)

Companies can use GRI guidelines in several ways with varying degrees of stringency. For example, they may elect to use them for informal reference or to apply them incrementally. Or they may decide to report their corporate sustainability information based on the more demanding *in accordance* level. The move from *informal* to *in accordance* under GRI standards occurs through enhancements of transparent reporting, reporting coverage across the company and reporting structure (see www.globalreporting.org/ services/report/inaccordancechecks for more information). As

EXECUTIVE SUMMARY

- To **satisfy the information needs** of external and internal stakeholders, more organizations are measuring and reporting on their social and environmental performance. CPAs can play an important role in providing the needed information and helping to verify its accuracy.
- **Corporate sustainability reporting (CSR)** involves reporting financial and nonfinancial information to key stakeholders on the company's operational, social and environmental activities and its ability to deal with related risks.
- **The most dominant CSR regulations** are those of the Global Reporting Initiative (GRI), which issued its first comprehensive reporting guidelines in 2002 and its G3 Reporting Framework in October 2006. As of October 2006, more than 1,000 international companies had registered with the GRI and issued corporate sustainability reports using its standards.
- **An opportunity exists for CPAs** to audit the information companies present in corporate sustainability reports. As of yet interested parties have not fully agreed on what information can and should be audited. Concern exists about the suitability of the criteria used to prepare the reports and what performance and reporting standards the auditor should use.
- **A joint task force of the AICPA** and the Canadian Institute of Chartered Accountants (CICA) concluded the 2002 GRI standards had not yet reached a point where they were suitable criteria to be considered generally acceptable and allow a set of generally accepted assurance standards for CSR reports to be developed. Two exposure drafts offered by accountants in the Netherlands on assurance engagements related to sustainability reporting are currently under review by international accounting organizations including the AICPA.

of July 2006, just over 20% of the organizations issuing CSR reports using GRI guidelines did so at the *in accordance* level. This percentage has been increasing since 2002, suggesting organizations issuing CSR reports recognize an increasing market value for *in accordance* reports. The new G3 Reporting Framework is designed to improve the process whereby organizations become *in accordance*.

Opportunities to Provide Assurance for CSR

As with any information an organization reports, the lack of an accompanying independent assurance report reduces the quality and informational usefulness of a CSR. (See "Fraud Risk in CSR.") Consider the reaction should public companies begin to issue unaudited financial statements. Aspects of CSRs are auditable because they are quantitative and verifiable. However, the current lack of reliable metrics for all stakeholder measures results in many qualitative statements about risk management and performance and quantitative measures that are not reliable enough to audit. Thus, the reports that are audited generally are limited in scope (a report might be accompanied by a legend stating which measures are audited).

The GRI's new reporting framework addresses the issue of assurance for CSRs. Exhibit 3 provides details on the framework's choices on assurance. In 2005 KPMG reported that accounting firms prepared more than 50% of the assurance reports for CSRs.

Exhibit 4 shows the CSR audit opinion for Royal Dutch/Shell's 2003 fiscal year. It was jointly audited by PricewaterhouseCoopers LLP (London) and KPMG LLP (The Hague). The opinion points out that only certain measures in the report were audited and describes the type

of procedures performed. The last statement in the scope paragraph provides negative assurance for the remainder of the corporate sustainability report (the accounting firms read that part of the report and noted no material inconsistencies).

The majority of information on which assurance currently is being provided is nonfinancial, quantitative performance measures. For example, Pricewaterhouse-Coopers and KPMG provided assurance on these performance measures in the Shell report:

- Global warming potential.
- Energy efficiency.
- Total spills.
- Flaring in exploration and production activities.
- Fatal accident rate.
- Injury frequency.
- Carbon dioxide release.
- Methane release.
- Regulatory, health, safety and environmental fines.

While there are many other performance measures in the report, their auditability was not at the level the firms could audit with a high enough level of assurance to provide an opinion.

Other assurance approaches that accounting firms use include a review level engagement or limited assurance based on the policies in place and the results of evidence-gathering procedures, as well as verification reports that refer to existing international assurance and attestation standards. For example, exhibit 5 contains the independent auditors' report for Starbucks' 2005 CSR. Moss Adams LLP issued it as being prepared using international standards approved by the IAASB and issued in 2005 as a guideline. The firm's conclusion says Starbuck's CSR was prepared consistent with its internal policies and report

Exhibit 2

U.S. COMPANIES REGISTERED WITH THE GRI FOR CORPORATE SUSTAINABILITY REPORTING

3M	Ecolab	Nike
Abbott Labs	EDS	Office Depot
AMD	Exxon Mobil	Pepsico
AES Corporation	Ford	Pinnacle West Capital
Agilent	Freescale Semiconductor	Plan A
Alcoa	GAP	Polaroid
Allegan	Genecor	Procter & Gamble
Alliant Energy	GE	R J Reynolds
Amerada Hess	GM	Reebok
American Standard Companies	Georgia-Pacific	Rio Tinto Borax
Anheuser-Busch	Gillette (now P&G)	SC Johnson & Son
Applied Materials	Green Mountain Energy	Seventh Generation
Avon Products	Haworth	Smithfield Foods
Bank of America	Heinz	Staples
Baxter	Hewlett-Packard	Starbucks
Ben & Jerry's	Intel	State Street
Bristol-Myers Squibb	IBM	Sunoco
Brown & Williamson	International Finance	Target
Calvert Group	International Paper	Temple-Inland
Cascade Eng.	Johnson & Johnson	Texas Instruments
Catholic Healthcare West	Kimberly Clark	Timberland
CH2M Hill	Louisiana Pacific	Time Warner
Chevron	Lucent	Tyco
Chiquita Brands	Masco	Tyson Foods
Cinergy (now Duke)	Mattel	UPS
Cisco Systems	McDonald's	United Technologies
Citigroup	MeadWestvaco	Visteon
Coca-Cola Enterprises	Merck	Wells Fargo
Cummins	Microsoft	Weyerhaeuser
Dell	Mirant	Wisconsin Energy
Dow Chemical	Motorola	World Bank Group
Dow Coming	National Grid	Wyeth
Du Pont	Newmont Mining	YSI Incorporated

Source: As of October 2006, www.globalreporting.org.

information was reasonably supported by documentation, internal processes and activities, and information provided by external parties. This type of report, while only referring to established criteria (standards approved by the IAASB) still improves the quality of information for external users.

Shell's 2005 CSR report was ranked no. 1 by Pleon's 2005 Global Stakeholder Report (www.pleon.com), which asked stakeholders worldwide to give examples of companies that do a good job of CSR reporting. Interestingly, Shell changed its approach for its 2005 report from using independent accounting firms to an independent panel of experts who reviewed the CSR and offered praise and criticism (see exhibit 6 for excerpts from the panel's report). While this change does not mean the independent accounting firms were ineffective, it suggests organizations should consider a range of methods for providing assurance about the information in the CSR. If accountants fail

to act on the opportunity to provide assurance, companies will begin to adopt other, less rigorous, means.

Challenges of Providing Auditor Assurance

There are two major challenges in providing a sustainability report with auditor assurance: the suitability of the criteria management uses to prepare its sustainability report and the performance and reporting standards the auditor uses. International and national standard setters should not let these challenges deter them from seeking a solution—there is need for these reports, as well as to protect the public through auditor verification.

While the GRI appears to have the most commonly adopted criteria for sustainability reporting and is the organization likely to evolve as providing generally accepted

Exhibit 3

ASSURANCE GUIDANCE IN THE GRI G3 REPORTING FRAMEWORK

Assurance

Choices on assurance

Organizations use a variety of approaches to enhance the credibility of their reports. Organizations may have systems of internal controls in place, including internal audit functions, as part of their processes for managing and reporting information. These internal systems are important to the overall integrity and credibility of a report. However, the GRI recommends the use of external assurance for sustainability reports in addition to any internal resources.

A variety of approaches are currently used by report preparers to implement external assurance, including the use of professional assurance providers, stakeholder panels, and other external groups or individuals. However, regardless of the specific approach, it should be conducted by competent groups or individuals external to the organization. These engagements may employ groups or individuals that follow professional standards for as-

surance, or they may involve approaches that follow systematic, documented, and evidence-based processes but are not governed by a specific standard.

The GRI uses the term *external assurance* to refer to activities designed to result in published conclusions on the quality of the report and the information contained within it. This includes, but is not limited to, consideration of underlying processes for preparing this information. This is different from activities designed to assess or validate the quality or level of performance of an organization, such as issuing performance certifications or compliance assessments.

Overall, the key qualities for external assurance of reports using the GRI Reporting Framework are that it:

- Is conducted by groups or individuals external to the organization who are demonstrably competent in both the subject matter and assurance practices;
- Is implemented in a manner that is systematic, documented, evidence-based, and characterized by defined

procedures;
- Assesses whether the report provides a reasonable and balanced presentation of performance, taking into consideration the veracity of data in a report as well as the overall selection of content;
- Utilizes groups or individuals to conduct the assurance who are not unduly limited by their relationship with the organization or its stakeholders to reach and publish an independent and impartial conclusion on the report;
- Assesses the extent to which the report preparer has applied the GRI Reporting Framework (including the Reporting Principles) in the course of reaching its conclusions; and
- Results in an opinion or set of conclusions that is publicly available in written form, and a statement from the assurance provider on their relationship to the report preparer.

As indicated in Profile Disclosure 3.13, organizations should disclose information on their approach to external assurance.

Source: www.globalreporting.org.

Fraud Risk in CSR

Thomas Golden is one of the leading forensic accounting partners at PricewaterhouseCoopers. He believes individuals who perpetrate financial reporting fraud generally fit one of two profiles. The first is otherwise honest individuals who misrepresent the numbers by rationalizing that what they are doing is best for the company. The second group is individuals who are well aware of what they are doing and who are attempting to attain goals dishonestly. Golden says such individuals exhibit a "rampant disregard for the truth." With either pattern, the pressure to misrepresent information is not entirely alleviated by the Sarbanes-Oxley Act or any other act by a government agency or regulator.

In fact, Golden believes that in the case of financial statement reporting, the rules put in place by Sarbanes-Oxley are analogous to squeezing a balloon. Although they make misrepresenting a company's financial reports more difficult (it's harder to "cook the books"), the pressure on the organizational balloon to perform well remains intense and causes misrepresentations to pop out in other areas.

One rather obvious area where this misinformation can pop out is through largely unaudited reports containing mainly nonfinancial information about an organization, such as the success of a company's new drug in Southeast Asia or the number of subscribers in its system. While the auditor reads communications such as press releases, letters to shareholders and the management discussion & analysis section of annual reports for consistency with the financial statements, nonfinancial information in these communications, as well as corporate sustainability reports, provide tempting opportunities for misrepresentations because they are unaudited.

Another intriguing example Golden offers is that of certain prisoners who, even in solitary confinement, have successfully continued to run their gang's activities on the outside. Unfortunately, these prisoners don't stop communicating illegal and dangerous information to individuals willing to listen. Instead, they adapt to their situation in solitary, which might be difficult at first but becomes easier with practice.

In much the same way, a fraudster might no longer be able to manage earnings or misapply GAAP as easily as before Sarbanes-Oxley, but he or she can find other ways to accomplish the same objectives. And these methods will

(Continued)

get easier over time with practice. The use of unaudited communications that contain nonfinancial and other operations data in a misrepresentative manner might be challenging at first, but that will become easier with practice, too.

Golden says that as long as there is an abundance of investors with too much money chasing too few investment opportunities offering high returns, the temptation to misrepresent a company's performance or future prospects based on nonfinancial and other information will be too great to ignore. He says this is a huge hole in the corporate reporting process and if the accounting profession fails to take a leadership role in plugging it, a new market entrant could emerge to capitalize on providing assurance services for corporate sustainability reports.

"Individuals and firms in our profession need to realize they are in the 'assurance,' not simply the 'auditing' business," Golden says, "and investors need assurance on nonfinancial as well as financial data."

Exhibit 4

INDEPENDENT AUDITORS' REPORT FOR ROYAL DUTCH/SHELL 2003 CORPORATE SUSTAINABILITY REPORT

Assurance report

To: Royal Dutch Petroleum Company and the "Shell" Transport and Trading Company, p.l.c.

Introduction

We have been asked to provide assurance on selected data, graphs and statements of the Royal Dutch/Shell Group of Companies (the "Group") contained in The Shell Report 2003. The Shell Report is the responsibility of management. Our responsibility is to express an opinion on the selected data, graphs and statements indicated below based on our assurance work performed.

Assurance work performed

For the safety and environmental parameters identified with the symbol ● on pages 22 to 26, we obtained an understanding of the systems used to generate, aggregate and report the data for these parameters at Group, Business, Zone and Operating Unit level. We assessed the completeness and accuracy of the data reported in respect of 2003 by visiting Operating Units to test systems and review data. We assessed date trends in discussion with management. We tested the calculations mode at Group level. We also completed assurance procedures on the Refinery Energy Index and reported our findings to management.

For the Sakhalin Location Report on pages 16 and 17 we visited the location to inspect documentary evidence and held interviews with Business and in-country management and with three mojar Russian contracting companies to understand and test the systems, procedures, and evidence in place supporting the assertions and matters discussed within this Location Report. We also performed assurance procedures in relation to China West-East pipeline project and reported our findings to management.

We read the whole Report to confirm that there are no material inconsistencies based on the work we have performed.

Basis of opinion

There are no generally accepted international environmental, social and economic reporting standards. This engagement was conducted in accordance with the International Standards for Assurance Engagements. Therefore, we planned and carried out our work to provide reasonable, rather than absolute, assurance on the reliability of the selected data, graphs and statements that were subject to assurance. We believe our work provides a reasonable basis for our opinion.

Considerations and limitations

It is important to read the data and statements in the context of the basis of reporting provided by the management as set out below and the notes below the graphs. Environmental and social data and assertions are subject to more inherent limitations than financial data, given both their nature and the methods used for determining, calculating of estimating such data.

Our assurance scope is limited to those specific matters mentioned in our opinion below. We have not provided assurance over the contents of the entire Shell Report 2003, nor have we undertaken work to confirm that all relevant issues are included. In addition, we have not carried out any work on financial and economic performance data and data reported in respect of future projections and targets. Accordingly, no opinion is given in respect of them. Where we have not provided assurance over previous years' data this is clearly disclosed. We have not performed work on the maintenance and integrity of information from The Shell Report published on the Group's website.

To obtain a thorough understanding of the financial results and financial position of the Group, the reader should consult the Group's audited Financial Statements for the year ended 31 December 2003.

In our opinion:

—The safety and environmental historical data and graphs (together with the notes) on pages 22 to 26, marked with the symbol ●, properly reflect the performance of the reporting entities for each of these parameters;

—The assertions and matters discussed in the Sakhalin Location Report, on pages 16 and 17, are fairly described and supported by underling documentary or other evidence.

22 May 2004

Source: The Shell Report 2003, Royal Dutch/Shell Group of Companies, www.shell.com.

Is Corporate Sustainability Reporting a Valuable Corporate Reporting Tool? by Barnes and Smith **213**

Exhibit 5

AUDITORS' REPORT OF STARBUCKS CORPORATION SUSTAINABILITY REPORT

To the Stakeholders of Starbucks Coffee Company:

We have been engaged to provide assurance on the Corporate Social Responsibility ("CSR") Fiscal 2005 Annual Report (the "Report") of Starbucks Coffee Company ("Starbucks"), for the fiscal year ended October 2, 2005. We have performed evidence-gathering procedures on the following subject matter:

- Key Performance Indicators Summary and Fiscal 2005 Highlights;
- Information and data provided in each area of focus of the Report (World of Products, Society, Environment, and Workplace); and
- The management and reporting for the preparation of this information and data.

We have considered the subject matter against the following evaluation criteria:

- The procedures by which the CSR information and data were prepared, collated and compiled internally; and
- The control environment over the quality of the information and data.

Our statement should be considered in conjunction with the inherent limitations of accuracy and completeness for CSR data, as well as in connection with Starbucks internal reporting guidelines.

The Board of Directors of Starbucks is responsible for both the subject matter and the evaluation criteria.

Our responsibility is to report on the internal reporting processes, information and data for CSR based on our evidence-gathering procedures. Currently there are no statutory requirements or generally accepted verification standards in the United States of America that relate to the preparation, presentation, and verification of CSR reports. There are international standards for the CSR reports that were approved by the International Auditing and Assurances Standards Board (IAASB) in January 2005. Using the IAASB approved standards as a guideline, we planned and performed evidence-gathering procedures to provide a basis for our conclusion. However, we have not performed an audit in accordance with the International Standards on Auditing. Accordingly, we do not express such an opinion.

Our evidence-gathering procedures included, among other activities, the following:

- Testing the effectiveness of the internal reporting system used to collect and compile information on each area of focus in the Report;
- Performing specific procedures, on a sample basis, to validate the CSR data;
- Visiting Starbucks coffee buying operations in Switzerland;
- Visiting Starbucks corporate headquarters in Seattle, Washington;
- Interviewing partners responsible for data collection and reporting;
- Interviewing partners at retail locations;
- Assessing the information gathering and compiling process of each area of focus in the Report;
- Reviewing relevant documentation, including corporate policies, management and reporting structures; and
- Performing tests, on a sample basis, of documentation and systems used to collect, analyze and compile reported CSR information and data.

In our opinion, based on our work described in this report, the CSR information contained in the Report gives a fair representation of CSR performance and activities of Starbucks Coffee Company for the fiscal year ended October 2, 2005. Statements, assertions and data disclosed in the Report are reasonably supported by documentation, internal processes and activities, and information provided by external parties.

Moss Adams LLP
Seattle, Washington
January 27, 2006

Source: Starbucks 2005 Corporate Social Responsibility Report, www.starbucks.com.

CSR guidelines, it has yet to be recognized in this role by a regulatory body. One reason GRI standards are not generally accepted is the nature of the measures included in its earlier 2002 reporting guidelines, which faced issues associated with relevance, reliability, auditability and the like. The

GRI says one of its goals in issuing the new G3 guidelines was to improve the relevance and auditability of measures.

In 2002 the AICPA and the Canadian Institute of Chartered Accountants (CICA) formed a joint task force on sustainability reporting. While the task force concluded in

Exhibit 6

EXPERT PANEL REPORT FOR SHELL GROUP 2005 CORPORATE SUSTAINABILITY REPORT

Panel of Experts:

Margaret Jungk, Business Department Director, Danish Institute For Human Rights

Dr. Li Lailai, National Programme Director, Leadership For Environment And Development (Lead)—China: Director, Institute For Environment And Development, Beijing

Jermyn Brooks (Review Committee Chair), Board Member, Transparency International

Roger Hammond, Development Director, Living Earth

Jonathan Lash, President, World Resources Institute.

Shell invited us to assess on two counts. Firstly, does it contain the right information about the full range of issues that Shell stakeholders care most about? Secondly, how well does it reflect understanding of stakeholders' expectations? We were guided in our appraisal by the AA1000 Assurance Standard, an independent standard for evaluating sustainability reports against three basic principles: materiality, completeness and responsiveness to stakeholders. We met twice during the final stages of Shell's report drafting process. We interviewed senior Shell staff, including the Chief Executive, and individuals involved with the biggest projects and issues in the Report. In recognition of our time and expertise, an honorarium was offered, payable to us individually or to the organisation of our choice. This is our assessment of the *2005 Shell Sustainability Report,* unedited by Shell. We speak here as individuals, not for our organisations.

Shell's Sustainability Reporting

Since 1998, Shell's reporting has been judged by many external experts as among the best in its sector and overall. Shell has made a serious effort to compile a full and informative report that responds to the needs of the company's international stakeholders, while keeping it concise and readable. The Report's combination of descriptions of the energy challenge and Shell's business strategy, along with environmental and social performance data, documents Shell's concern with sustainability issues and performance. The Report is frank and honest. The company discusses successes as well as challenges and mistakes made (for example, in the accounts of the Corrib and Sakhalin projects).

[*Detailed Comments on Specific Sections Excluded—see Shell.com for complete report*]

We suggest the following ways Shell might improve future Sustainability Reports:

- In selecting subjects for inclusion in the Report, Shell prioritises issues which have the greatest impact on Shell and are highlighted by pressure groups. These measures may fail to take sufficiently into account impacts on wider society, that are not currently the subject of pressure group or media campaigns, but where the company has a substantial and sustained impact. We recommend that these be considered as key selection criteria in future Reports.
- Shell is increasing the number of upstream projects. It is important for the company to comment on how the Shell Project Academy and biodiversity knowledge management system will contribute to the capture and transfer of project experience and skills. Emphasis should be on stakeholder dialogue and conflict-management skills.
- Key performance indicators are presented in the data section of the Report. We believe they could be improved by inclusion of additional metrics, for example relating to pay discrepancies between nationals and non-nationals, the average number of hours worked annually, and the use of hotlines to report breaches of Shell's General Business Principles.
- The annual spend on researching and developing renewables would be more helpful than cumulative figures for the last five years.

Conclusion

We want to thank Shell for its commitment to reporting and its willingness to seek external review of the results. We are impressed by the Report's quality and the care with which it has been compiled. Our critical comments in no way diminish this. We are unanimous in encouraging Shell to make progress on this path.

The Hague, April 3, 2006

Source: The Shell Report 2005, The Shell Group, www.shell.com.

2003 that the GRI had not yet developed to a point where its criteria were suitable, it also recognized the importance of working with the GRI and international standard setters to develop performance and reporting criteria. The task force took an important step in the United States by developing the first attestation engagement on environmental reporting. With the approval of the AICPA Auditing Standards Board, the task force issued Statement of Position 03-2, *Attest Engagements on Greenhouse Gas Emissions Information*. The AICPA also is participating in the Enhanced Business Reporting Consortium (www.ebr360.com), which is examining how to improve information for public company stakeholders.

In January 2005 the professional body of accountants in the Netherlands published two exposure drafts—ED 3410, *Assurance Engagements Relating To Sustainability Report*, and ED 3010, *Practitioners Working With Subject Matter Experts From Other Disciplines On Non-Financial Assurance Engagements* (presumably referenced in the Starbucks CSR assurance report). These documents were built on International Assurance Standards, which are similar to the attestation standards the ASB issues. In response the International Audit and Assurance Standards Board (IAASB) formed a sustainability advisory expert panel (which includes members from the AICPA/CICA task force) to review the EDs and provide comments and suggestions to the Netherlands. The EDs and the IAASB comment letter can found at www.ifac.org.

The letter focused on several key aspects of the EDs that needed refinement before they would be acceptable to the IAASB and ASB. Those include

- Judgments around the suitability of criteria decision.
- The use of experts in performing these types of engagements.
- The work effort necessary to distinguish between reasonable or high assurance vs. limited or moderate assurance.
- Materiality factors to consider in planning the scope of the engagement and when deciding on the type of report to issue.
- The completeness of the sustainability report.

Adding further to the auditor's challenge is the realization that the information in such reports usually is generated by a diverse set of measurement techniques. Information may be gathered from various sources, some of which are outside the reporting organization because of the specialized expertise required to accurately measure certain items. These circumstances may require the auditor to become familiar with the measurement procedures, management practices, systems and integrity of the other organization(s), in addition to those of the reporting organization. As Shell notes in its 2003 CSR, "environmental and social data and assertions are subject to more inherent limitations than financial data, given both their nature and the methods used for determining, calculating or estimating such data."

An alternate set of assurance standards has been developed by AccountAbility, which has no relationship with the AICPA, IFAC or other well-established assurance organizations. In 2002 AccountAbility issued its AA1000Assurance Standards, which represented the first assurance standard covering sustainability reporting and performance based on principles of materiality, completeness and responsiveness (www.accountability.org.uk). Some 120 organizations used the AA1000 standard in 2004.

Growth Opportunity

Corporate sustainability reporting is a rapidly growing way to address stakeholder demands for risk management and more performance measurement information. There are tremendous opportunities for CPAs in industry to be involved with the preparation and disclosure of these reports. The GRI G3 Reporting Framework might emerge as the one most likely to be generally accepted. With organizations issuing corporate sustainability reports at a rapid rate using GRI guidelines, stakeholders for all public companies will come to expect these reports at some point in the future.

There also are tremendous opportunities for CPAs in public practice to provide independent assurance on these reports. However, they face several challenges, including the development of performance and reporting standards. The ASB is supportive of and is working with the IAASB to develop international standards that can be tailored for U.S. auditors. Addressing these challenges will satisfy the growing needs of investors who are demanding the information and who would benefit from auditor assurance. In the 2005 Pleon report, researchers Thomas Lowe and Jens Clausen said CSR report credibility is best achieved by external accountants providing formal external report verification. However, as Shell's change to an expert panel illustrates, accountants might only have a finite amount of time to step forward and provide the expected assurance.

BRIAN BALLOU is an associate professor of accounting at Miami University (OH, USA) and co-director of the Center for Governance, Risk Management and Reporting at the Richard T. Farmer School of Business.

DAN L. HEITGER is an assistant professor of accounting at Miami University (OH, USA) and co-director of the Center for Governance, Risk Management and Reporting at the Richard T. Farmer School of Business.

CHARLES E. LANDES is vice-president AICPA professional standards and services.

S. Prakash Sethi  **NO**

Corporate Sustainability Reporting: Tackling Credibility and Conflicts of Interest

It's time to inject a dose of reality and integrity into corporate social responsibility and sustainability reports, argues Prakash Sethi.

A large number of major corporations, notably the large multinational corporations, have been publishing non-financial reports that describe a company's activities pertaining to issues of major concern to various socio-political groups and public-at-large.

For example, in a database generated by SICCA and containing over 1200 companies from around the world, in 2008 there were 490 companies that had published corporate social responsibility/sustainability (CSR-S) reports including 13 companies that had created web-based CSR-S reports.

All available evidence suggests that the trend toward publishing CSR-S reports will increase as companies are confronted by public demand, and peer group pressure, to provide greater information about social and environmental impact of their business practices in all parts of the world.

Significance

We should not, however, rush to judgment by concluding that corporations have significantly increased their CSR activities especially when they go beyond corporate charity and philanthropy and where CSR-S reports are loaded with pictures of beautiful landscapes and smiling children waving happily to their corporate benefactors.

The new emphasis in the CSR-S reports instead focuses on a company's core business activities and their impact on the sustainability of the planet's environment and preservation of the quality of life and survivability of its inhabitants.

The widespread corporate embrace of CSR-S reports is one example of this growing and pertinent trend. CSR-S (or non-financial) reports provide corporations a number of important advantages.

1. The company has total control over the medium, i.e., CSR-S report, to ensure that its message is presented in the most favorable surrounding context.
2. The message is communicated as intended with no independent external or un-controlled assessment.

The nature of corporate control over the medium and the message also places enormous burden on the corporate sponsor to ensure that its message contains a high level accuracy, specificity, and materiality to engender public trust in the corporate message.

The Model Is Broken

Companies are spending millions of dollars annually to publish and disseminate their CSR-S reports.

And yet, rather than enhancing corporate credibility, these reports have tended to exacerbate public distrust and skepticism because they lack credible evidence as to the accuracy and comprehensiveness of the information contained in these reports.

Under the circumstances, it would seem logical that companies would take their lead from their publication of financial reports where they are required by law to provide external measures of assurance as to the quality and accuracy of information.

Unfortunately, our analysis of the current state of CSR-S reports suggests that companies have largely misused this opportunity by loading their reports with generally non-substantive information asserting companies performance on issues of environment, society, and governance (ESG).

Our analysis shows that of the companies publishing CSR-S reports, 61% did not make any mention of integrity assurance; 11% made some reference to assurance but provided no information; and only 28% of the companies provided some type of formal assurance statement.

A content analysis of assurance statements was based on a 10 point score. Of these, [s]even (7) points were allocated to the comprehensiveness of the investigation and verification process, and three (3) points were assigned to the scope of the integrity assurance.

The data shows that level of integrity assurance, and indeed the overall quality of CSR-S reports, was not confined to a particular industry or region, although some industries and regions displayed overall results.

In general, companies were more inclined to provide details as to the comprehensive[ness] of the investigation and verification process than the scope of the integrity assurance itself.

For example, 49% of the companies (67) scored between [5 and 7] points on the details on the investigative process, and only 6 companies received the top score of 3 on the scope of integrity assurance.

There [are] 9 companies with the best performing scores of 9–10 with regard to Assurance Statements.

Big Four Accounting Firms and Conflicts of Interest

A large number of assurance statements were provided by the big four certified public accounting firms (63%). However, assurance statement providers also included specialized integrity assurance organizations, for-profit NGOs and other third-party monitoring groups.

Our analysis of assurance providers for CSR-Sustainability reports revealed a disturbing trend with regard to assurance audits conducted by the Big Four Financial Auditing Firms, i.e., the firm providing assurance statements for CSR-Sustainability reports was also responsible for conducting financial audit for the same company.

Moreover, this situation was found to exist in the case of 43 companies (49%) where CSR-Sustainability reports had assurance statements provided by the Big Four financial auditing firms, i.e., PricewaterhouseCoopers (15 companies), KPMG (12 companies), Ernst & Young (9 companies), and Deloitte (7 companies).

In the U.S. and European Union, financial auditing firms have faced increased scrutiny and criticism where they have provided additional advisory-consulting services to the corporations in addition to conducting financial audits.

It seems ironic that corporations and financial auditing firms would not avoid even the appearance of conflict of interest and thereby avoiding public distrust.

At the risk of stating the obvious, it behooves on the corporate community to substantially increase their efforts and improve the quality of their CSR-S reports in terms of comprehensiveness and relevance of the information provided these reports, and also to ensure their accuracy through independent and credible verification of information that is disseminated to the public with maximum transparency. Otherwise, corporations would be faced with a further diminution in the public trust and a degradation of their reputation.

S. PRAKASH SETHI is the president of the Sethi International Center for Corporate Accountability, and university distinguished professor at Baruch College/CUNY, New York.

EXPLORING THE ISSUE

Is Corporate Sustainability Reporting a Valuable Corporate Reporting Tool?

Critical Thinking and Reflection

1. What could be done to improve the reporting process?
2. Are the reports really valuable?
3. From a corporate perspective, what do the reports represent, especially given their present state and format?
4. What should a CSR report consist of?
5. Who should monitor and verify the information contained in these reports?
6. Should corporations have to respond to and report on nonfinancial factors?

Is There Common Ground?

Both sides of this debate recognize that the trend for reporting on sustainability issues is on the rise and the demand for these reports does not appear to be weakening. The heart of this issue however lies in the details or content of these reports. Specifically, what information should be included, how should it be reported, and should there be any auditing or formal assessment of these reports. Given the evolutionary nature of this type of reporting, it is anticipated that these discussions and this debate will continue well into the next decade.

Additional Resources

Aras, G. and Crowther, D. (2008). "Corporate Sustainability Reporting: A Study in Disingenuity," *Journal of Business Ethics*, Spring, pp. 279–288.

Buhr, N. (2007). "Histories and Rationales for Sustainability Reporting," in Jeffrey Unerman, Jan Bebbington, and Brendan O'Dwyer (Eds.), *Sustainability Accounting and Accountability*, London, UK: Routledge, pp. 57–69.

Hess, D. (2008). "The Three Pillars of Corporate Social Reporting as New Governance Regulation:

Disclosure, Dialogue, and Development," *Business Ethics Quarterly*, 18(4), pp. 447.

Kolk, A. (2004a). "A Decade of Sustainability Reporting: Developments and Significance." *International Journal of Environment and Sustainable Development*, 3(1), pp. 51–64.

Kolk, A. (2004b). "More Than Words? An Analysis of Sustainability Reports." *New Academy Review*, 3(3), pp. 59–75.

MacLean, R. and Rebernak, K. (2007). "Closing the Credibility Gap: The Challenges of Corporate Responsibility Reporting." *Environmental Quality Management*, Summer, pp. 1–6.

Pounder, B. (2011). "Trends in Sustainability Reporting," *Strategic Finance*, December, pp. 21–23.

Reilly, A.H. (2009). "Communicating Sustainability Initiatives in Corporate Reports: Linking Implications to Organizational Change," *SAM Advanced Management Journal*, Summer, pp. 33–43.

Sherman, R.W. (2012). "The Triple Bottom Line: The Reporting of 'Doing Well' & 'Doing Good'," *The Journal of Applied Business Research*, July/August, pp. 673–681.

Internet References . . .

New Group Aims to Set Sustainability Reporting Standards

Connor, M. (2012). "New Group Aims to Set Sustainability Reporting Standards," October 1.

http://business-ethics.com/2012/10/01/1750-new-group-to-set-sustainability-standards-for-business/

Carrots and Sticks: Promoting Transparency and Sustainability

Global Reporting Initiative (GRI) (2012a). "Carrots and Sticks: Promoting Transparency and Sustainability."

www.globalreporting.org/resourcelibrary/Carrots-And-Sticks-Promoting-Transparency-And-Sustainbability.pdf

Global Reporting Initiative

Global Reporting Initiative (GRI) (2012b).

www.globalreporting.org/reporting/Pages/default.aspx

The Future of Corporate Social Responsibility Reporting

Maguire, M. (2011). "The Future of Corporate Social Responsibility Reporting," January.

www.bu.edu/pardee/files/2011/01/PardeeIIB-019-Jan-2011.pdf

Mandatory Social Responsibility

Oxford Analytica (2010). "Mandatory Social Responsibility," May 5.

www.forbes.com/2010/05/04/corporate-social-responsibility-csr-business-oxford.html

Does Corporate Social Responsibility Increase Profits?

Robins, R. (2011). "Does Corporate Social Responsibility Increase Profits?" May 12.

http://business-ethics.com/2011/05/12/does-corporate-social-responsibility-increase-profits/

The Rising Global Interest in Sustainability and Corporate Social Responsibility Reporting

White, S.E. (2012). "The Rising Global Interest in Sustainability and Corporate Social Responsibility Reporting," October 5.

http://sustainability.thomsonreuters.com

Selected, Edited, and with Issue Framing Material by:
Kathleen J. Barnes, *East Stroudsburg University*
and
George E. Smith, *Albright College*

ISSUE

Is It Really Possible to Create Sustainable Businesses?

YES: Chris Boyd, from "Sustainability Is Good Business," *The OECD Observer* (September 2001, pp. 35–37)

NO: Pamela Laughland and Tima Bansal, from "The Top Ten Reasons Why Businesses Aren't More Sustainable," *Ivey Business Journal* (January/February 2011), www.iveybusinessjournal.com/topics/social-responsibility/the-top-ten-reasons-why-businesses-aren%E2%80%99t-more-sustainable

---

Learning Outcomes

After reading this issue, you should be able to:

- Describe barriers to sustainability practices in corporations.
- Discuss potential opportunities afforded by a sustainability agenda and strategy.
- Explain what sustainability is and means to supporters of corporate sustainability.
- Appreciate the challenge of building and operating a sustainable business.

ISSUE SUMMARY

YES: Chris Boyd argues that there "is no fundamental contradiction between concern for the environment or social responsibility and the profit motive" and that "it is good business for companies to act in a more sustainable way."

NO: Pamela Laughland and Tima Bansal surveyed 15 organizations "on the leading edge of sustainability" asking them why more firms are not committing to the sustainability. This brief article lists and describes the Top 10 hurdles for business sustainability resulting from that work.

In an October 2011 *Harvard Business Review* article on sustainability, Chouinard, Ellison, and Ridgway explain:

> No one these days seriously denies the need for sustainable business practices. Even those concerned about only business and not the fate of the planet recognize that the viability of business itself depends on the resources of healthy ecosystems—fresh water, clean air, robust biodiversity, productive land—and on the stability of just societies. Happily, most of us also care about these things directly (Chouinard, Ellison, & Ridgway, 2011).

The sentiment conveyed in this quotation illustrates the importance that is being given to sustainability and sustainable business. In trying to define and frame the issue of sustainability, the following information can be found on an MIT Sloan Management Review web page (http://sloanreview.mit.edu/what-is-sustainability/):

What does sustainability mean?
Depends whom you ask. (Debates about it can get warm.) But at root it's the idea that systems—including natural and human ones—need to be regenerative and balanced in order to last. We believe that that means all kinds of systems: economic, environmental, societal, and personal. The sustainability question is: How can we design and build a world in which the Earth thrives and people can pursue flourishing lives?

Are there other definitions?
Yes—too many to count. Some focus on environmental impact alone, or emphasize the idea of the triple bottom line (measuring performance of organizations or communities on separate economic, environmental, and social dimensions). One of the best known general definitions emerged from a 1987 United Nations report about sustainable development, which was described as development "meeting the needs of the present

without compromising the ability of future generations to meet their own needs." Increasingly, attempts at definition are recognizing that the needs of natural, economic, and social systems are so interdependent that [they] have to be considered in an integrated way.

Based on this information, sustainable businesses then are those that seek to address the needs of business, society, and the environment in the present without adversely impacting the future. These corporations are concerned with conservation, minimizing their "environmental footprints," and becoming responsible stewards of the resources that they have been provided. In building upon this idea, many organizations have adopted and are adopting "green policies" to reduce waste, make better use of energy, and limit their impact on the environment that will ultimately be left to and passed on to future generations.

The articles included in this issue seek to examine the issue of developing and maintaining a sustainable business. First, Chris Boyd presents his view that sustainability is good business. In his opinion, "there is no fundamental contradiction between concern for the environment or social responsibility and the profit motive." He views the pursuit of sustainability and sustainable business practices as being strategic concepts and issues that businesses should account for and include.

Ms. Laughland and Professor Bansal illustrate challenges and obstacles to Mr. Boyd's views in their article. These authors cite evidence from other studies that indicate the potential benefits of pursing a sustainability agenda and proceed to ask why there aren't more companies following this path. To better understand the dynamics, issues, and challenges confronting businesses, Laughland and Bansal conducted a survey with 15 organizations on the "leading edge of sustainability" and asked them to provide their thoughts on why there were not more organizations committing to sustainability. Based on their survey data, they present the top 10 hurdles for business sustainability in 2011.

YES ⬅

Chris Boyd

Sustainability Is Good Business

Sustainability, the triple bottom line of economic profitability, respect for the environment and social responsibility: these are the new buzzwords of many a corporate annual report. Global companies everywhere are falling over themselves to declare their adherence to the principles of sustainable development. Is this a new moral crusade on the part of big business, or simply the result of pressure from demonstrators like those in Seattle and Genoa?

For some, either of these arguments may be true, but on the whole, sustainability is largely a question of good business. In fact, there is no fundamental contradiction between concern for the environment or social responsibility and the profit motive that has largely created the developed world as we know it today. In short, greed is still good for you.

Not that unrestrained market forces will deliver sustainability. There is clearly a role for government in setting the right framework for markets to deliver those broader based outcomes we all want for our planet. On the environment side, there are externalities—costs not borne by the polluter—that are excluded from influencing the market at present. This has occurred for various reasons, but mainly because resources, like fresh air and clean water, were simply treated as costless until recently. Historically, we have seen examples of such externalities being successfully internalised—the bringing of common grazing lands into private ownership, thereby creating the incentive to conserve, is one case—though not without conflict. Greenhouse gas emissions that cause global warming are an obvious environmental externality that we now know needs to be internalised. Only in a few countries are emissions regulated or taxed in some way. In most countries, it is "costless" for firms to emit CO_2, so of course there is little incentive for them to change their behaviour unless governments act. Indeed, many companies support efforts to reach worldwide agreement on combating climate change in order to make the necessary economic adjustments in an orderly fashion.

Governments also have a crucial role to play in setting the right framework for markets to function in socially responsible ways. Tax and spending policies should be set in ways that complement the market economy by providing public goods efficiently. More controversially perhaps, governments are mainly responsible for ensuring human rights and fighting corruption, although companies, especially large global ones, cannot and do not ignore these issues.

However, it is good business for companies to act in a more sustainable way, even where the market does not yet provide the appropriate signals. Take climate change as an example. The cement industry is a significant producer of CO_2, the principal greenhouse gas, causing about 5% of the world's emissions. As the world's largest cement producer, Lafarge has an interest in reducing its carbon intensity, not only to prepare itself for a future carbon-constrained world, but also to help avoid rushed and poorly designed legislation. Not only Lafarge in the cement industry, but also companies such as BP and Shell in the oil industry, TransAlta in the power sector and Dupont in chemicals have a similar view of climate change.

On the social side too, our concern for sustainability is grounded in good business reasons. Our cement plants and our quarries often dominate other industries in their local communities. Lafarge has learned over its almost 170 years of existence that the implicit "license to operate" from local communities, gained through actions coming out of dialogue and transparency, is as important as the regulatory permits from the authorities. Without the support and understanding of local communities, changes such as quarry extensions or fuel switches to use waste fuels like used tires, which reduce costs and save fossil fuels, would be more difficult if not impossible to obtain. Our business would become precarious and less flexible.

Acting in a sustainable way can make firms more competitive, more resilient to shocks, nimbler in a fast-changing world, more unified in purpose, more likely to attract and hold customers and the best employees, and more at ease with regulators and financial markets.

Financial markets are beginning to notice these positive effects. Between 1 January 1999 and 30 June 2000, the Dow Jones Sustainability Group World Index—composed of sustainability-driven companies including Lafarge— outperformed the Dow Jones Global World Index by 127 basis point in US dollar terms. The index consists of the top 10% of companies seen as leaders in sustainable development. Their value advantage held in both bull and bear markets.

A Strategy That Pays

The main business drivers of sustainability for manufacturing firms make a good strategic concept for improving business performance:

- Eco-efficiency: Reducing inputs of limited natural raw materials or fuel consumption, reducing waste production and utilising by-products from other industries, allow firms to cut costs;

- Improving product added value: With a sustainability approach, firms expect to be able to expand their product lines to sell more complex and technological products, with more value added (licenses, exclusive technology, etc.). Links with customers and users will become closer and better established in the long term and loyalty will be improved;
- Creating new market opportunities: A sustainability policy should facilitate firms' expansion into new countries or regions through more sensitive and proactive methods of integration and an enhanced environmental approach. New products will allow firms to respond better to the emerging expectations of their customers;
- Strengthening socially responsible management: Such a policy will strengthen corporate culture, help firms to maintain the loyalty of their employees and attract high-potential new employees;
- Improving reputation: A proactive strategy will help firms keep their "license to operate," and improve their corporate image in order to maintain brand value, as well as their relationships with local authorities and communities. This helps to reduce the prospect of inappropriate new taxes and regulations and avoid crises.

Smart Markets

Given the right framework, competitive and open markets are the right way to move towards sustainability. Markets, with all their imperfections, are nevertheless the best means that man has found to produce innovation and efficiency. By rewarding success, markets harness creative energy. It is difficult to imagine that government officials, however well-meaning or efficient, will be better at organising a route to sustainability than the market mechanism, as long as this is properly framed to encourage sustainability.

Certainly, sustainable development should not become an excuse for governments to impose yet more heavy-handed regulation and yet more taxes. Just look at the French government's attempts to impose sustainability reporting by law with over thirty indicators proposed

in the social field alone or the US Superfund legislation, which benefits mostly lawyers. More energy should be spent on getting the price and other signals right so that markets work in a more sustainable fashion. This means convincing, not coercing. After all, sustainability will not progress if those that are meant to implement it are alienated from the concept. It also means that governments should take a comprehensive approach. Sustainable development is by its very nature not amenable to the partial, unco-ordinated methods that different government departments tend to employ. An example is the enormous subsidies still paid to fossil fuels in many countries, which conflict with climate change concerns.

No one has a monopoly of knowledge on how to progress towards sustainability. Dialogue and partnership, between governments and civil society in general on the one hand and business on the other, is the way forward. Who knows exactly what will emerge in terms of agreements and initiatives? But what is clear is that markets can and must be made to work for the benefit of all. Without them progress towards global sustainable development will be much more difficult, if not impossible, to achieve.

References

Forum: "OECD Guidelines for Multinational Enterprises," series of opinion articles, in *OECD Observer*, No. 225, March 2001. Also see Policy Brief at www.oecd.org/publications/Pol_brief/

Schmidheiney, Stefan, *Changing Course: A Global Perspective on Development and the Environment*, Business Council for Sustainable Development, MIT Press, Cambridge, 1992.

Sustainable America, The President's Council on Sustainable Development, US Government Printing Office, Washington D.C., 1996.

Witherell, B., Maher, M., "Responsible corporate behaviour for sustainable development," *OECD Observer* No. 226/227, Summer 2001. See www.oecdobserver.org

---

CHRIS BOYD is senior vice-president of environment and public affairs at Lafarge. Lafarge is a world leader in building materials with 85,000 workers employed in 75 countries.

PLEASE NOTE: To access the "NO" selection, please refer to "The Top Ten Reasons Why Businesses Aren't More Sustainable by Pamela Laughland and Tima Bansal immediately following this issue.

EXPLORING THE ISSUE

Is It Really Possible to Create Sustainable Businesses?

Critical Thinking and Reflection

1. In what ways are customers benefited by sustainable business practices?
2. How do businesses benefit from pursuing corporate strategies focused on sustainability?
3. Will customers send market signals to businesses engaged in sustainability that will reward those efforts? Why or why not?
4. How could the degree of a business's commitment to sustainability be measured?
5. Are there corporate stakeholders that could assist businesses in pursuing sustainability?

Is There Common Ground?

The common ground on this particular issue appears to be the recognition that businesses need to consider new models that will protect the environment and society. There is a growing commitment to the idea that the environment businesses operate and exist in has a finite set of resources, and responsible use of those resources should be taken into account as businesses develop and execute their strategies. The challenge here is the viability of these ideas for sustaining business. Boyd believes sustainability should be an integral part of a business's strategy and that sustainability practices reward businesses, especially in the long run. Laughland and Bansal maintain that while there is evidence of the success spoken of by Boyd, the transition has been slow and their research provides 10 reasons for this lag. Given these contrasting viewpoints, it is likely that the issue of business sustainability will continue to receive attention and be a topic of discussion and debate for some time.

Additional Resources

Chouinard, Y., Ellison, J., and Ridgeway, R. (2011). "The Big Idea: The Sustainable Economy," *Harvard Business Review*, October, http://hbr.org/2011/10/the-sustainable-economy/ar/1

Crew, D.E. (2010). "Strategies for Implementing Sustainability: Five Leadership Challenges," *SAM Advanced Management Journal*, Spring, pp. 15–21.

Haanaes, K., Balagopal, B., et al. (2011). "First Look: The Second Annual Sustainability & Innovation Survey," *MIT Sloan Management Review*, Winter, pp. 77–83.

Haanaes, K., Balagopal, B., et al. (2011). "New Sustainability Study: The 'Embracers' Seize Advantage," *MIT Sloan Management Review*, Spring, pp. 23–35.

Internet References . . .

What Is Sustainability?

MIT Sloan Management Review (2012). "What is Sustainability?"

http://sloanreview.mit.edu/what-is-sustainability/

IVEY BUSINESS JOURNAL

The Top Ten Reasons Why Businesses Aren't More Sustainable

By Pamela Laughland and Tima Bansal

Reprint# 9B11TA03

RICHARD IVEY SCHOOL OF BUSINESS FOUNDATION January/February 2011
COPYRIGHT © 2011

Ivey Business Journal
is published by Richard Ivey School of Business Foundation a division of
The Richard Ivey School of Business.
For subscription information, please contact:
Ivey Business Journal
P.O. Box 10, Station Q
Toronto, Ontario M4T 2L7

Email: www.iveybusinessjournal.com   Phone: (416) 923-9945

The Top Ten Reasons Why Businesses Aren't More Sustainable

By Pamela Laughland and Tima Bansal

Pamela Laughland is a Research Associate at the Richard Ivey School of Business and Knowledge Coordinator for the Network for Business Sustainability.

Tima Bansal is Professor, Richard Ivey School of Business. She is Director, Ivey's Centre for Building Sustainable Value, and Executive Director, Network for Business Sustainability.

"It doesn't fit the business case," or "How are we supposed to measure the impact?" are just two of the most common excuses corporations offer for not drawing up and implementing sustainability initiatives in all aspects of their operations. These authors met with some of the leading practitioners of sustainability and identified how organizations can stop making excuses and start building sustainability into everything from supply chain activities to HR practices.

The evidence is in: Firms that invest in sustainability are no worse off financially than those that do not.[1] Plus, their employees, customers, and investors are happier and more committed.[2] Even the simplest of activities, such as philanthropy, can yield financial rewards.[3] So, why isn't every firm jumping on the sustainability bandwagon?

We asked 15 organizations that are on the leading edge of sustainability to tell us why. In fact, every year, we assemble representatives from leading corporations in different industries to brainstorm and discuss the reasons why Canadian firms don't take action on social and environmental issues. The top 10 reasons they identified are listed below.

Top 10 hurdles for business sustainability in 2011

1. There are too many metrics that claim to measure sustainability—and they're too confusing.
2. Government policies need to incent outcomes and be more clearly connected to sustainability.
3. Consumers do not consistently factor sustainability into their purchase decisions.
4. Companies do not know how best to motivate employees to undertake sustainability initiatives.
5. Sustainability still does not fit neatly into the business case.
6. Companies have difficulty discriminating between the most important opportunities and threats on the horizon.
7. Organizations have trouble communicating their good deeds credibly, and avoid being perceived as greenwashing.
8. Better guidelines are needed for engaging key stakeholders, such as aboriginal communities.
9. There is no common set of rules for sourcing sustainably.
10. Those companies that try leading the sustainability frontier often end up losing.

What is Business Sustainability?

Business sustainability is often defined as managing the triple bottom line – a process by which firms manage their financial, social, and environmental risks, obligations and opportunities. We extend this definition to capture more than just accounting for environmental and social impacts. Sustainable businesses are resilient, and they create economic value, healthy ecosystems and strong communities. These businesses survive external shocks because they are intimately connected to healthy economic, social and environmental systems.

The Process for Identifying The Top 10

Fifteen representatives of leading organizations across different sectors gathered for a one-day roundtable in Toronto to identify the top 10 sustainability issues facing Canadian business for 2011. This Leadership Council, which convenes annually to set priorities for the Network for Business Sustainability, included BC Hydro, Canadian Pacific, Environment Canada, Holcim Canada Ltd., the International Institute for Sustainable Development, Industry Canada, The Pembina Institute, Research In Motion Limited, SAP Canada Inc., Suncor Energy Inc., TD Bank Group, Teck, Telus, Tembec, and Unilever Canada Inc. These firms identify global priorities from the Canadian perspective, to ensure that the priorities have global relevance. These representatives engaged in a 3-stage process:

1) Identifying their own individual issues;
2) Aggregating and refining the issues into meaningful categories; and,
3) Ranking priorities by importance.

This process yields a set of issues that is representative, prioritized, and agreed-upon. Current and past priorities for the Network for Business Sustainability can be found here.

We discuss each of these hurdles below.

1. There are too many metrics that claim to measure sustainability—and they're too confusing.

What gets measured gets managed. Issues or goals without obvious metrics are much harder to tackle. Sustainability initiatives can be particularly difficult to measure because they often affect people and society at a macro level, and their organizational implications are unclear. Further, their impacts are not immediately obvious and they depend on who implements them and how. Many suites of metrics and measurement systems—such as the Global Reporting Initiative, ecological footprint, and life-cycle assessment—currently exist to help managers measure their sustainability.

The range of options often results in more problems than solutions. What makes one metric or suite of metrics better than another, and how can businesses judge which is most appropriate for their needs? As one manager said: *"It's important to know which sustainability metrics are most meaningful and integrate them with traditional business metrics."* Managers recognize that different metrics serve different purposes: some are most relevant to particular sectors, such as manufacturing, while others focus on specific issues, such as carbon. Some metrics focus on products whereas others focus on organizations; some set common benchmarks, whereas others inspire leadership. It seems as if there is a veritable cacophony of metrics, standards, and certifications. Even leading businesses need guidance on which ones will help them benchmark, signal their commitment to sustainability, and identify areas that need improvement.

2. Government policies need to incent outcomes and be more clearly connected to sustainability.

Governments have several tools at their disposal, such as taxes, regulations, and markets, to encourage businesses to steward environmental resources. However, they are often applied in piecemeal fashion, poorly measured, or used ineffectively. Businesses and management often want to "do the right thing", and appropriate policy can support this mindset. Leading businesses want policies that push all organizations to improved sustainability outcomes. In doing so, firms can put into place long-term measures and innovate new products and practices that move them closer to those goals.

Businesses also want to know the best practices for collaborative consultation and policy development involving government, business, and other stakeholders. They do not want to be adjuncts, but to work with government collaboratively and meaningfully. One manager asked, *"How can we build bridges between government and business that will allow for knowledge sharing and a solid foundation for future business sustainability-related policies?"* In other words, business wants to be involved in the process such that the resulting policy is effective, efficient, and consistent with both the needs of business and society.

3. Consumers do not consistently factor sustainability into their purchase decisions.

Many decisions consumers make—from what food to buy to how much energy to use—involve sustainability-related tradeoffs. We constantly trade off different types of impacts (social, environmental, or economic) at different levels (personal, communal, or societal) over different time periods (now or later). In the words of one manager: *"Many people demand cleaner energy but refuse, for example, to allow windmills in their community. How can we help consumers make informed tradeoffs when it comes to sustainability?"*

Understanding how consumers value sustainability in the context of other product attributes would help businesses develop products that meet their needs. Further, there may be a role for business in educating consumers on issues and product attributes, resulting in more informed purchasing decisions.

Still, this doesn't just apply to consumers—it also applies to investors. Shareholders and lenders must decide where to invest their money. How do they choose between different companies, which requires trading off one set of corporate attributes for another? Should they invest in a power producer using cheap coal or another moving towards renewable or alternative energy? Understanding how people make tradeoffs will help businesses make sustainable choices.

4. **Companies do not know how best to motivate employees to undertake sustainability initiatives.**

    Survey research shows employees would rather work for sustainable firms—and some would even forego higher earnings to do so.[4] Firms must better leverage this knowledge to attract and retain the best employees. To do this, sustainability managers want to know which employee incentive plans are most valued, and so likely to be effective. One manager clearly identifies this need, asking: *"What does the cumulative experience of business tell us about how best to incorporate sustainability performance targets into employee incentives?"*

    These mechanisms should allow firms to leverage their sustainability initiatives and values, building the right capacity internally and ensuring progress is made towards sustainability goals. An enduring commitment to sustainability, one that can only be achieved over a long time horizon, may separate those companies that are truly committed to leading change from those that are only keeping pace with their peers. One manager at a leading firm points out: *"It's easy to generate ideas and start initiatives at the grassroots level. But how do we sustain that momentum for fruitful innovation across the entire organization—and over the long term?"* However, such commitment requires the buy-in and sustained interest of employees. In this way, good employees attract other good employees, and the firm moves towards a virtuous and enduring cycle of sustainability.

5. **Sustainability still does not fit neatly into the business case.**

    Most sustainability managers are beyond asking if it pays to be good (or green). However, they are often called on to explain and defend sustainability activities. Current financial decision-making does not fully capture the value of sustainability-related investments. These investments are often based on long-term and intangible rewards, whereas many investments made are based on the short-term impact on the bottom line. One manager pointed out that the payback period for sustainability investments often exceeds that required to approve projects. Sustainability executives may resort to intangibles to justify corporate environmental and social investments. Initiatives are often treated therefore, as 'off-grid' or 'one-offs', rather than a recurring component in all decision-making activities. Another manager said: *"We need to be able to value brand, reputation and the externalities arising from our business activities."*

    Sustainability managers want to know exactly how returns on sustainability investments can be measured and seen. What are the short-term and long-term ways to assess and justify these investments? How can sustainability executives demonstrate the value of sustainability within the decision-making language and framework of finance executives? Until sustainability becomes accepted as a legitimate—and value-creating—activity, it may lose out to projects that are more easily understood and evaluated.

6. **Companies have difficulty discriminating between the most important opportunities and threats on the horizon.**

    Numerous threats are looming for business—from financial crises, to climate change, to local land issues, to health pandemics. It is difficult to judge which of these risks warrants attention, and often more challenging to prioritize them. Businesses need guidance on how to evaluate the materiality of an issue, both for disclosure purposes and for strategic planning. One manager points to the complexity facing their business: *"There are myriad opportunities and risks we could tackle as an organization. We need to understand where to focus our attention to advance our practices now and in the future."*

    Equipped with an understanding of which risks and opportunities are most material to their organization, managers can then prioritize material issues, translate them into internal strategies, and communicate them to stakeholders.

7. Organizations have trouble communicating their good deeds credibly, and avoid being perceived as greenwashing.

Claims made by some businesses and NGOs regarding sustainability are perceived to be credible, whereas others are met with skepticism or disbelief. The different reactions are likely related to attributes of the organization making the claims—its size, its structure, its actions, or its motivations. Even leading businesses are wary of touting their successes, as such communications can invite public criticism for the things that they aren't doing.

Companies want to know how to communicate their message credibly, so the integrity of their efforts is clear. This issue is critically important as most of the benefit of CSR activities can depend on whether stakeholders believe the message to be truthful. One manager noted: *"Polls show people consider academics and NGOs more credible than corporations and government. What sincere action can organizations undertake to foster public credibility?"*

8. Better guidelines are needed for engaging key stakeholders, such as aboriginal communities.

Many businesses have experienced very positive interactions with aboriginal groups, resulting in benefits for both parties. Other businesses—sometimes operating in the same regions—have had negative interactions. One manager recognizes the unique viewpoint that is required to navigate such situations: *"Organizations need to understand the aboriginal perspective on sustainable development—which extends the traditional view of sustainability in resource development beyond the environmental, social and economic pillars to include cultural and spiritual dimensions."*

By building a more robust understanding of the aboriginal perspective on sustainability, the relationship between the business and the aboriginal community can be built on mutual respect and trust, which is more likely to lead to positive engagement. Furthermore, this understanding may inform the business community of new approaches to sustainability and stakeholder engagement, both within the aboriginal communities and outside of them.

9. There is no common set of rules for sourcing sustainably.

Businesses want to purchase products and services that are environmentally and socially responsible. But the process of identifying sustainable suppliers is not always straightforward, and the means for comparing products is not always obvious. Sustainable sourcing decisions may also require industry-specific knowledge and practices, or data that just may not be available.

Identifying a set of best practices for sustainable sourcing would provide organizations with targets for benchmarking as well as guidance on managing their supply chains. It would also yield an opportunity for leading businesses to showcase their good practices. One manager says: *"Sustainable sourcing is key for us. How can we get people to understand what it means for our business? Are there lessons from what we've done that can help other industries?"* Sustainable sourcing is not just about sustainability—it is also about managing and mitigating risks. This issue is clearly one in which the business case and societal good are aligned, and yet many businesses remain perplexed about how to manage their supply chains sustainably.

10. Those companies that try leading the sustainability frontier often end up losing.

Leadership in any field—sustainability included—carries with it some clear rewards. For instance, leading organizations can attract new customers, and foster loyalty with employees and community stakeholders. But there are also risks associated with being on the cutting edge. For example, sustainability leaders may overinvest in technologies that never yield the expected rewards, be overtaken by a second-mover who builds on the leader's ideas to leapfrog into the lead, or lose the support of internal stakeholders with shifting corporate priorities.

One manager highlights this paradox: "*Being a leader means sticking your head above the parapet: it exposes you to criticism internally and externally, but the potential rewards are great. Executives introducing new sustainability targets have to do their homework.*" The ability of companies to benefit from the potential upside and deflect risks will be key to ensuring that there are always businesses willing to raise the bar.

The Business Model for the 21st Century

In most discussions about the business case for sustainability, the emphasis has been on the bottom line. The value of sustainability has been analyzed from every direction—revenues, profits, and share prices—and it is clear that, in some circumstances, sustainability can pay off. However, sustainability is more than just about firm-level benefits. Businesses, business schools, and society recognize that the current course of production and consumption cannot be sustained within our natural resource limits.

Businesses develop the products and services consumed by individuals around the world. The vast resources extracted by business for society's use have created waste streams that find their way into our land, air and water and compromise human health. New businesses are being built on an understanding of the problems that have emerged through the 20th century. Increasingly, old businesses are evolving to use fewer resources, intensify the resources they do use, and renew and reuse the products they sell. New relationships are forming between businesses as firms realize synergies from interdependence; one firm can profit from another's waste, or several firms can benefit through flexible supply chain relationships built on common interest.

The 21st century will reveal a new paradigm in which business is no longer separate from society. Realizing the new "business-as-society" paradigm will require the efforts and ingenuity of organizations across sectors and industries. It will challenge the current generation of business leaders to apply their hard-won knowledge to novel problems, and the next generation to cut their teeth on issues of unprecedented importance and complexity. Those businesses that identified the hurdles and challenges described in this report, along with those businesses that aim to overcome them, will help to shape this new business landscape. The concept of sustainability is undeniably compelling. Done right, both business and society benefit.

---

[1] Orlitzky, Marc, Frank L. Schmidt and Sara L. Rynes, (2003). Corporate Social and Financial Performance: A Meta-Analysis. *Organizational Studies,* 24(3): 403-441.

[2] Grant, Adam M. and Sabine Sonnentag. (2010) Doing good buffers against feeling bad: Prosocial impact compensates for negative task and self-evaluations. *Organizational Behavior and Human Decision Processes,* 111 p13-22.

Harrison, Jeffrey S., Douglas A. Bosse and Robert A. Phillips. (2010) Managing for stakeholders, stakeholder utility functions, and competitive advantage. *Strategic Management Journal,* 31:58-74.

Jacobs, Brian W., Vinod R. Singhal and Ravi Subramanian (2010) An empirical investigation of environmental performance and the market value of the firm. *Journal of Operations Management,* 28: 430-441.

[3] Lev, Baruch, Christine Petrovits and Suresh Radhakrishnan. (2010) Is doing good good for you? How corporate charitable contributions enhance revenue growth. *Strategic Management Journal,* 31: 182-200.

[4] Montgomery, David B., and Catherine A. Ramus (2007) Including Corporate Social Responsibility, Environmental Sustainability, and Ethics in Calibrating MBA Job Preferences. Stanford Graduate School of Business, Research Paper No. 1981.

Selected, Edited, and with Issue Framing Material by:
Kathleen J. Barnes, *East Stroudsburg University*
and
George E. Smith, *Albright College*

ISSUE

Are Cap-and-Trade Policies Effective?

YES: **Richard Conniff,** from "The Political History of Cap and Trade," *Smithsonian* Magazine (August 2009), www.smithsonianmag.com/science-nature/Presence-of-Mind-Blue-Sky-Thinking.html

NO: **Martin Feldstein,** from "Cap-and-Trade: All Cost, No Benefit," *The Washington Post* (2009), www .washingtonpost.com/wp-dyn/content/article/2009/05/31/AR2009053102077_pf.html

Learning Outcomes
After reading this issue, you should be able to: • Understand and be able to explain what a cap-and-trade program is and how it works. • Discuss the potential pros and cons of cap-and-trade programs. • Describe some of the potential challenges and barriers to instituting cap-and-trade programs. • Appreciate the potential implications or economic impact these programs have on or for organizational stakeholders.

ISSUE SUMMARY

YES: Richard Conniff presents a brief history of cap-and-trade as a pollution reduction strategy in the United States. In this discussion he describes the approach and anticipated goals and outcomes of such a program. Additionally, he observes that the passage and outcomes of the Clean Air Act of 1990 serve as evidence that cap-and-trade approaches to pollution reduction can be successful.

NO: Martin Feldstein, a Harvard University economist, responds to a proposed Federal government cap-and-trade proposal aimed at lowering carbon dioxide (CO_2) emissions and addressing global warming. In Feldstein's estimation, the policy as proposed would have little effect on global warming and prove costly to the nation's inhabitants. At issue is how the permits or credits would be distributed under the proposed legislation.

"**P**ollution is the presence of substances in the environment that inconvenience or endanger humans" (Steiner & Steiner, 2012). Government, society, and business have explored many different options for controlling pollution. These options have had varied and different outcomes and results. At present society, business, and government are having extensive discussions regarding the reduction of "green house gases" (GHGs). These gases are problematic in that they are believed to be contributors to global warming. A proposed solution to reduce the emission of GHGs is the implementation of cap-and-trade programs on those industries contributing to the GHG problem.

The idea to use a cap-and-trade program is not necessarily a recent phenomena. Cap-and-trade approaches were used during the 1980s to 1990s to reduce CO_2 emissions that contributed to acid rain. The adoption of this approach in the United States was made official with the Clean Air Act of 1990. Presently states such as California and Massachusetts have added additional state laws and regulations to control emissions. The European Union has also adopted cap-and-trade programs to control pollution.

Norman Wei explains the basic mechanics of cap-and-trade:

> Here's how cap-and-trade works: The regulatory agency places a maximum amount of emission that a facility can emit for a particular pollutant—say CO_2. That's the cap part. Once this cap is in place, the agency provides an emission allowance to industries that can be applied against the cap. The allowance may be as large as the cap during the first few years of the program. It then gradually decreases over time. This decrease in allowance has the effect of reducing the amount of CO_2 that can be emitted each year.

> The whole idea of cap-and-trade is to provide a disincentive to industry to continue to emit harmful pollutants such as greenhouse gas (primarily CO_2 from coal power plants).

Faced with this decreasing allowance—which is in effect a more restrictive limit on emission over time—the regulated industry has two options to comply with the cap. It can install pollution control equipment to reduce its emission to make up for the decreasing allowance to meet the cap. Or it can purchase credit in an open market to make up for any short fall. That's the trading part. Conversely, if a facility comes in below the cap as a result of installing pollution control devices, it may have "surplus allowance" that it can sell in the open market and make money. (www.pollutionengineering.com, 2009)

Those supportive of cap-and-trade policies view the approach as a means for using human nature to find solutions that reduce environmental problems. In this approach, the incentive to individuals and companies is to find ways to increase profitability and rewards by reducing the costs of negative environmental effects. As standards tighten and outputs are decreased, companies seek out approaches that will reduce their related costs. The overarching objective of these programs is to strive for voluntary compliance by enticing companies to consider the potential profit or economic impact associated with a change (or lack of change) in behavior.

Perhaps the most vocal concerns with this approach to environmental regulation are first, who ultimately carries the burden of the cap-and-trade approach to pollution reduction and second, how, or if the shares of a particular substance are disbursed initially and reduced over time. In the case of who bears the burden the argument is often that the corporation has the capacity to pass on the burdens associated with cap-and-trade approaches to the consumer. Thus, rather than changing corporate behavior, it becomes an added tax on the end user or consumer which is one of the points that Professor Feldstein makes in his article.

The second issue is twofold. First, how does the initial distribution of shares or credits occur? Professor Feldstein is skeptical about the proposed approach in the legislation he is reacting to in his article. In his opinion, the program as proposed does not get to the biggest abusers or generators of the problem the proposed strategy is attempting to address. Second, for this approach to work there has to be a goal of reducing output over time. In some cases, these approaches have been employed without the inclusion of this piece which has led critics to question how any reduction will or could be made without including a process that incrementally calls for a reduction of pollutants over time.

YES ↵

Richard Conniff

The Political History of Cap and Trade

John B. Henry was hiking in Maine's Acadia National Park one August in the 1980s when he first heard his friend C. Boyden Gray talk about cleaning up the environment by letting people buy and sell the right to pollute. Gray, a tall, lanky heir to a tobacco fortune, was then working as a lawyer in the Reagan White House, where environmental ideas were only slightly more popular than godless Communism. "I thought he was smoking dope," recalls Henry, a Washington, D.C. entrepreneur. But if the system Gray had in mind now looks like a politically acceptable way to slow climate change—an approach being hotly debated in Congress—you could say that it got its start on the global stage on that hike up Acadia's Cadillac Mountain.

People now call that system "cap-and-trade." But back then the term of art was "emissions trading," though some people called it "morally bankrupt" or even "a license to kill." For a strange alliance of free-market Republicans and renegade environmentalists, it represented a novel approach to cleaning up the world—by working with human nature instead of against it.

Despite powerful resistance, these allies got the system adopted as national law in 1990, to control the power-plant pollutants that cause acid rain. With the help of federal bureaucrats willing to violate the cardinal rule of bureaucracy—by surrendering regulatory power to the marketplace—emissions trading would become one of the most spectacular success stories in the history of the green movement. Congress is now considering whether to expand the system to cover the carbon dioxide emissions implicated in climate change—a move that would touch the lives of almost every American. So it's worth looking back at how such a radical idea first got translated into action, and what made it work.

The problem in the 1980s was that American power plants were sending up vast clouds of sulfur dioxide, which was falling back to earth in the form of acid rain, damaging lakes, forests and buildings across eastern Canada and the United States. The squabble about how to fix this problem had dragged on for years. Most environmentalists were pushing a "command-and-control" approach, with federal officials requiring utilities to install scrubbers capable of removing the sulfur dioxide from power-plant exhausts. The utility companies countered that the cost of such an approach would send them back to the Dark Ages. By the end of the Reagan administration, Congress had put forward and slapped down 70 different acid rain bills, and frustration ran so deep that Canada's prime minister bleakly joked about declaring war on the United States.

At about the same time, the Environmental Defense Fund (EDF) had begun to question its own approach to cleaning up pollution, summed up in its unofficial motto: "Sue the bastards." During the early years of command-and-control environmental regulation, EDF had also noticed something fundamental about human nature, which is that people hate being told what to do. So a few iconoclasts in the group had started to flirt with market-place solutions: give people a chance to turn a profit by being smarter than the next person, they reasoned, and they would achieve things that no command-and-control bureaucrat would ever suggest.

The theory had been brewing for decades, beginning with early 20th-century British economist Arthur Cecil Pigou. He argued that transactions can have effects that don't show up in the price of a product. A careless manufacturer spewing noxious chemicals into the air, for instance, did not have to pay when the paint peeled off houses downwind—and neither did the consumer of the resulting product. Pigou proposed making the manufacturer and customer foot the bill for these unacknowledged costs—"internalizing the externalities," in the cryptic language of the dismal science. But nobody much liked Pigou's means of doing it, by having regulators impose taxes and fees. In 1968, while studying pollution control in the Great Lakes, University of Toronto economist John Dales hit on a way for the costs to be paid with minimal government intervention, by using tradable permits or allowances.

The basic premise of cap-and-trade is that government doesn't tell polluters how to clean up their act. Instead, it simply imposes a cap on emissions. Each company starts the year with a certain number of tons allowed—a so-called right to pollute. The company decides how to use its allowance; it might restrict output, or switch to a cleaner fuel, or buy a scrubber to cut emissions. If it doesn't use up its allowance, it might then sell what it no longer needs. Then again, it might have to buy extra allowances on the open market. Each year, the cap ratchets down, and the shrinking pool of allowances gets costlier. As in a game of musical chairs, polluters must scramble to match allowances to emissions.

Getting all this to work in the real world required a leap of faith. The opportunity came with the 1988 election of George H.W. Bush. EDF president Fred Krupp phoned Bush's new White House counsel—Boyden Gray—and suggested that the best way for Bush to make good on his pledge to become the "environmental president" was to fix the acid rain problem, and the best way to do that was by using the new tool of emissions trading. Gray liked the marketplace approach, and even before the Reagan administration expired, he put EDF staffers to work drafting legislation to make it happen. The immediate aim was to break the impasse over acid rain. But global warming had also registered as front-page news for the first time that sweltering summer of 1988; according to Krupp, EDF and the Bush White House both felt from the start that emissions trading would ultimately be the best way to address this much larger challenge.

It would be an odd alliance. Gray was a conservative multimillionaire who drove a battered Chevy modified to burn methanol. Dan Dudek, the lead strategist for EDF, was a former academic Krupp once described as either "just plain loony, or the most powerful visionary ever to apply for a job at an environmental group." But the two hit it off—a good thing, given that almost everyone else was against them.

Many Environmental Protection Agency (EPA) staffers mistrusted the new methods; they had had little success with some small-scale experiments in emissions trading, and they worried that proponents were less interested in cleaning up pollution than in doing it cheaply. Congressional subcommittee members looked skeptical when witnesses at hearings tried to explain how there could be a market for something as worthless as emissions. Nervous utility executives worried that buying allowances meant putting their confidence in a piece of paper printed by the government. At the same time, they figured that allowances might trade at $500 to $1,000 a ton, with the program costing them somewhere between $5 billion and $25 billion a year.

Environmentalists, too, were skeptical. Some saw emissions trading as a scheme for polluters to buy their way out of fixing the problem. Joe Goffman, then an EDF lawyer, recalls other environmental advocates seething when EDF argued that emissions trading was just a better solution. Other members of a group called the Clean Air Coalition tried to censure EDF for what Krupp calls "the twofold sin of having talked to the Republican White House and having advanced this heretical idea."

Misunderstandings over how emissions trading could work extended to the White House itself. When the Bush administration first proposed its wording for the legislation, the EDF and EPA staffers who had been working on the bill were shocked to see that the White House had not included a cap. Instead of limiting the amount of emissions, the bill limited only the *rate* of emissions, and only in the dirtiest power plants. It was "a real stomach-falling-to-the-floor moment," says Nancy Kete, who was

then managing the acid rain program for the EPA. She says she realized that "we had been talking past each other for months."

EDF argued that a hard cap on emissions was the only way trading could work in the real world. It wasn't just about doing what was right for the environment; it was basic marketplace economics. Only if the cap got smaller and smaller would it turn allowances into a precious commodity, and not just paper printed by the government. No cap meant no deal, said EDF.

John Sununu, the White House chief of staff, was furious. He said the cap "was going to shut the economy down," Boyden Gray recalls. But the in-house debate "went very, very fast. We didn't have time to fool around with it." President Bush not only accepted the cap, he overruled his advisers' recommendation of an eight million-ton cut in annual acid rain emissions in favor of the ten million-ton cut advocated by environmentalists. According to William Reilly, then EPA administrator, Bush wanted to soothe Canada's bruised feelings. But others say the White House was full of sports fans, and in basketball you aren't a player unless you score in double digits. Ten million tons just sounded better.

Near the end of the intramural debate over the policy, one critical change took place. The EPA's previous experiments with emissions trading had faltered because they relied on a complicated system of permits and credits requiring frequent regulatory intervention. Sometime in the spring of 1989, a career EPA policy maker named Brian McLean proposed letting the market operate on its own. Get rid of all that bureaucratic apparatus, he suggested. Just measure emissions rigorously, with a device mounted on the back end of every power plant, and then make sure emissions numbers match up with allowances at the end of the year. It would be simple and provide unprecedented accountability. But it would also "radically disempower the regulators," says EDF's Joe Goffman, "and for McLean to come up with that idea and become a champion for it was heroic." Emissions trading became law as part of the Clean Air Act of 1990.

Oddly, the business community was the last holdout against the marketplace approach. Boyden Gray's hiking partner John Henry became a broker of emissions allowances and spent 18 months struggling to get utility executives to make the first purchase. Initially it was like a church dance, another broker observed at the time, "with the boys on one side and the girls on another. Sooner or later, somebody's going to walk into the middle." But the utility types kept fretting about the risk. Finally, Henry phoned Gray at the White House and wondered aloud if it might be possible to order the Tennessee Valley Authority (TVA), a federally owned electricity provider, to start buying allowances to compensate for emissions from its coal-fired power plants. In May 1992, the TVA did the first deal at $250 a ton, and the market took off.

Whether cap-and-trade would curb acid rain remained in doubt until 1995, when the cap took effect.

Nationwide, acid rain emissions fell by three million tons that year, well ahead of the schedule required by law. Cap-and-trade—a term that first appeared in print that year—quickly went "from being a pariah among policy makers," as an MIT analysis put it, "to being a star—everybody's favorite way to deal with pollution problems."

Almost 20 years since the signing of the Clean Air Act of 1990, the cap-and-trade system continues to let polluters figure out the least expensive way to reduce their acid rain emissions. As a result, the law costs utilities just $3 billion annually, not $25 billion, according to a recent study in the *Journal of Environmental Management*; by cutting acid rain in half, it also generates an estimated $122 billion a year in benefits from avoided death and illness, healthier lakes and forests, and improved visibility on the Eastern Seaboard. (Better relations with Canada? Priceless.)

No one knows whether the United States can apply the system as successfully to the much larger problem of global warming emissions, or at what cost to the economy. Following the American example with acid rain, Europe now relies on cap-and-trade to help about 10,000 large industrial plants find the most economical way of reducing their global warming emissions. If Congress approves such a system in this country—the House had approved the legislation as we went to press—it could set emissions limits on every fossil-fuel power plant and every manufacturer in the nation. Consumers might also pay more to heat and cool their homes and drive their cars—all with the goal of reducing global warming emissions by 17 percent below 2005 levels over the next ten years.

But advocates argue that cap-and-trade still beats command-and-control regulation. "There's not a person in a business anywhere," says Dan Esty, an environmental policy professor at Yale University, "who gets up in the morning and says, 'Gee, I want to race into the office to follow some regulation.' On the other hand, if you say, 'There's an upside potential here, you're going to make money,' people do get up early and do drive hard around the possibility of finding themselves winners on this."

Richard Conniff is a 2009 Loeb Award winner for business journalism.

Martin Feldstein   → **NO**

Cap-and-Trade: All Cost, No Benefit

The Obama administration and congressional Democrats have proposed a major cap-and-trade system aimed at reducing carbon dioxide emissions. Scientists agree that CO_2 emissions around the world could lead to rising temperatures with serious long-term environmental consequences. But that is not a reason to enact a U.S. cap-and-trade system until there is a global agreement on CO_2 reduction. The proposed legislation would have a trivially small effect on global warming while imposing substantial costs on all American households. And to get political support in key states, the legislation would abandon the auctioning of permits in favor of giving permits to selected corporations.

The leading legislative proposal, the Waxman–Markey bill that was recently passed out of the House Energy and Commerce Committee, would reduce allowable CO_2 emissions to 83 percent of the 2005 level by 2020, then gradually decrease the amount further. Under the cap-and-trade system, the federal government would limit the total volume of CO_2 that U.S. companies can emit each year and would issue permits that companies would be required to have for each ton of CO_2 emitted. Once issued, these permits would be tradable and could be bought and sold, establishing a market price reflecting the targeted CO_2 reduction, with a tougher CO_2 standard and fewer available permits leading to higher prices.

Companies would buy permits from each other as long as it is cheaper to do that than to make the technological changes needed to eliminate an equivalent amount of CO_2 emissions. Companies would also pass along the cost of the permits in their prices, pushing up the relative price of CO_2-intensive goods and services such as gasoline, electricity and a range of industrial products. Consumers would respond by cutting back on consumption of CO_2-intensive products in favor of other goods and services. This pass-through of the permit cost in higher consumer prices is the primary way the cap-and-trade system would reduce the production of CO_2 in the United States.

The Congressional Budget Office recently estimated that the resulting increases in consumer prices needed to achieve a 15 percent CO_2 reduction—slightly less than the Waxman–Markey target—would raise the cost of living of a typical household by $1,600 a year. Some expert studies estimate that the cost to households could be substantially higher. The future cost to the typical household would rise significantly as the government reduces the total allowable amount of CO_2.

Americans should ask themselves whether this annual tax of $1,600-plus per family is justified by the very small resulting decline in global CO_2. Since the U.S. share of global CO_2 production is now less than 25 percent (and is projected to decline as China and other developing nations grow), a 15 percent fall in U.S. CO_2 output would lower global CO_2 output by less than 4 percent. Its impact on global warming would be virtually unnoticeable. The U.S. should wait until there is a global agreement on CO_2 that includes China and India before committing to costly reductions in the United States.

The CBO estimates that the sale of the permits for a 15 percent CO_2 reduction would raise revenue of about $80 billion a year over the next decade. It is remarkable, then, that the Waxman–Markey bill would give away some 85 percent of the permits over the next 20 years to various businesses instead of selling them at auction. The price of the permits and the burden to households would be the same whether the permits are sold or given away. But by giving them away the government would not collect the revenue that could, at least in principle, be used to offset some of the higher cost to households.

The Waxman–Markey bill would give away 30 percent of the permits to local electricity distribution companies with the expectation that their regulators would require those firms to pass the benefit on to their customers. If they do this by not raising prices, there would be less CO_2 reduction through lower electricity consumption. The permit price would then have to be higher to achieve more CO_2 reduction on all other products. Some electricity consumers would benefit, but the cost to all other American families would be higher.

In my judgment, the proposed cap-and-trade system would be a costly policy that would penalize Americans with little effect on global warming. The proposal to give away most of the permits only makes a bad idea worse. Taxpayers and legislators should keep these things in mind before enacting any cap-and-trade system.

MARTIN FELDSTEIN is a professor of economics at Harvard University and president emeritus of the nonprofit National Bureau of Economic Research.

EXPLORING THE ISSUE

Are Cap-and-Trade Policies Effective?

Critical Thinking and Reflection

1. How could a cap-and-trade policy be implemented in the United States?
2. What might be the costs of a cap-and-trade policy to the nation, consumers, and corporations?
3. Is there a guarantee that enacted policies will lead to anticipated outcomes?
4. What does the future hold for cap-and-trade?
5. What alternatives are there to the cap-and-trade approach?

Is There Common Ground?

The common ground that exists on this issue appears to be that there is some agreement that corporate behavior needs to change. Specifically that the view of the environment and the use of natural resources need to be considered from the perspective that we are not simply consumers of that environment, but stewards. The challenge here is finding an approach that all relevant stakeholders can agree upon and see merit in. This issue will undoubtedly be a topic of debate and discussion in the near future as not only the United States, but the global community hammer out measures that will result in practices that represent efforts to practice good stewardship over global natural resources.

Additional Resources

Buntin, J. (2010). "Cap & Fade," *Governing*, December, pp. 26–31.

Duesterberg, T.J. (2009). "Cap-and-Trade Would Be a Major Mistake," *Industry Week*, July, p. 12.

Fugazy, D. (2009). "Considering a Cap-and-Trade System," *Mergers & Acquisitions*, May, pp. 24–25.

Gray, C.B. (2010). "The Problem with Cap and Trade," *The American Spectator*, June, pp. 56–58.

Matisoff, D.C. (2010). "Making Cap-and-Trade Work: Lessons from the European Union Experience," *Environment*, January/February, pp. 10–19.

Schakenbach, J., Vollaro, R., and Forte, R. (2006). "Fundamentals of Successful Monitoring, Reporting, and Verification under a Cap-and-Trade Program," *Journal of the Air & Waste Management Association*, November, pp. 1576–1583.

Stavins, R.N. (2008). "Cap-and Trade or a Carbon Tax?" *The Environmental Forum*, January/February, p. 16.

Steiner, J.F. and Steiner, J.A. (2012). *Business, Government, and Society*, 13th ed., New York: McGraw-Hill Irwin, p. 438.

Wade, J. (2009). "Cap & Trade," *Risk Management*, October, pp. 18–19.

Internet References . . .

What Is Cap and Trade?

(2009). "What Is Cap-and-Trade?" August, p. 11.

www.pollutionengineering.com

UNIT 5

UNIT

International Management Issues

*A*s the worldwide recession intensifies, governments of many countries are enacting protectionist economic policies as a means of helping their domestic economies. According to many economists, however, both theory and practice strongly indicate that protectionist actions do more harm than good. Nevertheless, President Obama and the Democratic-controlled legislative branch appear to be receptive to protectionist suggestions, leading many intellectuals and social commentators to wonder if such policies might actually be beneficial to U.S. business interests. Thus, in the final Taking Sides text section, newsworthy and important issues facing many managers and executives today are discussed.

Selected, Edited, and with Issue Framing Material by:
Kathleen J. Barnes, *East Stroudsburg University*
and
George E. Smith, *Albright College*

ISSUE

Do Unskilled Immigrants Hurt the American Economy?

YES: Steven Malanga, from "How Unskilled Immigrants Hurt Our Economy," *City Journal* (Summer 2006)

NO: Diana Furchtgott-Roth, from "The Case for Immigration," *The New York Sun* (September 22, 2006)

Learning Outcomes
After reading this issue you should be able to:
• Understand the positive and negative consequences of unskilled immigrants on the American economy.   • Explain how unskilled immigrants can be used as an effective workplace tool.   • Understand the policies that might be implemented concerning unskilled immigration.   • Appreciate the practical implications of unskilled immigrants use in the workplace.

ISSUE SUMMARY

YES: Steven Malanga believes the influx of unskilled immigrants results in job loss by native workers and lower investment in labor-saving technology. He also contends that illegal immigration taxes our already-strained welfare and social security systems.

NO: Diana Furchtgott-Roth, senior fellow at the Hudson Institute and a former chief economist at the U.S. Department of Labor, points out that annual immigration represents a small portion of the U.S. labor force, and, in any event, immigrant laborers complement, rather than replace, legal American citizens in the workplace.

In April 2010 Arizona Governor Jan Brewer signed the "Support Our Law Enforcement and Safe Neighborhoods Act" (SB1070). While many decried the signing of this act by Governor Brewer and raised issues regarding the potentially discriminatory actions of the law, the underlying intent of the act was to impose additional controls on immigration in the state of Arizona beyond those performed by the federal government. Despite the fact that parts of the Arizona act have been struck down in court, 36 additional states have followed Arizona's lead in proposing similar laws. In 31 instances the states rejected or refused to advance the bills. In five states—Utah, Indiana, South Carolina, Georgia, and Alabama—those bills have been voted into law and in many cases have been observed to mirror or even surpass the Arizona law. Some observers believe that this current trend—the passing of immigration law—will continue in the future. This issue focuses on examining the question of whether or not unskilled immigrants threaten the U.S. labor force and ultimately harm the American economy.

According to the Cato Institute, over the past 200 years, the United States has welcomed more than 60 million immigrants to its shores (www.freetrade.org/issues/immigration.html). Although the vast majority of those immigrants entered the country legally, in recent decades, the number of people entering the country illegally has grown tremendously. Estimates currently put the number of illegal immigrants in the United States somewhere between 10 and 15 million. Regardless of the actual figure, there is no question that the continued growth of illegal aliens has important ramifications both politically and socially; indeed, one need only observe the behaviors of the two political parties to verify the truth of this statement.

Of particular importance to this text is the impact of the growth of illegal aliens on the American workplace. Those that believe the overall effect of these unskilled workers is generally beneficial to the U.S. economy provide numerous points in support of their position. They point, for example, to research showing that immigrants and natives frequently do not compete for the same jobs. Interestingly, in areas where demand for labor is high

relative to supply, hiring immigrants results in a comple-
mentary outcome rather than a competitive situation.
Thus, supporters contend, the view that illegal aliens and
other immigrants take jobs from native workers is simple-
minded. An often-overlooked fact is that many immigrants arrive in the United States with strong skill sets
and a burning desire to make something of themselves.
Indeed, many employers have found that there is a large
degree of overlap between the characteristics of an individual willing to accept the risks and dangers of relocat-
ing to a foreign land to make a better life for him(her)self
and the characteristics of a loyal, dependable, and driven
employee. Finally, supporters note that illegal aliens contribute mightily to our economy in ways beyond their
physical labor: As a group, they contribute billions of dollars to social security through payroll taxes. For example,
The Washington Post estimated that during the period from
1990 to 1998, illegal aliens paid more than $20 billion in
payroll taxes (Washingtonpost.com). However, owing to
fears of being caught and deported, few actually collect
payments, thus providing the social security program with
a huge net gain.

On the other side of the debate are those who are
against corporations being allowed to hire illegal aliens
because of the detrimental effects doing so may have on
the American labor force. Central to their position is the
argument that illegal immigration disproportionately
affects poor American natives because the immigrants are
willing to work the unskilled jobs typically held by poor

Americans and do so for much less pay. They further argue
that from this perspective, firms that hire illegal aliens
are anti-American because they are effectively displacing
legitimate American citizens from these jobs. Another
charge frequently leveled at supporters is the negative
impact on the economy due to illegal immigration, particularly in the area of taxes. On the one hand critics point
out, states lose billions of dollars each year in the form of
unpaid taxes. On the other, states are faced with growing
demands for governmental services driven by the increase
in their populations, some of which is the result of illegal
immigration. The net result? States have to raise taxes to
meet these needs; thus, the law-abiding American citizen
foots the bill for the illegal immigrants. It's hard to see
how this outcome can be viewed as anything but harmful
to the U.S. economy.

Thus, the question posed here is whether the U.S.
economy suffers when American businesses hire unskilled
illegal aliens. Answering in the affirmative is columnist Steven Malanga. He believes the influx of unskilled
immigrants results in job loss by native workers and lower
investment in labor-saving technology. Arguing the other
side of the debate is Diana Furchtgott-Roth, a senior fellow
at the Hudson Institute and a former chief economist at
the U.S. Department of Labor. She points out that annual
immigration represents a small portion of the U.S. labor
force and immigrant laborers complement, rather than
replace, legal American citizens in the workplace.

YES ↵

Steven Malanga

How Unskilled Immigrants Hurt Our Economy

The day after Librado Velasquez arrived on Staten Island after a long, surreptitious journey from his Chiapas, Mexico, home, he headed out to a street corner to wait with other illegal immigrants looking for work. Velasquez, who had supported his wife, seven kids, and his in-laws as a *campesino,* or peasant farmer, until a 1998 hurricane devastated his farm, eventually got work, off the books, loading trucks at a small New Jersey factory, which hired illegals for jobs that required few special skills. The arrangement suited both, until a work injury sent Velasquez to the local emergency room, where federal law required that he be treated, though he could not afford to pay for his care. After five operations, he is now permanently disabled and has remained in the United States to pursue compensation claims. . . .

Velasquez's story illustrates some of the fault lines in the nation's current, highly charged, debate on immigration. Since the mid-1960s, America has welcomed nearly 30 million legal immigrants and received perhaps another 15 million illegals, numbers unprecedented in our history. These immigrants have picked our fruit, cleaned our homes, cut our grass, worked in our factories, and washed our cars. But they have also crowded into our hospital emergency rooms, schools, and government-subsidized aid programs, sparking a fierce debate about their contributions to our society and the costs they impose on it.

Advocates of open immigration argue that welcoming the Librado Velasquezes of the world is essential for our American economy: our businesses need workers like him, because we have a shortage of people willing to do low-wage work. Moreover, the free movement of labor in a global economy pays off for the United States, because immigrants bring skills and capital that expand our economy and offset immigration's costs. Like tax cuts, supporters argue, immigration pays for itself.

But the tale of Librado Velasquez helps show why supporters are wrong about today's immigration, as many Americans sense and so much research has demonstrated. America does not have a vast labor shortage that requires waves of low-wage immigrants to alleviate; in fact, unemployment among unskilled workers is high—about 30 percent. Moreover, many of the unskilled, uneducated workers now journeying here labor, like Velasquez, in shrinking industries, where they force out native workers, and many others work in industries where the availability of cheap workers has led businesses to suspend investment in new technologies that would make them less labor-intensive.

Yet while these workers add little to our economy, they come at great cost, because they are not economic abstractions but human beings, with their own culture and ideas—often at odds with our own. Increasing numbers of them arrive with little education and none of the skills necessary to succeed in a modern economy. Many may wind up stuck on our lowest economic rungs, where they will rely on something that immigrants of other generations didn't have: a vast U.S. welfare and social-services apparatus that has enormously amplified the cost of immigration. Just as welfare reform and other policies are helping to shrink America's underclass by weaning people off such social programs, we are importing a new, foreign-born underclass. As famed free-market economist Milton Friedman puts it: "It's just obvious that you can't have free immigration and a welfare state."

Immigration can only pay off again for America if we reshape our policy, organizing it around what's good for the economy by welcoming workers we truly need and excluding those who, because they have so little to offer, are likely to cost us more than they contribute, and who will struggle for years to find their place here.

Hampering today's immigration debate are our misconceptions about the so-called first great migration some 100 years ago, with which today's immigration is often compared. . . . If America could assimilate 24 million mostly desperate immigrants from that great migration—people one unsympathetic economist at the turn of the twentieth century described as "the unlucky, the thriftless, the worthless"—surely, so the story goes, today's much bigger and richer country can absorb the millions of Librado Velasquezes now venturing here.

But that argument distorts the realities of the first great migration. . . . Those waves of immigrants—many of them urban dwellers who crossed a continent and an ocean to get here—helped supercharge the workforce at a time when the country was going through a transformative economic expansion that craved new workers, especially in its cities. A 1998 National Research Council report noted "that the newly arriving immigrant nonagricultural work force . . . was (slightly) more skilled than the resident American labor force": 27 percent of them were skilled laborers, compared with only 17 percent of that era's native-born workforce.

Many of these immigrants quickly found a place in our economy, participating in the workforce at a higher rate even than the native population. Their success at finding work sent many of them quickly up the economic ladder: those who stayed in America for at least 15 years, for instance, were just as likely to own their own business as native-born workers of the same age, one study found. . . .

What the newcomers of the great migration did not find here was a vast social-services and welfare state. They had to rely on their own resources or those of friends, relatives, or private, often ethnic, charities if things did not go well. That's why about 70 percent of those who came were men in their prime. It's also why many of them left when the economy sputtered several times during the period. . . .

Today's immigration has turned out so differently in part because it emerged out of the 1960s civil rights and Great Society mentality. In 1965, a new immigration act eliminated the old system of national quotas, which critics saw as racist because it greatly favored European nations. Lawmakers created a set of broader immigration quotas for each hemisphere, and they added a new visa preference category for family members to join their relatives here. Senate immigration subcommittee chairman Edward Kennedy reassured the country that, "contrary to the charges in some quarters, [the bill] will not inundate America with immigrants," and "it will not cause American workers to lose their jobs."

But, in fact, the law had an immediate, dramatic effect, increasing immigration by 60 percent in its first ten years. Sojourners from poorer countries around the rest of the world arrived in ever-greater numbers, so that whereas half of immigrants in the 1950s had originated from Europe, 75 percent by the 1970s were from Asia and Latin America. And as the influx of immigrants grew, the special-preferences rule for family unification intensified it further, as the pool of eligible family members around the world also increased. Legal immigration to the U.S. soared from 2.5 million in the 1950s to 4.5 million in the 1970s to 7.3 million in the 1980s to about 10 million in the 1990s.

As the floodgates of legal immigration opened, the widening economic gap between the United States and many of its neighbors also pushed illegal immigration to levels that America had never seen. In particular, when Mexico's move to a more centralized, state-run economy in the 1970s produced hyperinflation, the disparity between its stagnant economy and U.S. prosperity yawned wide. Mexico's per-capita gross domestic product, 37 percent of the United States' in the early 1980s, was only 27 percent of it by the end of the decade—and is now just 25 percent of it. With Mexican farmworkers able to earn seven to ten times as much in the United States as at home, by the 1980s illegals were pouring across our border at the rate of about 225,000 a year, and U.S. sentiment rose for slowing the flow.

But an unusual coalition of business groups, unions, civil rights activists, and church leaders thwarted the call for restrictions with passage of the inaptly named 1986 Immigration Reform and Control Act, which legalized some 2.7 million unauthorized aliens already here, supposedly in exchange for tougher penalties and controls against employers who hired illegals. The law proved no deterrent, however, because supporters, in subsequent legislation and court cases argued on civil rights grounds, weakened the employer sanctions. Meanwhile, more illegals flooded here in the hope of future amnesties from Congress, while the newly legalized sneaked their wives and children into the country rather than have them wait for family-preference visas. The flow of illegals into the country rose to between 300,000 and 500,000 per year in the 1990s, so that a decade after the legislation that had supposedly solved the undocumented alien problem by reclassifying them as legal, the number of illegals living in the United States was back up to about 5 million, while today it's estimated at between 9 million and 13 million.

The flood of immigrants, both legal and illegal, from countries with poor, ill-educated populations, has yielded a mismatch between today's immigrants and the American economy and has left many workers poorly positioned to succeed for the long term. . . . Nearly two-thirds of Mexican immigrants, for instance, are high school dropouts, and most wind up doing either unskilled factory work or small-scale construction projects, or they work in service industries, where they compete for entry-level jobs against one another, against the adult children of other immigrants, and against native-born high school dropouts. Of the 15 industries employing the greatest percentage of foreign-born workers, half are low-wage service industries, including gardening, domestic household work, car washes, shoe repair, and janitorial work. . . .

Although open-borders advocates say that these workers are simply taking jobs Americans don't want, studies show that the immigrants drive down wages of native-born workers and squeeze them out of certain industries. Harvard economists George Borjas and Lawrence Katz, for instance, estimate that low-wage immigration cuts the wages for the average native-born high school dropout by some 8 percent, or more than $1,200 a year. . . .

Consequently, as the waves of immigration continue, the sheer number of those competing for low-skilled service jobs makes economic progress difficult. A study of the impact of immigration on New York City's restaurant business, for instance, found that 60 percent of immigrant workers do not receive regular raises, while 70 percent had never been promoted. . . .

Similarly, immigration is also pushing some native-born workers out of jobs, as Kenyon College economists showed in the California nail-salon workforce. Over a 16-year period starting in the late 1980s, some 35,600 mostly Vietnamese immigrant women flooded into the industry, a mass migration that equaled the total number of jobs in the industry before the immigrants arrived. Though the new workers created a labor surplus that led to lower prices, new services, and somewhat more demand, the economists estimate that as a result, 10,000 native-born workers either left the industry or never bothered entering it.

In many American industries, waves of low-wage workers have also retarded investments that might lead to modernization and efficiency. Farming, which employs a million immigrant laborers in California alone, is the prime case in point. Faced with a labor shortage in the early 1960s, when President Kennedy ended a 22-year-old guest-worker program that allowed 45,000 Mexican farmhands to cross over the border and harvest 2.2 million tons of California tomatoes for processed foods, farmers complained but swiftly automated, adopting a mechanical tomato-picking technology created more than a decade earlier. Today, just 5,000 better-paid workers—one-ninth the original workforce—harvest 12 million tons of tomatoes using the machines.

The savings prompted by low-wage migrants may even be minimal in crops not easily mechanized. Agricultural economists Wallace Huffman and Alan McCunn of Iowa State University have estimated that without illegal workers, the retail cost of fresh produce would increase only about 3 percent in the summer-fall season and less than 2 percent in the winter-spring season, because labor represents only a tiny percent of the retail price of produce and because without migrant workers, America would probably import more foreign fruits and vegetables. . . .

As foreign competition and mechanization shrink manufacturing and farmworker jobs, low-skilled immigrants are likely to wind up farther on the margins of our economy, where many already operate. For example, although only about 12 percent of construction workers are foreign-born, 100,000 to 300,000 illegal immigrants have carved a place for themselves as temporary workers on the fringes of the industry. In urban areas like New York and Los Angeles, these mostly male illegal immigrants gather on street corners, in empty lots, or in Home Depot parking lots to sell their labor by the hour or the day, for $7 to $11 an hour. . . .

Because so much of our legal and illegal immigrant labor is concentrated in such fringe, low-wage employment, its overall impact on our economy is extremely small. A 1997 National Academy of Sciences study estimated that immigration's net benefit to the American economy raises the average income of the native-born by only some $10 billion a year—about $120 per household. And that meager contribution is not the result of immigrants helping to build our essential industries or making us more competitive globally but instead merely delivering our pizzas and cutting our grass. Estimates by pro-immigration forces that foreign workers contribute much more to the economy, boosting annual gross domestic product by hundreds of billions of dollars, generally just tally what immigrants earn here, while ignoring the offsetting effect they have on the wages of native-born workers.

If the benefits of the current generation of migrants are small, the costs are large and growing because of America's vast range of social programs and the wide advocacy network that strives to hook low-earning legal and illegal immigrants into these programs. A 1998 National Academy of Sciences study found that more than 30 percent of California's foreign-born were on Medicaid—including 37 percent of all Hispanic households—compared with 14 percent of native-born households. The foreign-born were more than twice as likely as the native-born to be on welfare, and their children were nearly five times as likely to be in means-tested government lunch programs. Native-born households pay for much of this, the study found, because they earn more and pay higher taxes—and are more likely to comply with tax laws. Recent immigrants, by contrast, have much lower levels of income and tax compliance (another study estimated that only 56 percent of illegals in California have taxes deducted from their earnings, for instance). The study's conclusion: immigrant families cost each native-born household in California an additional $1,200 a year in taxes.

Immigration's bottom line has shifted so sharply that in a high-immigration state like California, native-born residents are paying up to ten times more in state and local taxes than immigrants generate in economic benefits. Moreover, the cost is only likely to grow as the foreign-born population—which has already mushroomed from about 9 percent of the U.S. population when the NAS studies were done in the late 1990s to about 12 percent today—keeps growing. . . . This sharp turnaround since the 1970s, when immigrants were less likely to be using the social programs of the Great Society than the native-born population, says Harvard economist Borjas, suggests that welfare and other social programs are a magnet drawing certain types of immigrants—nonworking women, children, and the elderly—and keeping them here when they run into difficulty.

Not only have the formal and informal networks helping immigrants tap into our social spending grown, but they also get plenty of assistance from advocacy groups financed by tax dollars, working to ensure that immigrants get their share of social spending. Thus, the Newark-based New Jersey Immigration Policy Network receives several hundred thousand government dollars annually to help doctors and hospitals increase immigrant enrollment in Jersey's subsidized health-care programs. Casa Maryland, operating in the greater Washington area, gets funding from nearly 20 federal, state, and local government agencies to run programs that "empower" immigrants to demand benefits and care from government and to "refer clients to government and private social service programs for which they and their families may be eligible." . . .

Almost certainly, immigrants' participation in our social welfare programs will increase over time, because so many are destined to struggle in our workforce. Despite our cherished view of immigrants as rapidly climbing the economic ladder, more and more of the new arrivals and their children face a lifetime of economic disadvantage, because they arrive here with low levels of education and with few work skills—shortcomings not easily overcome. Mexican immigrants, who are up to six times more likely to be high school dropouts than native-born Americans, not only earn substantially less than the native-born median, but the wage gap persists for decades after they've arrived. A study of the 2000 census data, for instance, shows that the cohort of Mexican immigrants between 25 and 34 who entered the United States in the late 1970s were earning 40 to 50 percent less than similarly aged native-born Americans in 1980, but 20 years later they had fallen even further behind their native-born counterparts. Today's Mexican immigrants between 25 and 34 have an even larger wage gap relative to the native-born population. Adjusting for other socioeconomic factors, Harvard's Borjas and Katz estimate that virtually this entire wage gap is attributable to low levels of education. . . .

One reason some ethnic groups make up so little ground concerns the transmission of what economists call "ethnic capital," or what we might call the influence of culture. More than previous generations, immigrants today tend to live concentrated in ethnic enclaves, and their children find their role models among their own group. Thus the children of today's Mexican immigrants are likely to live in a neighborhood where about 60 percent of men dropped out of high school and now do low-wage work, and where less than half of the population speak English fluently, which might explain why high school dropout rates among Americans of Mexican ancestry are two and a half times higher than dropout rates for all other native-born Americans, and why first-generation Mexican Americans do not move up the economic ladder nearly as quickly as the children of other immigrant groups.

In sharp contrast is the cultural capital transmitted by Asian immigrants to children growing up in predominantly Asian-American neighborhoods. More than 75 percent of Chinese immigrants and 98 percent of South Asian immigrants to the U.S. speak English fluently, while a mid-1990s study of immigrant households in California found that 37 percent of Asian immigrants were college graduates, compared with only 3.4 percent of Mexican immigrants. Thus, even an Asian-American child whose parents are high school dropouts is more likely to grow up in an environment that encourages him to stay in school and learn to speak English well, attributes that will serve him well in the job market. Not surprisingly, several studies have shown that Asian immigrants and their children earn substantially more than Mexican immigrants and their children.

Given these realities, several of the major immigration reforms now under consideration simply don't make economic sense—especially the guest-worker program favored by President Bush and the U.S. Senate. Careful economic research tells us that there is no significant shortfall of workers in essential American industries, desperately needing supplement from a massive guest-worker program. Those few industries now relying on cheap labor must focus more quickly on mechanization where possible. Meanwhile, the cost of paying legal workers already here a bit more to entice them to do such low-wage work as is needed will have a minimal impact on our economy.

The potential woes of a guest-worker program, moreover, far overshadow any economic benefit, given what we know about the long, troubled history of temporary-worker programs in developed countries. They have never stemmed illegal immigration, and the guest workers inevitably become permanent residents, competing with the native-born and forcing down wages. Our last guest-worker program with Mexico, begun during World War II to boost wartime manpower, grew larger in the postwar era, because employers who liked the cheap labor lobbied hard to keep it. By the mid-1950s, the number of guest workers reached seven times the annual limit during the war itself, while illegal immigration doubled, as the availability of cheap labor prompted employers to search for ever more of it rather than invest in mechanization or other productivity gains.

The economic and cultural consequences of guest-worker programs have been devastating in Europe, and we risk similar problems. When post–World War II Germany permitted its manufacturers to import workers from Turkey to man the assembly lines, industry's investment in productivity declined relative to such countries as Japan, which lacked ready access to cheap labor. When Germany finally ended the guest-worker program once it became economically unviable, most of the guest workers stayed on, having attained permanent-resident status. Since then, the descendants of these workers have been chronically underemployed and now have a crime rate double that of German youth. . . .

"Importing labor is far more complicated than importing other factors of production, such as commodities," write University of California at Davis professor Philip Martin, an expert on guest-worker programs, and Michael Teitelbaum, a former member of the U.S. Commission on Immigration Reform. "Migration involves human beings, with their own beliefs, politics, cultures, languages, loves, hates, histories, and families."

If low-wage immigration doesn't pay off for the United States, legalizing illegals already here makes as little sense as importing new rounds of guest workers. The Senate and President Bush, however, aim to start two-thirds of the 11 million undocumented aliens already in the country on a path to legalization, on the grounds that only thus can America assimilate them, and only through assimilation can they hope for economic success in the United States. But such arguments ignore the already poor economic performance of increasingly large segments of the *legal* immigrant population in the United States. Merely granting illegal aliens legal status won't suddenly catapult them up our mobility ladder, because it won't give them the skills and education to compete. . . .

If we do not legalize them, what can we do with 11 million illegals? Ship them back home? Their presence here is a fait accompli, the argument goes, and only legalization can bring them above ground, where they can assimilate. But that argument assumes that we have only two choices: to decriminalize or deport. But what happened after the first great migration suggests a third way: to end the economic incentives that keep them here. We could prompt a great remigration home if, first off, state and local governments in jurisdictions like New York and California would stop using their vast resources to aid illegal immigrants. Second, the federal government can take the tougher approach that it failed to take after the 1986 act. It can require employers to verify Social Security numbers and immigration status before hiring, so that we bar illegals from many jobs. It can deport those caught here. And it can refuse to give those who remain the same benefits as U.S. citizens. Such tough measures do work: as a recent Center for Immigration Studies report points out, when the federal government began deporting illegal Muslims after 9/11, many more illegals who knew they were likely to face more scrutiny voluntarily returned home.

If America is ever to make immigration work for our economy again, it must reject policies shaped by advocacy groups trying to turn immigration into the next civil rights cause or by a tiny minority of businesses seeking cheap labor subsidized by the taxpayers. Instead, we must look to other developed nations that have focused on luring workers who have skills that are in demand and who have the best chance of assimilating. Australia, for instance, gives preferences to workers grouped into four skilled categories: managers, professionals, associates of professionals, and skilled laborers. Using a straightforward "points calculator" to determine who gets in, Australia favors immigrants between the ages of 18 and 45 who speak English, have a post–high school degree or training in a trade, and have at least six months' work experience as everything from laboratory technicians to architects and surveyors to information-technology workers. Such an immigration policy goes far beyond America's employment-based immigration categories, like the H1-B visas, which account for about 10 percent of our legal immigration and essentially serve the needs of a few Silicon Valley industries.

Immigration reform must also tackle our family-preference visa program, which today accounts for two-thirds of all legal immigration and has helped create a 40-year waiting list. Lawmakers should narrow the family-preference visa program down to spouses and minor children of U.S. citizens and should exclude adult siblings and parents.

America benefits even today from many of its immigrants, from the Asian entrepreneurs who have helped revive inner-city Los Angeles business districts to Haitians and Jamaicans who have stabilized neighborhoods in Queens and Brooklyn to Indian programmers who have spurred so much innovation in places like Silicon Valley and Boston's Route 128. But increasingly over the last 25 years, such immigration has become the exception. It needs once again to become the rule.

STEVEN MALANGA is a contributing editor to City Journal and a senior fellow at the Manhattan Institute, which publishes *City Journal*. His primary area of focus is economic development within dense urban centers, with a particular emphasis on those areas in and surrounding New York and the Tri-State Area.

Diana Furchtgott-Roth   → **NO**

The Case for Immigration

It was raining in Washington last week, and vendors selling $5 and $10 umbrellas appeared on the streets. They had Hispanic accents, and were undoubtedly some of the unskilled immigrants that Steven Malanga referred to in his recent *City Journal* article, "How Unskilled Immigrants Hurt Our Economy."

I already had an umbrella. But the many purchasers of the umbrellas did not seem to notice that the economy was being hurt. Rather, they were glad of the opportunity to stay dry before their important meetings.

The *City Journal* article is worth a look because it reflects an attitude becoming more common these days in the debate. The article speaks approvingly of immigrants from Portugal, Asia, China, India, Haiti, and Jamaica. But it also makes it clear that we have too many Mexicans, a "flood of immigrants" who cause high unemployment rates among the unskilled. They work in shrinking industries, drive down wages of native-born Americans, cost millions in welfare, and retard America's technology.

These are serious charges indeed. Similar charges, that immigrants have caused native-born Americans to quit the labor market, have been made by Steven Camarota of the Center for Immigration Studies. But are they true?

Annual immigration is a tiny fraction of our labor force. The Pew Hispanic Center Report shows that annual immigration from all countries as a percent of the labor force has been declining since its recent peak in 1999.

Annual immigration in 1999 equaled 1% of the labor force—by 2005 it had declined to 0.8%. Hispanics, including undocumented workers, peaked in 2000 as a percent of the labor force at 0.5%, and by 2004 accounted for only 0.4% (0.3% for Mexicans) of the labor force.

Looking at unskilled workers, Hispanic immigration as a percent of the American unskilled labor force (defined as those without a high school diploma) peaked in 2000 at 6%, and was 5% in 2004 (4% for Mexicans). Five percent is not "floods of immigrants."

Mr. Malanga writes that America does not have a vast labor shortage because "unemployment among unskilled workers is high—about 30%." It isn't. In 2005, according to Bureau of Labor Statistics data, the unemployment rate for adults without a high school diploma was 7.6%. Last month it stood at 6.9%.

Data from a recent study by senior economist Pia Orrenius of the Dallas Federal Reserve Bank show that foreign-born Americans are more likely to work than native-born Americans. Leaving their countries by choice, they are naturally more risk-taking and entrepreneurial.

In 2005 the unemployment rate for native-born Americans was 5.2%, but for foreign-born it was more than half a percentage point lower, at 4.6%. For unskilled workers, although the total unemployment rate was 7.6%, the native-born rate was 9.1% and the foreign-born was much lower, at 5.7%.

According to Mr. Malanga, unskilled immigrants "work in shrinking industries where they force out native workers." However, data show otherwise. Low-skilled immigrants are disproportionately represented in the expanding service and construction sectors, with occupations such as janitors, gardeners, tailors, plasterers, and stucco masons. Manufacturing, the declining sector, employs few immigrants.

One myth repeated often is that immigrants depress wages of native-born Americans. As Professor Giovanni Peri of the University of California at Davis describes in a new National Bureau of Economic Analysis paper last month, immigrants are complements, rather than substitutes, for native-born workers. As such, they are not competing with native-born workers, but providing our economy with different skills.

Education levels of working immigrants form a U-shaped curve, with unusually high representation among adult low- and high-skilled. In contrast, the skills of native-born Americans form a bellshaped curve, with many B.A.s and high school diplomas but relatively few adult high school drop-outs or Ph.D.s

Low-skill immigrants come to be janitors and housekeepers, jobs native-born Americans typically don't want, but they aren't found as crossing guards and funeral service workers, low-skill jobs preferred by Americans. Similarly, high-skilled immigrants also take jobs Americans don't want. They are research scientists, dentists, and computer hardware and software engineers, but not lawyers, judges, or education administrators.

Because immigrants are complements to native-born workers, rather than substitutes, they help reduce economic bottlenecks, resulting in income gains. Mr. Peri's new study shows that immigrants raised the wages of the 90% of native-born Americans with at least a high school degree by 1% to 3% between 1990 and 2004. Those without a high school diploma lost about 1%, an amount that could be compensated from the gains of the others.

If immigrants affect any wages, it's those of prior immigrants, who compete for the same jobs. But we don't see immigrants protesting in the streets to keep others out, as we see homeowners in scenic locations demonstrating against additional development. Rather, some of the biggest proponents of greater immigration are the established immigrants themselves, who see America's boundless opportunities as outweighing negative wage effects.

Mr. Malanga cites a 1998 National Academy of Sciences study to say, "The foreign-born were more than twice as likely as the native-born to be on welfare." Yet this study contains estimates from 1995, more than a decade ago, and mentions programs such as Aid to Families with Dependent Children that no longer exist. Even so, the NAS study says that foreign-born households "are not more likely to use AFDC, SSI, or housing benefits."

The NAS study concludes that, since the foreign-born have more children, the "difference in education benefits accounts for nearly all of the relative deficit . . . at the local government level." Mr. Malanga, writing about how unskilled immigrants hurt the economy, would likely be in favor of these immigrants trying to educate their children, especially since these children will be contributing to his Social Security benefits.

Mr. Malanga suggests that the availability of low-wage immigrants retards investments in American technology. He cites agriculture as an example where machines to pick produce could be invented if labor were not available. Or, Mr. Malanga says, we could import produce from abroad at little additional cost.

Although consumers don't care where their food comes from, farmers certainly do. Farms provide income to farmers as well as to other native-born Americans employed in the industry as well as in trucking and distribution, just as immigrants in the construction industry have helped fuel the boom that sent employment of native-born construction workers to record levels. It makes little sense to send a whole economic sector to other countries just to avoid employing immigrants.

If unskilled immigrants don't hurt our economy, do they hurt our culture? City Journal editor Myron Magnet writes that Hispanics have "a group culture that devalues education and assimilation." Similar concerns about assimilation were made about Jews, Italians, Irish, Germans, Poles, and even Norwegians when they first came to America. All eventually assimilated.

Moreover, for those who are concerned with Spanish-speaking enclaves, a September 2006 paper by a professor at Princeton, Douglas Massey, shows that within two generations Mexican immigrants in California stop speaking Spanish at home, and within three generations they cease to know the language altogether. He concludes, "Like taxes and biological death, linguistic death seems to be a sure thing in the United States, even for Mexicans living in Los Angeles, a city with one of the largest Spanish-speaking urban populations in the world."

Legalizing the status of the illegal immigrants in America by providing a guest-worker program with a path to citizenship would produce additional gains to our economy. This is not the same as temporary worker programs in Germany, which did not have a path to citizenship, and so resulted in a disenfranchised class of workers.

With legal status, workers could move from the informal to the formal sector, and would pay more taxes. It would be easier to keep track of illegal financial transactions, reducing the potential for helping terrorists.

For over 200 years, American intellectual thought has included a small but influential literature advocating reduced immigration. The literature has spawned political parties such as the Know-Nothing Party in the mid-19th century and periodically led to the enactment of anti-immigrant laws. Immigrants, so the story goes, are bad for our economy and for our culture.

The greatness of America is not merely that we stand for freedom and economic prosperity for ourselves, but that we have consistently overcome arguments that would deny these same benefits to others.

DIANA FURCHTGOTT-ROTH is a senior fellow at the Manhattan Institute. She is also a contributing editor of RealClearMarkets.com, and a columnist for the *Washington Examiner,* MarketWatch.com, and *Tax Notes.*

EXPLORING THE ISSUE

Do Unskilled Immigrants Hurt the American Economy?

Critical Thinking and Reflection

1. What might be the goals of an unskilled immigrant policy?
2. How might an unskilled immigrant policy be implemented in the United States?
3. What might be the costs to consumers, corporations, and the nation of an unskilled immigrant policy?
4. What is the likelihood that an enacted unskilled immigrant policy will lead to anticipated outcomes?
5. What does the future hold for immigration policy?

Is There Common Ground?

One reason the issue of an unskilled immigrant policy is so contentious is that both sides can cite data in support of their position. While finding common ground on even basic aspects of this important management topic is difficult, there is consensus that an unskilled immigrant policy is a highly charged topic that will continue to be examined and debated for quite some time.

Additional Resources

Passel, J.S. (2005). "Estimates of the Size and Characteristics of the Undocumented Population," Pew Hispanic Center, March 21.

Tom Tancredo. (2005). "Illegal Aliens Taking American Jobs," House of Representatives, November 17.

Internet References . . .

Immigration Quotas vs. Individual Rights: The Moral and Practical Case for Open Immigration

Binswanger, H. (2006). "Immigration Quotas vs. Individual Rights: The Moral and Practical Case for Open Immigration," *Capitalism Magazine*, April 2.

http://capmag.com/article.asp?ID=4620

Immigration Law Should Reflect Our Dynamic Labor Market

Griswold, D. (2008). "Immigration Law Should Reflect Our Dynamic Labor Market," The Cato Institute, April 27.

www.cato.org/pub_display.php?pub_id=9360

Q & A Guide to State Immigration Laws

Immigration Policy Center. (2012). "Q & A Guide to State Immigration Laws," February 16.

www.immigrationpolicy.org/special-reports/qa-guide-state-immigration-laws

Amnesty for All Undocumented Immigrants and Full Labor Rights for All Workers!

Open World Conference of Workers, "Amnesty for All Undocumented Immigrants and Full Labor Rights for All Workers!" OWC Continuations Committee.

www.owcinfo.org/campaign/Amnesty.htm

American Brain Drain

Wall Street Journal Opinion. (2007). "American Brain Drain," *Wall Street Journal Review and Outlook*, November 30.

http://online.wsj.com/article/SB119638963734709017.html?mod=opinion_main_review_and_outlooks

Selected, Edited, and with Issue Framing Material by:
Kathleen J. Barnes, *East Stroudsburg University*
and
George E. Smith, *Albright College*

ISSUE

Is Economic Globalization Good for Humankind?

YES: Paul A. Gigot and Guy Sorman, from "Foreword" (2008), www.heritage.org/index/PDF/2008/Index2008_Foreword.pdf

NO: Branko Milanovic, from "Why Globalization Is in Trouble—Parts 1 and 2" (August 31, 2006), http://yaleglobal.yale.edu/display.article?id=8073

Learning Outcomes

After reading this issue you should be able to:

- Understand the positive and negative consequences of economic globalization.
- Understand both corporate and national motives driving economic globalization.
- Understand what policies might be implemented with regard to economic globalization.
- Appreciate the practical implications and limitations of economic globalization.

ISSUE SUMMARY

YES: Arguing that globalization is good for humankind are Paul A. Gigot and Guy Sorman. They outline seven ways in which globalization has positively impacted life and what needs to be done to further its advancement.

NO: Branko Milanovic, an economist with both the Carnegie Endowment for International Peace and the World Bank, is against globalization. Milanovic addresses several reasons for his views while emphasizing the incompatibility of globalization with the ages-old ethnic and religious traditions and values that characterize much of the world.

According to a leading international business textbook, globalization is "the inexorable integration of markets, nation-states, and technologies . . . in a way that is enabling individuals, corporations, and nation-states to reach around the world farther, faster, deeper, and cheaper than ever before" (Griffin and Pustay, 2010). Globalism is a phenomenon that has its roots in the rebuilding of Europe and Asia in the aftermath of World War II. As a measure of how powerful a phenomenon it has become, consider that the volume of international trade has increased over 3,000 percent since 1960! Most of this tremendous growth has occurred in the TRIAD, a free-trade market consisting of three regional trading blocs: Western Europe in its current form as the European Union, North America, and Asia (including Australia). Increasingly, however, the developing nations of the world are contributing to the expansion in world trade. Foreign investment has grown at a staggering rate as well: over three times faster than

the world output of goods. In the early part of the twenty-first century, it is not a stretch to say that virtually all businesses in industrialized nations are impacted to some degree by globalization.

It seems pretty clear that globalization will continue to grow as a dominant force in international relations among countries, particularly as more Second and Third World countries open their borders to international trade and investment. What may be less clear, however, is whether or not this is a positive development. In other words, is economic globalization good for humankind?

Globalization invokes strong arguments and strong emotions from supporters on each side. Those who believe globalization is a beneficial force for humans have a plethora of reasons for their view. From an economic perspective, the spread of free trade and free markets across the globe has liberated hundreds of millions from poverty over the past 40 years. Studies on economic freedom consistently show that countries that embrace globalization are more economically free and, as a direct result, enjoy higher per capita wealth than countries that are more isolated economically. Supporters also note that the growth in globalization has been accompanied by a growth in democracy as well. Along with these two benefits, globalization enhances the cultures of those countries that embrace it.

Guy Sorman, one of the authors of the YES selection in this debate, points out: "Through popular culture, people from different backgrounds and nations discover one another, and their 'otherness' suddenly disappears." Increases in cultural tolerance and openness to different worldviews is part-and-parcel of globalization. A tangentially related benefit involves the spread of respect for the rights of women and minorities around the globe. Discrimination is incompatible with freedom and democracy, and the spread of globalization brings pressure to bear on governments to recognize and protect the rights of all their citizens.

Detractors of globalization raise several important points. Echoing anti-outsourcing advocates, they argue that globalization results in a loss of jobs due to competition with low-wage countries. Indeed, the major economic force driving the tremendous growth of the Indian and Chinese economies over the past 15 years is their competitive advantage of access to cheap labor. Many antiglobalization supporters argue that corporations are becoming too powerful politically and economically and believe that the search for overseas profits and markets is the primary cause.

Opponents also raise concerns over national safety and security issues. As the globe continues to shrink and the ease and speed of information exchange continues to increase, the likelihood of cyber-attacks and the theft of sensitive military, technological, and economic information is assumed to increase. The threat of terrorism has grown dramatically in the past 30 years due in large part, say the globalization critics, to the spread of globalization driven by the United States and other western, First-World civilizations. As the recent Swine Flu outbreak reminds us, the threat of a worldwide health pandemic grows larger the more integrated the world becomes.

YES ↵

Paul A. Gigot
and Guy Sorman

Foreword

I don't know who first used the word "globalization," but he was probably no friend of capitalism. The word is bureaucratic and implies that the world economy is subject to the control of some vast, nefarious force beyond human influence. The reality is that the world economy is enjoying its strongest run of prosperity in 40 years thanks to the greater ability of billions of individuals to make free choices in their own self-interest. The *Index of Economic Freedom* has been encouraging this trend for 14 years, and at the end of 2007, we can happily say it continues.

The world economy extended its multiyear run of 5 percent or so annual GDP growth this year, notwithstanding an American slowdown due mainly to the housing correction. As I write this, the U.S. economy seems to have survived the August credit crunch related to the collapse of the sub-prime mortgage market. The summer squall showed once again how interrelated financial markets have become, with sub-prime losses popping up around the world and even causing an old-fashioned bank run at Northern Rock in the United Kingdom.

The episode is naturally leading to soul-searching about the stability of this brave new world of global finance—including the spread of asset securitization, the rise of hedge funds, and an explosion in derivatives. This introspection ought to be healthy. The sub-prime fiasco has, at the very least, exposed the need for more careful vetting by investors, but regulators and bankers are also sure to examine the rules for transparency and capital requirements to prevent the spread of problems throughout the financial system. The event also shows the need for more careful driving by America's Federal Reserve, whose easy-money policy in the first half of this decade was the root cause of the housing boom and bust. The good news is that, at least so far, there hasn't been a regulatory overreaction that could stymie growth.

The irony of the year has been the shifting economic policy trends in America and France, of all places. The U.S. political debate is moving in a negative direction as "fairness" and income redistribution replace growth as the policy lodestar and proposals for tax increases proliferate. The Bush tax cuts of 2003 were crucial to kicking the economy out of its post-9/11, post-dot.com doldrums. But they expire after 2010 and are in serious jeopardy. The free-trade agenda has also stalled as bilateral pacts with Latin America and South Korea face heavy going on Capitol Hill. The 2008 election will be as much a referendum on economic policy as on foreign policy.

Perhaps the rest of the world will have to teach America a policy lesson or two. As the *Index* shows, Europe overall has moved in a freer direction this decade. This is due in large part to reform in the former Eastern Europe, as well as to the policy competition caused by the success of the euro. With capital and people free to move and governments no longer able to inflate their way out of fiscal difficulty, the trend has been toward lower tax rates and labor market liberalization.

Miracle of miracles, even France has been mugged by this reality. Nicolas Sarkozy made the revival of the French economy a main theme of his successful campaign for president, and he has followed with proposals for what he called "a new social contract founded on work, merit and equal opportunity." We should all hope he succeeds—not merely to compensate for any slowdown in America, but for its own sake to help Europe break away from its self-imposed sense of diminished expectations. In any event, this policy churning in Europe shows how the ability to move capital freely across borders imposes a price on bad government decisions.

The larger point is that if we step back from the daily turmoil, we can see that we live in a remarkable era of prosperity and spreading freedom. Hundreds of millions of people are being lifted out of poverty around the world as global trade and investment expand and countries like India and China liberalize parts of their economies. The International Monetary Fund reported in early 2007 that every country in the world, save for a couple of small dictatorships, was growing. This prosperity can itself create discontent due to the rapidity of change, and it certainly poses a challenge to political leaders who are obliged to explain and manage its consequences. The *Index of Economic Freedom* exists to help in that explanation, and we hope readers continue to find it a source of comparative policy wisdom.

Globalization Is Making the World a Better Place

What we call "globalization," one of the most powerful and positive forces ever to have arisen in the history of mankind, is redefining civilization as we know it. This is one of my hypotheses. To be more specific, I will try to describe what globalization is, its impact on world peace, and the freedom it brings from want, fear, and misery.

Globalization has six major characteristics: economic development, democracy, cultural enrichment, political and cultural norms, information, and internationalization of the rule of law.

Economic Development

Usually, globalization is described in terms of intensified commercial and trade exchanges, but it is about more than just trade, stock exchanges, and currencies. It is about people. What is significant today is that through globalization many nations are converging toward enhanced welfare.

This convergence is exemplified by the 800 million people who, in the past 30 years, have left poverty and misery behind. They have greater access to health care, schooling, and information. They have more choices, and their children will have even more choices. The absolutely remarkable part is that it happened not by accident but through a combination of good economic policy, technology, and management.

Of course, not all nations are following this path, but since the fall of the Berlin Wall, more and more are coming closer. Only Africa's nations have yet to join, but who would have hoped and predicted 30 years ago that China and India, with such rapidity and efficiency, would pull their people out of misery? There is no reason why Africa, when its turn comes, will not do the same. Convergence should be a source of hope for us all.

Democracy

In general, since 1989, the best system to improve the welfare of all people—not only economically, but also in terms of access to equality and freedom—appears to be democracy, the new international norm. As more and more countries turn democratic or converge toward democratic norms, respect for other cultures increases.

Democracy has guaranteed welfare far better than any dictatorship ever could. Even enlightened despots cannot bring the kind of safety democracy is bringing. Sometimes a trade-off between economic allotment and democracy occurs. Sometimes the economy grows more slowly because of democracy. Let it be that way. Democracy brings values that are as important for the welfare of the human being as [the] economy is.

After all, as history shows, the chance of international war diminishes step by step any time a country moves from tyranny to democracy, as democracies do not war against one other. That more and more nations are turning democratic improves everyone's way of life.

Cultural Enrichment

Critics of globalization frequently charge that it results in an "Americanization of culture" and concomitant loss of identity and local cultural values. I would propose a more optimistic view, and that is that globalization leads to never-ending exchange of ideas, especially through popular culture, since it affects the greatest number of people.

Through popular culture, people from different backgrounds and nations discover one another, and their "otherness" suddenly disappears. For example, a popular Korean television sitcom now popular in Japan has shown its Japanese viewers that, like them, Koreans fall in love, feel despair, and harbor the same hopes and fears for themselves and for their children. This sitcom has transformed the image Japanese have of the Korean nation more profoundly than any number of diplomatic efforts and demonstrates that globalization can erode prejudices that have existed between neighboring countries for centuries.

Furthermore, this process of better understanding allows us to keep our identity and add new identities. The Koreans absorb a bit of the American culture, a bit of the French, a bit of other European societies. Perhaps they have become a different sort of Korean, but they remain Korean nonetheless. It is quite the illusion to think you can lose your identity. And it goes both ways. When you look at the success of cultural exports out of Korea—this so-called new wave through music, television, movies, and art—Korea becomes part of the identity of other people.

Now, as a Frenchman, I am a bit Korean myself. This is how globalization works. We do not lose our identity. We enter into the world that I call the world of multi-identity, and that is progress, not loss.

Political and Cultural Norms

One of the most significant transformations in terms of welfare for the people in the globalized world is the increased respect given to the rights of women and minorities. In many nations, to be a woman or to belong to a minority has not been easy. In the past 30 years, however, women and minorities everywhere have become better informed and have learned that the repression they suffered until very recently is not typical in a modern democracy.

Let us consider India, where a strong caste system historically has subjugated women and untouchables.

Thanks to the globalization of democratic norms, these minorities are better protected; through various affirmative action policies, they can access the better jobs that traditionally were forbidden to them. This transformation has positive consequences for them, of course, and also creates better outcomes for their children's welfare and education. We are entering into a better world because of their improved status, thanks to the cultural and democratic exchanges generated by globalization.

Information

Through legacy media and, more and more, through the Internet and cellular phones, everyone today, even in authoritarian countries, is better informed. For one year, I lived in the poorest part of China, and I remember well how a farmer, in the most remote village, knew exactly what was happening not only in the next village, but also in Beijing and New York because of the Internet and his cellular phone. No government can stop information now. People know today that, as they say, "knowledge is power."

Now let us imagine if the genocide in Darfur had happened 20 or 30 years ago. The Darfur population would have been annihilated by the Sudanese government, and no one would have known. Today we all know about the genocide. The reason why the international community has been forced to intervene is because of the flood of information. Knowledge is proving to be the best protection for oppressed minorities and, thus, one of the most vital aspects of globalization.

Internationalization of the Rule of Law

Internationalization of rule of law, of course, has limitations. The institutions in charge of this emerging rule of law, whether the United Nations or the World Trade Organization, are criticized. They are not completely legitimate. They are certainly not perfectly democratic, but you cannot build a democratic organization with non-democratic governments. It becomes a trade-off.

In spite of all the weaknesses of international organizations, the emergence of a real international rule of law replaces the pure barbarism that existed before, which had consisted of the most powerful against the weak. Even though globalization cannot suppress war, it is remarkably efficient at containing war. If you examine the kinds of wars we have today, compared to the history of mankind, the number of victims and number of nations involved are very few. We are all safer because of both this emerging rule of law and the flow of information provided by globalization.

Invented by Entrepreneurs

We also need to remember that globalization is not some historical accident but has been devised and built by those who wanted it. Diplomats did not invent it. Entrepreneurs did.

Let us look at Europe. After World War II, the Europeans discovered that they had been their own worst enemies. For 1,000 years, we were fighting each other. Why? We do not remember very well. Every 30 years, we went to war. The French killed the Germans. The Germans killed the French. When you try to explain this history to your children, they cannot understand. Diplomats and politicians from the 18th century onward unsuccessfully made plans to avoid this kind of civil war within Europe.

Then, in the 1940s, a businessman came along named Jean Monnet. His business was to sell cognac in the United States, and he was very good at it. The idea Jean Monnet had was that perhaps the unification process of Europe should not be started by diplomats. Maybe it should be started by business people. He proceeded to build the European Union on a foundation of commerce. He started with coal and steel in 1950, and it was through the liberation of that trade that he conceived the unification of Europe, which has played a crucial role in the globalization process.

Monnet's guiding principle was that commercial and financial ties would lead to political unification. The true basis of European solidarity has come through trade. Through this method, all of the benefits of globalization have been made possible, because free trade has been at the root level. An attack on free trade is an attack on both globalization and the welfare of the peoples of the world, so we must be very cautious when we discuss trade, as it is the essential key allowing the rest to happen.

None of this is to imply that trade is easy. In the case of Europe, it was made easier because all of the governments were democratic. It is much more complicated to build free trade with non-democratic governments, but because globalization starts with the construction of this materialistic solidarity, ideals must come afterwards.

Two Threats to Globalization

Perhaps what I have presented so far is too optimistic a picture of globalization, but I believe we have good reason to be upbeat. However, there are two threats to globalization that may be taken too lightly today.

Global epidemics. In terms of health care, we are more and more able to cope with the current illnesses of the world. Though Africa still poses a problem, through global efforts it will be possible in the years to come to reduce the major epidemics there: AIDS and malaria.

But new epidemics are threatening the world. If we remember what happened in China some years ago with the SARS epidemic, which was very short, and then the avian flu threat in 2005, you understand that there are new threats somewhere out there and that the modern world is not really prepared. One of the consequences of globalization is that people travel more, which means that viruses travel more and adapt.

Therefore, I think globalization should require the international community to develop ever more sophisticated systems to detect and cure the new epidemics that have been a negative consequence of globalization.

Terrorism. Although wars these days are more limited, new forms of warfare have emerged, which we call terrorism. Terrorism today can seem like a distant menace somewhere between the United States and the Middle East. Because of the global progress of the rule of law, however, violent groups know that it is no longer possible to wage war in the traditional way; therefore, people driven by ideological passions are increasingly tempted by terrorist methods as a way of implementing their agenda.

Those are the true negative aspects of globalization: epidemics and terrorism. Regretfully, we are too focused on the traditional problems like free trade. We are not focused enough on the future threats.

I wish globalization were more popular, but it is our fault if it is not. Perhaps we should use different words. "Globalization" is ugly. We should find a better word, and we should try to explain to the media and students that we are entering into a new civilization of welfare, progress, and happiness, because if they do not understand the beauty of globalization, they will not stand up for it when it is threatened.

Paul A. Gigot is the editor of *The Wall Street Journal* Editorial Page.

Guy Sorman is a French journalist and author.

Branko Milanovic   ➡ **NO**

Why Globalization
Is in Trouble—Parts 1 and 2

Part I

Washington: Historically, the dominant power tends to support globalization as a way to increase the ambit of its influence, expand trade and gain economic advantage, co-opt new citizens and possibly show the advantages of its own pax. This was the case with the Roman, British and now American-led globalizations. But recently, the rich West—which saw globalization as a prelude to "the end of history"—is having second thoughts.

Two fears drive this unease with globalization: The first is a fear of job loss due to competition from low-wage countries. The second is the fear of ethnic and cultural dilution due to increased immigration.

The cause of the first fear is a fast reemergence on the world stage of China and India. For students of history, the rise of China and India is not a surprise. The two countries are just recapturing the ground lost during the 19th and most of the 20th century. Before the Industrial Revolution, China's and India's combined output accounted for one half of the world's total. Now, after a quarter-century of China's spectacular growth, and more than a decade of India's growth acceleration, the two countries contribute less than a fifth of total world output. Although their share is, in the long-term historical sense, still below what it used to be, it has nevertheless increased dramatically compared to where it was 30 years ago. The rise of the two Asian giants, reflected in their dynamic trade, large Chinese export surpluses and India's role as an outsourcing center and a potential leader in information technology, has made the West wonder whether it can compete with such hardworking, cheap, plentiful and yet relatively skilled labor.

While the fear of job loss is driven by fast economic growth of the two giants, the fear of immigration is, ironically, caused by the slow economic growth of the rest of the developing world. The people who try to reach the shores of Europe or cross from Mexico into the US come from the countries that have disastrously fallen behind Western Europe and the US during the last quarter century. In 1980, Mexico's real per-capita income, adjusted for the differential price level between Mexico and the US, was a third of that in the US. Today, the ratio is almost 4.5 to 1. The poor Africans who land daily on beaches of the Spanish Canary Islands come from the countries that

have seen no economic growth in 50 years. Take Ghana, a country often touted as an African success case: Around its independence, in 1957, its income was one half of Spain's; today, it is one tenth.

Immigration puts a similar pressure on low- or medium-skilled jobs in the West as do cheap imports from China and outsourcing to India. And indeed, wages of low- and medium-skilled workers in the rich countries have failed to keep pace with incomes of educated workers at the top of the pyramid. While the median US real wage has not risen in real terms over the last 25 years, real wages of the top 1 percent have more than doubled. The richest 1 percent of Americans today controls almost 20 percent of total US income, a proportion higher than at any time since the Roaring Twenties. The U-turn of inequality—a sharp increase that started during the Thatcher-Reagan era, after a long decline—has affected, to a varying extent, all Western countries.

But at stake is something more profound than a threat to jobs and stagnant wages in a few "exposed" sectors. After all, the West is no stranger to structural change. Ricardo in his "Principles" written in 1815 discusses labor dislocation "occasioned" by the introduction of machinery. The Western countries handled the decline of powerful industries like coal, textile and steel. Economists have never been sympathetic to the protection arguments of sunset industries: In an expanding economy, structural change is necessary and inevitable; jobs lost in one industry will reappear as new jobs in another industry.

The difference now is that the twin challenge undermines the consensus upon which the West's welfare state was built since World War II. To understand why, recall that the Western welfare states rest on two building blocks: those of ethnic and social solidarity. The first building block implies that one is willing to be taxed if certain that aid will flow to somebody who is ethnically or culturally similar. But once large stocks of immigrants with different, and not easily adaptable, social norms, arrive, that certainly is no longer. More immigrants will strain the already-tattered solidarity among citizens of rich European countries.

The second building block of the welfare state is class solidarity. For it to exist, there must be relatively similar economic conditions between classes so that one can reasonably expect that for social transfers paid out of his pocket today, he may be compensated—if the need arose—by a similar benefit in the future. If, for example, unemployment rates are relatively equal across skill levels, then the highly skilled will pay for unemployment benefits; but if unemployment rates are different, the highly skilled may opt out. As the income divide widens in the West between the rich and the highly educated who have done well, and the middle classes and the unskilled who are merely scraping by, the second building block on which welfare capitalism was built crumbles. Economic inequality also translates into a cultural divide. "Ethnic" migrants who fill the rungs of low-paid workers are not the only ones economically and culturally different from today's Western elites; the elites are also growing more different from their own poorer ethnic brethren.

So far reaching, these developments require an entirely new social contract, a redefinition of capitalism no less. Such fundamental changes are not easy to come by when the threat is subtle, continuous, incremental and far from dramatic in a daily sense. Difficult decisions can be postponed, and neither politicians nor the electorate have an appetite for change. A battle of attrition regarding who would bear the costs of adjustment ensues, and this is at the heart of Europe's present immobilism.

Why is the development of "new capitalism" and rethinking of the old social contract so much more difficult for Europe than for the US? First, for an obvious reason, because Europe's welfare state is much more extensive, more embedded in ordinary life, and its dismantlement is more socially disruptive. Second, because a low population growth—or in many countries, a decline—necessitates continuing large immigration. But, and this is the crux of the matter, Europe struggles more in absorbing immigrants than the US. Historically, of course, Europe was not a society of immigrants. Europeans were happy to receive foreign workers as long as they would do low-paying jobs and stay out of the way. This quasi-apartheid solution preserved immigrants' culture, which then, most famously in the Netherlands, was found to clash with some European values. Immigrants, more so their daughters and sons, were not happy to remain in subaltern jobs. And while Europe was good about welcoming them to its soccer and basketball teams, it was more stingy when it came allowing them to direct operating rooms or boardrooms.

The bottom line is that Europe needs no less than a social revolution: replacement of its welfare state, and acceptance that Germans, French or Italians of tomorrow will be much darker in their skin color, composed of individuals of various religions, and in many respects indeed a different people. As fusion of Frankish ethnicity and Latin culture created France, a similar Christiano-Islamic and Afro-European fusion may create new European nations, perhaps with a different outlook on life and social norms. No society can accomplish such epochal transformation quickly and painlessly.

Part II

Washington: In the rich world globalization had driven the wedge between social classes, while in the poor world, the main divide is between countries: those that adjusted to globalization and, in many areas, prospered and those that adjusted badly and, in many cases, collapsed.

Indeed the Third World was never a bloc the way that the first and second worlds were. But it was united by its opposition to colonialism and dislike for being used as a battlefield of the two then-dominant ideologies. As the Second World collapsed and globalization took off, the latter rationale evaporated, and a few countries, most notably India and China, accelerated their growth rates significantly, enjoying the fruits of freer trade and larger capital flows. And although these two countries adapted well to globalization, there is little doubt that their new-found relative prosperity opened many new fissure lines. Inequality between coastal and inland provinces, as well as between urban and rural areas, skyrocketed in China. So did, and perhaps by even more, inequality between Southern Indian states, where the hub cities of Mumbai, Chennai and Bangalore are located, and the slow-growing Northeast. For China, which still may face political transition to democracy, widening inequality between different parts of the country, could have disastrous consequences.

But another large group of Third World countries, from Latin America to Africa to former Communist countries, experienced a quarter century of decline or stagnation punctuated by civil wars, international conflicts and the plight of AIDS. While between 1980 and 2002, the rich countries grew, on average, by almost 2 percent per capita annually, the poorest 40 countries in the world had a combined growth rate of zero. For large swaths of Africa where about 200 million people live, the income level today is less than it was during the US presidency of John F. Kennedy.

For these countries the promised benefits of globalization never arrived. The vaunted Washington consensus policies brought no improvement for the masses, but rather a deterioration in the living conditions as key social services became privatized and more costly as was the case, for example, with water privatizations in Cochabamba, Bolivia, and Trinidad, electricity privatization in Argentina and Chad. They were often taken over by foreigners, and to add insult to injury, Western pundits arrived by jets, stayed in luxury hotels and hailed obvious worsening of economic and social conditions as a step toward better lives and international integration. For many people in Latin America and Africa, globalization appeared as new, more attractive label put on the old imperialism, or worse as a form of re-colonization. The left-wing reaction sweeping Latin America, from Mexico to Argentina, is a direct consequence of the fault lines opened by policies that were often designed to benefit Wall Street, not the people in the streets of Lima or Caracas.

Other Third World states—particularly those at the frontline of the battle between communism and capitalism, with ethnic animosities encouraged during the Cold War, efforts by Washington and Moscow to get the upper hand in the conflict—exploded in civil wars and social anomies. That part of the world associates globalization with disappointment (because Washington consensus never delivered), resentment (because others got ahead) and poverty, disease and war. In several sub-Saharan African countries, life expectancy at the turn of the 21st century is not only where it was in Europe almost two centuries ago but is getting worse. In Zimbabwe, between 1995 and 2003, life expectancy declined by 11 years to reach only 39 years.

Ideologies which proposed some economic betterment and offered self-respect to many people in Africa (from Kwame Nkrumah's African socialism to Julius Nyerere's "cooperative economy") and parts of the former Communist bloc (Tito's "labor management") all collapsed and have given way to self-serving oligarchies that justified their policies, not by calling on their own citizens, but by publishing excerpts from reports written by the World Bank and the International Monetary Fund.

In the Third World as a whole, globalization, at best, produced what Tocqueville, with a touch of aristocratic disdain, called a government of the commercially-minded middle classes, "a government without virtue and without greatness"; at worst, it produced governments of plutocrats or elites unconcerned about their own populations. Globalization thus appeared in the poorest and weakest countries at its roughest.

Perhaps the greatest casualty of the money-grubbing global capitalism was loss of self-respect among those who have failed economically—and they are preponderantly located in the poorest countries. The desperate African masses who want to flee their own countries leave not only because incomes are low and prospects bleak, but also because of a lack of confidence that either they or their governments, no matter who is in power, can change life for the better. This despondency and loss of self-respect is indeed a product of globalization. In the past one could feel slighted by fortune for having been born in a poor country, yet have as compensation a belief that other qualities mattered, that one's country offered the world something valuable, a different ideology, a different way of life. But none of that survives today.

The problem was, strangely, noticed by Friedrich Hayek. Market outcomes, Hayek argued, must not be presented as ethically just or unjust because the market is ethically neutral. But to buttress the case for global capitalism, its proponents insist in an almost Calvinist fashion that economic success is not only good in a purely material sense, but reveals some moral superiority. Thus winners are made to feel not only richer but morally superior, and the converse: The losers feel poor and are supposed to be ashamed of their failure. Many people do, but understandably not all take gladly to such judgment.

An interesting coincidence of interests emerges between the desperate masses and the rich in advanced countries. The latter, educated and with considerable property "interests," are, economically, often in favor of greater Third World competitiveness and migration since, either as investors abroad or consumers of cheap labor services at home, they benefit from low-wage labor. This unlikely coincidence of interest lends some superficial justification to the claims of George Bush and Tony Blair that the opponents of free-trade pacts work against the interests of the poor. The problem that the president and the prime minister fail to acknowledge, or perhaps even to realize, is that many of the policies urged by their governments on poor countries in the last two decades have indeed brought people to their current point of desperation.

Sandwiched between this unlikely "coalition" of the global top and the global bottom, are globalization's losers: the lower and middle classes in the West, and those in the "failed" states, not yet sufficiently desperate to board the boats to Europe or cross the US border at night. They too lost in terms of their national sovereignty and personal income. They may not gladly accept, though, that they are morally inferior. At first sight, they do not seem likely to derail globalization because their power is limited. Yet in a more interdependent world with an easy access to deadly weapons, politics of global resentment may find many followers.

BRANKO MILANOVIC is an economist with the Carnegie Endowment for International Peace. Milanovic's most recent book is *Worlds Apart: Measuring International and Global Inequality.*

EXPLORING THE ISSUE

Is Economic Globalization Good for Humankind?

Critical Thinking and Reflection

1. What might be the goals of an economic globalization policy for corporations and nations?
2. How might an economic globalization policy be implemented? Could such a policy be implemented on a global scale?
3. What is the likelihood that an enacted economic globalization policy will lead to anticipated outcomes?
4. What might be the costs to consumers, corporations, and countries of an economic globalization policy?
5. What does the future hold for an economic globalization policy?

Is There Common Ground?

One reason the issue of an economic globalization policy is so contentious is that both sides can easily cite data in support of their position. The underlying balancing act that appears to exist with this particular issue is that of balancing corporate profit motives with socially responsible business practices that truly address various societal needs. While finding common ground on even basic aspects of this topic is difficult, it is anticipated that discussions of an economic globalization policy will continue to be highly charged and ongoing for quite some time.

Additional Resources

Griffin, R.W. and Pustay, M.W. (2010). *International Business*, 6th ed., Prentice Hall.

Nikiforuk, A. (2007). *Pandemonium: How Globalization and Trade Are Putting the World at Risk*, University of Queensland Press.

Investor's Business Daily (2007). "The Backlash Against Globalization."

Stoylarov, G. (2009). "Globalization: Extending the Market and Human Well-Being," *The Freeman*, 59 (3).

Internet References . . .

Strength in Numbers for Globalization's Critics

Elsaeßer, C. (2007). "Strength in Numbers for Globalization's Critics," *Deutch Welle*, September 5.

www.dw-world.de/dw/article/ 0,2144,2473215,00.html

Findings of *Freedom in the World 2008*— Freedom in Retreat: Is the Tide Turning?

Puddington, A. (2008). "Findings of *Freedom in the World 2008*—Freedom in Retreat: Is the Tide Turning?" Freedom House.org.

www.freedomhouse.org/template .cfm?page=130&year=2008

Selected, Edited, and with Issue Framing Material by:
Kathleen J. Barnes, *East Stroudsburg University*
and
George E. Smith, *Albright College*

ISSUE

Are Protectionist Policies Beneficial to Business?

YES: Ha-Joon Chang, from "Protecting the Global Poor," *Prospect Magazine* (July 2007)

NO: Robert Krol, from "Trade, Protectionism, and the U.S. Economy: Examining the Evidence," *Trade Briefing Paper No. 28* (The Cato Institute, September 16)

Learning Outcomes

After reading this issue you should be able to:

- Understand the positive and negative consequences of protectionist policies on American corporations.
- Understand how protectionist policies can be used as an effective corporate strategy.
- Understand what policies might be implemented to support an effective protectionist corporate strategy.
- Appreciate the practical implications of corporate protectionist strategy use in the workplace.

ISSUE SUMMARY

YES: In support of the idea that protectionist policies help business, Ha-Joon Chang focuses attention on developing industries in poor countries. Further, he describes and advocates historical protectionist policies from around the world.

NO: In the NO selection, Robert Krol describes the findings of various economic studies of international trade. The areas that he surveys include the effect of trade on employment and wages as well of the costs of trade restrictions. He concludes that overall the benefits from protectionist policies are overshadowed by their negative effects.

It is understandable that a country would want to take care of its own citizens first. To this end, many countries adopt policies that prop up domestic industries and limit foreign organizations from engaging in business in their country. Generally speaking, such policies are typically labeled "protectionism." A formal definition of protectionism is the "National economic policies designed to restrict free trade and protect domestic industries from foreign competition" (Cavusgil, Knight, and Riesenberger, 2008, p. 620). Protectionist policies include governmental actions such as tariffs (taxes on imported goods), quotas (limits on the amount of goods that can be imported), subsidies (government support of certain domestic businesses or industries), and other policies like the "Buy American" requirements in the United States.

Let's take a look at a couple of broad examples. When foreign competitors in a particular industry operate with a lower cost basis, home governments will frequently provide funds (subsidies) to that industry in their own country to help the domestic companies compete against foreign competitors. The ultimate goals of such policies are many and may include keeping specific domestic industries competitive, keeping the country's workers employed, and keeping them employed at higher wages than would be the case without subsidies. Another protectionist strategy is to assess tariffs on foreign goods. The addition of the tariff causes foreign competitors to charge higher prices than they would otherwise desire in order to remain profitable.

For a more concrete example, we can look at the U.S. steel industry. To address increasing fears that foreign steelmakers will increase market share in the United States, politicians and U.S. steel industry advocates want to implement economic stimulus legislation requiring that infrastructure projects in the United States use domestic steel (Hardy and Buley, 2009). Further, there is concern that market share increases from foreign competitors will hurt not only the steel industry but also have negative effects on the environment. Consider the following comments from a union leader in the U.S. steel industry: "In congressional testimony in March [2009], United Steelworkers boss Leo Gerard explained how unfettered trade in steel would both ship jobs abroad and make the world's pollution worse. Ton for ton, he said, Chinese steel leaves a carbon footprint three times as large as American steel" (Hardy and Buley, 2009).

Although many believe that protectionism may indeed afford some advantages for domestic business, opponents of protectionism argue that due to the interdependence of global trade and financial systems, these advantages are offset by many negative consequences (Kerr, 2009). For instance, an unintended, and unavoidable, consequence of subsidies and tariffs is higher prices for products available to consumers. Protectionist policies also tend to lower the overall quality of goods available and ultimately increase the tax burden on the general public.

Writing in the NO selection for this debate topic, Robert Krol describes the findings of various economic studies of international trade. Krol looks at the effect of trade on employment and wages as well as examining the costs of trade restrictions. From his research, he concludes that "Although international trade forces significant adjustments in an economy, as the evidence shows, the costs of international trade restrictions on the economy outweigh the limited benefits these restrictions bring to import-competing industries" (p. 10).

The opposing view, taken from *Prospect Magazine*, is provided by Ha-Joon Chang, who focuses attention on the benefits of protectionism for infant, or developing industries in poor countries. Chang describes and advocates historical protectionist policies from all around the world. Interestingly, the selection contains many examples taken from the histories of today's wealthiest countries. The point behind this approach is that history shows that for today's poorer nations to succeed, they need to be allowed to adopt regulations that protect their fledgling key industries.

YES ↵

Ha-Joon Chang

Protecting the Global Poor

Once upon a time, the leading car-maker of a developing country exported its first passenger cars to the US. Until then, the company had only made poor copies of cars made by richer countries. The car was just a cheap subcompact ("four wheels and an ashtray") but it was a big moment for the country and its exporters felt proud.

Unfortunately, the car failed. Most people thought it looked lousy, and were reluctant to spend serious money on a family car that came from a place where only second-rate products were made. The car had to be withdrawn from the US. This disaster led to a major debate among the country's citizens. Many argued that the company should have stuck to its original business of making simple textile machinery. After all, the country's biggest export item was silk. If the company could not make decent cars after 25 years of trying, there was no future for it. The government had given the car-maker every chance. It had ensured high profits for it through high tariffs and tough controls on foreign investment. Less than ten years earlier, it had even given public money to save the company from bankruptcy. So, the critics argued, foreign cars should now be let in freely and foreign car-makers, who had been kicked out 20 years before, allowed back again. Others disagreed. They argued that no country had ever got anywhere without developing "serious" industries like car production. They just needed more time.

The year was 1958 and the country was Japan. The company was Toyota, and the car was called the Toyopet. Toyota started out as a manufacturer of textile machinery and moved into car production in 1933. The Japanese government kicked out General Motors and Ford in 1939, and bailed out Toyota with money from the central bank in 1949. Today, Japanese cars are considered as "natural" as Scottish salmon or French wine, but less than 50 years ago, most people, including many Japanese, thought the Japanese car industry simply should not exist.

Half a century after the Toyopet debacle, Toyota's luxury brand Lexus has become an icon of globalisation, thanks to the American journalist Thomas Friedman's book *The Lexus and the Olive Tree*. The book owes its title to an epiphany that Friedman had in Japan in 1992. He had paid a visit to a Lexus factory, which deeply impressed him. On the bullet train back to Tokyo, he read yet another newspaper article about the troubles in the middle east, where he had been a correspondent. Then it hit him. He realised that "half the world seemed to be . . . intent on building a better Lexus, dedicated to modernising, streamlining and privatising their economies in order to thrive in the system of globalisation. And half of the world—sometimes half the same country, sometimes half the same person—was still caught up in the fight over who owns which olive tree."

According to Friedman, countries in the olive-tree world will not be able to join the Lexus world unless they fit themselves into a particular set of economic policies he calls "the golden straitjacket." In describing the golden straitjacket, Friedman pretty much sums up today's neoliberal orthodoxy: countries should privatise state-owned enterprises, maintain low inflation, reduce the size of government, balance the budget, liberalise trade, deregulate foreign investment and capital markets, make the currency convertible, reduce corruption and privatise pensions. The golden straitjacket, Friedman argues, is the only clothing suitable for the harsh but exhilarating game of globalisation.

However, had the Japanese government followed the free-trade economists back in the early 1960s, there would have been no Lexus. Toyota today would at best be a junior partner to a western car manufacturer and Japan would have remained the third-rate industrial power it was in the 1960s—on the same level as Chile, Argentina and South Africa.

Had it just been Japan that became rich through the heretical policies of protection, subsidies and the restriction of foreign investment, the free-market champions might be able to dismiss it as the exception that proves the rule. But Japan is no exception. Practically all of today's developed countries, including Britain and the US, the supposed homes of the free market and free trade, have become rich on the basis of policy recipes that contradict today's orthodoxy.

In 1721, Robert Walpole, the first British prime minister, launched an industrial programme that protected and nurtured British manufacturers against superior competitors in the Low Countries, then the centre of European manufacturing. Walpole declared that "nothing so much contributes to promote the public wellbeing as the exportation of manufactured goods and the importation of foreign raw material." Between Walpole's time and the 1840s, when Britain started to reduce its tariffs (although it did not move to free trade until the 1860s), Britain's average industrial tariff rate was in the region of 40–50 percent, compared with 20 percent and 10 percent in France and Germany, respectively.

The US followed the British example. In fact, the first systematic argument that new industries in relatively backward economies need protection before they can compete with their foreign rivals—known as the "infant industry" argument—was developed by the first US treasury secretary, Alexander Hamilton. In 1789, Hamilton proposed a series of measures to achieve the industrialisation of his country, including protective tariffs, subsidies, import liberalisation of industrial inputs (so it wasn't blanket protection for everything), patents for inventions and the development of the banking system.

Hamilton was perfectly aware of the potential pitfalls of infant industry protection, and cautioned against taking these policies too far. He knew that just as some parents are overprotective, governments can cosset infant industries too much. And in the way that some children manipulate their parents into supporting them beyond childhood, there are industries that prolong government protection through clever lobbying. But the existence of dysfunctional families is hardly an argument against parenting itself. Likewise, the examples of bad protectionism merely tell us that the policy needs to be used wisely.

In recommending an infant industry programme for his young country, Hamilton, an impudent 35-year-old finance minister with only a liberal arts degree from a then second-rate college (King's College of New York, now Columbia University) was openly ignoring the advice of the world's most famous economist, Adam Smith. Like most European economists at the time, Smith advised the Americans not to develop manufacturing. He argued that any attempt to "stop the importation of European manufactures" would "obstruct . . . the progress of their country towards real wealth and greatness."

Many Americans—notably Thomas Jefferson, secretary of state at the time and Hamilton's arch-enemy—disagreed with Hamilton. They argued that it was better to import high-quality manufactured products from Europe with the proceeds that the country earned from agricultural exports than to try to produce second-rate manufactured goods. As a result, Congress only half-heartedly accepted Hamilton's recommendations—raising the average tariff rate from 5 percent to 12.5 percent.

In 1804, Hamilton was killed in a duel by the then vice-president Aaron Burr. Had he lived for another decade or so, he would have seen his programme adopted in full. Following the Anglo-American war in 1812, the US started shifting to a protectionist policy; by the 1820s, its average industrial tariff had risen to 40 percent. By the 1830s, America's average industrial tariff rate was the highest in the world and, except for a few brief periods, remained so until the second world war, at which point its manufacturing supremacy was absolute.

Britain and the US were not the only practitioners of infant industry protection. Virtually all of today's rich countries used policy measures to protect and nurture their infant industries. Even when the overall level of protection was relatively low, some strategic sectors could get very high protection. For example, in the late 19th and early 20th centuries, Germany, while maintaining a relatively moderate average industrial tariff rate (5–15 percent), accorded strong protection to industries like iron and steel. During the same period, Sweden provided high protection to its emerging engineering industries, although its average tariff rate was 15–20 percent. In the first half of the 20th century, Belgium maintained moderate levels of overall protection but heavily protected key textile sectors and the iron industry.

Tariffs were not the only tool of trade policy used by rich countries. When deemed necessary for the protection of infant industries, they banned imports or imposed import quotas. They also gave export subsidies—sometimes to all exports (Japan and Korea) but often to specific items (in the 18th century, Britain gave export subsidies to gunpowder, sailcloth, refined sugar and silk). Some of them also gave a rebate on the tariffs paid on the imported industrial inputs used for manufacturing export goods, in order to encourage such exports. Many believe that this measure was invented in Japan in the 1950s, but it was in fact invented in Britain in the 17th century.

It is not just in the realm of trade that the historical records of today's rich countries burst the bindings of Friedman's golden straitjacket. The history of controls on foreign investment tells a similar story. In the 19th century, the US placed restrictions on foreign investment in banking, shipping, mining and logging. The restrictions were particularly severe in banking; throughout the 19th century, non-resident shareholders could not even vote in a shareholders' meeting and only American citizens could become directors in a national (as opposed to state) bank.

Some countries went further than the US. Japan closed off most industries to foreign investment and imposed 49 percent ownership ceilings on the others until the 1970s. Korea basically followed this model until it was forced to liberalise after the 1997 financial crisis. Between the 1930s and the 1980s, Finland officially classified all firms with more than 20 percent foreign ownership as "dangerous enterprises." It was not that these countries were against foreign companies per se—after all, Korea actively courted foreign investment in export processing zones. They restricted foreign investors because they believed—rightly in my view—that there is nothing like learning how to do something yourself, even if it takes more time and effort.

The wealthy nations of today may support the privatisation of state-owned enterprises in developing countries, but many of them built their industries through state ownership. At the beginning of their industrialisation, Germany and Japan set up state-owned enterprises in key industries—textiles, steel and shipbuilding. In France, the reader may be surprised to learn that many household names—like Renault (cars), Alcatel (telecoms equipment), Thomson (electronics) and Elf Aquitaine (oil and gas)—have been state-owned enterprises. Finland, Austria and Norway also developed their industries through extensive state ownership after the second world war. Taiwan has achieved its economic "miracle" with a state sector more than one-and-a-half times the size of the international average, while Singapore's state sector is one of the largest in the world, and includes world-class companies like Singapore Airlines.

Of course, there were exceptions. The Netherlands and pre-first world war Switzerland did not adopt many tariffs or subsidies. But they did deviate from today's free-market orthodoxy in another, very important way—they refused to protect patents. Switzerland did not have patents until 1888 and did not protect chemical inventions until 1907. The Netherlands abolished its 1817 patent law in 1869, on the grounds that patents created artificial monopolies that went against the principle of free competition. It did not reintroduce a patent law until 1912, by which time Philips was firmly established as a leading producer of lightbulbs, whose production technology it "borrowed" from Thomas Edison.

Even countries that did have patent laws were lax about protecting intellectual property (IP) rights—especially those of foreigners. In most countries, including Britain, Austria, France and the US, patenting of imported inventions was explicitly allowed in the 19th century.

Despite this history of protection, subsidy and state ownership, the rich countries have been recommending to, or even forcing upon, developing countries policies that go directly against their own historical experience. For the past 25 years, rich countries have imposed trade liberalisation on many developing countries through IMF and World Bank loan conditions, as well as the conditions attached to their direct aid. The World Trade Organisation (WTO) does allow some tariff protection, especially for the poorest developing countries, but most developing countries have had to significantly reduce tariffs and other trade restrictions. Most subsidies have been banned by the WTO—except, of course, the ones that rich countries still use, such as on agriculture, and research and development. And while, of course, no poor country is obliged to accept foreign inward investment (and most receive none or very little), the IMF and the World Bank are always lobbying for more liberal foreign investment rules. The WTO has also tightened IP laws, asking all but the poorest developing countries to comply with US standards—which even many Americans consider excessive.

Why are they doing this? In 1841, Friedrich List, a German economist, criticised Britain for preaching free trade to other countries when she had achieved her economic supremacy through tariffs and subsidies. He accused the British of "kicking away the ladder" that they had climbed to reach the world's top economic position. Today, there are certainly some people in rich countries who preach free trade to poor countries in order to capture larger shares of the latter's markets and to pre-empt the emergence of possible competitors. They are saying, "Do as we say, not as we did," and act as bad samaritans, taking advantage of others in trouble. But what is more

worrying is that many of today's free traders do not realise that they are hurting the developing countries with their policies. History is written by the victors, and it is human nature to reinterpret the past from the point of view of the present. As a result, the rich countries have gradually, if often sub-consciously, rewritten their own histories to make them more consistent with how they see themselves today, rather than as they really were.

But the truth is that free traders make the lives of those whom they are trying to help more difficult. The evidence for this is everywhere. Despite adopting supposedly "good" policies, like liberal foreign trade and investment and strong patent protection, many developing countries have actually been performing rather badly over the last two and a half decades. The annual per capita growth rate of the developing world has halved in this period, compared to the "bad old days" of protectionism and government intervention in the 1960s and the 1970s. Even this modest rate has been achieved only because the average includes China and India—two fast-growing giants, which have gradually liberalised their economies but have resolutely refused to put on Thomas Friedman's golden straitjacket.

Growth failure has been particularly noticeable in Latin America and Africa, where orthodox neoliberal programmes were implemented more thoroughly than in Asia. In the 1960s and the 1970s, per capita income in Latin America grew at 3.1 percent a year, slightly faster than the developing-country average. Brazil especially was growing almost as fast as the east Asian "miracle" economies. Since the 1980s, however, when the continent embraced neoliberalism, Latin America has been growing at less than a third of this rate. Even if we discount the 1980s as a decade of adjustment and look at the 1990s, we find that per capita income in the region grew at around half the rate of the "bad old days" (3.1 percent vs 1.7 percent). Between 2000 and 2005, the region has done even worse; it virtually stood still, with per capita income growing at only 0.6 percent a year. As for Africa, its per capita income grew relatively slowly even in the 1960s and the 1970s (1–2 percent a year). But since the 1980s, the region has seen a fall in living standards. There are, of course, many reasons for this failure, but it is nonetheless a damning indictment of the neoliberal orthodoxy, because most of the African economies have been practically run by the IMF and the World Bank over the past quarter of a century.

In pushing for free-market policies that make life more difficult for poor countries, the bad samaritans frequently deploy the rhetoric of the "level playing field." They argue that developing countries should not be allowed to use extra policy tools for protection, subsidies and regulation, as these constitute unfair competition. Who can disagree?

Well, we all should, if we want to build an international system that promotes economic development. A level playing field leads to unfair competition when the players are unequal. Most sports have strict separation by age and gender, while boxing, wrestling and weightlifting have weight classes, which are often divided very finely. How is it that we think a bout between people with more than a couple of kilos' weight difference is unfair, and yet we accept that the US and Honduras should compete economically on equal terms?

Global economic competition is a game of unequal players. It pits against each other countries that range from Switzerland to Swaziland. Consequently, it is only fair that we "tilt the playing field" in favour of the weaker countries. In practice, this means allowing them to protect and subsidise their producers more vigorously, and to put stricter regulations on foreign investment. These countries should also be allowed to protect IP rights less stringently, so that they can "borrow" ideas from richer countries. This will have the added benefit of making economic growth in poor countries more compatible with the need to fight global warming, as rich-country technologies tend to be far more energy-efficient.

I am not against markets, international trade or globalisation. And I acknowledge that WTO agreements contain "special and differential treatment" provisions which give poor country members certain rights, and which permit rich countries to treat developing countries more favourably than other rich WTO members. But these provisions are limited and generally just give poor countries longer time periods to liberalise their economic rules. The default position remains blind faith in indiscriminate free trade.

The best way to illustrate my general point is to look at my own native Korea—or, rather, to contrast the two bits that used to be one country until 1948. It is hard to believe today, but northern Korea used to be richer than the south. Japan developed the north industrially when it ruled the country from 1910–45. Even after the Japanese left, North Korea's industrial legacy enabled it to maintain its economic lead over South Korea well into the 1960s.

Today, South Korea is one of the world's industrial powerhouses while North Korea languishes in poverty. Much of this is thanks to the fact that South Korea aggressively traded with the outside world and actively absorbed foreign technologies while North Korea pursued its doctrine of self-sufficiency. Through trade, South Korea learned about the existence of better technologies and earned the foreign currency to buy them. In its own way, North Korea has managed some technological feats. For example, it figured out a way to mass-produce vinalon, a synthetic fibre made out of limestone and anthracite, which has allowed it to be self-sufficient in clothing. But, overall, North Korea is technologically stuck in the past, with 1940s Japanese and 1950s Soviet technologies, while South Korea is one of the most technologically dynamic economies in the world.

In the end, economic development is about mastering advanced technologies. In theory, a country can develop such technologies on its own, but technological self-sufficiency quickly hits the wall, as seen in the North Korean case. This is why all successful cases of economic development have involved serious attempts to get hold of advanced foreign technologies. But in order to be able to import technologies from developed countries, developing nations need foreign currency to pay for them. Some of this foreign currency may be provided through foreign aid, but most has to be earned through exports. Without trade, therefore, there will be little technological progress and thus little economic development.

But there is a huge difference between saying that trade is essential for economic development and saying that free trade is best. It is this sleight of hand that free-trade economists have so effectively deployed against their opponents—if you are against free trade, they imply, you must be against trade itself, and so against economic progress.

As South Korea—together with Britain, the US, Japan, Taiwan and many others—shows, active participation in international trade does not require free trade. In the early stages of their development, these countries typically had tariff rates in the region of 30–50 percent. Likewise, the Korean experience shows that actively absorbing foreign technologies does not require a liberal foreign investment policy.

Indeed, had South Korea donned Friedman's golden straitjacket in the 1960s, it would still be exporting raw materials like tungsten ore and seaweed. The secret of its success lay in a mix of protection and open trade, of government regulation and free(ish) market, of active courting of foreign investment and draconian regulation of it, and of private enterprise and state control—with the areas of protection constantly changing as new infant industries were developed and old ones became internationally competitive. This is how almost all of today's rich countries became rich, and it is at the root of almost all recent success stories in the developing world.

Therefore, if they are genuinely to help developing countries develop through trade, wealthy countries need to accept asymmetric protectionism, as they used to between the 1950s and the 1970s. The global economic system should support the efforts of developing countries by allowing them to use more freely the tools of infant industry promotion—such as tariff protection, subsidies, foreign investment regulation and weak IP rights.

There are huge benefits from global integration if it is done in the right way, at the right speed. But if poor countries open up prematurely, the result will be negative. Globalisation is too important to be left to free-trade economists, whose policy advice has so ill served the developing world in the past 25 years.

HA-JOON CHANG is one of the leading heterodox economists and institutional economists specializing in development economics. Currently a reader in the political economy of development at the University of Cambridge, Chang is the author of several widely discussed policy books, most notably 2002's *Kicking Away the Ladder: Development Strategy in Historical Perspective.*

Robert Krol    **NO**

Trade, Protectionism, and the U.S. Economy: Examining the Evidence

Introduction

America's trade with the rest of the world expanded significantly after World War II. U.S. goods (exports plus imports) increased from 9.2 percent of gross domestic product in 1960 to 28.6 percent in 2007. This expansion of international trade has benefited the United States and its trading partners considerably. The benefits include a higher standard of living, lower prices for consumers, improved efficiency in production, and a greater variety of goods.

The expansion of international trade raises concerns about the impact on domestic firms. In particular, many people fear that international trade reduces job opportunities for workers and depresses wages. These fears create political support for protectionist policies. However, international trade restrictions are costly to consumers as well as producers.

A recent survey found that 59 percent of Americans have a favorable view of international trade, although survey trends also indicate that a growing number of Americans now view international trade less favorably. When asked about their attitudes concerning the expansion of U.S. trade relations with the rest of the world, 36 percent thought it was "somewhat bad" or "very bad" in 2007 compared with 18 percent in 2002.

In this presidential election year, interest in the international trade views of the likely Democratic and Republican nominees is high. A meaningful way to determine the candidates' thinking on international trade is to look at their legislative voting records.

According to the Cato Institute's Center for Trade Policy Studies, Republican Sen. John McCain (R-AZ) voted against trade restrictions 88 percent of the time over his career. He is classified as a free trader based on his voting record. Sen. Barack Obama (D-IL) voted against trade barriers only 36 percent of the time. Clearly, the outcome of the November election could significantly affect future U.S. trade policy. Whether the United States continues to promote free trade will depend in part on who is elected president.

Opinion surveys and congressional voting records suggest Americans disagree strongly about the costs and benefits of international trade. This paper reviews empirical studies that examine the evidence on how international trade affects the economy. The goal of this paper is to discuss the evidence with respect to four important areas of international trade: the causes of expanded international trade, the benefits of trade, the impact of trade on employment and wages, and the cost of international trade restrictions.

The following points summarize the evidence from a survey of major research in the field:

- Comparative advantage remains the major driver of global trade flows.
- Income growth accounts for two-thirds of the growth in global trade in recent decades, trade liberalization accounts for one-quarter, and lower transportation costs make up the remainder.
- Trade expansion has fueled faster growth and raised incomes in countries that have liberalized. A 1-percentage-point gain in trade as a share of the economy raises per capita income by 1 percent. Global elimination of all barriers to trade in goods and services would raise global income by $2 trillion and U.S. income by almost $500 billion.
- Competition from trade delivers lower prices and more product variety to consumers. Americans are $300 billion better off today than they would be otherwise because of the greater product variety from imports.
- International trade directly affects only 15 percent of the U.S. workforce. Most job displacement occurs in sectors that are not engaged in global competition.
- While trade has probably caused a net loss of manufacturing jobs since 1979, those losses have been more than offset by employment gains in other sectors of the economy. Net payroll employment in the United States has grown by 36 million in the past two decades, along with a dramatic increase in imports of goods and services.
- Growing levels of trade do not explain most of the growing gap between wages earned by skilled and unskilled workers. The relative decline in unskilled wages is mainly caused by technological changes that reward greater skills. Demand for unskilled workers has been in relative decline in all sectors of the economy, not just those exposed to trade.
- Trade barriers impose large, net costs on the U.S. economy. The cost to the economy per job saved in protected industries far exceeds the wages paid to workers in those jobs.

From *Trade Briefing Paper*, No. 28, September 16, 2008, pp. 2–10 (notes omitted). Copyright © 2008 by Cato Institute/Center for Trade Policy Studies. Reprinted by permission.

- Protectionism persists because small, homogeneous, and concentrated interests are better able to lobby the government than the large, heterogeneous, and dispersed mass of consumers.

Why Countries Trade

Comparative advantage remains the basis of international trade. Differences in production costs within countries determine much of the flow of goods and services across international borders. Economists use the term "comparative advantage" to indicate that a country has a cost advantage in producing certain goods relative to other goods that could be produced within that same country. In other words, what spurs trade and specialization is not the absolute cost advantage that one country's producers have over their competitors in another country, but the relative advantage they have compared to other sectors within their own country.

Consider the example of a more-developed Country A and a less-developed Country B. Country A may be able to produce t-shirts twice as efficiently as Country B; but if it can produce computers 10 times more efficiently, it will make economic sense for Country A to specialize in producing and exporting computers while importing t-shirts from Country B. Trade allows both countries to direct their internal resources—principally labor and capital—to those sectors where they are relatively more productive compared to other sectors in the domestic economy.

Comparative advantage can spring from multiple sources. A country can have a cost advantage in the production of a particular good because of superior production technology. This superiority can include better ways to organize the production process or a climate that allows the country to grow certain crops, such as bananas and mangos, more cheaply. It can also include greater investments in skilled labor and equipment that can result in a comparative advantage in such areas as computer software.

The United States has proportionately more skilled labor than unskilled labor compared with most countries. This makes the United States the low-cost producer for goods that rely on skilled labor and sophisticated machinery. Therefore, the United States exports high-tech manufactured goods that can be produced using relatively more skilled labor and imports shoes and apparel that are produced using a large amount of unskilled labor.

However, sometimes trade involves similar goods. For example, the United States both exports and imports golf clubs. This type of trade occurs in markets where businesses differentiate their products and experience declining average costs as production expands. In this setting, opening an economy to international trade increases the size of the market. Average costs fall, resulting in lower prices and a wider array of products being sold in each of the trading countries. Consumers can select from products produced by domestic as well as foreign firms. Lower prices and greater variety increase consumer welfare.

Global trade has expanded significantly since World War II for a number of reasons, including lower transportation and information costs, higher per capita income, and changes in government policies. The containerization of shipping has reduced loading times, improving efficiency, just as less expensive air transportation has increased international trade in perishable items. Improvements in information technology have made it less costly for consumers to determine the characteristics of products produced abroad. Information technology has also made it easier for producers to assess consumer preferences, allowing better customization of products and services for buyers in foreign markets. Income growth in developed countries and even in some less-developed countries has increased the demand for goods and services produced domestically as well as from abroad. Finally, trade restrictions have decreased significantly since World War II.

Evidence is now available that quantifies the relative contribution of these different factors to the growth of world trade. Scott Baier and Jeffrey Bergstrand attribute 67 percent of the increase in international trade to income growth, another 25 percent to tariff reductions, and the remaining 8 percent to falling transportation costs. Critics of trade blame trade agreements for spurring global competition, when in fact most trade growth simply stems from rising global incomes. A reversion to protectionism would not necessarily stop the growth of global trade, but it would sacrifice the considerable economic benefits of more open competition.

Benefits from International Trade

Since World War II, multilateral and unilateral tariff negotiations have reduced barriers to international trade. Several attempts have been made to quantify the resulting welfare gains to consumers and producers. In brief, trade leads to specialization based on comparative advantage, which lowers production costs, allowing for greater levels of output and, therefore, consumption. Individuals are able to purchase products at lower prices, resulting in higher real incomes and a higher standard of living. In addition, trade allows countries to import products that embody new technologies which are not produced at home.

One way to assess the gains from international trade is to compare the level of welfare (measured imperfectly by real per capita GDP) before and after trade restrictions are dropped. A dramatic example of this type of trade reform occurred in Japan during the early 1850s. For 200 years up until then, Japan had almost no economic or cultural contact with other countries. Then the Japanese government signed a treaty with the United States that was designed to shift the country from a no-trade to a free-trade regime in seven years. Daniel Bernhofen and John Brown estimate that, with the increase in international trade, Japan's real GDP was 8 percent higher by the end of the seven-year period than if the economy had remained closed. Furthermore, by opening its economy to the rest of the world, Japan was able to import capital goods, new technologies, and new production methods that promoted faster economic growth and even higher living standards over time.

In another historical episode, the United States closed its borders to international trade in 1807 when President Thomas Jefferson imposed a trade embargo to avoid conflicts with the warring British and French navies. Dartmouth economist Douglas Irwin estimates the embargo reduced U.S. GDP by about 5 percent in one year. Jefferson quickly ended the embargo because of the high economic cost it imposed on the country.

Research economists have used computer models of the economy to capture the industry adjustments and aggregate GDP gains from trade liberalization. Work by Drusilla Brown, Alan Deardorff, and Robert Stern represents this type of study. They estimate that a one-third reduction in agricultural, manufacturing, and service-sector trade restrictions worldwide would increase world GDP by $686 billion (measured in 1995 dollars) over a prereduction baseline. In the United States, GDP would rise 1.8 percent. If all trade barriers were eliminated, world GDP would increase by more than $2 trillion and U.S. GDP would be $497 billion, or 4.8 percent, higher than before liberalization.

Although the association between free trade and prosperity has been well documented, the correlation between international trade and increased per capita income has been difficult to illustrate—perhaps because countries with higher per capita income choose to trade more. In a well-known study, Jeffrey Frankel and David Romer examined the relationship between international trade and per capita income using 1985 data for a large cross-section of countries. To deal with the causality issue, Frankel and Romer used geographic variables correlated with international trade but not per capita income. This approach isolates the portion of international trade not caused by growth in per capita income. They found that, as the share of exports-plus-imports to GDP rises by 1 percentage point, per capita income increases by 2 percentage points.

However, Frankel and Romer's work has been criticized because the geographic variables they used may be correlated with other geographic factors that influence GDP. For example, distance from the equator correlates with per capita income, possibly invalidating the results. Marta Noguer and Marc Siscart used an improved specification to reestimate the relationship. Controlling for distance from the equator, they found that a 1-percentage-point increase in trade share raises per capita income by 1 percentage point. Noguer and Siscart concluded that trade does indeed raise a country's standard of living.

More recently, Romain Wacziarg and Karen Horn Welch examined the relationship between trade and economic growth for 133 countries over most of the post–World War II period. Using country case studies and trade policy indicators, they identified the year countries in the study liberalized their trade policies. They found that, on average, countries grew 1.5 percentage points faster per year following trade liberalization during the period 1950 to 1998. Focusing on a subgroup of countries that had at least eight years of data before and after liberalization, they found 54 percent of these countries grew faster. Of the remaining countries examined, 21 percent did not experience faster growth while 25 percent of the countries grew more slowly.

Wacziarg and Welch found that the countries that experienced faster economic growth maintained their liberalization polices while the others did not. Also, some of the countries that did not grow faster following trade liberalization experienced political instability and restrictive macroeconomic policies that hindered growth in the post-trade-liberalization period. Obviously, trade liberalization alone is not always enough to overcome other factors inhibiting growth.

Economists have also turned to individual factory-level data to better understand the connection between international trade and a country's standard of living. Looking at U.S. manufacturing data from 1987 to 1997, Andrew Bernard, J. Bradford Jensen, and Peter Schott found that a one-standard-deviation decrease in tariffs and transportation costs increased productivity growth by 0.2 percentage points per year, primarily as a result of a shift in production from low- to high-productivity plants. Many low-productivity plants closed. At the same time, however, exports from plants already exporting increased, and high-productivity plants that previously produced only for the domestic market entered the export market.

Daniel Trefler found productivity gains of 1.9 percent per year in Canadian manufacturing following the implementation of the 1989 free trade agreement with the United States. Average manufacturing employment fell by 5 percent in the seven years following the agreement. Those job losses were disproportionally in manufacturing plants that received the greatest tariff protection prior to the trade agreement. However, employment growth in more efficient manufacturing plants helped to reemploy displaced workers over time. These studies show that the short-run adjustment costs and job displacement associated with the closing of inefficient plants can be offset by greater productivity and higher standards of living in the longer-run.

These estimates of the gains from international trade probably underestimate the improvement in well-being that increased trade brings. Moving to freer international trade also increases the variety of goods and services individuals can choose from. If consumers value variety, then welfare improves in an open economy. This welfare gain may not show up in income data, but it does make people better off. In addition, greater variety in intermediate capital goods benefits producers. Better intermediate goods improve efficiency and speed productivity growth, resulting in a higher standard of living for workers.

Christian Broda and David Weinstein examined the benefits of greater import variety in the United States over the period 1972 to 2001. They estimated that the variety of international goods imported into the United States tripled over the period. One traditional measure of the welfare gain from international trade is the decline in prices as measured by an import price index. However, Broda and Weinstein point out that the United States' import price index is not adjusted for changes in variety. If greater variety increases a consumer's satisfaction and standard of living without raising prices, then consumers should be able to achieve the same level of welfare while spending less. When Broda and Weinstein adjusted the U.S. import price index for changes in variety, they estimated the U.S. welfare gain from a greater variety of imports to be approximately 2.8 percent of GDP, or $300 billion per year.

These empirical studies provide evidence that international trade raises income and productivity. They also show that the greater product variety brought about by expanding international trade improves welfare.

Trade's Effect on Employment

People concerned about trade worry that gains in productivity and product variety come at the expense of domestic employment. Yet, the evidence shows little relationship between greater imports and any change in aggregate employment. Over the past 20 years, U.S. *aggregate* net employment has increased from 102 million jobs to nearly 138 million jobs, while imports of goods and services have gone from a little over $500 billion to $2.35 trillion. As shown in Figure 1, employment tends to rise along with imports. Demographic trends, worker education and skill levels, labor-market regulations, and business-cycle developments—not trade—are the dominant factors influencing the overall level of employment and the unemployment rate in the U.S. economy.

International trade does have distributive effects. Although the country as a whole is better off, individual groups of workers or industries may be worse off. This occurs because, once a country opens itself up to international trade, import prices fall because of greater competition and export prices rise because producers can sell to a larger global market. Domestic production of import-competing goods contracts while production in export industries expands, changing the real earnings of inputs employed in these sectors.

What are the implications for the United States? As noted earlier, the United States exports goods that use relatively more skilled labor and imports goods that use relatively more unskilled labor. As the economy adjusts to changing trade patterns, the demand for skilled labor increases and the demand for unskilled labor decreases. Thus, as the United States opens its economy to greater international trade, real wages of skilled labor rise relative to the real wages of unskilled labor. Making matters more difficult for unskilled laborors, displaced workers may also experience a period of unemployment before they find a new job.

Researchers who investigate the impact of international trade on employment and wages find that, despite public rhetoric, international trade has a relatively small impact on wages and employment in the United States. Growth in wage inequality over the last 25 years has apparently been driven more by technological change than international trade.

Two facts shed some light on this general conclusion. First, international trade directly affects only 15 percent of the U.S. workforce. This suggests that international competition is an issue for only a minority of workers. Second, high rates of job loss occur in sectors of the economy that are not engaged in international trade, indicating that factors other than international trade play an important role in labor-market disruptions.

In addition, the decline in employment in the manufacturing sector has been driven primarily by greater labor

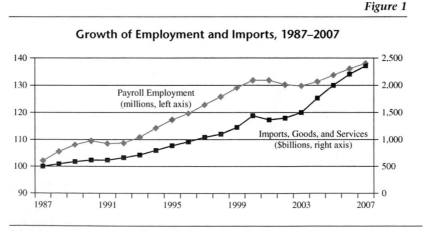

Figure 1

Growth of Employment and Imports, 1987–2007

Sources: Economic Report of the President, 2008; Bureau of Labor Statistics, and U.S. Department of Commerce.

productivity rather than by growth in international trade. The net employment impact of international trade on manufacturing is small because the United States is both an importer and exporter of manufactured goods.

In a series of studies, Lori Kletzer examined the impact of increased imports on gross U.S. industry employment. For industries most affected by imports, she estimated 7.45 million *gross* manufacturing jobs were lost between 1979 and 2001, or 28,219 per month. This represents a loss of 15 percent of all manufacturing jobs during the 22-year period.

Kletzer points out that data limitations make it difficult to determine if displaced workers have lost their jobs because of imports or for some other reason. Other factors, such as changes in technology or consumer tastes, can also result in job loss. For example, high labor-productivity growth has resulted in a long-run decline in manufacturing jobs—independent of foreign competition. These studies also ignore the jobs created from exporting or from the lower business costs that result from imports, which can expand employment in other sectors.

The more important finding is the *net* effect of imports and exports on employment. Economists at the Federal Reserve Bank of New York have estimated the number of workers needed to produce U.S. goods—imports and exports—with the difference representing the net number of jobs gained or lost in the goods sector because of international trade. Because imports are greater than exports, the calculation shows a net loss in jobs from trade. For the period 1997–2003, they found that net job loss from trade averaged 40,000 per month, or 2.4 percent of total employment. However, the study does not capture employment gains in other sectors, like services, which result from access to lower cost inputs and new technology embedded in imports. It is important to recognize that total net employment in the United States increased by 7.2 million jobs over this period, which indicates that job creation in nonmanufacturing sectors more than offset job losses in manufacturing.

Trade's Impact on Wages

A more contentious labor-market issue concerns the increase in wages of skilled workers relative to unskilled workers. Is this trend the result of changes in information technology, or is international trade to blame? Most studies conclude that international trade has played only a modest role in rising wage inequality. The empirical evidence suggests that skill-biased technological change has had a bigger impact.

First, the demand for skilled labor has increased relative to the demand for unskilled labor in most industries, even those not heavily engaged in international trade. If international trade were driving this trend, we would not observe high relative demand for skilled labor in all sectors, or in sectors that do not engage in significant international trade.

If international trade was driving the growing wage inequality between skilled and unskilled workers, then import prices of unskilled-labor-intensive goods should be declining over time and export prices of skilled-labor-intensive goods should be rising over time as trade expands. That is, import prices should decline as we replace higher-cost, domestically produced products with similar products produced at lower cost from countries that have a comparative advantage in those items. Similarly, export prices should be higher in foreign markets because those markets tend to be high-cost producers of the products we export due to our comparative advantage. Using aggregate export and import price indices, Robert Lawrence and Matthew Slaughter found this not to be the case over the 1979 to 1991 period. Their result is consistent with many (though not all) studies that take this approach. A few studies did find a shift in relative international prices in the 1970s, but they still concluded that the relative wage change was driven primarily by technological change rather than shifting international prices.

More recently, using a similar approach for the period 1981 to 2006, Robert Lawrence found a 12 percentage-point decline in the ratio of blue- to white-collar compensation which he attributed to greater international trade. Most of the decline occurred during the 1980s, a period of fairly stable import-to-export price ratios. The evidence from the 1980s is inconsistent with the theory that international trade is the primary driver of greater wage inequality.

Robert Feenstra and Gary Hanson argue that the outsourcing of less-skilled jobs does reduce demand for unskilled workers in the United States (lowering relative wages), but it is not the primary cause. They examined the impact of this type of outsourcing for 435 U.S. manufacturing industries from 1972 to 1990. For the 1972–1979 period, they found that changes in wage inequality were not related to outsourcing. For the 1979–1990 period, outsourcing appeared to explain about 15 percent of the increased wage inequality, while the introduction of computers explained 35 percent.

Expanding international trade can influence employment patterns and relative wages in an economy. The evidence reviewed in this paper indicates that trade is not the primary source of U.S. job displacement or wage inequality. Technological change and faster productivity growth play the dominant role in these developments.

Cost of Protectionism

Countries can influence international trade by using tariffs and quotas. The purpose of an import tariff is to reduce imports and expand domestic production in the protected industry. With higher output, industry profits and employment expand. However, that expansion comes at a cost. Domestic consumers pay more for products, and domestic resources are used less efficiently. Downstream industries that would use imported products as an input face higher costs, lowering output and employment in those industries.

Gary Hufbauer and Kimberly Elliott examined the welfare gains from the elimination of tariffs and other quantitative restrictions in 21 major sectors of the U.S. economy in the 1980s. Perhaps the most interesting and striking result they reported is their calculation of the consumer gains per job lost if the United States were to eliminate tariffs on an industry. They estimated the dollar cost savings for consumers relative to the total number of jobs lost due to the elimination of an international trade restriction. The average for all 21 sectors was $168,520 per job annually—far higher than the annual earnings of an individual worker. The dollar cost savings ranged from a high of more than $1 million per job in the ball bearings industry to a low of $96,532 per job in costume jewelry. For the sugar sector, the figure was $600,177 per job. For each job "saved," consumers paid three times the average wage in manufacturing. In other words, trade restrictions impose costs on consumers three times the gain to protected workers.

Why do these costly international trade restrictions remain in place? The simple explanation is that the benefits from these types of policies are concentrated in the affected labor force while the costs are spread out over the entire population of consumers.

Producers tend to be a small, relatively homogeneous group. Often they are geographically concentrated. As a result, the costs per person associated with organizing and lobbying for protection from imports are low. Because they form a small group, the benefits per person (higher profits and wages) from import protection are high. The benefit-cost ratio or payoff associated with lobbying government officials is high. Producers and workers find it worthwhile to organize in order to place political pressure on governments for protection from imports. Since elected officials are interested in reelection, they respond by providing protection in exchange for political support.

For consumers, the benefit-cost ratio per person is low. Consumers are a large, geographically diverse, heterogeneous group. As a result, the costs of organizing to lobby against international trade restrictions are high. Furthermore, although the total cost to consumers of these restrictions is high, the cost is typically low on a per-person basis. The benefit-cost ratio or payoff associated with lobbying elected officials is low. Consumers are less likely to expend the resources needed to generate political action in their favor. For example, in the sugar industry

the benefits per producer for import restrictions are more than $500,000 per year. For sugar consumers, although the total costs are high, the per-person cost comes to only $5 per year. Not surprisingly, sugar producers actively lobby for import protection and sugar consumers take few steps to oppose it, despite the high total cost to consumers.

Conclusion

International trade has expanded dramatically since World War II. Recent polls and political rhetoric suggest support for continued trade liberalization may be waning—and that is of concern. A movement away from the relatively open global trading system that is currently in place would impose significant economic costs on the United States and the rest of the world.

This paper has provided a comprehensive review of the important empirical studies that quantify the impact of trade on the economy. The evidence is clear: International trade raises a country's standard of living. Lower prices on imported products and greater product variety enhance consumer well-being. Specialization based on comparative advantage and increased competition from foreign businesses improves production efficiency, raising GDP. Firms also get access to foreign capital goods that often contain new technologies, further improving productivity.

Concerns over international trade often center on the effect on jobs and wages. The evidence shows trade can result in the displacement of workers in industries that must compete with imports. However, the impact is modest relative to overall employment growth. Although displaced workers do face adjustment costs, overall the United States has experienced robust total employment growth in the presence of expanded trade. Furthermore, studies show that international trade has a relatively small affect on wages. Greater wage inequality has been driven more by skill-biased technological change than by international trade.

Although international trade forces significant adjustments in an economy, as the evidence shows, the costs of international trade restrictions on the economy outweigh the limited benefits these restrictions bring to import-competing industries.

ROBERT KROL is a professor of economics at California State University, Northridge.

EXPLORING THE ISSUE

Are Protectionist Policies Beneficial to Business?

Critical Thinking and Reflection

1. What might be the tactics of a protectionist strategy?
2. How might a protectionist strategy be implemented in a corporation?
3. What might be the costs to consumers, corporations, and the nation of corporations following an unmitigated protectionist strategy?
4. What is the likelihood that an enacted protectionist strategy will lead to anticipated outcomes?
5. What does the future hold for industries following protectionist strategies?

Is There Common Ground?

One reason the issue of protectionist policies is so contentious is that both sides can easily cite data in support of their position. While finding common ground on basic aspects of this important management topic is difficult, there is consensus that protectionist policies are an important topic that will be debated for quite some time, especially in certain industries.

Additional Resources

Cavusgil, S.T., Knight, G. and Riesenberger, J.R. (2008). *International Business*, Pearson, p. 620.

Hardy, Q. and Buley, T. (2009). "The Greening of Trade Wars," *Forbes*, May 10, 2009, Forbes.com, p. 26.

Johnson, I. (2009). "World News: Foreign Businesses Say China Is Growing More Protectionist," *Wall Street Journal* (Eastern Edition), April 28, p. A8.

Kerr, W.A. (2009). "Recession, International Trade and the Fallacies of Composition," *The Estey Centre Journal of International Law and Trade Policy:* Special Section on Geographical Indicators, 10(1), pp. 1–11.

The Economist (2009). "Low Expectations Exceeded."

Internet Reference . . .

Buy American Is About Building Jobs, Not Protectionism

Connell, T. (2009). "Buy American Is About Building Jobs, Not Protectionism," *AFL-CIO NOW*, February 20.

http://blog.aflcio.org/2009/02/20/buy-american-is-about-building-jobs-not-protectionism/

CPSIA information can be obtained
at www.ICGtesting.com
Printed in the USA
EDOW021458200513
1620ED